RED THEOLOGY: ON THE CHRISTIAN COMMUNIST TRADITION

Studies in Critical Research on Religion

Haymarket Books is proud to be working with Brill Academic Publishers (www.brill.nl) to republish the *Studies in Critical Research on Religion* book series in paperback editions. This peer-reviewed book series offers insights into our current reality by exploring the content and consequences of power relationships under capitalism, and by considering the spaces of opposition and resistance to these changes that have been defining our new age. Our full catalog of *SCRR* volumes can be viewed at https://www.haymarketbooks.org/series_collections/6-studies-in-critical-research-in-religion.

RED THEOLOGY: ON THE CHRISTIAN COMMUNIST TRADITION

ROLAND BOER

Haymarket Books
Chicago, IL

First published in 2019 by Brill Academic Publishers, The Netherlands.
© 2019 Koninklijke Brill NV, Leiden, The Netherlands

Published in 2020 by
Haymarket Books
P.O. Box 180165
Chicago, IL 60618
773-583-7884
www.haymarketbooks.org
info@haymarketbooks.org

ISBN: 978-1-64259-372-3

Distributed to the trade in the US through Consortium Book Sales and
Distribution (www.cbsd.com) and internationally through Ingram Publisher
Services International (www.ingramcontent.com).

This book was published with the generous support of Lannan Foundation and
Wallace Action Fund.

Special discounts are available for bulk purchases by organizations and
institutions. Please call 773-583-7884 or email info@haymarketbooks.org for
more information.

Cover design by Jamie Kerry and Ragina Johnson.

Printed in United States.

Library of Congress Cataloging-in-Publication data is available.

10 9 8 7 6 5 4 3 2 1

For Dick Boer

Contents

Preface

When asked in different contexts what my position is in relation to Christianity, I say that I identify as a Christian communist. Perhaps this is a confession, perhaps not, but it is an indelible part of the tradition that has shaped me. Often my answer to the question is invoked when I am with people who would subscribe to the adage: Christianity is Christianity and communism is communism and never the twain shall meet. Thus, Christian communism is impossible, they think, an oxymoron. The discussions that ensue are lively and intriguing. This book is in many respects an effort at explaining this position, in light of some two millennia of a complex tradition of Christian communism. The study is a less a history per se than a series of case studies, some more theoretical and others more historical, but usually from an unexpected angle. More of that in what follows.

The idea for the book was first suggested many years ago by Dick Boer, who urged me to undertake a study of engagements with Marxism by Christian theologians. But that is a study only Dick could undertake. This book may be seen as my own response to Dick's urging, keeping this form of communism at the centre, even if I approach the topic from a number of angles. Indeed, Dick and I have followed a path first taken by none other than Friedrich Engels and Kim Il Sung, from Reformed theology to communism, although neither of us would claim anywhere near the same stature as our forebears, nor indeed the need to give up one tradition for the sake of the other.

Others too have been witting and unwitting contributors. Given that the initial ideas were developed in a number of different contexts – although nearly all of it has either been rewritten or indeed written anew – I would like to thank Dick Horsley, Neil Elliott, Janelle Watson, Agon Hamza, Marion Maddox, Geoff Boucher, Matt Sharpe, Li Yazhi, Sun Xiuli, Yu Min, Lu Shaochen, Zhang Jing, Zang Fengyu, Zhang Shuangli, Zhu Yanming and Zhu Caihong – to name but a few. I also appreciate deeply the careful and detailed work of Warren Goldstein, one of the best editors on the planet and one of the most insightful. Each person has in their own way made suggestions, challenged me and encouraged me to develop my thoughts further. In all this, Christina Petterson and I continue our common project, to whatever unexpected part of the world it might take us.

The Hill
January 2018

Series Editor's Preface

When it comes to the relationship between Marxism and religion or theology, Roland Boer is the leading expert. With over twenty monographs and hundreds of peer reviewed articles and book chapters, the volume of his scholarly output is only matched by its high quality. With a background in European classics and biblical studies, he not only approaches Marxist texts with the eye for detail of the biblical critic but approaches biblical texts from the perspective of the historical materialist. I am therefore incredibly pleased to have Professor Boer contribute this book to this series "Studies in Critical Research on Religion." This volume brings together much of his corpus with many of the chapters being a synopsis of earlier works. In addition, Chapters 8, 10, and 14 (on Marxist-Christian Dialogue, Farnham Maynard, and on Religion in North Korea) are previously unpublished; the last is particularly impressive since it helps shed light on a country whose image is distorted by Western news media. Boer's research on the interconnections between Marxism and religion brings to light that both have a cold and a warm stream and that it is the latter that can illuminate the path toward a more humane future.

Warren S. Goldstein, Ph.D.
Center for Critical Research on Religion
www.criticaltheoryofreligion.org

Introduction

'All things in common' has been the slogan of Christian communists for some two millennia. It originally comes from Acts 2:44, with a variation in Acts 4:32. But it was actually a Marxist, Karl Kautsky, who established that there is a distinct tradition of this form of communism, inspired by these biblical texts and constituting the longest continuous form of communism in the world. I will have more to say about Kautsky in the first chapter, for I have long been intrigued by his massive work from 1895, *Forerunners of Modern Socialism*, which traces the history of Christian communism through European history. Given its relative obscurity, I set about rereading Kautsky as a preparation for writing this book, especially since much of the work remains untranslated. As is the way with such re-readings, I saw it in a way I had not seen before, identifying new insights and avenues of thought.

This experience led me to change the original plan of the book, which I had imagined would take shape as a volume of collected essays that I had written earlier, with some mild editing for the sake of the present work. Instead, I revised and rewrote most of what I had studied earlier, in the light of new research and thought. Only a few of the chapters have come through somewhat unscathed: those on the novel *Q*, Calvin, Luther, Althusser, and Chinese Christian communism. The remainder is almost or completely new, especially since I have delved into areas I had not researched before, such as the Marxist-Christian dialogue of the 1960s and 1970s and the distinct developments of Christian communism in the Democratic People's Republic of Korea (informally known as North Korea). The result is a largely new work with its own logic.

I have organised the chapters in a geographical manner, following the intriguing path of Christian communism. After a careful reassessment of Kautsky's identification of the tradition itself, I focus on the West Asian provenance of Christianity. This entails an examination of the nature of early Christian communism and the debates that swirl around this phenomenon, before engaging with its appropriation and transformation in a European context. By this time, my preferred approach should become clear, for I deal with the manifestations of Christian communism from different angles, whether a popular novel concerning the revolutionary currents during the Reformation, Calvin's struggles over whether one should overthrow ungodly rulers, or the engagements with Luther by Marx and Engels. In the modern era, I engage with debates over whether Marxism is a 'secularised' form of 'salvation history', the Marxist-Christian dialogue, and the intriguing efforts by a young Louis Althusser to develop a form of spiritual revolution. My love of finding unexamined corners of the tradition appears yet again with a chapter on the Australian Christian communist and priest, Farnham Maynard. This chapter provides the first step into other parts of the world, with studies of the consistent need for the Russian Bolsheviks to engage with new forms of Christian communism, its initial appearance in China with the Taiping Revolution in the nineteenth century, the development of a distinct Chinese tradition in the early twentieth century, and then the unexpected but fascinating transformations on the Korean peninsula, with a focus on Kim Il Sung.

A couple of major themes appear early in my analysis, so let me identity them here. The first is that Christian communism is predicated on profound criticisms of the state of the world, usually from a sense of radical divine transcendence. For some, the answer has been to establish alternative and inevitably small communities that seek to embody a different way of living out their belief and practice within the world. They may wish to provide alternative models, hoping that others will see the benefits and thereby gradually transform society as a whole. Or they may distance themselves from the world, desiring to be left in peace so as to develop their communities. For others, the answer has been revolutionary. The theologically inspired criticisms of the injustices and oppressions of the status quo have led them to the position that the only answer is a revolutionary overthrow. At times, we find that both of these elements – the communal and the revolutionary – come together, while at other times a peaceful community is forced to engage in revolutionary action in response to oppression from outside forces. The only path left to achieve their desired communism is to engage in revolutionary violence.

The second theme concerns the political ambivalence of Christian thought and practice, embodied above all in the biblical texts that picture early Christian communism and those that advocate obedience to and support of the rulers of this world. I argue that this tension should not be seen in terms of a core-periphery model. According to this model, one may argue that either Christianity's conservative or revolutionary dimensions constitute the core and that the other is thereby a peripheral element, or perhaps even a distortion of the basic truth. Instead, it is clear that Christianity struggles with a tension between these two positions. The same sacred texts and the same doctrinal positions can easily support the status quo or they can inspire profound criticism, if not revolutionary action. We see this dynamic time and again through the history of Christianity.

It remains to offer a synopsis of the fourteen chapters in the book. The first chapter provides a critical engagement with Kautsky's landmark *Forerunners of Modern Socialism*, identifying his key structuring assumptions (which are not always consistent), the nature of his engagement with the many historical manifestations of Christian communism, with specific attention given to his enthusiasm for the 1525 Peasant War (Thomas Müntzer) and the 1534–1535 Anabaptist revolution in Münster. Apart from establishing a tradition of Christian communism, which moves well past Engels's initial efforts, Kautsky also hints at a key insight: the biblical and theological nature of this communism was not a mere cloak for more central political and economic issues. Instead, its theological form was integral to its political nature.

Now we can turn to the West Asian origins of Christianity. Chapter 2 entails a more detailed study of early Christian communism, focusing initially on Kautsky's comparatively well-known *Foundations of Christianity* (1908). Kautsky wrote the book – the first Marxist study of Christianity – in response to criticisms of his briefer and earlier outline. But I am also interested in Rosa Luxemburg's reconstruction, which shares much with Kautsky, but seeks more explicitly to address the concerns of the many workers joining the Social-Democratic party who were also believers. Both of them make the specific argument that this early communism was one of consumption rather than production, which meant that there was no change in the mode of production itself. Only modern communism, they argue, proposes such a shift, but the argument faces some difficulty when one tracks carefully through Kautsky's work to find that a significant number of communist movements before the modern era also engaged in distinctly new productive activities. The final argument of this chapter concerns political myth. Given that the historical evidence for early Christian communism is not conclusive, I propose that it functions as this type of myth: it offers an image and promise of a community that produced distinct and concrete historical manifestations.

In the third chapter, I pick up the other side of the political ambivalence noted earlier. In this case, my concern is a key text that continues to be used to support the powers that be: Romans 13:1-7. After an assessment of efforts to deal with this troublesome text, I examine the many contradictions in the texts of the Apostle Paul so as to develop a Mao-inspired contradiction analysis. This takes me to economic realities. As in the previous chapter (and based on earlier work), I examine the relevant aspects of the ancient economy of the Greco-Roman world, concluding that Paul's many contradictions are simultaneously formal traces and persuasive efforts to provide an imaginary resolution – with distinct historical effects – of the profound tensions of the socio-economic situation.

Chapter 4 moves into the European sixteenth century (Reformation), but from a different angle. It examines the translations between theology and radical politics in the popular novel *Q*, originally published in Italian in 1999. Written by the Italian collective, Luther Blissett (now Wu Ming), this long novel provides a skilful and engaging retelling of the revolutionary waves of the time, working around a central and unnamed character (shadowed by a Vatican agent) who is involved in the Peasant and Münster revolutions, the radical groups in the northern Netherlands and in Antwerp, as well as the possibility of revolution in Italy itself. I seek to situate the novel within the Marxist approach to Christian communism, which includes – apart from Engels and Kautsky – Anatoly Lunacharsky and Ernst Bloch. Antonio Gramsci also peers over the pages of *Q*, especially in his wish that Italy too might have experienced the Reformation. From there, I analyse four themes or tensions with which the novel deals, themes that are inherited from that tradition but to which it gives new angles: passion and reason, rupture and communalism, the political ambivalence of Christianity, and the issue of translation between radical politics and theology.

The next chapter moves to another expected corner – the work of John Calvin, especially the last chapter of his *Institutes* (4.20.32). Why Calvin? Is he not an arch-conservative, a proponent of predestination, and at the roots of so much evangelical conservatism today? In this part of the *Institutes*, we find a somewhat different Calvin. Despite his strenuous efforts to advocate obedience to rulers (Romans 13), he is too careful a student of the Bible to avoid the conclusion that one is duty-bound to disobey any ungodly and tyrannical ruler. By focusing on the literary structure of Calvin's argument, I analyse his struggles over this question: his assertions that rulers should be obeyed come what may and the recognition that God and God's appointed agents may under certain conditions punish and remove tyrannical rulers. All of this leads to his final recommendation not to obey ungodly rulers. In this matter, Calvin reveals the tension mentioned earlier, between radical and conservative elements of Christian theology.

The sixth chapter concerns the other great leader of the 'magisterial' Reformation, Luther, but it does so via another angle. I examine the engagements with Luther by Marx and Engels, doing so in three sections. The first focuses on human nature, showing how the Augustinian focus of Lutheranism contrasts with the tendency towards a more Pelagian position in Marxism. The second turns to Engels's assessment of the German Peasant revolution of 1525, in which Engels seeks to characterise Luther as the champion of a fledgling bourgeoisie (burghers and reforming princes), only to signal his awareness of Luther's more radical, if not revolutionary edge that inspired leaders like Thomas Müntzer. The third and longest section concerns Marx, who, somewhat surprisingly, offers a critically dialectical engagement with Luther. For Marx, Luther marks the necessary first stage of the German revolution, without whom the second stage could not happen.

By now we have moved into the modern era in Europe, when Christian communism and Marxism found themselves in constant, albeit often uneasy, interaction. In this light, Chapter 7 focuses on the abiding question as to whether Marxism is a form of 'secularised' Jewish and Christian *Heilsgeschichte*, or salvation history. The answer turns out to be negative, although this entails analysing specific materials from Marx and Engels. These include Marx's close interactions with Bruno Bauer, Engels's lifelong fascination with the biblical book of the Apocalypse (usually designated 'Revelation') and the apocalyptic and biblically inspired forms of communism with which Marx and Engels engaged. In each case, we find that both of the founders of modern communism opposed those forms that were shaped by biblical models. The key, however, is the lengthy and oft-ignored polemic against Max Stirner in *The German Ideology*. Finding that Stirner is still beholden to Christian themes, Marx and Engels begin to develop the first and rough outlines of what would become historical and dialectical materialism. The fulcrum of history becomes contradiction, understood in a dialectical fashion that cuts a path away from *Heilsgeschichte* to a new model of history, albeit one that still relies on a fulcrum. In the process, they offer a radical relativisation of the claims that theologians and philosophers have often made concerning the ontological and historical priority of theology.

The eighth chapter concerns the Marxist-Christian dialogue of the 1960s and 1970s. This is a topic that has interested me for more than three decades, although this is the first opportunity to assess its insights and shortcomings, with a view to current debates. While it was born from a sense of crisis, in terms of profound changes brought about by the anti-colonial struggles, the realities of potential nuclear war and the sense that both communist and capitalist societies had stagnated, it was also a very European debate on which the rest of world only impinged in certain ways. Of less interest now are their concerns over theism and atheism in relation to Marx's works, as well as *praxis*, which they interpreted from Marx's early theses on Feuerbach as 'sensuous human activity'. Indeed, this emphasis reveals the profound influence that the publication of Marx's early 'humanistic' works had on the debate. Both the 'Economic and Philosophic Manuscripts' of 1844 and *The German Ideology* had been collated, organised and published in 1932. Here was a Marx many felt shed a new light on the whole tradition, so much so that they could talk about humanism, alienation, protest (via Prometheus) and the future. Here too theologians found much that could be appropriated, transformed and criticised. However, my treatment of these issues shifts the register, dealing now with human nature, the need for a materialist doctrine of evil, the question of how protest appears under socialism in power, and the possibility that the development of proleptic theology at the time was actually due to the influence of Marxism.

I close by suggesting – contrary to the participants – that the opening for the dialogue was actually created, belatedly, by the decade long compact between the Soviet Union's communist government and the Russian Orthodox Church between 1943 and 1953.

One of the traps of the Marxist-Christian dialogue was to assume that a person was either a Marxist or a Christian, but not both at the same time. The reality was that some were indeed both, so this chapter and the next examine two examples. In Chapter 9, I engage with Louis Althusser, particularly an important text, a 'Matter of Fact', written in 1948. In this essay, Althusser attempts to develop a theory of the revolution of religious life. It appeared at an important juncture of his life, for he was still a member of the Roman Catholic Church, but had recently joined the Communist Party of France. The tensions of that conjunction are clear, but I am interested in his attempt to extend, by analogy, the Marxist theory of social revolution into a revolution of personal spiritual life. In this effort, the context is the apparent untranscendable horizon of the Roman Catholic Church. So Althusser begins by outlining the condition of an ailing, out-of-date, and reactionary church. He then focuses on the conditions for wider social revolution, with which progressive members among the faithful must join in a politics of alliance. Finally, he attempts – all too briefly – to outline what a personal religious revolution might be. In his own way, Althusser finds himself part of the long tradition of revolutionary Christianity.

The other person who embodies both dimensions within his own thought and action, thereby carrying on the dialogue internally, is the Australian priest, Farnham Maynard (1882–1973). Long the Anglican priest at St Peter's Eastern Hill in Melbourne, he was not only a proponent of the spiritual revival embodied in Anglo-Catholicism, but also one who had trained in science. So his approach to Christian communism was via a method that may be called a dialectic of science and prayer. With this method, Maynard – in papers usually written for conferences at which Marxists, Christians and Christian communists were involved – develops his own understandings of the tension between reaction and revolution, seeking to address both communists who were somewhat sceptical of religion and Christians who had their reservations about 'godless' communism. That Maynard felt they should work together is obvious, but he also retained a distinct role for Christian theology in constructing socialism. It could provide what Marxism could not, namely, answers to the deeper questions of existence and the purpose of life. My interest in Maynard is not merely due to the fact that he was an Australian priest, but that he was also enthusiastic about socialism in power, visiting both the Soviet Union and China at a time when travel to such places was banned by the Australian government.

Maynard's travels – apart from the fact that we have already moved outside Europe – takes me to both places. Chapter 11 deals with the Russian Revolution and the effort to construct socialism in that part of the world. Although I draw on earlier research, the shape of the chapter is new. It begins with the constant need for the Bolsheviks and especially Lenin to come to terms with Russian peasant socialism, embodied in the simple but profound slogan, 'the land is God's'. The next section analyses Lenin's complex engagements with Tolstoy, the most well-known exponent of this tradition of peasant Christian communism. While Lenin seeks to identify the distinct insights from Tolstoy, especially in terms of the profound criticisms of feudal and capitalist exploitation in Russia, he dismisses Tolstoy's Christian communism as simplistic, spiritualised and impractical. But Lenin misses the way Tolstoy deploys both the revolutionary and communal dimensions of the tradition I have identified. In Tolstoy, they are inseparable. The third section engages with Anatoly Lunacharsky, who offers the most unique Russian contribution to the whole tradition. As a resolute atheist, Lunarcharsky developed 'God-building', by which he meant that the gods of religion were ideal models to which human beings should strive through socialist construction. Lunarcharsky saw revolutions as high points of this God-building, but his lasting contribution was to structure the world's first socialist educational system in terms of God-building, leaving a legacy for later socialist education policies.

In the twelfth chapter, I move back in time a little to the Chinese Taiping Revolution in the mid-nineteenth century. It was not only the largest revolutionary movement in the world at the time, but also one that was inspired by Christianity. Indeed, it marks the moment when the revolutionary religious tradition arrived in China. My account of the revolution stresses the role of the Bible, its radical reinterpretation by the Taiping revolutionaries, and the role it played in their radical acts and their reconstruction of economic and social relations. My assessment of the Taiping Revolution needs to engage with the many interpretations offered in both Chinese and foreign works, since I seek to provide a distinct interpretation in light of the Christian communist tradition. To this end, I identify a number of key features: its revolutionary nature, challenging the whole imperialist system in China; its effort at constructing a different social order; its constitutive use of unorthodox or 'heterodox' interpretations of the Bible; its emphasis on dreams and visions; its deep contextualisation or 'sinification'; and its primary appeal to peasants and disaffected labourers, especially miners. I close the chapter by considering Mao Zedong's cautious assessment, particularly since it is so often seen as the first modern revolution in China.

Still in China, the thirteenth chapter moves to the first part of the twentieth century when a number of Christian theologians engaged actively with communism and Marxist theory. I focus on the work of Wu Leichuan (1870–1944), Wu Yaozong (1893–1979) and Zhu Weizhi (1905–1999), who creatively sought engagements between Christianity and historical materialism and thereby articulated a unique Chinese development, although they also drew on international currents of thought. The chapter analyses their varying methods of doing so, their reconstructions of the figure of Jesus and early Christianity, and the efforts to see both the links and differences between Christianity and communism.

The final chapter concerns Korea, or more specifically the Democratic People's Republic of Korea. That this part of the world is in our own time somewhat demonised and misunderstood is perhaps an understatement. But this situation has meant that very little serious study has been undertaken. My analysis begins by considering the role of Chondoism, a uniquely Korean form of religion that arose in the nineteenth century. Not only does it reveal that religion and revolution are not restricted to Christianity, but it also enables me to delve into the work of Kim Il Sung. He offers a knowledgeable assessment, seeking to emphasise the deeply revolutionary credentials of Chondoism. The next section continues with Kim Il Sung, now in terms of his extensive assessments of Protestant Christianity. While he is in two minds about how much he was part of the Presbyterian Church in his youth, he is certainly appreciative of the sustained support he received from the close family friend, the Reverend Son Jong Do. At times, he deploys classic Reformed theological arguments, leading him to assert that there is 'no law preventing religious believers from making the revolution'. The final section analyses the situation in the DPRK today, drawing on some insightful studies that show how Christianity has survived and flourished once again in this part of the world – contrary to many unfounded assertions that would have us believe otherwise. Most intriguingly, it is a form of Christianity that is part of the socialist construction in the DPRK and one of its main avenues of international diplomacy.

Two final comments: First, a book such as this does not seek to deal with every aspect of the Christian communist tradition, for this would require an encyclopaedia. For example, I do not engage in detail with either messianism or the Essenes. In terms of messianism, I have dealt elsewhere and in-depth with Ernst Bloch, who was instrumental in bringing a reworked category of messianism – as an aspect of what he called utopia – into Marxism. As for the Essenes, they were for many the Jewish forerunners of early Christian communism. They appear in my treatment of Kautsky and Lunacharsky, although since the time of their treatments much has been discovered (the Dead Sea

Scrolls) and scholarly work has multiplied. I also do not offer an assessment of Latin American Liberation theology, which for many is the most well-known recent manifestation of the tradition. Since this subject has been tackled competently by many others, I have nothing to add. Instead, I prefer to focus on different angles, forgotten works and unexpected corners, such as Kautsky's *Forerunners*, Farnham Maynard or the DPRK. Second, as I mentioned earlier, a few of the chapters have appeared in earlier publications, with some moderate editing to render them suitable for the longer format of a monograph. Permission has been granted for their use here. They are: "'All Things Are in Common": Theology and Politics in Luther Blissett's *Q' International Socialism: A Quarterly Journal of Socialist Theory* 141 (2014): 139–59; 'Marxism and Eschatology Reconsidered', *Mediations* 25.1 (2011): 39–60; 'Althusser's Religious Revolution', *Althusser and Theology: Religion, Politics and Philosophy*, ed. Agon Hamza. Leiden: Brill, pp. 18–30; 'Chinese Christian Communism in the Early Twentieth Century' (with Chin Kenpa), *Religion, State and Society* 44.2: 96–110.

The remaining chapters – the majority – have either been completely re-written or appear here for the first time.

Karl Kautsky's *Forerunners of Modern Socialism*

The first comprehensive effort to establish a tradition of Christian communism was by neither a theologian nor a church historian. Instead, it was the Marxist Karl Kautsky. A towering figure among the second generation of Marxists and leading light in the massive German social-democratic movement, Kautsky and Engels had been discussing this question for a few years. However, while Engels had established an initial and basic framework in his studies of the Peasant Revolution and the revolutionary origins of Christianity (1850a, 1850b, 1894–95a, 1894–95b),[1] Kautsky and his collaborators took the project much, much further.[2] Although he contributed the lion's share of the final work, we also find contributions from Eduard Bernstein, Paul Lafargue, Hugo Lindemann and Morris Hillquit (Kautsky 1895, Kautsky et al. 1895).[3]

Despite its importance, *Forerunners* has often been neglected (although this is not the case with the earlier work by Ernst Troeltsch).[4] It would be easy to

---

[1] Following in Engels's footsteps is the work by Bebel (1876).

[2] Although Engels and Kautsky corresponded in the early 1890s concerning the Bible and Christianity, especially in light of Engels's forthcoming article on early Christianity but also other aspects of the development of Christianity (Engels 1891a, 174, 1891b, 88, 1891c, 200, 1891d, 114, 1892a, 1892b, 1892c, 493–94, 1892d, 422–23, 1894a, 314, 1894b, 260, 1894c, 321, 1894d, 268, 1894e, 328–29, 1894f, 276), Engels was curiously unaware of the forerunners project. He found out only after it was published, prompting initially a hurting and sharp response and then appreciation, along with a few quibbles (Engels 1895a, 1895b). By this time, the throat cancer that would soon end Engels's life on 5 August was well advanced.

[3] A comparison between the two-volume version of 1895 and the four volumes of 1922 reveal some editorial revisions. The material up to Thomas More remains the same, as it had all been written by Kautsky. However, in the 1922 edition, volume three has removed the contribution by Bernstein, keeping only the chapter on More by Kautsky and two chapters by Lafargue on Campanella and the Jesuits in Paraguay (Kautsky and Lafargue 1922). The final volume keeps the chapter on French socialism in the seventeenth and eighteenth centuries, but the final chapter on the various communist communities in North America is completely rewritten by Morris Hillquit (Lindemann and Hillquit 1922). Since my focus is on Kautsky, my references are to the original edition.

[4] Troeltsch (1992, 1912) felt called upon to take Kautsky's Marxist approach to task, although he follows a similar line in relation to the medieval and reformation groups. For a detailed and insightful study, see Goldstein (2014: 475–76, 478–83). By contrast, more recent work devoted to Müntzer at best mentions Kautsky in passing but usually prefer to ignore him, as do those that focus on the Münster Revolution (Gritsch 1989; Scott 1989; Friesen 1990; Goertz 2000; Bak et al. 2013, 90, 99). Marxist scholars too have been rather keen to dismiss his work (Löwy 1996, 10–11; Toscano 2010a, 76, 2010b, xiv).

point out that significant new historical materials have been uncovered in the last 120 years or more, or that critical work has moved beyond Kautsky. But that is to miss the point of Kautsky's inaugural act in identifying a tradition of Christian communism. So in what follows, I offer a critical exposition of the work as a whole. The process entails dealing with a mix of sources in German and English. Indeed, a signal of – if not also a contributor to – the neglect of the work is that only part of the work has been translated, more than a century ago: *Communism in Central Europe in the Time of the Reformation* (1897) comprises an abridged version of the original first volume published in German. It leaves out a swathe of material from Plato to the Beghards, as well as later chapters on medieval movements from the Waldensians to the Dulcinians, the Beghards and the Lollards. For this reason, my references are at times only to the German material, while in other moments I am able to refer to both English and German texts. My exposition seeks to present the main topics covered, noting Kautsky's enthusiasms (especially the Peasant Revolution of 1525 and that of Münster in 1534–1535) but above all drawing out and focusing on the key analytic categories deployed.

To wit, Kautsky deploys a number of distinctions that attempt to organise his narrative. The first concerns communal organisation and revolutionary action. Kautsky identifies communistic formations in all of the groups or proposals he studies, from Plato and early Christian communism onwards. However, it becomes somewhat secondary with the first militant group, the Dulcinians, at the beginning of the fourteenth century. This revolutionary militancy will characterise nearly all of the groups that follow, down to the Anabaptists at Münster, although he puts due emphasis on the latter's communal dimensions. In Kautsky's hands, this distinction becomes a historical one. I will not say more concerning the distinction here, for it will be subjected to analysis and criticism in what follows. A closely related distinction is between, on the one hand, the unpolitical and passive, and, on the other, the politically active and rebellious (Kautsky 1897, 27–28, 1895, 135, 138). While the former he finds with early Christian communism, the latter type appears with the Dulcinians, fuelled both by economic developments and a burning desire to read the Bible for themselves. Thus far, Kautsky has not provided any feature that distinguishes modern communism from pre-modern forms. He may observe that early Christian and heretical forms of communism are one with the modern variety in terms of their international, or rather 'interlocal [*interlokal*]', nature.[5] But they are different in one crucial area: the pre-modern

---

5   Like their modern comrades, the earlier communists were united everywhere in struggling against oppression and exploitation: if a communist 'finds comrades he is at home' (Kautsky 1897, 26, 1895, 135).

forms were all varieties of a communism of consumption rather than production. They sought to share their goods, abrogating private property in favour of common property that was distributed to any as had need (Acts 2 and 4). But this approach did little to change the actual means of production in the economic processes at large. For Kautsky, only modern communism attempts such a transformation. Again, I will note this distinction where it appears and its problems (it will also be addressed in Chapter 3). The final distinction is not raised directly by Kautsky, but it emerges from both the previous point and the whole project. This concerns continuity and discontinuity, which is endemic to the task he and his collaborators set themselves. The appeal of such a project is obvious, for it sought to show that the struggle for communism in its many forms was a long one indeed, finally coming to fruition after Marx. But the danger is that modern socialism becomes merely a phase of a longer history, with relatively little to set it apart from its forerunners.

The final introductory question concerns terminology: what should these pre-modern movements be called? Kautsky distinguishes between different types of communism, particularly 'Christian communism [*christliche kommunismus*]', 'monastic communism [*klösterliche kommunismus*]', 'heretical communism [*ketzerische kommunismus*]', and 'modern communism [*neuere kommunismus*]' (Kautsky 1897, 24–28, 1895, 133–38).[6] Of these, my – and indeed Kautsky's – focus is the common ground between Christian and heretical communism, so I use 'Christian communism' to cover both types. Indeed, when concluding his detailed treatment of the Reformation era (with the account of Münster), Kautsky uses the term 'Christian communism' for the whole period up to the sixteenth century (Kautsky 1897, 293, 1895, 436).[7] So also with my text.

1   The Manifold Types of Heretical Communism

The first volume of *Forerunners* – completely written by Kautsky – sets the scene by discussing briefly Plato's *Republic*, summarises the main points concerning early Christian communism, sets up the socio-economic context of the European Middle Ages, delves into the many radical movements from the Waldensians to the Bohemian Brethren and then focuses intently on the Peasant Revolution and the Anabaptists in Münster. His concern is to establish – in good historical-materialist fashion – the socio-economic background to each

---

6 Monastic communism is in some respects an offshoot of Christian communism, although it raises some intriguing problems for Kautsky, which I will address in the next chapter.

7 Note also, in the untranslated German text, the generic '*religiös-kommunistischen Gemeinde* [religious-communist communities]' (Kautsky 1895, 108).

of the movements he analyses, which then enables analysis of the ideological and political dimensions. Thus, with regard to Plato, he initially covers the political, economic, historical (Peloponnesian War) and even philosophical (pre-Socratic) context of Plato's thought, before engaging with *The Republic*. Here Kautsky finds the first systematic and philosophical outline of communism. However, unlike later forms of communism, it is what he calls '*gleichheitskommunismus*', or egalitarian communism (the term comes from Engels) – forerunner of later, liberal versions.[8] Already at this point do we find the distinction I mentioned earlier, between a communism of production and one of consumption. In what will become a refrain throughout the work, he finds a communism of consumption in Plato, with the outcome that it did nothing to change the actual economic relations of exploitation.

Christian communism appears next, after a leap of some 500 years. Here Kautsky agrees to some extent with Engels's thesis: we find the influence of chiliasm, with its revolutionary concerns, and the appeal of the Christian message to the poor – slaves, labourers and urban unemployed. But on two crucial points, Kautsky goes beyond Engels, with each point raising a further question. First, he argues that early Christian communities were communist in organisation (Acts 2:44-45 and 4:32-35), albeit focused on consumption. Although this proposal is relatively brief in *Forerunners*, it generated significant controversy, with theologians and socialists criticising the argument. This criticism prompted Kautsky to develop the comprehensive analysis found in *Foundations of Christianity* (1908a, 1908b), which I will analyse in more detail in the next chapter. But what is the question raised by this proposal? It concerns the passive-active distinction I mentioned earlier. For Kautsky, early Christian communism tended to be passive and non-political, while medieval 'heretical' communism was active and political. By this he means a contrast between communal life, often in retreat from the world, and revolutionary action. Only with some forms of medieval 'heretical' communism do we find the latter, appearing first with the Dulcinians. As we will see, the distinction is not so much one of either-or, but often both-and. At times, a movement evinces both features, while at other times it may focus on one or the other. This argument leads to Kautsky's second difference from Engels. The latter had argued that Christianity's revolutionary credentials appeared with its conquest of the Roman Empire. Kautsky demurs. Instead, he sees this 'conquest' in terms of a narrative of betrayal, if not a 'Fall' narrative (Genesis 3). The betrayal in question was the transformation of Christianity from a communist movement to the religion of

---

8   It should also be distinguished from 'Salon communism', characteristic of Roman rulers playing with philosophy. As Kautsky writes in a sharp sentence: 'Aber dieser Salonkommunismus des Modephilosophen bildete nur eine der zahlreichen Spielereien' (Kautsky 1895, 21).

empire by the fourth century CE, with all of the attached privileges. Formally, this narrative is endemic to both reform and socialist movements. At some point, so the narrative goes, the church or a socialist revolution loses its way, becoming corrupted by the trappings of power. What is needed, then, is not only a recovery of the initial impulse, but also an effort to understand how the betrayal took place. However, I am not sure that a 'Fall' narrative is the best argument (Kautsky will use it from time to time in his treatment of medieval movements), for it assumes an authentic and original core that is then undone. Instead, I will develop later an initial and constitutive contradiction that can lead in either a reactionary or a revolutionary direction.

Let us stay with this problem a little longer. According to Kautsky's account (1895, 35–39), he seeks to explain how the European Christian Church[9] became in the Middle Ages a possessor of massive property and enmeshed with slavery. Given that he analyses this development in terms of a narrative of betrayal, Kautsky has to account for the rise of radical communist movements in the Middle Ages and the Reformation era. He sees these movements as recovering the initial impulse of early Christian communism, albeit transforming this impulse from a passive to an active role. This shift, he argues, was due to crucial economic changes. Thus, in the second chapter of *Forerunners* he sets the context for later radical developments. Here we find treatments of various wage-workers and nascent classes: artisans, guilds and journeymen, the roles of apprentices and masters, the organisation of groups in what would later be called class struggle, the village-communes with land held in common (*Markgenossenschaft*) and the 'mining right [*Bergrecht*]', the tensions between town artisans and miners, the rise of early capitalist engagement with mining, and the miners themselves. What emerges from this analysis is that the Middle Ages was certainly not stagnant in terms of economic changes and that class struggle was already becoming a paramount issue.

Now Kautsky delves into the long history of Christian communist movements. Since one can find outlines of each movement in other places, I do not need to repeat such outlines here: Arnold of Brescia, Waldensians, Apostolic Brethren, Dulcinians, Beghards, Lollards, Bohemian Brethren, running from the twelfth to the fifteenth centuries. Instead, let me return to the distinction between communal practice and revolutionary action. Although a key insight of the study, Kautsky deploys it in different ways. At times, it takes the form of a passive-active opposition, used to distinguish early Christian communism from the 'heretical' communism of the Middle Ages; at other times, the term 'communist' applies to communal organisation; and at others he distinguishes

---

9 He does not deal with the large Church of the East and its push across into China, let alone Eastern Orthodoxy or the Coptic Church.

between movements in terms of one or the other tendency. I am particularly interested in the last distinction, for reasons that will become clear. Thus, Arnold of Brescia, the Waldensians and Apostolic Brethren focused on communal organisation, while the Dulcinians, the early stages of the Bohemian Reformation (Taborites) and at times the Lollards were more revolutionary.[10]

So we find: Arnold of Brescia's call for the Roman Catholic Church to renounce temporal possessions and return to apostolic simplicity, as well as his leadership role in the Commune of Rome from 1145 to 1155 (he was rewarded for his efforts with hanging, burning and having his ashes thrown into the Tiber River). Or the Waldensians, who initially gathered around Peter Waldo in Lyon (1173). Crucial for them too was voluntary poverty (*freiwillig Armut*), selling all one has and having property in common (Acts 2 and 4 and the Sermon on the Mount), relative gender equality, and – due to systemic persecution – a retreat to the countryside, especially the valleys of the Piedmont. Here they took on what Kautsky (1895, 147) calls the 'character of small-peasant democracy'. Or the Apostolic Brethren (Apostolici), inspired by Gerardo Segarelli, a poor dealer from Parma in Italy. He and his followers too renounced possessions (first in 1260) and had goods in common, but they also dressed as they thought the first apostles might have done, going about begging and preaching repentance (inspired by Mark 6:7-13 and Luke 10:1-12). Or the Beguines and then the Beghards, or 'Sisters and Brothers of the Free Spirit' (Kautsky focuses more on the latter), who emerged in the twelfth century around Liège and spread into the Netherlands and the regions around Cologne. Condemned and persecuted from time to time, women and men of the movement persisted until the seventeenth century. Although they formed voluntary communities, focusing on spirituality and communal living, they differed from many of the others by continuing their types of skilled labour, often as weavers. Kautsky dubs their movement as one of a 'communist cooperative'. They formed, in other words, local units of production, gaining a reputation for diligent labour that was to become a characteristic feature of the Taborites, Bohemian Brethren and Anabaptists in Moravia. Of course, this productive emphasis questions Kautsky's efforts to characterise all of the pre-modern movements as determined by a communism of consumption (upon which he will elaborate some years later in *Foundations of Christianity* – see the next chapter). Clearly, they were focused on production – an issue to which I will return. But at this point, let me ask another question: how do these movements differ from similar earlier examples, which also renounced wealth and sought to recover apostolic

---

10   The next three chapters are omitted from the English translation: Chapter 3 (of Part 3) on heretical communism in Italy and Southern France; Chapter 4 on the Beghards; Chapter 5 on the Lollards.

simplicity (the Franciscans being the most notable example)? Simply put, each of them drew the ire of the pope. Had they been approved, they would have fallen into a monastic pattern and developed into 'aristocratic communism'. But this was not to be. Instead, the plethora of such movements was resisted, condemned as heretical and persecuted, to the extent of a ban on all new mendicant movements at the Second Council of Lyon in 1274. Radicalisation was the natural response, in which religious symbols (Eucharist in both elements and vernacular Bibles being the most common) were championed against a Rome that became the evil and idolatrous 'Babylon' of the book of Revelation.

Radicalisation was not restricted to communal life and the rejection of Rome. At a certain point, armed resistance would also appear in the form of the Dulcinians. Indeed, for Kautsky (1895, 153) they mark 'the first attempt at an armed communist uprising [*der erste Versuch einer bewaffneten kommunistischen Erhebung*]'. So they were not merely brigands or even guerrilla fighters, holding out against crusaders sent to crush them in their fortress on Monte Rubello in the Piedmont. And it was not merely because Fra Dolcino of Novarra (1250–1307), who took over leadership of the Apostolic Brethren in 1300 and turned them in a militant direction, had a liking for the millenarian theories of Joachim of Fiore (although these theories also have venerable revolutionary credentials after the work of Ernst Bloch). Kautsky is keen to emphasise how the revolutionary approach also arose from changing socio-economic conditions, affecting peasants and wage-workers and leading them to a nascent sense of class consciousness. It helps that four letters from the erudite Dolcino have survived, in which he advocated liberation from feudal and ecclesial hierarchies, as well as the communistic organisation of society with which we have become familiar – property in common, mutual aid and respect. Clearly, the two sides Kautsky has identified – communal life and revolution – come together with the Dulcinians. It is not for nothing that they later became seen as early socialist champions in the Italian Left, with workers erecting a monument on Monte Rubello.

A new phase had dawned with the Dulcinians, which enables Kautsky to deal with a number of revolutionary Christian communist movements. These include that peculiarly English development, Lollardy. Emerging late in the twelfth century, their symbols were the vernacular Bible to be studied by all and refusal of the standard hallmarks of the Roman Catholic Church. Due to repeated persecution, the Lollards eventually became revolutionary, especially in the Peasant's Revolution of 1381 (although it included apprentices, artisans, gentry and clergy), under the inspiration of John Ball and Wat Tyler and driven by the economic upheavals of the fourteenth century. Kautsky gives more time to what is often called the Bohemian Reformation, focusing mostly on the major group known as the Taborites (from their base in Tabor). Emerging in the fourteenth century under the inspiration of Jan Hus (who was promptly burnt at the stake for his teachings), their biblically-based theological and liturgical criticisms of Rome were closely connected with their communistic organisation and formidable military might. Not to be neglected here are the economic developments in Bohemia, in terms of mining, an emerging money economy, enclosures and deep changes in the class relations of the peasantry and nobility. Indeed, class provides the key to the initial success of the Taborites and their undoing, at least in their first phase. Focused on peasants and relatively new wage workers, it was able to develop both 'democratic' organisation and forms of production,[11] indicating once again that a communism of production could arise before modern communism – so much that the Taborites gained a reputation for their diligent labour and productivity. Let me return to the question of class, for here Kautsky also locates the undoing of the Taborites. In light of their stunning military successes, they attracted more and more other class elements, such as disaffected minor nobility, freebooters, brigands and so on. This had the effect of diluting the initial communistic impetus and introducing divisions in the movements. All of which took place while their opponents were regrouping and in the context of their inability to effect a full transformation in mode of production. The time, in other words, was not ripe. The effective end of the Taborites came at the Battle of Lipany, 30 May, 1434, in which their army was all but wiped out. Three years later the remainder capitulated to Emperor Sigismund.

The final movement before the era of the German Reformation is the Bohemian Brethren, who both continued the spirit of the Bohemian Reformation of the fifteenth century and fell decisively on the side of communistic social organisation. Kautsky seems to have relatively little interest in this group, for his analysis is somewhat superficial. Making their first appearance in 1457, they eschewed revolutionary violence and focused on radical communistic settlements. Even under persecution, forcing them to flee into the forests and caves, they continued their form of collective life, which also entailed diligent attention to labour. Here lies the source of their 'Fall', according to Kautsky: such labour produces relative wealth, putting pressure on the community. After some internal struggle, the Bohemian Brethren succumbed to the temptations of wealth and became too bourgeois (and relatively pacifist) for Kautsky's

---

11   Kautsky use of 'democracy' here seems to be influenced by the close connection between democracy and communism at the turn of the twentieth century in Europe and Russia (Kolonitskii 2004). At the same time, Kautsky (1897, 177) also uses 'democracy' to refer to incipient bourgeois forms in the towns as 'town democracy'.

interest in their later development (especially after their rejuvenation in Saxony from 1722). Although we have encountered this 'Fall' narrative on more than one occasion, I have not as yet commented on its inherent problems. Given its biblical provenance, it is common indeed in the history of Christianity. But it faces significant problems. Let me put it this way: such a narrative entails a claim to return to the original teachings and social practices that have been distorted by the many layers of institutional corruption. This tendency may manifest itself as moderate reform or radical revolution, but it is predicated on the claim to originality. The perpetually new monastic movements in the Middle Ages through to the Protestant Reformation and especially the Peasant and Münster Revolutions all evince the same pattern with myriad variations. Of course, there is no singular account of origins in the sacred texts, so that each reform movement could and still does lay claim to a different origin. But Kautsky's use of this narrative is not restricted to his treatment of Christian communism, for, like so many 'Western' Marxists, he also has a tendency to deploy an analogous 'Fall' narrative in relation to Marxism itself, predicated on finding the 'original' meaning of the texts of Marx and Engels. To return to the Bohemian Brethren in their later incarnation, under the auspices of Count Zinzendorf in Herrnhut, Saxony: is an alternative to a narrative of betrayal possible? It may be the case that the path of these reformers was, particularly in Eastern Europe, a complex transition to capitalism rather than a simple betrayal.[12] In breaking with the re-feudalisation of Eastern Europe, working in early forms of industrial production (in village houses) and highly mobile, they may well have enabled such a transition (Petterson In press).

Since I would like to focus for the rest of this chapter on Thomas Müntzer and the Anabaptists in Münster, let me deal briefly with the remainder of *Forerunners* first. Kautsky's last contribution to the collection concerns his beloved Thomas More, who was also the topic of a separate earlier study (Kautsky 1888a, 1888b). More's *Utopia* he regards as one of the major socialist texts before Marx and Engels. More too was inspired by Christian communism, which he found in old popular Roman Catholicism and the monastic tradition. Indeed, More was the last representative of this tradition, dying as a martyr. But More also criticised economic exploitation in the England of Henry VIII, offering *Utopia* as an economic, political and social alternative to what he experienced. At this level, he was also a materialist critic, thereby becoming the crucial link between older Christian communism and modern communism, between medieval religiosity and historical materialism. Christian communism may have come to an end with the Münster Revolution, but More

---

12   Another way of putting it is that the early movement made the transition from 'sect' to 'church', but I seek to emphasise the economic dimension.

provides the moment of transition, in which the first glimpses of modern socialism begin to emerge. Later studies include those of Thomas Campanella (1568–1639), who sought to establish a movement based on the community of goods with a distinctly apocalyptic tone – revising Joachim of Fiore's work, Campanella anticipated the Age of the Spirit in 1600. But this contribution was written by Paul Lafargue, Marx's son-in-law, who also wrote the section on the autonomous indigenous communities established by the Jesuits in Paraguay in the seventeenth and eighteenth centuries. A substantial study of the seventeenth-century English (bourgeois) revolution was written by Eduard Bernstein (excised from the revised edition of 1922), who covers the Calvinist inspiration of the Puritans, the Quakers, Francis Bacon, Hobbes's *Leviathan*, Harrington's *Oceania*, and especially the biblically-inspired communist utopia proposed by Gerrard Winstanley and the True Levellers (Winstanley 1983). The final contributions come from Hugo Lindemann on the socialist developments in France and North America, from the seventeenth into the eighteenth century (although the North American chapter was later rewritten, with much greater detail, by Morris Hillquit). Here the focus is as much on the spate of utopian socialist literature as it is on communities themselves, or rather, in the French context, literature abounded while in North America one community after another was established, either to come to an end in a few short years or to transform into fully-fledged capitalist enterprises. By this time, capitalism already had a couple of centuries to establish itself. North America may have presented a curious 'state of nature', where one could experiment anew, but the reality was experiments that lent themselves towards fostering capitalist enterprises. By this time, the vast project bumps into the period when modern socialism emerges.

2   Müntzer and Münster

To return to Kautsky's reconstruction: if Thomas More's was his personal favourite, then 'in popular consciousness [*Volksbewußtsein*] Müntzer was and is the most brilliant embodiment of heretical communism' (Kautsky 1897, 154, 1895, 312).[13] Engels's influence, from his essay of 1850, is one reason, but so also is the ability to claim an earlier hero for the struggles of workers and peasants. In light of this tradition, Kautsky devotes far more space to this theologian of the revolution, as well as the Anabaptist Revolution in Münster a decade later (1534–1535). The structure of his reconstruction follows the pattern already established: attention to the socio-economic conditions; concern with

---

13   Translation modified.

the myriad currents, especially now in the context of the German Reformation; and the connection between theological positions and social acts. On at
least one key feature, the accounts of both revolutions differ from most of the
earlier ones. Since they came to a violent end, crushed by the combined forces
of the powers that be, Kautsky does not need to deploy a narrative of betrayal.
Indeed, the 'failure' of the revolutionary moment means that they could die
martyrs, holding on to their principles to the end.

Saxony, Kautsky begins, had experienced an economic boom from its mining and weaving activities. Indeed, if one travels through Saxony and Thuringia
today, preferably by bicycle or on foot, one can still find mines across the countryside, some operating and others no longer so. Old weaving centres still bear
traces of their past, especially in the Lusatian League.[14] While this boom meant
that Friedrich III (1463–1525), Elector of Saxony, became powerful indeed and
was able to refuse bribes (for his vote in elections for the Holy Roman Emperor),
the miners, weavers and indeed peasants found that conditions were not so
beneficial. They also discovered the power of armed force, for their resistance
had direct economic repercussions. The situation in Saxony was favourable to
Luther, protected by the Elector, but also for the more radical Müntzer, who
found the miners, weavers and peasants responsive to his message. Kautsky
later returns to the question of socio-economic conditions, as the revolution
itself draws near. Now he focuses on the deteriorating conditions for peasants
in light of early commodity production and primitive accumulation of capital
in the fifteenth century, the wave of enclosures and the consequent indigence
of peasants seeking work. To be added here are changes in methods of warfare,
with relatively well-trained mercenaries and the spread of gunpowder use.
With these developments, the time was increasingly ripe for revolution, which –
argues Kautsky – must have been obvious to someone like Müntzer.

Significant here is that despite Kautsky's tendency at times to see religious
language as a cloak (here he follows Engels's study of Müntzer), he pays careful
attention to what Müntzer actually thought. These include the first liturgy in
German, published in Allstedt (also spelled Allstätt and Allstädt), and associated documents, leaflets and letters. Kautsky is particularly interested in their
democratic (communistic) and revolutionary features. The earlier texts, suggests Kautsky, tend to focus on church and community organisation, evincing
a relatively peaceful tone. This included a democratic approach to worship,

---

14   Dating from 1346, the league included Görlitz, Bautzen, Löbau, Zittau, Kamenz and Lau-
      ban, all of them in the Sorbian minority nationality area. Already from the fourteenth
      century, the economic strength of the towns was in cloth manufacture, rising to a signifi-
      cant force in the late fifteenth century. Radical tendencies have run through the area for
      centuries.

with all participating, counsels to discipline so as not to cause undue trouble, a form of what Kautsky calls 'pantheistic mysticism' (Müntzer's predilection for dreams and visions is duly noted), and religious tolerance for the variety of religious practices in sovereign states (Kautsky 1897, 113–16, 1895, 268–72).

The turn comes at the famous sermon delivered to the princes, with the title 'Interpretation of the Second Chapter of Daniel' (Müntzer 1988, 230–52). It was delivered in Allstedt on 13 July, 1524, to Duke Johann (John) of Saxony, brother and soon successor of Friedrich III, the Elector of Saxony who had done so much to enable Luther's efforts. Others too were present, including Johann's son, Johann Friedrich. The sermon offers a skilful exegesis of Daniel 2, setting up sharp distinctions between the elect and damned, prophet and soothsayer, Christ and Antichrist, so as to call on the princes to destroy the oppressors and evil ones so as to liberate the poor and oppressed, who are humiliated now in a manner similar to Christ. Drawing on a full range of biblical texts, Müntzer then quotes Christ: 'I am not come to bring peace, but the sword' (Matthew 10:34). 'But what is one to do with the sword? Exactly this: sweep aside those evil men who obstruct the gospel! Take them out of circulation!' But if the princes will not carry out their divinely appointed task, 'the sword will be taken from them' (Müntzer 1988, 246, 250).[15] Despite sympathetic ears, Müntzer's call was to no avail, although he was given room to move on and was not overly restricted (apart from limiting some printing presses from publishing his works). As Kautsky points out, Müntzer had moved from seeking to persuade others to rousing his associates and comrades. This is the tone of the later letters quoted by Kautsky, as well as the *Confession*. Indeed, here we find the crucial combination of both communal organisation and insurrection. As Kautsky quotes:

> In regard to what was to be understood by 'the Gospel', he asserts: 'It is an article of our creed, and one which we wish to realise, that all things are in common [*omnia sunt communia*], and should be distributed as occasion requires, according to the several necessities of all. Any prince, count, or baron who, after being earnestly reminded of this truth, shall be unwilling to accept it, is to be beheaded or hanged'.[16]
>
> KAUTSKY 1897, 130, 1895, 284

---

15   'On Counterfeit Faith' from December of 1523 already speaks of the need 'to root out, tear
     down and scatter the counterfeit Christians' (Müntzer 1988, 218).
16   The text translated by Matheson reads: 'All things are to be held in common [*omnia sunt
     communia*] and distribution should be to each according to his need, as occasion arises.
     Any prince, count, or gentleman who refused to do this should first be given a warning,
     but then one should cut off his head or hang him' (Müntzer 1988, 437).

Omnia sunt communia is of course the Latin translation of the slogan 'all things in common' in Acts 2:44 and 4:32, the core inspiration – as I have already noted earlier – for Christian communism itself. Kautsky also stresses the organisational ability of Müntzer, for he was far from being a somewhat deluded visionary. Although he was one of a number of the complex and interweaving currents at the time, Kautsky (1897, 110, 1895, 266) emphasises that his significant contribution was due 'to his extravagant communistic enthusiasm, combined with an iron determination, passionate impetuosity, and statesmanlike sagacity'. On this matter Kautsky (1897, 145, 1895, 300) stresses the already existing networks, maintained through the 'indefatigable interlocal activity of the communistic "apostles"', of peasants, townspeople and especially the militant miners. In the end, it was not to be enough, for time was too short, plans were not sufficiently developed and the divisions too strong. But not for want trying. All of this was inseparable from Müntzer's theological engagements, with a view to overthrowing oppressors and freeing those burdened in the name of a thoroughly democratic and communist project. It was certainly not Ernst Bloch who first stressed the integral role of biblical interpretation and theological engagement with Müntzer's and indeed the peasants' revolutionary activity.[17] We find it very much in Kautsky's detailed reconstruction, so much that he can mention the Gospel and democracy (communism) as one and the same: Müntzer 'urged them to stand fast to the Gospel (i.e., by the democratic cause), and to resist its enemies' (Kautsky 1897, 129, 1895, 283).

Overall, Kautsky's analysis of Müntzer is rather astute for its time, going well beyond Engels's effort and despite a tendency to glide over material at other times. He is judicious when using secondary sources, attempting to address their anti-Müntzer bias, as we also find with his treatment of the revolution at Münster. And he offers a gentle – and somewhat heretical in a German context – downgrading of Luther's contribution to the German Reformation. Luther emerges as the lesser theologian, a man buffeted and overtaken by events and innovations. All he could do much of the time was appropriate the initiatives of others and claim them as his own.[18] In this light, I find it strange – as mentioned earlier – that subsequent engagements with Müntzer rarely acknowledge Kautsky's work, making at best a passing reference. Of all those I have been able to consult, only Bloch (1969) acknowledges and draws upon Kautsky for his own analysis. This neglect, especially over the last decade or so, is all the more curious since Müntzer has been reappropriated by elements

---

17   As Toscano mistakenly suggests (2010b, xv–xvi).
18   Perhaps the only item missing is an appreciation of the ambiguity in Luther's own thought, which the radicals took further and from which Luther recoiled when he saw the implications.

of the anti-capitalist movement, featuring above all in the fascinating novel, *Q* (see Chapter 3). All this is taking place when the country where he was most acknowledged, being held up as a pre-modern revolutionary hero, has not only been erased from the map but almost erased from the memory of the European Left. I speak here of the DDR, East Germany, where – under the influence of Engels, Bebel, Kautsky, Mehring (1931) and Bloch – Müntzer was known by everyone. Indeed, the elaborate celebrations of the 500th year since Müntzer's birth – with more than a decade's preparation of sculptures, vast murals (especially in Bad Frankenhausen), marking of historical sites, publications and festivities – took place in September, 1989, only weeks before the DDR was enveloped, if not colonised, by West Germany. All of this does not rate a mention in more recent appropriations of Müntzer; the same – curiously – applies to Kautsky's analysis.

The treatment of the Anabaptists at Münster is the most thorough of all, with Kautsky finding himself drawn into far more detail than he at first planned. Tracking back, he opts primarily for what became known later as the 'monogenesis'[19] position: Anabaptism began as a peaceful movement in the context of the Swiss Reformation, focused on Zurich. Due to intense persecution, in which Protestant and Roman Catholic bodies often worked together, they spread into the Tyrol, Moravia (where their communist organisation flourished most fully until persecution set in), Southern Germany, The Netherlands and north-western Germany. While Kautsky sees little direct connection with Müntzer and the Peasant Revolution,[20] partly to counter anti-Anabaptist polemic, he does see a strong continuity within Anabaptism through to Münster. He prefers to understand this militant, well-nigh apocalyptic event as a response to repeated persecution. Perhaps a better angle is to see it as part of the complexity of the movement itself. Indeed, as I have argued earlier in this chapter, the revolutionary and the communal were two parts of the longer tradition of Christian communism. Other elements also appear, such as 'mysticism [*Schwärmer*]', anti-clericalism, radical concerns with origins, and of course a resolute focus on the Bible.

In many respects, Kautsky sees the Anabaptists as the greatest forerunners to modern socialism,[21] not least because many of the more recent accounts

---

19   This has become the majority approach to Anabaptist origins (Bender 1944; Friedmann 1973; Estep 1995).
20   A common tenet of the monogenetic position, although later polygenetic work indicates the complexity of interconnections, which included those with Müntzer and the radical Karlstadt (Klaassen 1973; Packull 1977a; Seebaß 2002).
21   Revealed also in his allusive language, which evokes modern socialist organisation: 'Greater importance, however, attaches to the second Congress in August, 1527, which was attended by more than sixty delegates from Germany, Austria, and Switzerland. Its chief

took these Anabaptists as models of the evils of communism. So his defence of the Anabaptists is as much a defence of the modern socialist movement. This includes his efforts to uncover the bias of his sources through a favoured move: revealing the contradictions in their narratives that show how unfounded are the depictions of debauchery, excess and sheer hypocrisy of the leadership.[22] It also leads him to emphasise the disciplined communal life instigated even under duress, as well as the basic desire for peace so as to be able to work at constructing their alternative social and economic organisation. In doing so, he must counter a wave of efforts to depict the Anabaptists as depraved monsters, who let loose the most primal of human passions once the fetters of 'respected order' had been cast aside.[23] Kautsky carefully reconstructs the limited nature of wealth redistribution (from the old order), the management of popular governance in democratic forms, the persistent enthusiasm and devotion to the cause even in the final hours (especially by the women), the desire for celebration even under siege and, perhaps the most contentious issue of all, the economic and social need for what has been called 'polygamy'. And old calumny indeed, levelled against all manner of socialist movements: the community of goods meant the communal 'use' of women by men – or so the detractors were ever fond of pointing out (assuming thereby the possession of women by men). Kautsky argues for the economic necessity in a town under prolonged siege: of about 10,000 defenders, 8,000 were women. Given that household structures were not dismantled, women were free to choose a household with a man 'in charge', and leave if it was unsuitable.

On this matter, Kautsky develops what may well be his most profound insight: any form of socialism is a work in progress, seeking the correct path to the unknown. Noting that there was no definitive statement on marriage, he traces the various reflections, announcements, backtracking and reformulations, pointing out that they 'never got beyond the *search* for a suitable form of marriage that met the extraordinary circumstances in which they found themselves' (Kautsky 1897, 269–70, 1895, 418). This observation applies not merely to

---

task was the organisation of the propaganda work, the sending of "apostles" into different districts, and perhaps also the settling of the programme, or "Confession"' (Kautsky 1897, 181; 1895, 341).

22 This is especially so of Gresbeck's eyewitness account, coloured by the fact that he went over to the besiegers and advised them of the best way to attack the beleaguered defenders. This account is now available in an excellent English translation of the original German (Mackay 2016). The bias Kautsky seeks to counter continues to appear in more recent works (Arthur 1999).

23 The great symbol was adult or believers' baptism, which Kautsky sees as a trenchant form of resistance against the political, cultural, and theological hegemony of the ruling class (Kautsky 1897, 170–72, 1895, 329–31).

relations between the sexes but to all forms of socialist construction. Too often do critics assume that socialism should be implanted perfectly in the blink of an eye, failing to understand that any such effort involves much trial and error for what can only be a work in progress. Kautsky also stresses the realities of Christian communism under siege, a lesson repeated time and again when any later efforts to construct socialism appear. Apart from the profound challenges of attempting to do so in what would later be an overwhelmingly capitalist context (Kautsky 1897, 214, 1895, 371–72), the ferocity of opponents is usually unbounded, as the punishments meted out to the defeated defenders at Münster already show. So also with international blockades, economic sanctions, fostering of civil wars and anti-socialist forces within, if not outright invasions that are found in the history of modern socialism. Kautsky does not opt for the position that the Anabaptist effort at Münster was thereby distorted by the necessity of dealing with counter-revolution, preferring to emphasise that they achieved far more than could be expected in the circumstances. But he also does not opt for the position that such a situation is normal for any effort at socialism, which is in our time perhaps much clearer.

3   Theology and Revolution

I have sought to provide a critical overview of Kautsky's much-neglected contributions to *Forerunners of Modern Socialism*, stressing certain aspects and problems. The main achievement is to establish a distinct tradition of what may be called Christian communism, in which he goes far beyond Engels's initial efforts. In doing so, his contribution is far indeed from the caricatures of Marxist approaches as 'reductionist' (Friesen 1965). Instead, Kautsky's work shows clearly that a Marxist framework is inclusive rather than reductionist. The economic base does not necessarily provide the sole key, for one can understand a movement fully only when economic, social, cultural, political and religious factors are taken into account. As his reconstruction unfolds, he introduces a number of key distinctions, which are useful but contain problems of their own. The first of these concerns communal organisation and revolutionary militancy. The first Kautsky finds already in Plato (in limited fashion) and early Christianity, running through until the breakthrough to militancy by the Dulcinians. Related is his distinction between passive and active forms, with the former most notable among the early Christian communists and the latter with the Dulcinians, Taborites, Lollards, the Peasant Revolution and Münster. However, as I have made clear on a number of occasions, the distinction is too sharp in Kautsky's analysis. The reason is relatively straightforward: organising a community along even some communist lines entails rejection and criticism of wider social norms. While some communities – even today – hope that their example may influence others, and while they prefer peaceful existence, unmolested by outsiders, the reality is that profound criticism (whether for theological or other reasons) also underlies revolutionary militancy. The latter may arise out of force of circumstances, such as persecution, but it may also arise from an awareness that any profound and long-lasting change requires that one needs to face the forces of counter-revolution, which are usually far more brutal in their efforts to suppress socialism, Christian or otherwise (as Kautsky notes in the ferocity of the forces arrayed against Münster, but of which one can find myriad examples since). Here too biblical texts come to the fore. Acts 2 and 4 may provide a model for collective life, but – as Kautsky notes – texts such as the Apocalypse, the Old Testament denunciations of tyrants and oppressors, and the words of Jesus that speak of bringing not peace but a sword, provided more than enough inspiration for revolutionary uprisings (Kautsky 1897, 27, 1895, 137). The communal life of the Beguines and Beghards is thus on a continuum with the Dulcinians and Lollards, if not Müntzer's peasants and the extraordinary effort at Münster. For these reasons, I have argued earlier that communal organisation along communist lines and revolutionary action are really two parts of the same reality, with one or the other coming to the surface depending on the circumstances. To go a little further, even when a community or even a whole country is able through whatever means to begin the process of constructing socialism, it requires military, economic and political strength, as well as allies, to withstand the constant pressure from its opponents.

I would like to close with a final question: what is the role of theology? At times Kautsky speaks of the *'religiöse Hülle'* or 'shell of religion' (1895, 124), much like Engels in the latter's assessment of Müntzer.[24] Yet Kautsky is also fully aware of the force of ideas from another age, if not the 'weight of religion'. The most insightful approach appears in a couple of pages in the midst of his long engagement with the Anabaptists. He writes: 'At the time of the Reformation, the general tone of thought was not legal, but theological, and, in consequence, the more radical a social movement, the more theological were its forms of expression' (Kautsky 1897, 221, 1895, 377).[25] Immediate concerns, notes Kautsky, are more obviously economic: a grievance over corn prices, hoarding by the rich, service demanded by a lord, restrictions to traditional rites of access to common lands, an increase in taxes that were already beyond the means of peasants and workers. But when those local protests gain more

---

24   The English translation of Kautsky's text has 'veil of religion' (1897, 11). Friesen's study (1965) can hardly get past this point.

25   Translation modified.

widespread and organised support, they typically take on modes of expression that go deeper, seeking underlying causes and expressing common grievances. At the time of the Reformation that was primarily in terms of theology, but in our own day it may be expressed in terms of particular political ideologies. In that formulation, he may seem to draw closer to Engels's suggestion concerning the 'cloak' or code of theological language for expressing political aspirations. But he does not do so, for no one language provides the authentic core, for which others are cloaks. Instead, his point is that theology and political thought are both modes through which radicalisation gains traction and grips the masses.[26]

---

[26]   In this respect, Kautsky anticipates more recent Marxist-inspired studies of the radical dimension of the Reformation (Brendler 1989; Vogler 1989).

CHAPTER 2

Early Christian Communism as a Political Myth

The enduring appeal of early Christian communism requires more attention, so in the present chapter I focus on this specific feature of Kautsky's construction of the long tradition of radical Christianity. Indeed, it was precisely this argument in *Forerunners* that he was prompted, due to criticism, to defend and elaborate in a work that followed a little over a decade late, *Foundations of Christianity* (1908) – the first historical and dialectical materialist account of the Bible as such.[1] Kautsky was not the only Marxist of the time to devote attention to this question, for a few years before his tome was published, Rosa Luxemburg published an essay on the same topic. Consideration of both their proposals leads me to assess in more detail a core feature of their reconstruction: the proposal that early Christian communism was one of consumption rather than production. Although I have broached this question in the previous chapter, it requires more critical attention here. Also running through their work is the question of history, specifically in relation to how much can be known of early Christianity, a question that leads me to deal with other scholarly work relating to the foundational texts of Acts 2 and 4. Curiously, biblical scholars and historians are less interested in whether we can reliably ascertain the existence or otherwise of early Christian communism, for they are almost all focused on denying that it was a form of communism, or may at most admit that it was a form of 'love communism' (Weber and Troeltsch – see Goldstein 2014). But I am interested in historical matters at two other levels: first, how the economic context leaves its mediated traces in the text; second, how this text gains a historical force of its own as an authoritative story, in terms of the history of scholarship itself, as the motivation for repeated and actual attempts at Christian communism, and through the suggestion – by Luxemburg – that modern communism would complete what early Christian communism began.

---

1 The book was immensely popular and influential, with translations – to give a few examples – into Finnish, English, Dutch, Hungarian, Greek, Russian, Polish, Romanian, Serbo-Croatian, Japanese and Chinese, with subsequent editions in German and then in many translations (Bentley 1982, 43).

1   **Reconstruction: Kautsky**

In the introduction to *Foundations*, Kautsky mentions the criticisms of his earlier *Forerunners of Modern Socialism*, criticisms that found 'fault mainly' with
the 'brief account of the communism of primitive Christianity' (Kautsky 1908a,
xxi, 1908b, 3). As a response, he felt the need for a fuller elaboration, which led
him to a work that was much larger than he initially intended.[2] In *Foundations*,
Kautsky draws heavily on the latest (German) biblical scholarship, so that he
is wary of written texts and treads carefully in historical reconstruction. After detailing the difficulties in delineating a historical Jesus, he seeks out the
economic and political backgrounds: not merely of the Greco-Roman context,
with its slave economy[3] and imperial state, but also of ancient Israel, with its
trade, peasant impoverishment, Babylonian exile (determinative for the production of religious beliefs and literature), and later movements, especially
Sadducees, Pharisees, Zealots and Essenes. Far from offering a reductionist account (Meeks 2003, 3), Kautsky does not explain everything in terms of the
economic base, but includes economics, class, politics, culture and ideas in a
comprehensive Marxist analysis.

With the Essenes, Kautsky nears his most significant but controversial topic:
early Christian communism, for which the Essenes provide a broader context.
If the Zealots evinced the active, revolutionary side of religious communism,
the Essenes developed the other, focusing on communal living away from urban centres. Kautsky uses the available sources, especially Josephus, to depict
a religious community that had all things in common, segregated the sexes and
foreswore sexual relations (although he notes that children were produced by
those in another, albeit lower, level of Essene organisation). Most importantly,
he argues that the Essenes had a communism of consumption rather than production. This hermeneutic principle had already been developed in his earlier
Forerunners, which he applied (although not without difficulty) to all forms
of pre-modern communism. The same applies to early Christianity, entailing
that they did nothing to change the socio-economic structures of the Greco-
Roman world. Only a communism that alters production rather than modes of
consumption would have a lasting effect.

---

2   For a detailed analysis of the influence of Kautsky's study on Max Weber, see Goldstein (2014:
    486–501).
3   Kautsky stresses that the slave economy or 'Ancient mode of production' inhibited innova-
    tion and rapidly stagnated. This argument resonates through the Marxist tradition, finding
    articulate expression in Anderson's later study (1974, 25–28). The reconstruction also tracks
    back to the socio-economic context of the Hebrew Bible, thereby providing the first histori-
    cal materialist overview of the whole Bible.

Where is the basis for this proposal? Kautsky engages in extensive biblical interpretation, of which I can give only a sample. Acts 2:44-45 and 4:32-35, with their 'all things in common', provide evidence for communal practices. Kautsky argues that the early Christian community, beginning with Jesus and then reflected in the Acts of the Apostles, was a communist one: 'At first the community had been permeated by an energetic though vague communism, an aversion to all private property, a drive toward a new and better social order, in which all class differences should be smoothed out by division of possessions' (Kautsky 1908a, 217, 1908b, 433). Added to this are the 'proletarian nature of the movement' (1 Corinthians 1:26-27), contempt for labour (Luke 12:22-31), destruction of the traditional family (Mark 3:31-25; Luke 9:59-62; 14:26; 1 Corinthians 7), and class hatred against the rich (Luke 6:20-25; 16:19-31; 18:18-28; the whole of the epistle of James). With this last item, he moves to the radical dimension, which appears in statements of conflict and the contradictory stories of disciples bearing swords (Matt 10:34; Luke 12:49-53; 22:38).[4] Two questions arise from this reconstruction. First, how did the Christian movement survive and grow, since it was one movement among many? The answer: the communistic organisation already in place around Jesus. Indeed, this was the secret of the success of Christianity, for only a 'communistic mutual aid organisation' '[*kommunistische Unterstützungsorganisation*]' (Kautsky 1908a, 198, 1908b, 407) would have enough impetus to move beyond the death of its founder. Second: how to account for accommodation with the rich and powerful that appears already in the New Testament? Kautsky is of two minds. On the one hand, he deploys a narrative of betrayal from an authentic core: the radical edge is softened, slavery embraced, hierarchies and division of labour

---

4   Kautsky also cites other texts from the Gospels. Even the 'revisionist' Matthew has some telling verses. For example: 'And everyone who has left houses or brothers or sisters or father or mother or children or fields, for my name's sake, will receive a hundredfold, and will inherit eternal life' (Matthew 19:29); 'I was hungry and you gave me food, I was thirsty and you gave me something to drink, I was a stranger and you welcomed me, I was naked and you gave me clothing, I was sick and you took care of me, I was in prison and you visited me' (Matthew 25:35–36); 'Truly I tell you, just as you did it to one of the least of these who are members of my family, you did it to me' (Matthew 25:40). The other Gospels are not to be outdone: 'Sell your possessions, and give alms' (Luke 12:33); 'none of you can become my disciple if you do not give up all your possessions' (Luke 14:33); 'When Jesus heard this, he said to him, "There is still one thing lacking. Sell all that you own and distribute the money to the poor, and you will have treasure in heaven; then come, follow me." But when he heard this, he became sad; for he was very rich. Jesus looked at him and said, "How hard it is for those who have wealth to enter the kingdom of God! Indeed, it is easier for a camel to go through the eye of a needle than for someone who is rich to enter the kingdom of God"' (Luke 18:22-25; see also Mark 10:17-31). See also the story of Lazarus and the rich man (Luke 16:19-31).

instituted, and the communist impulse weakened (due to the inadequacies of a communism of consumption). On the other hand, he notes the deep internal contradiction in Christianity, with contrasting historical conditions, teachings and social organisation, evincing both the 'organization of communism' and of the 'exploitation of all classes'. Kautsky closes by arguing that the 'communist impulse' could not be excised, for it kept turning up in Christian history – as he had already argued in *Forerunners*.

2   Reconstruction: Rosa Luxemburg

Since I have already devoted considerable attention to Kautsky in the first chapter, I would like to engage with another related approach to the same problem – Rosa Luxemburg's less-known argument in her essay, 'Socialism and the Churches' (1905a, 1905b). This piece appeared in 1905, ten years after Kautsky's initial and brief proposal in *Forerunners*, but three years before his extensive *Foundations of Christianity*. Clearly, Luxemburg's reconstruction was part of a wider socialist effort at claiming a longer radical heritage – although she does not directly reference Kautsky. For my purposes, her essay has three key features, which may be described as tactical, historical and differential. Luxemburg is tactically explicit in her argument, directing her message to the many workers with strong religious affiliations who were joining the Social Democratic Party of Lithuania and Poland (if not the German Party) and who were facing vociferous opposition from church leaders. Your faith, she points out to the workers, is not inconsistent with socialism, for early Christianity too was a radical movement with communistic social organisation. Thus, she deliberately uses 'proletarians' to speak of both the oppressed class in the Roman Empire and the workers ground down by capitalism. Her argument may be one of analogy, but she pushes it much further, making use of an argument from origins that is close to the agenda of radical groups throughout the history of Christianity: modern socialists are not merely analogous to early Christians, but the socialists actually embody – in a concrete way – the socially salvific agenda of the early Church. Should Jesus appear in her time, he would side with the socialists: 'And, if Christ were to appear on earth today, he would surely attack the priests, the bishops and archbishops who defend the rich and live by the bloody exploitation of millions, as formerly he attacked the merchants whom he drove from the temple with a whip so that their ignoble presence should not defile the House of God' (Luxemburg 1905a, 150, 1905b, 43).[5] As we

---

5   Translation modified.

will see later, she also argues that modern socialists will complete what was begun by the early Christians.

The second feature of her argument is historical, invoking references from a variety of sources to back up her reconstruction and situating the development of early Christianity in its socio-economic context. The expected text of Acts 4:32-35 appears, stressing 'they had everything in common' and that those who had lands and houses sold them and brought the proceeds to the apostles. As also does Acts 2:44-45, which summarises these two points: 'And all who believed were together and had all things in common; and they sold their possessions and goods and distributed them to all, as any had need'. She also emphasises the practice of having meals in common and the abolition of family life (1905a, 138–39, 1905b, 26), backing up her invocation of the book of Acts with references to secondary sources. For instance, she quotes from an unspecified 'contemporary' writer, the church historian Vogel (albeit from 1780) and then some Church Fathers, such as Saint Basil in the fourth century, John Chrysostom (347–407) and Gregory the Great from the sixth century. The other dimension of her historical reconstruction has recourse to Marxist arguments concerning socio-economic factors. Thus, the early appeal of Christianity was among the slaves forced to work the ever-larger estates of the ruling class, as well as the peasants impoverished by the process. Losing their small holdings to the estates of the absentee landlords, these apparently independent producers either succumbed to debt slavery or fled to cities like Rome. Without a manufacturing base, there was little work even in the cities, so they relied on the insufficient corn dole to feed themselves and their families. Their inability to organise themselves in any meaningful way was also the situation of the slaves, who found themselves ground down by crushing labour and were too dispersed to make any effective effort at changing the situation – despite frequent slave revolts. In this context, she argues, Christianity 'appeared to these unhappy beings as a life-belt [Rettungsplanke], a consolation and an encouragement, and became, right from the beginning, the religion of the Roman proletarians' (Luxemburg 1905a, 136, 1905b, 24). Given their economic situation, these early Christians demanded an equal share of all resources, especially those that the rich hoarded for themselves. It was a communism born of dire economic circumstances.

3   Consumption versus Production, or, Transition

Luxemburg's third argument is differential. The major problem is that the picture of early Christianity she has reconstructed is clearly a communism of consumption rather than one of production. The limitations appear in terms of size (it can only work with a small community) and duration, for such consumption is workable only as long as some members have riches to share and goods to sell:

> But this communism was based on the consumption of finished products and not on the communism of work, and proved itself incapable of reforming society, of putting an end to the inequality between people and throwing down the barrier which separated rich from poor. ...Suppose, for example, that the rich proprietors, influenced by the Christian doctrine, offered to share up between the people all their money and other riches which they possessed in the form of cereals, fruit, clothing, animals, etc. what would the result be? Poverty would disappear for several weeks and during this time the people would be able to feed and clothe themselves. But the finished products are quickly used up. After a short lapse of time, the people, having consumed the distributed riches, would once again have empty hands.[6]
>
> LUXEMBURG 1905a, 137–38, 1905b, 26–27

Apart from the Christian communities themselves, nothing has changed within the economic structures as a whole. In fact, it would rely on the rich producing more, by means of their slaves, so that they could once again share their wealth with the Christian community – 'That would be to draw water in a sieve!' (Luxemburg 1905a, 138, 1905b, 27). And if they relinquished their control over the current means of production, the Christian communities as a whole would soon starve.

This consumption-production distinction was also central for Kautsky's reconstruction of the tradition of Christian communism (as we saw in Chapter 1), so let me bring Kautsky back into the discussion to interrogate the permutations of this distinction. Kautsky identifies nearly all of the pre-modern forms of communism – from Plato to the Anabaptists – as ones of consumption. Only with modern socialism does one find a resolute focus on transforming the means of production, a position that Luxemburg affirms. But the distinction raises more questions than it answers.

To begin with, where does this proposal lead? Obviously, it opens up a qualitative difference between pre-modern and modern socialism. Both Luxemburg and Kautsky face a conundrum: the more one emphasises a long tradition of communist movements, the more difficult it becomes to identify what is distinct about the modern version. Here the consumption-production distinction plays a crucial role. In contrast to the early Christians, modern socialists work

---

6 Translation modified.

for a fundamental change in the means of production. For Luxemburg, while the Christian communists 'did not demand that the land, the workshops and the instruments of work should become collective property, but only that everything should be divided up among them, houses, clothing, food and finished products most necessary to life', the socialists seek to make into common property the actual 'instruments of work, the means of production, in order that all humanity may work and live in harmonious unity' (Luxemburg 1905a, 138, 1905b, 27). Kautsky, as we saw, attempts to draw a firm historical boundary between pre-modern and modern forms. With the destruction of Münster in 1535, Christian communism came to an end as a 'real, effective force in public life', replaced by the modern proletariat in the context of capitalism and the bourgeois state (Kautsky 1897, 291, 293, 1895, 435–36).

But this is by no means the only option they explore. For her part, Luxemburg also suggests a devolutionary narrative, in which the internal logic of the communism of consumption leads to almsgiving. If one already has a structure that relies on those with resources to keep on giving to the community's poor, it is a short step to the ethos of the imperial church and its form of welfare. In other words, this form of communism can be accommodated within, if not lead to, new structures of exploitation.[7] For his part, Kautsky offers two qualifications that trouble the effort at a sharp distinction between Christian communism and modern socialism. The first is his attraction to Thomas More, who becomes a crucial link between the two forms, providing a bridge between medieval religiosity and modern materialism:

> We believe that we have disclosed the most essential roots of More's Socialism: his amiable character in harmony with primitive communism; the economic situation of England, which brought into sharp relief the disadvantageous consequences of capitalism for the working class; the fortunate union of classical philosophy with activity in practical affairs – all these circumstances combined must have induced in a mind so acute, so fearless, so truth-loving as More's an ideal which may be regarded as a foregleam of Modern Socialism.
>
> KAUTSKY 1888a, 128, 1888b, 228–29; see SCHWARTZ 1989

---

7 Kautsky also notes this tendency with the variation of monastic communism, which simultaneously carried on the impulse of early Christian communism as Christianity became the religion of empire in the fourth century and provided a line that prompted and supported early capitalist production through its 'hausgenossenschaft [house cooperative]' (Kautsky 1895, 111–12).

Clearly, the distinction was not as sharp as Kautsky suggests with his over-arching narrative. Another strand is even more telling. As I indicated earlier, Kautsky notes again and again that some medieval and Reformation-era communities also engaged in substantial production. These include the Bohemian Brethren, the Taborites and the Anabaptists in Moravia and Münster (Kautsky 1897, 197, 208, 211–12, 1895, 357, 366, 369), but it is summed best in his earlier observation: 'Communism produces extraordinary diligence, an extraordinary willingness to work [*der kommunismus erzeugt außerordentlichen Fleiß, eine außerordentliche arbeitsfreudigkeit*]' (Kautsky 1895, 109). Perhaps the tradition of Christian communism was more of a forerunner than he is elsewhere willing to admit, so much so that I am tempted to invoke here a dialectic of continuity and rupture, much like Lenin's 'leaps, breaks in gradualness, leaps, leaps' (Lenin 1914–16a, 123, 1914–16b, 112).

4   The Question of History

Let me summarise my argument thus far, which has offered a critical over-view of the reconstructions by Kautsky and Luxemburg. By and large, they agree in terms of the overall picture, although Luxemburg has a greater tactical emphasis on religious workers who seek to join and are joining socialist parties. However, their differential arguments evince a few problems. Keen to distinguish between early Christian and modern forms of communism, they stress the consumption-production distinction. But the distinction faces a number of qualifications, whether devolution into alms-giving by an imperial church, the suggestion that early Christian communism was fulfilled only with modern socialism, softening the sharp difference between the two types of communism through a historical figure (Thomas More), or the presence of a communism of production in Christian communism itself.

Running through these tensions is the problem of history, to which I now turn. As should be clear by now, both Kautsky and Luxemburg argue that this form of communal organisation did take place, even if it came undone through its own dynamic. Biblical scholars and historians are somewhat more divided, moving back and forth over whether the foundational text of the Acts of the Apostles can be used for historical reconstruction or not.[8] Yet, when one delves into such material in regard to Acts 2 and 4, the question of history becomes

---

8 The range of possibilities is embodied in the unwavering confidence of Bruce (1990) in the historical reliability of Acts all the way to Koester's (2000, 49–52, 321–27) profound scepticism given the genre of romance or epic that Acts evinces.

sidelined – except for Montero (2017)[9] – for the sake of another concern: the effort to negate any suggestion of early communism. Many who assume a historical reference speak of a 'community of goods' or an 'alternative family', diverting quickly to contemporary examples from Qumran and the Essenes and citing other biblical verses that tend in the same direction, such as Deuteronomy 15:4, Luke 8:3, John 12:6, Acts 11:29 and Galatians 2:10 (Capper 1995, 1996; Bauckham 2007, 62; Bartchy 1991). Or they labour more strenuously to water down the import of the text, suggesting it was limited to small groups for a short time and that it entailed no more than 'some kind of sharing' that was not 'highly organised' (Barrett 1994, 167–70, 252). Or it involved the proper use of wealth to build 'relationships and community' (Talbert 2005, 50), was focused on the 'love feast' or '*agape*-meal' (Finger 2007), the need for 'reciprocity' (Malina and Pilch 2008, 36, 46–47) or simply an admonition to give alms (Haenchen 1985, 192, 231–33). Scholars with a more sceptical approach to the historical reliability of a biblical text like Acts end up with much the same result, preferring to describe these accounts as compositions by the author concerning 'ideal life' in the Jerusalem community (Koester 2000, 322), an 'idealisation' designed to encourage the rich to work harder to assist the poor (Esler 1987, 186, 196), or simply as a 'utopian' picture, with all of the associated negative assumptions (Pervo 2009, 88–95, 126–28).[10] It is difficult to escape the conclusion that they all share in various ways the assumption expressed explicitly by Walter Rauschenbusch more than a century ago, that it was 'not communism in any proper sense of the word' (Rauschenbusch 1907, 122; see also Walton 2008). Similar sentiments were expressed at the same time across the Atlantic. Not only was there the very liberal and middle-class movement, the Evangelisch-sozialer Kongress (from 1890), which sought to counter the appeal of socialism in Germany, but also scholars such as Adolf von Harnack and Adolf Deissmann. While Harnack argued that the gospel of Jesus brings justice and soothes the sorrows of the distressed, so much so that it was 'profoundly socialistic', it was also deeply inward and thereby beyond the world and politics. It was a socialism based not – as Kautsky had argued in 1895 – on a social movement with Christ as a social deliverer, but on the 'consciousness of a spiritual unity' (Harnack 1902, 3, 108). For his part, Deissmann roundly condemned Kautsky and the historical materialist method in general by suggesting that even if Christianity appealed primarily to the 'lower' classes, it by

---

9   See further below.
10 Pervo has perhaps the most complete discussion of these issues, providing ample references for those wishing to pursue the opinions that biblical scholars take on these verses. See also the examples given in Montero (2017, 110–13).

no means entailed a proletarian revolution (Deissmann 1908, 8, 395, 465–67; Blanton 2007, 119–20; Crossley 2008, 15).[11] Clearly, the spectre of early Christian communism haunts these efforts.

Throughout these efforts, the question of history is – perhaps surprisingly – sidelined, so let me take a novel approach and deal with history. This concern has two dimensions, one dealing with historical background and the other with historical effect. On the matter of background or context we need to look somewhat awry, or at least to the wider context of economic history rather than the immediate question as to whether early Christian communism was practised or not. One reason is – as with so much ancient history – that it is impossible to verify whether a specific event mentioned in texts occurred or not. The evidence is simply too patchy and dispersed to make such assessments – as we find with the practice of early Christian communism. All we can say is that it might have happened, in light of comparable practices at the same time (the Essenes, for instance, although this too is based on interpreting texts and archaeological materials), but it may also not have happened in the way depicted.

For these reasons, I prefer to focus on the wider background of economic history. Relevant here is what may be called subsistence-survival agriculture. The reason will become clear soon enough, but let me outline the nature of this economic activity. This form of agriculture shows remarkable consistency across vast time periods, with rural labourers returning to it whenever possible. Its primary location was in village-communes, where we find diverse and versatile mechanisms of animal husbandry, with 2:1 ratios of resilient sheep and goats so as to ensure herd survival in the case of disease, regular culling across the herd, use of all animal parts, and optimal use of water and fodder (Sasson 2010). Crop growing too shows diversity in types of grains and fruits grown, in terms of both seasonal and long-term crops such as grapes and olives (Hald 2008). This economic activity – for agriculture was by far the prime economic reality of the ancient world – was socially determined through and through. It was centred on what Soviet-era Russian scholars called the extended-family household commune or a village-commune (Diakonoff 1974, 1975, 1991, 34–35; Jankowska 1969, 1991, 253; Bartlett 1990), and what 'Western' scholars have dubbed *musha'* farming (Wilkinson 2003, 2010; Khalidi 1984; Firestone 1990; Palmer 1999; Schäbler 2000; Nadan 2003, 2006). Typically, farmers lived in a village cluster, with a population of 75 to 150 and coterminous with the clan, although smaller settlements often had less than seventy-five

---

11   By contrast, Rauschenbusch cites Kautsky's *Forerunners* favourably, but only in the sense that the impulse survived in terms of poverty alleviation.

(Knight 2011, 122–23). From here, farmers would go out to the fields to work, as archaeological investigation of settlements and their pathways indicates (Wilkinson 2003; Casana 2007). But the fields were not held in perpetual possession by the same farmers. Instead, non-contiguous strips of land were allocated to each household for cultivation. In the Bible, this is the *ḥelqat haśśādeh* of Genesis 33:19–20; Ruth 4:3; 2 Samuel 14:30–31; 2 Kings 9:21, 25; Jeremiah 12:10; Amos 4:7 (cf. the verb *ḥlq*, 'apportion', in Jeremiah 37:12). These were social units of measurements rather than clear demarcations of land for the purpose of ownership. They would usually be of considerable length (up to one kilometre, or along the twisting path of a terrace in areas such as the Judean highlands), but with a width of a few furrows. At set times, usually annually or biannually, those strips were reallocated on the basis of need, fertility and labour power. The means of such reallocation varied, whether by lot, by all the adult males, a council of elders or perhaps a village headman. Needless to say, the process involved unwritten rules and much argument, but the outcome was that the strips were reallocated. Collective activity was inescapable within the village and between villages that were two to four kilometres apart, for the individual was helpless in the face of natural and social disaster, needing cooperation and reciprocal aid to survive (Diakonoff 1976, 66; Hopkins 1985, 256). Thus, kinship, both highly flexible and embodied in the patriarchal household, was crucial. A further factor was the advantage of combined labour, whether with plough teams, sowing or harvesting. Finally, the close-knit village-commune, with its headman and council of elders, was also advantageous for protection and defence against raiders. We may, following Roberts (1996, 35–37), describe these three factors as the communality of assent, economizing and enforcement.

How might this economic practice – or what I prefer to call an institutional form or economic building block – manifest itself in the text of Acts? Intriguingly, the few verses where it appears (Acts 2:44-45, 4:32-35) are like traces that disappear as quickly as they appear. Nothing further is made of them, especially in a text that is clearly saturated with the cultural and class assumptions of the *polis*. Indeed, I suggest that this curious remnant may be seen as a trace of the colonial *chōra*, which designates all of the area outside the *polis* in colonised areas that had to provide the *polis* with the items it deemed necessary for a 'civilised' existence. It was precisely in the *chōra* that one found the practices I have described.[12] This subsistence form had in fact been dominant for a long period leading up to the emergence of classical Greece. The centuries from the late second millennium BCE into the middle of the first millennium are usually

---

12   For a rare but welcome emphasis on the *chōra* in Acts, at concrete and metaphorical levels, see Petterson (2012).

characterised as 'collapse' or a 'dark age', but this is the perspective of the ruling class and its records (and so also modern historians who rely on such sources or their absence). From the perspective of rural labourers, it was anything but a collapse, for the preferred subsistence-survival form could dominate, so much so that one can speak of a subsistence economic regime that was dominant for centuries. But with the emergence of classical Greece and its slave system, subsequently enhanced by the Romans, this subsistence regime was inexorably driven back. In the context of Greco-Roman colonisation of the eastern Mediterranean, it was reconstituted as the colonised *chōra*, dominated in various ways by the extractive economic demands of the *polis*. But even in texts like Acts, which overwhelmingly presents the perspective and assumptions of the *polis*, traces and representations of the *chōra* and its efforts at subsistence-survival agriculture appear from time to time. After all, the very possibility of the world inhabited by Acts (and indeed Luke, if not much of the New Testament), relied inextricably on that which it sought to deny. So it should not surprise us that the other world, normally outside the boundaries of a text like Acts, should have a fitful presence, even if disappears again all too rapidly.

At the same time, such representations are so often indirect rather than direct. They may be seen as mediated responses, filtered as it were through a diffracting lens, so we can hardly expect a mirror-like reflection of actual conditions. That such a mediated and metaphorical response makes it more difficult to discern the historical conditions of the trace should be obvious, but this is by no means a reason to avoid discerning these traces. In this light, the representation in Acts 2 and 4 presents a number of displacements. To begin with, we find this community displaced from the *chōra* to the *polis*, cut off from its roots and trying to grow in strange soil. In the *chōra* subsistence-survival agriculture was very much a matter of production and consumption, for otherwise it would not be viable. But in a *polis* context these practices were no longer possible, leaving only the social determination of the products of labour and not their production. Thus, the insight of Kautsky and Luxemburg into the communism of consumption inadvertently picks up this feature. But their insight also indicates the mediated and indirect nature of the picture in Acts. Other traces appear, such as the paths followed by peasants to the *polis*, paths fraught with apprehension and need. On a daily basis, some peasants had to make the journey to the *polis*, with beasts of burden laden with requirements,[13] only

---

13   For example, a small town like Sepphoris in Galilee, with a population of about 8,000, would require annually no less than 1,600,000 kilograms of grain, 2,000,000 liters of wine, and 160,000 liters of oil. How many animal loads would this entail? Evidence from Egyptian papyri indicates that a donkey could carry 90 kilograms (3 artabae). This means that

to find themselves under threat of the *angareia* (forced labour). They might either be mistaken for such a labourer or simply be dragged off to the latest building project.[14] Or they may be lured by the illusory promise of 'opportunity' for disrupted lives in the *chōra*, drifting to the *polis* only to eke out a living on the fringes, providing necessary services that had little benefit for themselves. Again, this may be the historical reality, but in the text of Acts it appears as a mediated trace of these transitions. One feature of Acts is notable: it does not present this early Christian communism in disparaging terms, in contrast to the way Greco-Roman sources overwhelmingly represent peasants in the countryside as ugly, misshapen and dirty (G.E.M. de Ste. Croix 1981, 208–10).

5   Political Myth

Thus far I have dealt with the historical background of the representations in Acts 2 and 4, so it remains to deal with the historical effect. By this I mean the concrete practices generated by a text, particularly one that became part of a sacred canon. Even if the practice of Christian communism did not take place exactly in the way it is all too briefly represented in Acts, it has and continues to have significant repercussions among religious movements. This historical effect or power has appeared in at least three ways.

First, the arguments of Kautsky in particular were widely discussed, refuted and supported, vilified and backed-up. Earlier, I pointed out that the spectre of Kautsky's and Luxemburg's argument concerning early Christian communism continues to haunt scholarship. This ghost (to gloss *The Manifesto of the Communist Party*) appears time and again when scholars attempt to downplay the claim in the biblical text that the early Christians had 'all things in common'. Here I would like to pick up another dimension of this legacy, which comes originally from Engels (1894–95a, 1894–95b): Christianity appealed primarily to peasants, slaves and unemployed urban poor. This became an assumed position in the early- to mid-twentieth century among New Testament scholars such as Adolf Deissmann (1908, 465–67, 1929, 64–65) and among sociologists like Troeltsch (1992, 1912). Both seek to counter Engels, Kautsky and Luxemburg by arguing for a religious origin for Christianity and yet they assume the argument concerning the class makeup of earliest Christianity. However, by the 1960s a conservative reaction set in, pointing out that the textual 'evidence'

Sepphoris required on a daily basis just under 115 donkey loads (48.7 of grain, 60.9 of wine, and 4.9 of oil), or 41,975 per year (Choi 2014).

14   The requisitioning of a donkey and its colt in Matthew 21:2-7 may be seen in this light.

suggests a mixed class basis for the Christian movement (Judge 1960, 2008, 1–56), a position elaborated by, among others, the sociological study of Wayne Meeks (2003), who does not pass up the opportunity to condemn Kautsky's work as 'reductionist', and the rational choice study of Rodney Stark (1996), who hypothesises that Christianity primarily appealed to the privileged ruling class (2011, 87–104) and misses no opportunity to praise the role of Christianity in fostering reason, individualism, freedom, capitalism and the 'success' of the 'West' (2006). Stark's is obviously an extreme and unsupportable hypothesis, but even his efforts witness to Kautsky's continuing influence on scholarship, not least in the way he feels called upon to dismiss Kautsky (who is named) and Marxist arguments. Yet, as these proposals were being aired, biblical scholars developed further arguments for what may be called a red thread, running through from prophetic indictments of exploitation, rural patterns of allocative economics, impulses from the Jesus movement (Gottwald 1992; Horsley 2014; Horsley and Hanson 1985), as well as the constitutive resistance of subsistence-survival economics in the Greco-Roman world (Boer and Petterson 2017). These debates within scholarship may be seen as another dimension of the historical effect of Kautsky's argument, keeping it alive in a way he may well not have expected.

The second historical effect is perhaps more obvious, for this early account in Acts 2 and 4 has inspired many movements since to emulate it in practice. Apart from the historical examples outlined by Kautsky in his *Forerunners* (see Chapter 1), the study by Montero may be seen in this light. While he seeks to draw parallels from the Essenes, Hellenistic assumptions concerning ideal friendship, as well as other New Testament texts, his evidence draws heavily upon material that comes from the centuries after the biblical texts (Montero 2017, 58–69, 76–82).[15] From other sources, we may add monastic cenobitic (communal) practices, evangelical poverty among the Franciscan 'rigorists' and the communist efforts of Gerrard Winstanley and the Diggers in seventeenth century England (Hornik and Parson 2017, 64, 75–77). As Winstanley put it: 'And when the Son of man, was gone from the Apostles, his Spirit descended upon the Apostles and Brethren, as they were waiting at *Jerusalem;* and Rich men sold their Possessions, and gave part to the Poor; and no man said, That

---

15   Montero deploys Graeber's (2011, 94–95) definition of 'baseline communism', premised on the basic and necessary principle of 'from each according to his abilities and to each according to his needs', which is necessary at a fundamental level since human society would cease to function without this everyday and low-level form of mutual cooperation. Notable also is Montero's emphasis on 'informal' communism enforced by moral expectation, which was unable to change the larger economic context – a point that echoes Kautsky's and Luxemburg's emphasis on a communism of consumption.

ought that he possessed was his own, for they had all things Common, *Act.* 4.32' (Winstanley 1983, 88). In the nineteenth century, they continued with the Icarian communities led by Étienne Cabet and Wilhelm Weitling,[16] who was not only involved in Communia (in Iowa from 1847 to 1858), but also referred explicitly to the *Gütergemeinschaft*, the community of goods of Acts 2 and 4. The condition of joining the early Christians was the sale of all one's possessions and sharing with the poor. So seriously, observes Weitling, was this condition taken that failure to do so had the divine penalty of death – as the story about Ananias and Sapphira in Acts 5:1-11 makes clear.[17]

The third historical effect is perhaps the most unexpected. Let us return to Luxemburg, who argues that modern socialism will complete what early Christianity began. The latter's intention may have been in the right place – an ardent belief in communism – but it needs to go a step further: not only do the products of an economy need to be held in common, but so also do the means of production. Her arresting conclusion is that modern communism may be seen as the logical outcome, if not the fulfilment of Christianity: 'What the Christian Apostles could not accomplish by their fiery preaching against the egoism of the rich, the modern proletarians, workers conscious of their class-position, can start working in the near future, by the conquest of political power in all countries by tearing the factories, the land, and all the means of production from the capitalists to make them the communal property of the workers' (Luxemburg 1905a, 148, 1905b, 40). This argument bears the potential trap of supersessionism, in which a qualitatively higher form replaces an earlier one: modern communism with its focus on production is a step beyond early Christian communism. The proposal may, of course, run the other way, connecting the initial impulse from early Christian communism with the movement in which Luxemburg was so much involved. Thus, modern communism seeks to negate the tendency towards almsgiving and charity, with its redistribution of wealth that has become so characteristic of later social democracy under capitalism. Instead, it seeks – for Luxemburg – to pick up the torch lit first by early Christian communism, a torch that has flickered to life at significant moments since but has only with modern communism flared the brightest.

---

16   Engels called Weitling the 'first German communist'. For a full discussion with references, see Boer (2014a, 135–40).

17   'Die Bedingung der Aufnahme in das Christenthum war der Verkauf der Güter des neu Aufzunehmenden und die Vertheilung derselben unter die Armen. Die Uebertreter dieses Gesetzes wurden schwer gestraft, und wir finden in der Bibel auf einen solchen Fall selbst die Todesstrafe. Vgl. Apostelgeschichte 5, 1-11' (Weitling 1838–1839, 12). See also his *Poor Sinner's Gospel* (Weitling 1845a, 1845b).

To sum up, the early Christian communism identified and indeed claimed by Kautsky and Luxemburg has three concrete historical effects: the continuing effect on scholarship concerning early Christianity; the efforts through history to establish communities based on the principles of Acts 2 and 4; and the claim by Luxemburg that modern communism will complete what early Christianity began. How might we understand this virtual power of early Christian communism? This pertinence of this question is enhanced by the fact that we cannot conclusively verify the historical reliability of the brief depiction of the early Christian community in Acts 2 and 4. I have argued that its brief appearance in this text functions as a trace – mediated and displaced – of subsistence-survival agriculture, but remains no more than a trace. To make sense of the aftereffects of this trace, I would like to deploy the category of political myth.[18] The term carries the double sense of a constructed and imagined narrative that simultaneously bears a deeper truth (Lincoln 2000). Further, this myth has an enabling and virtual historical power that is also and simultaneously proleptic – to deploy the future perfect, we may speak of a communism that will have been true, so much so that it is directly influential in the present (Boer 2007c). In other words, Christian communism may have appeared briefly in history, as part of the founding moment of Christianity, but this is enough to express a hope for the future. Once it became an authoritative and even sacred story, it was appropriated again and again as communities sought to re-enact and live up to the ideal. Thus it gains a power of its own with historical consequences. That many of the Christian communist movements have come to an end sooner or later should not be regarded as a 'failure', but rather as an indication of the continuing power of this political myth. Even more, the tendency for some Christian communist movements to enact a communism of production rather than merely one of consumption – as we saw in the early treatment of Kautsky's *Forerunners* – indicates that these movements may be seen as efforts to realise what the image of Acts 2 and 4 was unable to realise.

18   A more useful approach than Nettl's dismissal as a 'curious piece of historical sophistry' (1966, vol. 1, 323).

CHAPTER 3

Reaction and Revolution: How to Read the Apostle Paul

In light of the previous two chapters, it may seem that the radical dimension of the Bible and Christianity is determinative – at least as I have presented matters thus far. Obviously, this is not the case, for the history of this particular religious tradition is overflowing with examples of a distinctly conservative, if not reactionary approach. The tension between the reactionary and the revolutionary is a recurring theme of the book as a whole, so, as a contrast with my treatments of Kautsky and early Christian communism, here I tackle directly a core biblical text for the reactionary position: Romans 13:1-7. This text, among others, causes not a few problems for those who seek a radical message in Paul's texts, let alone other parts of the Bible. Its significance is not merely due to the role of sacred texts in a religion like Christianity, but also because it comes from none other than the Apostle Paul, the most significant ideologue in this tradition. The analysis of this chapter is mostly theoretical, dealing with the interpretation of literature and the core ideas of Christian theology. But it is necessary due to the importance of the topic.

1   Anti- or Pro-Empire?

It is difficult to avoid the sense of Paul's exhortation in Romans 13:1. 'Let every person [*pasa psychē*] be subject [*hypotassesthō*] to the governing authorities [*exousiais hyperechousais*]' is quite clear: all of us must subordinate ourselves to those with power, authority and control over our lives – those 'over above' us. Three points are worth noting in these verses: a hierarchy of power, a concern with insurrection, and taxes. I will leave taxes alone (vv. 6-7), since the point flows from the other two. As far as hierarchy is concerned, what runs through Paul's text is a chain of command (see v. 1b): God first, who bestows power and authority upon designated rulers, and then all the rest who must obey them. Here it seems to be earthly rulers, but the same hierarchy applies to the spirit world (1 Corinthians 15:24). Now emerges the concern with sedition. This is really the main focus of the text, covering four of its seven verses. And it turns on a play with *tassō*. Originally designating the proper ordering of troops, *tassō* has come to mean the correct arrangement and order, the determined sequence of things. Paul points out that authority has been ordered (*tetagmenai*; v. 1) by God and it requires one to 'be subordinate [*hypotassesthō*]' (vv. 1 and 5) to that authority. However, what one must not do is undermine or go against that order (*antitassō*), or more strictly be a disruptor of order or 'a rebel [*ho antitassomenos*]' (v. 2). In other words, Paul is all too keen to counter any possibility of civil disobedience, sedition and insurrection. Woe to the 'one who resists authority [*ho antitassomenos tē exousia*]' (v. 2), he writes, for the wrath, judgement, terror, punishment and sword of the ruler and thereby of God will soon follow (vv. 2-5). Be afraid, be very afraid if you engage in such acts. One wonders why Paul is so keen frighten his readers into obedience, into 'good conduct' in order to gain the authority's approval (*epainon ex autēs*; v. 3). Might it be that Paul and those who took up his message glimpsed the radical possibilities of what he proposed elsewhere, a possibility that caused him a good deal of apprehension?

More than one conservative or reactionary has found a text such as Romans 13 extraordinarily useful. To cull a few more notable examples from a very long list: there is the deal done with the state under Constantine and the resultant efforts at 'catholic' or 'orthodox' Christianity; or the 'holy' Roman emperors who followed through the Middle Ages; the uncanny ability of absolute monarchs to be, as Christ's representative on earth, both head of state and of the church; the class status of the Church throughout feudalism; Luther calling on everyone to slaughter any rebel peasant they might encounter in 1525; the *sine qua non* of deep religious commitment by as many presidents of the United States as one cares to remember; and the grovelling support of wealthy and powerful rulers by any number of ecclesiastical bodies.

Romans 13 was not the only text called upon to justify such reactionary readings. For instance, John Calvin added to this flagship text Titus 3:1 on obeying the powers, principalities and magistrates (Calvin 1856, 324), 1 Peter 2:13 on submission to kings and governors (Calvin 1855, 79–80), and 1 Timothy 2:1-2 on prayers and intercessions for all in authority (Calvin 1856, 51–53; see also Calvin 1559, 4.20.23; Calvini 1559, 5:494.6–26). As I argue later, Calvin gets himself into a massive knot, since he is too perceptive a student of the Bible not to see that there are a good many texts that advocate disobeying an ungodly ruler, if not overthrowing such a ruler, although Calvin prefers to leave that task to the 'magistrate'.

I will come back to this tension in a moment, but before doing so let me juxtapose Romans 13 with the positions taken by those who approach the New Testament from the perspective of 'empire' and post-colonial criticism.[1] What is striking about these texts is that they seek not merely to situate the New Testament within the Roman Empire as a response to the earlier emphasis on

---

1   The range of such works is now extensive, but the best survey covering the New Testament is
    a series of articles by Diehl (2011, 2012, 2013).

its deeply Jewish nature, but they also argue that these texts are deeply anti-imperial documents. Or at least one can find, they argue, a consistent anti-imperial theme running through them. Invariably the comparison is made with our own times, whether the imperialism of the United States, or the global ravages of trans-national corporations or the profound difference between the majority of impoverished peoples of the world and the small number of the obscenely rich.

This approach seems to be a long way from Romans 13, so let us see what some of them make of that text.[2] Most of the positions fall into standard patterns of interpretation, although all of them share the assumption that at some level Paul must be consistent and even coherent. Although some have toyed with the idea that Romans 13:1-7 is, without any evidence, an interpolation (Kallas 1965), most fall back on the position that the text is a particular injunction limited to a specific time and place (Käsemann 1980, 338–47; Tellbe 2001, 171; Carter 2006, 133–36; Ehrensperger 2007, 173–74; Elliott 2008, 154). This argument has all manner of variations, such as a temporal one in which Paul advocated submission while the Romans seemed all powerful and resistance would have meant immediate annihilation (Ehrensperger 2007), or that he took up a standard theme and repeated it without reflecting too much (Käsemann 1980), or that he distinguishes between being forced to obey and willingly doing so (Carter 2006; Ehrensperger 2007). The catch is that this position turns on a deeply theological and problematic distinction between universal and particular admonitions. One cannot help notice that it is more popular when there is a rather bad example of government in mind – the Nazis for German critics or the United States for some critics in that part of the world. A less popular and difficult line is to argue that Paul is being ironic, offering a subtle critique of Roman power (Carter 2004; Jewett 2007, 787–89). In contrast to these various twists and turns, the very non-postcolonial Voelz (1999) actually offers a novel argument: the text is perfectly clear but it refers only to good governments – he explicitly mentions Nazi Germany as a negative example. No one, however, countenances the possibility that Paul may be inconsistent. Or not quite, for Elliott (2008, 1997) argues that Paul shows signs of strain since he was under the influence of imperial ideological forces that produced ripples and disjunctions in his letters. In other words, Elliott recognises a contradiction or two in Paul's texts, contradictions that arise from the 'material and ideological conditions in which the letter was written and which the letter was an attempt to resolve' (Elliott 2008, 156). I seek to take Elliott's insight a step or two further.

---

2   This is a heavily interpreted text, as one would expect. See the survey of positions in Tellbe (2001, 177–78) and especially Riekkinen (1980).

2 Contradiction Analysis

We have arrived at the point where anti-imperial, if not radical, readings run up against and struggle with texts like Romans 13, offering what are often old exegetical responses. Except for Elliott's interpretation, none of these approaches countenance the possibility that Paul may have been openly ambivalent on this matter – that there is a basic and irresolvable opposition in his thought. It should actually be no surprise that there is a tension or two in Paul's thought since his whole theoretical framework turns on them. Yet the assumption is that Paul has managed to work through or overcome them. The usual challenge for interpreters who assume that Paul must be coherent is to determine how he does so, for it is far from clear. In this section, then, I explore these oppositions and tensions further.[3]

Let me tabulate the many tensions in Paul's letters, attempting to be as comprehensive as possible:

- Death and life: Romans 5-6; 7:10; 8:2, 6, 38; 2 Corinthians 2:16; 4:10-12; Philippians 1:20-24.
- Adam and Christ: Romans 5:12-21; 1 Corinthians 15:21-22.
- Elect and damned: Romans 8:28-31; 9:11; 11:7, 28.
- Spirit and flesh: Romans 7:5, 14, 18; 8:1-13; 13:11-14; 1 Corinthians 3:1-3; 5:5; 6:16-17; 15:50; Galatians 3:13; 4:23, 29; 5:16-26; 6:8; Philippians 1:21-24; 3:2-4.
- Grace and law: Romans 4:16; 5:20; 6:14-15; Galatians 2:21; 5:4.
- Grace and sin: Romans 5:20-21; 6:1, 14-15.
- Grace and works: Romans 11:6.
- Christ and law: Romans 7:4, 21-25; 8:2; 10:4; 1 Corinthians 9:21; Galatian 2:16, 21; 3:1, 13, 24; 5:4; 6:2; Philippians 3:9.
- Christ and sin: Romans 5:21; 6:1, 5-11, 23; 7:22-25; 8:2, 9-10; 13:14; 1 Corinthians 8:12; 15:3, 17; 2 Corinthians 5:19, 21; Galatians 2:17; 3:22.
- Righteousness through faith or works: Romans 1:17; 3:21-22; 4; 10:6; Galatians 3:10-14; Philippians 3:9.
- Law of sin and law of Christ or faith: Romans 3:27-31; 7:21-25; 8:2.
- Jews and Gentiles: Romans 2:8-10; 3:9, 29; 9:24; 10:12; 1 Corinthians 1:23; Galatians 2; 3:28.
- Slave and free: Romans 6; 1 Corinthians 7:20-22; 9:19; 12:13; Galatians 3:28; 5:13.
- Male and female: Galatians 3:28.

---

3   I am not the first to point out that the New Testament is a treacherous and highly ambivalent terrain if one wishes to find a clear anti-imperial message. See Stephen Moore's (2006) thorough discussions of Mark, John and the Apocalypse, where he focuses on their political ambiguity, albeit without offering any reasons for it. On Mark see also Liew (1999).

This list should dispel any doubts as to how consistent these oppositions are. Yet, Paul tackles them in different ways. Sometimes one side receives his approving nod and the other side not (these should be obvious). At other times, he mixes and matches: Christ and life are pivots for many of the terms Paul values, so we can line up Christ and life with redemption, grace, and faith and oppose them to sin, law, death, and works.[4] And at other times he mentions an opposition in order to point out that it no longer applies in light of Christ (the famous male and female, slave and free, Jew and Gentile of Galatians 3:28). At others, the opposition becomes the basis of further complication, undermining and rearranging, such as the reshaping of law versus grace in terms of the law of Christ versus the law of sin, or the jumbling of flesh and spirit in light of the body and in terms of death and life.

Let me explore the tensions I have been emphasising a little further in terms of content, before turning to the form of these multiple and overlaid contradictions. Returning initially to Romans 13:1-7, we find that it has no explicit counter-posing text, but it evinces its own tensions (Elliott 2008). The main one is between the higher or governing authorities and God's authority (*exousia*), the latter being the only authentic authority (v. 1). The text immediately seeks to connect the two in a derivative fashion: any existing authority apart from God has authority only through God. For the next few verses (vv. 2-6) it becomes a little ambiguous as to which authority Paul means. 'Whoever resists authority...', he writes, 'authority does not bear the sword in vain', and 'Do you wish to have no fear of the authority?' It is not entirely clear whether God or the rulers are in mind here. The text overall seems to tilt in the direction of the rulers who derive their authority from God, but the tension in terms of content remains. It also implies that should a ruler resist divine authority, that ruler should be in fear of incurring judgement. 'Then do what is good, and you will receive its approval' (v. 3) would then apply as much to a ruler as to one who is subject to a ruler given authority by God. Notably, Paul does not say that a person should refuse or resist a ruler who does not 'do what is good'. That would be a step too far, at least in terms of this text.

While we are still with matters of content, the discussion of authority in Romans 13 connects with the wider issue of grace and law, which is usually coupled with faith and works. Romans and Galatians produce sentences such as: 'you are not under law but under grace [*charin*]' (Romans 6:14); 'we know that a person is justified [*dikaiousthai*] not by the works of the law but through

---

4   At this point we could extend this mixing in a way that would reveal some of Paul's more problematic assumptions. For example, what do the reshuffled oppositions of elect versus female, or law versus spirit, or indeed Jews versus life say about Paul's own deeper patterns of thought?

faith in Jesus' (Galatians 2:16); 'we hold that a person is justified by faith apart from works prescribed by the law' (Romans 3:28). The problem with these statements is that they have and do run in a number of directions, such as: Calvinist predestination (since we are completely reliant on God's grace we are also reliant on his decisions as to who will be saved and who damned); the Arminian and Methodist tendency (God's grace is available to all but we can accept or reject it); license (if we are of the elect then nothing we do will change that); Puritanism (in response to grace we need to live lives acceptable to God); quietism (it is all up to God); activism (showing the fruits of grace); and political radicalism (grace is the theological version of revolution).

I have run ahead of myself, so let me go back to Paul. While Paul asserted freedom from the law because of grace, some of the groups that grew up around these letters took the idea much further than he anticipated, pushing Christian freedom from the law into different directions such as freedom in regard to sex, worship, and Roman law. As some of the classic studies of the Corinthian and Galatian correspondence indicate, Paul seems to be putting out fires for which he himself was initially responsible (Longenecker 1990; Martin 1999; Thistleton 2000; Martyn 2004; Keener 2005; Matera 2007; Fitzmyer 2008).[5] While the Galatians erred on the side of sticking with the law, the Corinthians pursued Paul's arguments further than he was willing to countenance. So we find the libertine response: if the law has been overcome, then it is no longer relevant for us. Alternatively, if our sins have been forgiven once and for all, then it matters not what we do. Or in an apocalyptic vein: since Christ has inaugurated the last days, the old world has passed and has no hold on us now.

Once these various readings became clear to Paul, he realized that this was not quite what he had in mind. The push towards Christian freedom that appears in the letter to the Galatians runs into the mud in the Corinthian correspondence. To his own chagrin, these developments could claim a logical beginning within his own thought. So we find him trying to rein in what had been let loose, setting boundaries on what grace, faith and freedom mean. He argues that one should not dispense with the law entirely, for it is good; indeed, there is another law, the law of Christ and faith. He bans the sexual license that some saw in the original idea of freedom from the law, limits the freedom that women were taking in some of the churches, and urges some concern for

---

5 For the sake of argument, I assume with the bulk of studies of Paul that his references to opponents and opposing positions refer to real opponents. It would be interesting (but a different study) to explore the possibility that Paul manufactures these opponents in a deft piece of rhetorical shadow-boxing. By doing so, he brings his readers onside by arraying himself against a range of imaginary opponents.

'weaker' brethren who still felt bound to the law in outward observance (for example, on the question of eating meat given to idols). Thus, we find that the same person who wrote 'not under the law, but under grace' (Romans 6:14 and 15) and 'now we are discharged from the law, dead to that which held us captive' (Romans 7:6) also wrote the text with which I began my discussion, 'Let every person be subject to the governing authorities ... whoever resists authority resists what God has appointed' (Romans 13:1-2). The same mouth that dictated 'all who rely on the works of the law are under a curse' (Galatians 3.10) also mentions that 'we uphold the law' (Romans 3:31), that the law is 'holy' and 'good' (Romans 7:11 and 16). One more: to the Galatians he writes 'There is no longer slave or free ... for all of you are one in Christ Jesus' (Galatians 3.28), while he tells the Corinthians, 'Let each of you remain in the condition in which you were called' (1 Corinthians 7:20). Paul would bequeath these tensions to whomever took up his ideas.

By now the situation has become rather complex, with overlapping opposi-tions playing off against one another. At the level of form, two realities emerge. First, Paul needs to multiply the oppositions in question, as my initial effort to tabulate them indicates. Second, when Paul delves into the tensions, his thought twists and turns as he seeks to deal with the conundrums of grace-Christ-law-sin-works in light of different situations. As my effort to articulate what happens with these items indicates, the complexity multiplies.

3   Imaginary Resolution

How might we understand this tendency to complicate the contradictions? This formal question – inescapably tied with that of content – needs a meth-odological pause. Thus far, three main responses have been offered as ways to solve Paul's tensions. One is to gather all the reactionary texts, argue that they are central, that Paul really did suck up to the powers that be and then show through some deft exegetical arguments that the texts which contradict such a position – the anti-imperial ones which declare war on corrupt rulers and powers of this age – only do so apparently. Or we may take the opposite tack and argue that Paul is really a progressive deep down, that he consistently critiques 'empire'. In this case, the exegetical procedure is reversed and texts like Romans 13 require careful exegesis. A third approach shows some promise. This entails searching Paul's context in order to identify some crucial third term outside his texts that provides the key. Proposals include, but are certainly not limited to, the particular historical situations in which Paul might or might not have written the – authentic – letters; the androgyne as the answer to the tension between universalism and dualism in Paul's writings (Boyarin 1994, 2004); the Stoics who provide the inescapable philosophical and social background for Paul's thought (Swancutt 2004), so much so that he is a philosopher first (Engberg-Pedersen 2000); Hellenistic perceptions of sexuality and the body that become the necessary background for reading Paul (Martin 1999); or the *psychagogia*, the 'leading of souls' that runs through the moral philosophy of Greece and Rome which helps us perhaps to understand Paul's arguments in Philippians (Smith 2005). Why do they show promise? Implicit in this third approach is an awareness that Paul's fleeting missives in some way cannot make sense on their own. Or rather, that the tensions they evince struggle to be resolved on their own. To be sure, many of the works that seek an external third term still assume that one can identify – precisely through the external register – an elusive coherence in Paul's arguments.

Now a further problem with many such approaches emerges: they seek an idealist solution to an idealist problem. In other words, Paul's theoretical conundrums require a theoretical solution – an approach favoured by intellectuals, whose approaches are determined by the very occupation in which they are engaged. For the sake of advancing the argument, let me invoke none other than Karl Marx in response:

> Feuerbach, consequently, does not see that the 'religious sentiment' is itself a social product, and that the abstract individual which he analyses belongs to a particular form of society.

Or more fully:

> Feuerbach starts out from the fact of religious self-estrangement [*der religiösen Selbstentfremdung*], of the duplication of the world into a religious world and a secular one. His work consists in resolving the religious world into its secular [*weltliche*] basis. But that the secular [*weltliche*] basis lifts off from itself and establishes itself as an independent realm in the clouds can only be explained by the inner strife and intrinsic contradictoriness of this secular basis.
>
> MARX 1845a, 4–5, 1845b, 6–7

Replace 'Feuerbach' with 'biblical scholar', if not 'intellectual' as such, and the point becomes clearer. One may read these theses and the consequent method in a one-directional 'vulgar' Marxist fashion. Even though Marx's work from time to time exhibits such a practice, and although this moment is needed at certain points, this line is not dominant in my analysis. Instead, I take up the other dimension of this approach, in which the 'social product', the 'independent realm' of thought and the text responds to the 'inner strife and intrinsic contradictoriness' of its social and economic basis. The response in question is certainly not direct in most instances, but indirect and mediated, appearing in form as well as content, but all the while seeking to resolve the contradiction in question. The catch is that the attempted resolution remains theoretical and cultural and thereby cannot solve directly the socio-economic contradiction in question – unless the theoretical proposal becomes a guide for action. Thus, the text in which it is expressed continues to manifest – at another level and perhaps in unexpected ways – the very contradictions it sought to solve.[6]

So my hypothesis: Paul's multiple-layered contradictions, if not his efforts at narrative, function as persuasive efforts at an imaginary resolution of wider political, but especially socio-economic tensions. Politically, the point is reasonably obvious (to invoke the 'vulgar' Marxist moment of a direct connection). Paul's prevarications over 'authority [*exousia*]' speak rather directly of the tensions between imperial and local authority. Rather than a simple opposition between divine and human, between Godly authority and the (derived) mundane version, the earthly variety was not uniform: the local ruling class, with all its internal conflicts and struggles, also had to deal with the colonising presence of Greek-speaking *poleis*. Some had been established during the Greek conquests, only to be taken over and extended when the Romans asserted their colonial control. At times, a local ruling class sets itself against an imperial master, presenting itself as a champion of all who suffer from the imperial yoke. At others, the local rulers work hand-in-glove with the imperial overlords, especially in situations where such an arrangement enhances their own power, however limited it might be. Often, these local aspiring potentates play a double game at one and the same time (the Herods come to mind).

However, far more was at stake than merely political realities, for these were interwoven with the economic situation. Paul's texts breathe the air of the *polis*, in his language, in the way he frames questions, in the very way he looked at the world. But the *polis*, as I have already pointed out, was the marker of colonial presence in the eastern parts of the Roman Empire.[7] Crucial to understanding this situation is the transformation of the *polis-chōra* – city-hinterland – relation from classical Greece to the time in which Paul and

---

6 More recent articulations of this approach may be found in the work of Claude Lévi-Strauss (1989, 229–56), Louis Althusser (1971, 127–86) and Fredric Jameson (1981, 77–80). See also my effort to develop this approach for dealing with biblical texts in relation to economics (R. Boer 2015a, 48–51).

7 The overview of the economic situation in what follows is drawn from *Time of Troubles*, which has all of the necessary references (Boer and Petterson 2017, 49–152).

others were moving about. In the earlier context, a *polis* was inconceivable without the agricultural land surrounding it: the *chōra* and its *kōmae*, or villages. Given the overwhelmingly agricultural nature of ancient economics, the very possibility of establishing a *polis* depended on arable land. However, with the emergence of Greek colonisation and then the conquests by Alexander of Macedon, *poleis* were also established in the conquered and colonised areas. Over time, the *chōra* came to be all of the lands under the sway of the *polis.* The basic purpose was the same: to supply the *polis* with its foodstuffs, materials, clean water and labour – except that the local people so engaged did so for imperial overlords. The economic situation was transformed into one of coercive exploitation, by both economic and extra-economic means. Add to this the fact that *polis* was culturally and socially distinct from its occupied context. The language was Greek, the architecture and town-planning Greco-Roman, the governance imposed from without. By contrast, the colonised peoples spoke their local languages, followed very different customs and forms of social organisation, and practiced older forms of governance when possible. This reshaping of the *polis-chōra* relation may be described as a colonial economic regime, one that the Romans were happy to take over from the Greeks and bend to their own preferences. Of course, the problem with describing the situation in terms of *polis-chōra* is that it uses the very terms of the *polis* itself – precisely what Paul does as well in his own way.

If this colonial regime had enough of its tensions and struggles (witness the regular uprisings in different parts of the eastern Roman Empire), then the situation was exacerbated by its intersections with another economic regime – the slave regime. In the crucial part of the Roman Empire conquered early and then appropriated at all levels, the slave regime emerged from the long era of 'crisis' that enveloped the ancient Mediterranean and Southwest Asia. I speak of Greece, which after more than half a millennium of what is often but mistakenly called a period of 'crisis' and 'collapse' arose in a series of self-contained *poleis* with slavery a fundamental feature of their socio-economic structures. The core production of surplus upon which the ruling class lived was produced by slaves, so much so that even the most modest 'big peasant' would have at least one or two slaves. Indeed, the very possibility of Greek democracy, predicated as it was on the fundamental distinction between freedom and lack of freedom, relied on slavery to function. Slave market economies began to arise for the purpose of supplying slaves. But the Romans 'perfected' the system, if I may use such a term. Although the New Testament overwhelmingly represents household slaves, the vast bulk of slaves actually worked in agriculture. In Italy, slave estates spread along the river valleys, often using multiple forms of labour when required, including tenured peasants or day workers. Crucially, the Romans saw all forms of labour within the framework of slavery, even at times when other forms of labour outnumbered slaves. The effect of such a system pervaded all interlocked levels of life, from economic realities of agricultural production and slave markets, through social relations mediated through slaves, to cultural and ideological assumptions. These assumptions appear most clearly when we realise that the Greeks and Romans could not imagine their world or history without slavery.

Thus far, we already have four overlayed tensions: between divine and human 'authority', imperial and local rulers, *polis* and *chōra*, and between slave and free in the slave regime. Indeed, if the concept of freedom arose in the context of slavery, where many human beings as 'things [*res*]' were not free, then Paul's approach to freedom should be understood in a similar way. These are by no means the only tensions, for the colonial and slave regimes often had a problematic relationship. For example, slaves had to be found, by whatever means – prisoners of war, reproduction (*vernae*), exposed infants, debt-slavery, children sold by parents, adults giving themselves up to slavery, sentences given to some criminals, kidnapping, slave-raiding and acquisition across the frontiers. One major source was in the eastern parts, with some of the largest slave markets found here, especially Ephesus.[8] Obviously, the constant search for more slaves put pressure on the peoples of the *chōra*. Not only did they need to supply both the local *polis* with all sorts of goods, even adjusting agricultural production for the sake of fine breads (*panis siligneus* versus the peasant *panis plebeius*) and the Hellenistic preference for wine, but the constant search for slaves by whatever means threatened to reduce the number of agricultural labourers in colonised areas.

The question of labour brings us to a final collection of economic and social contradictions. The begin with, both the colonial and slave regimes sought in their very mechanisms to negate the continuing appeal of a resilient subsistence regime (see the previous chapter). The long period of what many call 'crisis' and 'collapse' – which extended from the end of the second millennium BCE into the middle of the first in the Greek world, saw the long dominance of this particular regime. It was characterised by an allocatory rather than an extractive economic dynamic, with field shares, labour and produce carefully allocated and reallocated in a regular basis. Its primary focus was on ensuring the continued viability of village communities, which also entailed diversity of crops and herds (typically two-thirds sheep and one-third goats). And it preferred to avoid being enmeshed with extractive regimes where possible, relocating villages away from the wavering sway of power, refusing labour and actively engaging in the destruction of centres of power when the weakness

---

8   Others include Byzantium, Alexandria, Amphipolis, Mitylene (after the decline of Delos), Sardis, Thyatira, Samos, Rhodes, Xanthus, Myra, Side, Acmonia and Gaza.

of the latter became apparent. In ancient Southwest Asia, it had seen earlier periods of dominance, only to find itself once again subjected to extractive regimes. In the Greek world, the eventual emergence of the slave regime in the middle of the first century BCE may be seen as an alternative and even ingenious response to the subsistence regime. The later colonial regime added another dimension to this response, with the two extractive regimes exercising a reasonably effective suppression of the subsistence regime and the interests of rural labourers. In many respects, this struggle against the subsistence regime may be seen as the primary economic tension or contradiction. This is not to say that the subsistence regime did not have its own tensions, particularly between what may be called the 'big peasant' and the 'small' and 'middle' peasants. Here patronage played a role alongside traditional patterns of patriarchal village governance. The relatively wealthy and powerful 'big' peasant was tolerated as long as his control was seen as largely beneficial to the survival of village economies, but it could easily tip over into an extractive mode that undermined these communities and their subsistence drive. This was indeed the case with the rise of the slave regime in the Greek world, since it can be seen as the victory of the big peasants who became the model of the Greek 'citizen', participants in Greek democracy (with its many limitations and flaws), and the ideal of the rural-based 'free man' who reduced others to slavery.

Labour itself runs like a red thread through all of these developments. All of the evidence – from life expectancies of 25–30 to consistent patterns of laws – indicates that labour was consistently in short supply in the ancient world. Even with the agricultural methods at hand, land was usually in abundance, but the difficulty was in finding labour to work it. Or at least, this was so for extractive regimes like the colonial and slave regimes, since they sought to maximise production for the provision of those not gainfully employed (the ruling class). Some periods may have experienced population pressures, such as the time when the Greeks first began colonial settlements in Asia Minor, but even in this case land was found elsewhere. This constant search for able hands to work the land in both the colonial and slave regimes had the effect of producing periodic waves of chronic labour shortage. Much more can be said about this question, but my point here is that it led to constant tensions between the colonial and slave regimes, as each sought to secure labour for its own mechanisms. It also enabled the most potent weapon of those forced to labour for others: the removal of labour, if not rural labourers moving themselves away from control by the local colonial *polis*. But is also led inexorably to a final economic regime of this ancient mode of production, which was the shift to what may be called the land regime. The origins of this regime may be traced back to practices of tenure in the Greco-Roman world, in which an extractive relation ensured that land was worked (labour) for the sake of the one controlling the land. Increasing, landlords sought to tie labour to land, culminating in the dramatic reform of Justinian in the late third century CE. Labour was fixed to a particular place (*origo*) with the consequent restriction of movement. The stated purpose was reform of the Roman taxation system through a census (to enable effective poll taxes), but the real and long-lasting effect was to lock in – theoretically at first – the whole of the working agricultural population throughout the empire. To secure this shift over time, a large number of subsequent laws were enacted (Constantine, famed for his conversion to Christianity, was an enthusiastic propagator of these laws). An individual tenant and his extended family was tied to the farm or plot under rent and would remain so on a hereditary basis. Those subject to the new situation began to be designated in the tax rolls as *colonus originalis, originarius,* or *adscripticius,* and the new abstract noun, *colonatus,* began to be used. Further, individuals who lived in villages (the vast majority) were tied to their villages. This situation had been developing for some time and it took even more time to sort out its complexities, but it entailed a new method for securing labour, if not an admission that the slave and colonial regimes were ultimately not able to counter the constitutive resistance of peasants and their preferred subsistence mode. The land regime also laid the groundwork for the eventual emergence of a feudal system in Europe.

By now it should be clear that multiple economic tensions played off against and overlapped with one another: authority (divine and human, imperial and local); *polis* and *chōra*; slave and free; colonial and slave regimes and their combined efforts to counter a subsistence regime; internal tensions in a subsistence regime; and labour and land. How does this complicated socio-economic situation relate to Paul's theoretical, if not theological, tensions? At one or two points, we may identify direct homologies (Goldmann 1964), as I have indicated earlier in relation to 'authority'. Another direct connection is between the offer of 'life' at various levels and the reality of short lives often afflicted by exploitation and diseases, such as the ever-present malaria, which may not have killed immediately but produced a range of secondary afflictions to which the bearer was now more vulnerable. But I have also pointed out that the relation is usually more indirect and relates to formal issues. This means that the very complexity of Paul's oppositions, the way they cannot so easily be separated from one another and constantly interact, may be seen as a formal manifestation in the very patterns of his thought of the socio-economic tensions I have outlined. The interweaving of these oppositions, the linking of one with another, the overcoming or transformation of one term in light of another – these and more indicate not merely an increasing effort to overcome the oppositions themselves, but ultimately the impossibility of doing so. For instance, siding with one side of the equation becomes an ethical decision for one or the other – life over death, grace over law, faith over works. This taking of sides is really the first step, for Paul also suggests that 'in Christ' some of these oppositions are overcome. Here we have the famous trio of slave and free, Jew and Gentile, male and female. In this step, Paul makes an effort at mediating the oppositions. One negates them by positing a greater and higher reality into which they are absorbed. A third option goes even further: in this case Paul narrates a passage from one to the other, from death to life, from law to grace, from works to faith and from sin to redemption. In the process, the first term is appropriated and transformed: so death becomes part of resurrection, law is still needed within grace, and works are transformed in faith.

Let me pick up this final point, since Paul's distinct response to the wider situation was to attempt a way out: a passage from one state of existence to another; from a life of sin to a life of faith. Taking up a methodological suggestion from Mao Zedong (1937a, 1937b), I would like to ask: what is the most important or primary contradiction in Paul's thought, a contradiction to which the others are secondarily related in an often complicated fashion? While a number of candidates may be entertained, especially the pattern of grace and law that I analysed earlier in relation to Romans 13, I propose that it is death and life. In order to see how, I return once more to Paul's arguments to see how they relate to these two terms, which appears explicitly in the narrative of the death and resurrection of Christ. Paul writes, 'But if we have died with Christ, we believe that we will also live with him' (Romans 6:8). Or as Romans 6:5 puts it slightly more expansively: 'For if we have been united with him in a death like his, we will certainly be united with him in a resurrection like his'. But this tension is not isolated, for it immediately connects with Adam and Christ: through one comes death, through the other life (1 Corinthians 15:21-22). So also with election, for the elect are those called to life, while the damned are not so fortunate (Romans 8:28-31). And the flesh is overwhelmingly one that leads to death, while the spirit gives life (although note Philippians 1:22-24 where being in the 'flesh', in this world, has certain benefits for others). Thus far, the narrative of oppositions seems reasonably straightforward, but, as we saw earlier, Paul is not content to settle for clear-cut oppositions, with each side neatly arrayed against the other. Already with these terms we find others that soon join them: with Adam we find sin and law, while with Christ appear grace and justification. The latter term also sits side by side with election (Romans 8:30, 33). One could argue that grace, justification, Christ (as well as faith) are clearly on the side of life, especially through the cross and resurrection of Christ. And so they are, but they have a curious effect on their opposites. Superficially, grace-Christ negates sin-law-works. But law and works do not merely ensure the path to death. Thus, we return to Paul's notorious twisting over the law: the law exists apart from sin, but the law exacerbates sin; following the letter of the law leads nowhere, but if one happens to enact the law even without knowledge then one is reasonably fine; Christ does not negate the law, except perhaps in a dialectical fashion in which he fulfils it; one may indeed speak of a 'law of the Spirit of life in Christ', which is opposed to the 'law of sin and of death' (Romans 8:2). Even more, sin may be intensified through the law, but this in turn makes grace abound even more (although this should not read – Paul counsels – as a license to sin enthusiastically).

The point here is that through it all Paul offers a distinct narrative, promising an ideal new life that puts the old life-leading-to-death behind one. Yet, the very form of Paul's argument raises a question: does one really pass from sin to salvation, from law to grace, from works to faith, from death to life? Even Paul is not so sure. The law is also good, he says, and you should really obey those earthly rulers, for God has appointed them. Women should not let freedom go to their heads and as for sex, he counsels that Christians had better follow his example where possible. Further, believers may be dead to sin, Christ may have forgiven them, and they may have entered a new life, but for some reason they continue to sin, the new collective is split by strife and the cares of the world keep crowding in upon them. The promised transition is not as effective as Paul might have hoped. No certain passage is offered; instead, Paul's narrative of passing from one state to another is fraught with a significant degree of uncertainty, hesitating in the middle of the bridge, wavering between two states. Paul seems to be caught between the pull of a new home, so much so that he wishes to die immediately and join Christ, but he also longs to stay in the old place. He writes to the Philippians in 1:21-24 that he does not know which option he prefers. On the one hand, 'living is Christ and dying is gain'; on the other, 'if I am to live in the flesh, that means fruitful labour for me'. Thus, 'I am hard pressed between the two: my desire is to depart and be with Christ, for that is far better; but to remain in the flesh is more necessary for you'. Here Paul puts it in terms of his personal desire and his sense of duty for the wellbeing of the Philippians, but the text reveals in a direct fashion the problem I have been emphasising.

The result is a profound ambivalence, which Paul both identified and – as a result of the later canonical decision to identify him as the prime ideologue of Christianity – came to determine the nature of Christian thought and practice that was to follow. Without a clean break, caught in the messy state of transition, both sides of the oppositions have claimed a place in Christianity. So, we have law *and* grace, works *and* faith, flesh *and* spirit, Adam *and* Christ, death *and* resurrection. Thus, the early church might have appealed to the poor peasant or slave or tenant, but it also had much to say to the wealthy landlord, slave owner or political power. It may have offered a new way of experiencing communal life, but it also ensured that such a life was hierarchical and unequal. In short, where grace appeared, so did law; where faith, also works; where life, also death; where resistance, compromise.

4   Conclusion

I began this analysis with the challenge of Romans 13:1-7, particularly in light of the preceding chapters on Kautsky's initial mapping of a history of revolutionary Christianity and the question of early Christian communism. This led me, initially in response to efforts to find an anti-imperial message in Paul, to an examination of the multiple tensions and contradictions in Paul's texts. Intrigued, I set off to examine these tensions and found an increasing complexity, which suggested an inability to overcome them. To identify a way to understand – but not resolve – these tensions, I took up a methodological suggestion from Marxist analysis: the development of contradictions at an ideological level may be seen as both a manifestation of and a response – in terms of content and form – to wider socio-economic tensions. In light of this methodological framework, I analysed the multiple contradictions produced by the various economic regimes of the ancient mode of production, specifically the colonial, slave and land regimes. But this was only an initial step, indicating the possibility that Paul's multiple tensions may be seen as a formal manifestation, in patterns of thought, by one inescapably immersed in the world of the *polis*. The next step was to focus on Paul's response, his effort to narrate a way out of this situation. This proposed solution turns on the narrative of Christ's death and resurrection, but Paul hesitates. He is uncertain about the transition entailed by the narrative and equally unclear about its completion. It might be possible to describe this problem in terms of a spiritual solution to a real-world problem, but this would be too easy and somewhat foreign to Paul's more integrated approach. More to the point, the result was that Paul left an ambivalent legacy at many levels, opening up the possibility for radical, if not revolutionary readings of his and other texts, but also the real potential for reactionary interpretations that are more than happy to bolster power and prestige. Indeed, the ambivalent tradition that developed from Paul suited the Empire rather well, from Constantine onwards. Yet, those who identify a more radical dimension would find this development far from acceptable.

CHAPTER 4

Omnia Sunt Communia: Theology and Politics in Luther Blissett's *Q*

> In regard to what was to be understood by 'the Gospel', he asserts: 'It is an article of our creed, and one which we wish to realise, that all things are in common [*omnia sunt communia*], and should be distributed as occasion requires, according to the several necessities of all. Any prince, count, or baron who, after being earnestly reminded of this truth, shall be unwilling to accept it, is to be beheaded or hanged'.
>
> KAUTSKY 1897, 130, 1895, 284

We have already met this quotation within a quotation in the first chapter, from Kautsky's *Forerunners* in his assessment of the Peasant Revolution and the role of Thomas Müntzer. The reason for quoting it again is not fortuitous, for it indicates the way Kautsky's initial insights have been taken up once again in our own day. The present chapter moves forward in time, although this time it has a double register: it deals with a troubled European present that is attempting to reappropriate the revolutionary decades of the sixteenth century. My focus is the long and wildly popular novel, *Q*, which is a stunning reclamation of the revolutionary Christian tradition for a whole generation of anti-capitalist activists in the early decades of the twenty-first millennium. Written by the radical Italian collective, Luther Blissett (now Wu Ming, 'nobody'),[1] it was first published online in Italian in 1999. I would like to suggest that it is both an unexpected and lively contribution to the renewed debate over Marxism and religion and that it reveals some unexpected dimensions of the anti-capitalist movement.[2] In what follows, I analyse the tone of the novel, one that is set

---

1 Luther Blisset, the name of an English footballer who played for AC Milan in the 1990s, was a name used by hundreds of activists in order to play pranks on the capitalist media. Wu Ming (the new name of the collective from 2000 but earlier the name of a much wider movement), was deeply involved in the G8 protests in Genoa, where the police laid a trap and beat, tortured and imprisoned many protestors. For some further information, filtered through both the mouths of Wu Ming and of the reporter, see the interviews by Baird and Home and their own reflections in the Verso reprint of Müntzer's *Sermon to the Princes* (Baird 2006; Home 2013; Wu 2001, 2010).

2 There is a slightly personal dimension to this question, since I seek some answers to the popularity in the same circles of my five volume work, *The Criticism of Heaven and Earth*

by a tradition that begins with Engels, runs through Karl Kautsky and Ernst Bloch, and includes Antonio Gramsci. This is a tone of revolutionary appreciation of the Anabaptists and of Thomas Müntzer, but also one that sees the Reformation itself as a great revolutionary period. From its tone, I move to the issues raised by the novel. These are the tensions between passion and reason, rupture and communalism, as well as the deep political ambivalence of theology. What is intriguing about these tensions is that one finds them in both revolutionary political and religious traditions. Finally, I broach the matter of translation, offering both an alternative model to the relations between religious and political thought, and seeking a possible answer as to why many of those in the anti-capitalist movement have read *Q*, indeed why they are so interested in religious radicalism.[3]

Before proceeding, a brief outline of the novel is in order, a novel that shows all the signs that the authors thoroughly enjoyed the writing thereof. The revolutionary decades of the sixteenth century are connected by a multi-named protagonist, who at the same time has no name.[4] He may be of German extraction, but much of the revolutionary and religious ferment arises from the Netherlands – a welcome emphasis. He moves from the battlefield of Frankenhausen in 1525, where the peasants led by 'Magister Thomas' (Müntzer) were finally defeated, to owning a Venetian brothel in the 1540s, from the Anabaptist revolution of Münster to defrauding the Fugger's bank of 100,000 florins, from the war parties of Jan van Batenburg to the free spirits or Loists of Antwerp,

---

(Boer 2007–2014). From Morocco to China to Australia, I have encountered activists who have read these heavy tomes and have endless questions concerning theology itself.

3   The secondary literature on *Q* is rather thin. The study by De Donno (2013) touches on some of the issues raised here (and I refer to it from time to time), but it seeks a moral in the novel and is theologically tone-deaf, thereby missing central features of the novel. The studies of Garber (2006) and Zucchi (2007) focus on historical issues. Although both attempt to assess the historical reliability of the novel's representation of the Anabaptists and the Reformation era, Zucchi at least searches for some features of their play with history. In reply, it is worth quoting the authors: 'We make use of historians' work, their research and their interpretations, but then we go beyond the point at which they're constrained to stop' (Baird 2006, 255). The main focus of the other studies on the Wu Ming project concerns the political function of indeterminate identities and authorship, along with scattered interest in the role of media and the nature of Italian literature and intellectual activism in Italy, or the function of the indeterminacy of names, with little, if any, attention paid to the crucial matter of the intersections between theology and politics in *Q* (Habeck 2003; Ovan 2005; Thoburn 2011; Biasini 2010; Mecchia 2009; Piga 2010).

4   Here the authors both implicitly acknowledge Lukács's point (1971) that the novel needs a hero to provide a thread that links its disparate elements and challenge that point with the multi-named hero and the two characters – the hero and the Vatican agent Q. For some further reflection on the slipperiness of identity and anonymity, see the interview by Baird (2006, 252) and the studies by Habeck (2003), Ovan (2005) and Thoburn (2011).

from bringing Italy to the verge of Reformation to conspiring with Jewish bankers to spread Calvinism via the booklet, *Benefit of Christ Crucified*. Increasingly, he becomes a leader himself, a prophet with a canny ability for taking care of himself. Throughout friends and comrades meet grisly ends, loves are lost or left behind, battles are mostly lost, but some are won.

All the time, he is shadowed by an equally unnamed Vatican agent. Or rather, this agent has a consistent code name, signing his missives to his Vatican boss with 'Q' and those to Müntzer with 'Qoèlet'. On each revolutionary occasion, Q is in the thick of events. He persuades Müntzer to take to the battlefield at Frankenhausen, feeding false information concerning the supposed unpreparedness of the troops of Philip, Landgrave of Hesse. He turns up within the walls of Münster, seeking to ingratiate himself – now as Gresbeck (the actual author of a first-hand account and betrayer of the revolutionaries) – with the Anabaptist leaders and push them to extremes. He investigates the curious radical ferment in Italy itself, devoting himself to identifying its cause. He counters the efforts of moderate Roman Catholic cardinals and theologians who seek rapprochement with the Protestants. Continuously, he pens missives to his tireless boss, Cardinal Gianpietro Carafa, the head of the newly formed Inquisition and one who becomes Pope Paul IV at the end of the novel. These letters are a crucial component of *Q*. At once fawning and frank, they offer insights into the radical movements, propose daring counter-revolutionary moves and educate readers concerning the inner theologico-political workings of the Counter-Reformation. He also pens the letters that win over the confidence of Müntzer, showing a mastery of flattery and faux confidentiality (although we must wait quite a while to find out he is the author).[5] The formal opposition of these two characters, both men of action and ingenuity, will become crucial for my later assessment of the ambivalence of Christianity.

1   *Q* and the Marxist Tradition

Q breathes the spirit of those who have identified a profoundly revolutionary dimension to Christianity – from Friedrich Engels, through Karl Kautsky and Anatoly Lunacharsky and Ernst Bloch, to Antonio Gramsci.[6] For Engels,

---

5   The other letters are those – between Müntzer and other revolutionaries – in the old satchel rescued by the hero from the battlefield of Frankenhausen, as well as the few sent by Anton Fugger to the Inquisition boss, seeking the punishment for heretics – burning at the stake – of those who had defrauded the bank so successfully. They are of the same ilk as Q's letters.

6   I would add the occasional moment from Marx and Mao as well. From Marx we have of course the explanation of the economic mechanisms of capitalism, focused now on the 'Dutch miracle', that is, the first properly capitalist empire (Blissett 2004, 260–64).

the process of coming to terms with his Reformed background (he shared the strong faith of his Calvinist household in Wuppertal) involved the increasing awareness of the revolutionary nature of Christianity.[7] Developing a passing insight in the 1840s concerning 'the religious revolution of which the outcome was Christianity',[8] Engels first elaborated his position in an influential study of Müntzer and the Peasant Revolution (Engels 1850a, 1850b).[9] Although this work set in train a series of subsequent studies, especially by Kautsky and Bloch, so much so that Müntzer became a revolutionary hero in East Germany, it is not Engels's best study. Here Müntzer's fiery theological language becomes a mere external covering for a secular, revolutionary core. Müntzer spoke in theological terms to the larger groups of peasants, but to the inner circle he spoke in a directly political manner, untainted by theology. Other elements are of greater worth, such as: the identification of a tension in Luther's message, one that both set Müntzer on his revolutionary path and then led Luther to denounce the peasants; the clear appeal of Luther to the merchants of the towns; and the detailed discussion of military manoeuvres and battle plans (with a glorious map). The latter may not have been taken up by the novel, but the former becomes a crucial feature that enhances the theme of the political ambivalence of Christianity.

Since I have dealt with Kautsky's careful study of Müntzer and Münster in the first chapter, I do not need to reiterate the points made there, although I would like to emphasise two points. First, Kautsky goes well beyond Engels with his awareness that in the sixteenth century theology was inextricably entwined with the economic, social and cultural dimensions of the revolutionary movements (Kautsky 1897, 220, 1895, 377). Second, one soon realises that *Q* is deeply consonant with Kautsky's work, even to the point of a similar

---

Further: 'Luther stripped the priests of their black garb, only to put it on the hearts of all men' (Blissett 2004, 258; Marx 1844a, 182, 1844b, 177; see also Boer 2012, 145–50). And the Maoist moment appears when Ottilie Müntzer whispers, 'You were right. We can't do anything without the peasants' (Blissett 2004, 60; see further Chan 2003).

7   For a detailed discussion of these aspects of Engels's work, with complete references, see *Criticism of Earth: On Marx, Engels and Theology* (Boer 2012, 233–306).

8   This is from his *Letters from London* of 1843. Following the text I have quoted is a reinterpretation of a phrase from Jesus's Sermon on the Mount (Matthew 5:3): 'blessed are the poor, for theirs is the kingdom of heaven and, however long it may take, the kingdom of this earth as well' (Engels 1843a, 380, 1843b, 452). To this should be added his early roll call of revolutionary movements and their leaders inspired by Christianity, such as Thomas Müntzer, Étienne Cabet, Wilhelm Weitling and others (Engels 1843c).

9   I am not interested here in assessing Müntzer per se, but rather in the Marxist heritage. For those wishing to explore Müntzer further, a cluster of studies – of varying quality – appeared at what was generally agreed to be the fifth centenary of his birth in 1989 (Gritsch 1989; Scott 1989; Friesen 1990; Goertz 2000; Bak et al. 2013). The best, however, remain Bubenheimer (1989) and Vogler (1989).

narrative flow.[10] Indeed, I would suggest that the central slogan – *omnia sunt communia* – of Wu Ming, as also of some parts of the anti-capitalist and commons movement,[11] is mediated via Kautsky's text. For Kautsky emphasises that 'all things in common' – *omnia sunt communia*, the Latin translation of Acts 2:44 and 4:32 – was the definition of the Gospel given by Müntzer (Kautsky 1897, 130, 1895, 284). The intersections are many: the narrative flow from the Peasant Revolution, through the revolutionary currents and underground work of the Anabaptists, to the watershed of Münster itself;[12] the careful effort to read against the anti-revolutionary bias of the sources; the suspicious figure of Luther, whom Müntzer outshines; the energy and organisational brilliance of the peasants and their leader; the names, networks and arrests of the various Anabaptist leaders; as also the empathetic interpretation of the Anabaptist revolution at Münster. Indeed, Kautsky is even more sympathetic to these radical Anabaptists than is *Q*. For the novel, eventually Münster slips into madness under Jan Matthys and then Jan van Leyden, especially when our hero leaves the city, first to seek reinforcements and supplies, and then for good. Yet, as we saw earlier, Kautsky attempts to understand and interpret favourably the situation of a city of radical communists under siege. We also find the central figure of Gresbeck, who betrayed Münster to the massed Roman Catholic and Protestant forces. A native of Münster and a joiner, Gresbeck wrote one of the most detailed accounts of the events in the city, albeit from the perspective of one who betrayed it (Mackay 2016). So Kautsky's suspicions provide the creative link by which Gresbeck becomes, in the novel, a manifestation of the Vatican agent, Q.

Anatoly Lunacharsky and Ernst Bloch also share Kautsky's insight – that theology is itself crucial. The well-nigh forgotten Lunacharsky (through no fault of his own) was a Left Bolshevik, Commissar for Enlightenment after the Russian Revolution, and author of a stunning work, *Religion and Socialism*.[13]

---

10   I make this point fully cognisant of the fact that Wu Ming has stated that Bloch is the major influence on their reading (De Donno 2013, 40). On this matter, I would simply point out that authorial statements are not always the best guide to interpretation, especially when they attempt to guide such interpretation.

11   In their introduction to the Verso reprint of Müntzer's *Sermon to the Princes*, Wu Ming note the curious and even troublesome intersection between *Q* and the anti-capitalist movement, especially at the G8 meeting in Genoa in 2008. Apart from placards with *omnia sunt communia*, those involved used aliases such as 'Magister Thomas' and 'Gert-from-the-well' (Wu 2010, xxxiv).

12   Even the opening scene in which Müntzer is captured after the battle of Frankenhausen, a scene that vividly captivates the reader in the opening pages of *Q*, appears in Kautsky's text, albeit in a more concise form (Kautsky 1897, 151–52, 1895, 309–10).

13   This two-volume work has lain in obscurity ever since Lenin attacked it 1908. For the complex story and a detailed study of the work see my *Lenin, Religion, and Theology* (Boer 2013a, 74–83).

Here he writes: 'Great prophets are always on the borders and among seething social struggle. With eagle eyes peering into the future, they provide a slogan, generalize the struggle, scourge the enemies of their ideas, console supporters' (Lunacharsky 1908b, 70). This applies as much to Müntzer as it does to the tradition of revolutionary prophets that he traces from the Bible: Amos the firebrand, bright Hosea, Isaiah the democrat, Jeremiah the furiously eloquent, Paul the democratic internationalist, Jesus the scourge of the propertied and wealthy, the 'everlasting Gospel' of Joachim of Fiore, through to Müntzer (Lunacharsky 1908b, 165–78, 1911, 145–55).

In many respects, Lunacharsky anticipates the interests and emphases of Ernst Bloch, even though the latter does not seem to have known of his forerunner. Along with Engels and Kautsky, Bloch influenced the raising of Müntzer to the status of pre-revolutionary hero in the DDR (much like Jan Hus in Czechoslovakia). His *Thomas Münzer als Theologe der Revolution* first appeared in 1921, with its wholehearted embracing of Müntzer and the peasant revolt. The book follows Kautsky's main points, arguing for the centrality of theology in Müntzer's radical politics, as also the pre-Marxist forms of communism that are found in the radical tradition of Christianity. For Bloch, of course, it is part of his wider project to restore the 'warm stream' of Marxism – the one that appeals to heart, that fosters enthusiasm and commitment. It is not that he wished to dispense with 'cold' theory, but that both are necessary for Marxism. One of the main sources for that warm stream is religion, or more specifically the Bible (Bloch 1968; Boer 2007a, 1–56). However, Bloch's distinct contribution is to focus on the apocalyptic or millenarian dimension of Müntzer's message, although this too is part of a larger project to show how revolutionary such religiously-inspired apocalyptic movements can be. Not only was this an effort to introduce a distinct dimension that Marxism had missed, but it also pushed back against the desire by Marx and Engels to counter the apocalyptic fervour of many early communists (such as Moses Hess and Wilhelm Weitling). In Müntzer's hands, then, the revolutionary myth of Christian communism finds full expression. The Bible becomes the bad conscience of the Church, and it is precisely its vivid apocalyptic texts that breathe the fire of protest and revolution.

By now there is more than enough to indicate the tradition from which *Q* springs, the tone and feel that it conveys: revolutionary Anabaptists, Christian communism, theology itself as potentially revolutionary – all mediated through a distinctly Marxist tradition. However, the novel also breathes a curiously Italian air, that of Gramsci. It was Gramsci's lasting lament that Italy had not experienced the Reformation. Indeed, he wrote: 'Luther and the Reformation stand at the beginning of all modern philosophy and civilization' (Gramsci 1994, 365). By contrast, Italy had undergone, through the Renaissance, a series of 'reforms that touch only the upper classes and often only the intel-lectuals' (Gramsci 1996, 244). Never has there been an 'intellectual and moral reform' that shook up society from bottom to top (Gramsci 1996, 243–44). He goes so far as to align the Protestant Reformation with the communist revolu-tion, for the Reformation was the last great European mass movement. The solution: Gramsci searches for a comparable figure and finds him in Machia-velli's prince. The authors of *Q* give voice to the same longing, although they also correct Gramsci by constructing an account in which the reason why a Reformation did not take place may be found in the Inquisition. Our protago-nist undertakes, towards the close of the novel, a program of roving preaching, spreading the Anabaptist message, baptising and finding many adherents. In the end it fails, through the dual causes of the Inquisition and the cowardice of the newly found leaders. The authors also correct Gramsci by locating the truly revolutionary strain of the Reformation not with Luther but with the Radical Reformation. If this had taken root, then there would indeed have been a thor-ough shakeup of Italian society at all levels.

So *Q* breathes the air of this long tradition in Marxism, where religion itself can become a revolutionary force. Engels feeling his way, Kautsky providing a grand narrative, Lunacharsky and Bloch giving some depth and Gramsci an air of longing: these are the nutrients of rich engagement.

2 Issues

My analysis turns now to consider four themes that emerge from *Q*: the tension between passion and reason, that between rupture and communal-ism, the political ambivalence of Christianity, and the question of translation between politics and theology.[14] All of these may be seen as distinct features of political myth, the recreation of which is a crucial feature of Wu Ming's proj-ect. However, since I have written at length on political myth elsewhere and since De Donno has broached, in a limited way, the self-proclaimed 'mytho-poesis' of Wu Ming, as well as their allegory of the present (R. Boer 2009d, De Donno 2013; Baird 2006, 257–59),[15] I prefer to develop that discussion in terms

---

14 Others may also suggest themselves, such as the carnivalesque nature of revolution, or revo-lution as apocalypse, the perennial question of old and new, or the tension between utopian and dystopian dimensions of radical activism. Apart from the last point, which may be extracted from De Donno's study (2013), the remainder are the topics of another study.

15 Although De Donno's emphasis on mythopoesis is welcome, it misses the full dialectical complexity of political myth (R. Boer 2009d). More problematic is the way he follows a rather old-fashioned search for authorial intention, overlaid with moral concerns – a curious effort given Wu Ming's problematizing of authorship itself. That he falls into the

of these four themes. On the first point, the novel clearly focuses on what it is that motivates people to take up revolutionary politics. It is a passion enhanced at a narrative level by the immediacy of the filthy roughness of life, but especially in situations of war. Carefully argued assessments of the current state of economic oppression, with the requisite determination of what needs to be done, may be one thing, but that – while thoroughly necessary – is not what touches the heart for many. It is what Ernst Bloch called the 'cold stream' of Marxism, or what Anatoly Lunacharsky described as '"dry" economic theory' (Lunacharsky 1908b, 9). Instead, they preferred to stress the enthusiastic and emotional dimensions. For both of them, the cold stream was embodied in Second International Marxism, which had lost the sensitive and enthusiastic Marx – a Marx who provided alongside his scientific work an emotional appeal, saying, according to Lunacharsky, 'that poets need many caresses' (1967, 274). Indeed, this Marx was the one who brought about in Lunacharsky a distinct 'conversion to Marxism', a conversion to a 'deeply emotional impulse of the soul' (Lunacharsky 1908b, 9). Or in Bloch's characteristic style, 'To the *warm stream* [Wärmestrom] of Marxism, however, belong liberating intention and materialistically humane, humanely materialist real tendency, towards whose all these disenchantments are undertaken' (Bloch 1995, 209, 1985, 241).

The tough hero of *Q* is also one whose eye has the glint of promise and hope, and who finds that same gleam in Thomas Müntzer, 'the flame that set Germany ablaze' (Blissett 2004, 27), in the peasants who follow him, in the eyes of the radicals at Münster, in the apocalyptic prophets such as Jan Matthys, and in the free spirits of Antwerp. To be sure, he has his head on his shoulders and the survivor's instinct. His scars – 'the geographical map of lost battles' (Blissett 2004, 114) – tell enough of that story. Yet in the face of an almost unending stream of catastrophe and failure, when the 'army of the elect' is 'lost in the mud', the passion remains (Blissett 2004, 24). But whence does that enthusiasm come? Is it in the catharsis of violence, when his hopes are seemingly dashed time and again against superior forces? Is it in the hedonism that creeps through at different moments, with a wine flask and a woman or two? Is it the revolutionary promise, when 'everything was possible' (Blissett 2004, 27, see also 45, 78), that calls one back again. No, it is clearly from his faith, of a radical Anabaptist kind.

A Gospel of the poor it was, of the dregs who never imagined they would have the chance to decide history. Or rather, through a focus on the texts in which obedience to God's command was central and those who failed to live

---

trap of following Wu Ming's own efforts to guide and control interpretation of the novel only exacerbates the problem. Further, he tends to focus on Thomas Müntzer, which is the concern only of the first part of the novel, thereby giving scant attention to the longer and even more intriguing engagements with Münster, the Anabaptists in the Lowlands, the Brethren of the Free Spirit in Antwerp and the movements in Italy.

up to that law were to be condemned. Princes, bishops, barons, counts, anyone who oppressed the poor, especially the peasants, were subject to God's judgement. Anyone who saw themselves as higher than everyone else, who took on airs and powers and wealth, did so not only on the backs of the poor, but in contravention to the message of the Gospel. The Church of Rome falls short, as does Luther, whose message appealed to the wealthy merchants and burghers of the towns, let alone the princes who saw in Luther and his message a way of throwing off the burden of Rome and the Holy Roman Emperor.

This emphasis leads to the second tension in the novel, between rupture and communalism – a distinction I have already explored in relation to Christian communism. The first appears obviously with the opening scene, the graphic and first-hand account of the slaughter of the peasants at Frankenhausen, and it continues through the long story of the siege of Münster, a name that provokes 'a shiver that was once an earthquake' (Blissett 2004, 142), let alone the apocalyptic squads of Jan van Batenburg in the Netherlands, seeking to bring on the end by cutting a swathe of destruction. Each was the 'umpteenth Jerusalem, still populated with ghosts and crazed prophets' (Blissett 2004, 112). But I wish to focus here on the constant desire, at both the personal level of our hero and of the revolutions themselves, to break through to communal life, with all things in common, mutual aid and the banishment of exploitation. We find this above all at three moments, with differing emphasis but with the same underlying desire.

Apart from efforts at communal government, as explorations of proto-socialist formations in Mühlhausen and Münster (both towns seized by deft and popular revolutions), the most obvious treatment of communalism takes place when the hero spends a good deal of time – the middle section of the novel – with the Brethren of the Free Spirit in Antwerp. Lodewijck de Schaliedecker (alias Eloi Pruystinck) is their founder and guide, a man who had, like Müntzer, gone beyond Luther, but on a different tack. For Eloi, the key is not violent conflagration, but an antinomian reading of theology. 'Not under law, but under grace' (Romans 6:14) means that the old order no longer holds one down. The new order, of grace that goes beyond all that is, begins now, has been inaugurated and awaits the consummation with Christ's return. The upshot: a community of mutual aid, having all things in common, in cooperation rather than conflict, of sexual freedom, an oasis in the maelstrom of life and politics. Indeed, this is precisely how the hero first encounters them. He is rescued by Eloi after a severe beating at the hands of Spanish colonial soldiers, immediately after the execution of Jan van Battenberg. The vast house of the Brethren becomes a place of recuperation from his injuries, of finding again old handicraft skills, of peace and even of love (Kathleen). But how does Eloi fund the group? He is as innocent as a dove and as wise as a serpent (Matthew

10:16), persuading the rich merchants and bankers of Antwerp, who are all too keen to foster any movement that challenges Rome and the tax burdens of the Spanish crown. Yet he also has a grander scheme, not only of funding his movement, but of bringing the corrupt economic and ecclesial order of Europe to its knees. He enlists our protagonist and an old banker into a massive project that defrauds the Fugger's bank and nets them each 100,000 florins (an early instance of revolutionary expropriations, which the Bolsheviks would later perfect). The idea is that the scheme would throw doubt into the reliability of the Fugger's bank, but Anton Fugger calls Cardinal Carafa to investigate and try Eloi as a heretic. Eloi dies at the stake in 1544, but not before many among the Brethren – forewarned – escape overseas, or, in the case of our hero, to Italy.

Tellingly, he takes on the name of Lodewijck de Schaliedecker,[16] and recreates a very different communal life, now in Venice and as a shareholder (with his many florins) in a brothel. His hard-earned toughness enables him to provide the necessary threat of violence (and its occasional enactment) to ensure the women in the brothel can work in peace and under good conditions. Here is both an astute awareness that any communist venture requires a strong arm to keep its would-be destroyers at bay, but also a working out of what it actually means for Jesus to prefer the company of 'the disinherited, the whores and the panders', the dregs who had nothing to lose (Blissett 2004, 150). Of course, the brothel venture is connected with the antinomian sexual bent of the novel, in which the celebration of a very different, communal life, also means the earthiness of carnivalesque, sensual enjoyment – even Müntzer is known to like a drink, engage in sexual banter, and occasional public sex, such as the mutual masturbation with Ottilie (Blissett 2004, 51, 72).[17]

A final expression of the desire for communalism emerges through the contacts with the Jews and Muslims in the story. Initially, some Jewish bankers provide a glimpse of an alternative life, even while constantly watching their backs and prepared to pack up and move on at a moment's notice. And then, as the novel closes, the Muslims of the Ottoman world, with their superior culture and knowledge of what it means to live well, provide a glimpse of peace. A man now older and with a few too many creaky bones and stiff muscles finds at last a life on the other side of revolution.

Both elements – of violent revolution and communal life – come through strongly in the novel, at times as a stark contrast, but more often as a necessary pair (in contrast to Kautsky's effort to separate them too sharply). So also

---

16   In comparable moments, he takes on the names of Gerrit Boekbinder in Münster (thereby linking in with the historical Bartholomeus Boeckbinder) and Titian in Italy (the Italian heretic connected with *The Benefit of Christ Crucified*).

17   'Let the Carnival begin', is the call that notes the successful revolution in Münster (Blissett 2004, 211). Bakhtin's study of the carnivalesque may be read as both a search for its historic revolutionary role and as a code for the Russian Revolution (Bakhtin 1984; Boer 2007b).

with the Anabaptist tradition that is central to the novel. Its communal tendencies may have flourished during its period in Moravia (as Kautsky notices) and come to the fore in the pacifist propensities that have had the upper hand since the Münster Revolution, at least in those branches influenced by David Joris, Obbe Phillips and Menno Simons.[18] Yet Anabaptism embodies a tension between the two sides, a tension that is necessary for any movement that bases itself upon vanquishing a world of exploiters and fat cats for the sake of one that espouses communal life. Once again, the deep patterns of Kautsky's work show through here, for in his lengthy account he is keen to emphasise the superior communal life of the various strands of 'heterodox communism', during the relatively brief periods when they were given space to develop.[19]

I would like to focus briefly on a third distinctive feature of the novel: the tension between reaction and revolution that runs through the text, both in terms of form and content. I have already written of the political ambivalence inherent within the workings of Christian thought and practice in the previous chapter (see also Boer 2014a, 125–69), so I do not wish to reprise that whole argument here, save for a couple of observations. By political ambivalence I mean the ease which theology and the church may sidle up to tyrants and repressive economic orders, while at the same time giving continuous inspiration to revolutionary movements. Neither one is a core truth, for which the other then becomes a distortion, for both are genuinely possible within the logic of theology.[20]

This ambivalence emerges at multiple levels within the novel. It may be within Luther himself, for he is the one who set the radicals on their paths, especially Müntzer, who was 'more like Luther than Luther himself' (Blissett 2004, 38). That is, they sought to bring to its natural conclusion the message of salvation by grace through faith (Blissett 2004, 31). Luther soon became alarmed at what he had unleashed, seeking to rein in the radical tendencies of those who took

---

18   The debate turns up in the novel itself (Blissett 2004, 251). The argument that the communal side is the true core and the other an aberration is both mistaken and obviously an effort to gain the upper hand in a perpetual struggle. Garber's study (2006) is written from the perspective of ensuring that the pacifist story remains the core.

19   Nonetheless, a loss of the revolutionary edge risks two developments: an accommodation with the status quo for the sake of working within the system; and retreat from the world in somewhat self-contained communities that define themselves by offering an alternative to the degraded world that surrounds them. The reasons for such moves vary widely, some of them strategically justified, but too often do these moves become permanent, eschewing any form of revolutionary activity and finding all manners of justifications for doing so. At one point in the novel, a debate between Eloi and the hero turns on precisely these issues (Blissett 2004, 256–58).

20   De Donno's proposal (2013, 44–49) that the novel seeks to revitalise the radical utopian tradition while warning against its authoritarianism and the repressive nature of institutions may be seen as one element of this larger political ambivalence of Christianity.

him at his word, taking a position in line with the Roman church he opposed.[21] Melanchthon then expresses the position of both Rome and Wittenberg, that of Romans 13.[22] However, these issues remain at the level of content. By contrast, a more sustained manifestation of this political ambivalence appears in the form of *Q*. I think in particular of the doppelganger characters, of the name-changing Anabaptist revolutionary and his opposite, the Vatican agent Q, who works for the founder of the Inquisition, Cardinal Carafa. Struggling with one another at a distance or at close quarters, at times even cooperating (especially when Q is Gresbeck in Münster and then towards the close of the novel), it seems as though the agent mostly has the upper hand. He it is who persuades – through carefully crafted letters (as 'Qoèlet') that inspire trust[23] – Müntzer to lead the under-prepared peasants onto the battlefield at Frankenhausen. He too volunteers to go into Münster, in order to push the leaders to extremes so that the whole Anabaptist movement would be discredited. Here he becomes the historical figure of Gresbeck, who pens the most intimate account of the revolution and is instrumental in its betrayal (Mackay 2016). At this point, my own sense is that the authors overplay their hand, for Q is a little too involved in every event, a little too prescient, a little too able to influence the course of history. The result is that the agency of the peasants and Anabaptists dissipates somewhat, even with the realistic awareness of the perpetual threat of spies and agents. Given that the coherence of a novel such as this is strung together by the lead character – here a double character – the point is that reaction is exceedingly strong and devious. Yet, in the end, Q loses his sense of purpose, and realises how much he has both been used and how dispensable he really is. Finally, the hero and Q meet, cooperate for a moment to gain access to incriminating documents concerning the pope and the struggles in the church between moderates and hard-liners, only for Q and the documents to burn and die in the fire that consumes the Viennese brothel.

The man with many names and yet none embodies the revolutionary side of this tension. While the struggles between him and Q manifest the profound political ambivalence at the heart of Christianity, the novel closes with a hint

---

21   This insight is given to Q himself, who writes in one of his letters: 'The truth is that the portal that Luther has opened is one that he himself would now wish to be closed' (Blissett 2004, 36).

22   At one point, in debate with the radical Karlstadt, Melanchthon quotes Romans 13:1: 'Let every soul be subject to the governing authorities. For there is no power but of God: the powers that be are ordained by God' (Blissett 2004, 29).

23   The letters – a standard literary device – are another formal manifestation of the tension. Initially, it seems as though Q has the upper hand, with his long letters foreseeing new developments, if not precipitating them. Yet, Müntzer too has written and received letters, kept in the satchel our hero manages to rescue from the battlefield at Frankenhausen. In the end, these letters hold their own against those of Q.

that the latter has greater endurance. The passion never quite fades; the multitude of failures and disasters never quite dampens his desire and belief; many
ghosts may visit his dreams, but he wakes once again.[24] Here too form exhibits
this message even more than content. At the novel's opening, we are thrown
into the last moments of the bloody defeat at Frankenhausen.[25] Müntzer
and our man are hauled off the field by the miner-bodyguard, Elias, only for
Müntzer to be captured, Elias to be beheaded on the street, and the hero to
escape narrowly. Why begin with a crushing defeat? I suggest that the defeat
actually opens up the possibility of hope. New life follows death. Defeat is the
first word, the common denominator, a bitter lesson to be learned, but it is not
the end. Indeed, the structure of the novel that follows, at least for two-thirds
of its length, works its way between flashback (enabled at first by the rescued
letters of Müntzer and then by the questions of Eloi Pruystinck) and the present, filling out the story that led to the high-points of Frankenhausen and then
Münster, yet showing that the project continues beyond the defeat. A deft
switching back and forth between past aorist and present tenses in the narrative add yet another level of the formal emphasis of this feature. The novel
continues, with even more defeats, but those formal moves indicate that at
least one survives, learns, hopes and fights again. The revolutionary fire cannot
be extinguished so easily.

3   Conclusion: How to Be Truly Radical

I have argued that *Q* offers a comprehensive recovery of the radical, revolutionary dimensions of the Reformation, especially for a range of Left-wing
movements today. It is indebted to the Marxist tradition of identifying the revolutionary strain of Christian thought and practice, whether in terms of early
Christianity, Thomas Müntzer and the Peasants, or the Anabaptists at Münster.
Here the names of Engels, Luxemburg, Kautsky, Lunacharsky and Bloch are
central. I have also sought out the deeper issues raised by the novel, in terms of
the tensions between passion and reason, rupture and communalism, and the
political ambivalence of Christianity. I would like to close on a slightly different, albeit related note, and ask: how does all this have relevance to the appeal
of *Q* today, with its wholesale recovery of the radical theological tradition?

---

24   'Every time thunder shakes the heavens, I start at the memory of the cannon. Every time I
      close my eyes to sleep, I know that by the time I open them again I'll have been visited by
      many ghosts' (Blissett 2004, 399).
25   A similar approach is used with the death squads of Jan van Batenberg, for the narra-
      tive reopens after the execution of van Batenburg and the hero's narrow escape after a
      harrowing defeat (Blissett 2004, 103–4).

Apart from the issues explored earlier, I suggest that a significant part of Q's appeal lies in what may be called the translatability of religion and (especially) radical politics. That is, the semantic fields of key terms and ideas in both politics and theology offer the possibility of being translated into one another. On this point, the novel goes beyond Kautsky, who merely hints at this possibility with his juxtaposition of the radicalism of social movements and the deeper theological nature of its articulation: 'The more radical a social movement, the more theological were its forms of expression (Kautsky 1897, 220, 1895, 377). Q offers a thorough translatability of theology and radical politics. Terms such as revolution and miracle, obedience to the law of God and justice, the land as God's and land reform, adult (or believer's) baptism and the right of people to make their own political decisions, Christian communism and the abolition of private property – these and more have their own semantic fields that open out to one another. Let me give one example of many (note the biblical allusions):

> We were diligent sowers of the seed, lighting the spark of war against those who had usurped the word of God, the tormentors of His people. I saw scythes hammered into swords, hoes becoming lances and simple men leaving the plough to become fearless warriors. I saw a little carpenter carving a great crucifix and guiding Christ's troops like the captain of the most invincible army. I saw all this and I saw those men and women take up their own faith and turn it into a banner of revenge. Love seized our hearts with that one fire that flamed within us all: we were free and equal in the name of God, and we would smash the mountains, stop the winds, kill all our tyrants in order to realise His kingdom of peace and brotherhood. We could do it, in the end we could do it: life belonged to us.[26]
>
> BLISSETT 2004, 67

When they touch one another in the process of translation, the semantic fields overlap, albeit not completely. God may come out into the barricades, get drunk in taverns, sack churches and frighten the horses (Blissett 2004, 219), but that is not all God does. As any translator knows only too well, the overlap is never complete, for each semantic field has smaller or larger regions that do not intersect immediately, which lie outside and perhaps even resist the translating process. When such a translation process works well, both political and theological terms are enriched, but when it works less well, something is lost

---

26   Or, in the words of Bernard Rothmann, the preacher of Münster: 'Justice for us, brothers and sisters, justice for anyone who is held in servitude, forced to work for a starvation wage, anyone who has faith and sees the house of the lord sullied with images, and children being washed with holy water like dogs under a fountain' (Blissett 2004, 171). Note also Q's own words: 'Wherever there is a discontented, hungry or ill-treated peasant or craftsman, there is a potential heretic' (Blissett 2004, 98).

in the process of translation. Now the situation becomes more interesting, for translation never rests content with the initial overlap. For this reason, it constantly moves back and forth, from one term to the other, exploring possible alternatives. The dialectic is never satisfied with its achievement. And there remains often a dimension that cannot be translated, that resists the process and holds the other term to account. Theology may say to politics: you cannot express everything that I am able to express, especially in ontological terms. Politics may reply: ditto, except that I give fuller articulation to imminent forms of political desire.

The advantages of this model – which can be sketched out here only in a preliminary manner – are threefold. First, it challenges the narrative of secularisation, in which theology is the point of origin and political thought becomes the inheritor and transformer, emptying these terms of theological content and yet bound to the forms of expression. If we shift the model to one of translation, we are able to dispense with the linear narrative and gain a greater sense of the perpetual interplay between these two languages. Second, it negates the claims to absolute status by either code. For theology, it usually takes the form of absolute source, the origin and thereby determining mode of expression. Political thought may attempt a similar move (usually via the troubled classicist narrative that traces the origins of Western thought to that eastern European, Balkan country known as Greece), or it may urge that it is the basic form, for which theology is then a particular expression. By contrast, translation reminds each that theirs is a limited language, with some pluses and minuses.

Third, the model of translation provides a fruitful avenue for considering the popularity of a novel like Q among some – usually younger – elements of the European radical Left today. The novel does not spare readers the intricacies of the theological debates of the sixteenth century, for these are crucial for understanding its politics. It does so in a way that refuses absolute status to either code, for political aspirations were expressed in theological terms, while theological differences were in their turn articulated in political shape. The authors offer, if you will, a careful example of that translation process in action. For instance, the wonderful scene of feasting and sex in the early days of Münster (Blissett 2004, 177–79) is an expression both of the radical form of grace and of the freedoms unleashed when the people themselves take power. The scene cannot be understood without both codes intersecting at this point. This feature of the novel is replicated time and again throughout the text, all of which leads to the desire by those on the activist Left to understand the nature and intricacies of those debates. In this respect, they carry on a tradition that Q has recovered.

CHAPTER 5

John Calvin and the Problem of Ungodly Rulers

Müntzer, Münster and the Anabaptists were not the only manifestations of radical theology and politics during the European sixteenth century. In this chapter and the next, I turn my attention to the 'magisterial' Reformation – although Müntzer too was called Magister Thomas – with particular interest in Calvin and Luther. Above all, I am interested in the tensions that emerge between radical and conservative elements. As for Calvin, his natural proclivity was towards conservative positions that support the powers that be, but he perpetually struggles with the radical directions that he keeps finding in the Bible and at the heart of theological thought. It is not for nothing that Engels would follow a path from the Reformed (Calvinist) faith of his youth to what became known as Marxism, a path that is perhaps not as strange as it may at first seem (see also my final chapter on Kim Il Sung, who followed a similar path). A second, more underlying concern is the close connection between theology and politics in Calvin's texts, especially his *Institutes of the Christian Religion.* In our fragmented academies, we like to distinguish between little corners of specialization that rarely recognize one another. So also with the study of Calvin: it is too easy to distinguish discrete realms of thought, whether in terms of theology, politics, economics, society or even daily life (Höpfl 1982, 217; Dommen and Bratt 2007; Biéler 2006). By contrast, I seek the way these realms are interwoven with another, except that this is a somewhat perverse way of putting it, one that would be foreign to Calvin and his contemporaries (Graham 1978; Stevenson 1999; Van Kley 1999).

In this chapter, I focus on the famous last section of Calvin's *Institutes,* where we find politics and theology inseparably entwined. Every sentence of what is called 'Of Civil Government [*De Politica Administiatione*]' evinces a tension between radical and conservative, or revolutionary and reactionary elements of theology. Time and again Calvin espies the radical possibilities of the Bible and theology, only to try to contain it within his own carefully constructed boundaries, from where it breaks out once again. Structurally too there is something amiss with the chapter, indicating that he was unable to organise the material to his satisfaction. Calvin sets out in this last chapter of the *Institutes* to speak of three categories: the magistrate, the laws and the people (*Inst.* 4.20.3; *OS* 5:474.17-24).[1] Yet before long kings appear so that we

---

1 Following convention, *Inst* refers to the *Institutes of the Christian Religion,* and references are given in terms of book, chapter, and paragraph numbers. As for the Latin original, I have

find a competing structure: king, magistrate (and the laws), and people. One
feature is the ostensible structure of his chapter, while the other is the political
reality with which he tries to deal. They are at odds with each, clashing from
time to time, which suggests an inability to control what is happening with the
discussion (see further Bousma 1988, 204–13; Willis-Watkins 1989; Steinmetz
1995, 199–208; Stevenson 1999, 32–36, 2004). In sum, Calvin struggles between
strict stipulations to obey rulers and his closing realisation that one is duty-
bound to *disobey* any ungodly and tyrannical ruler. Through a close reading of
the literary structure of Calvin's argument, I follow his struggle concerning this
issue, moving through his assertions that one must obey at any cost, through
recognizing that God and his appointed agents may punish and overthrow
tyrannical rulers, to his direction not to obey any ungodly ruler.

I begin with the crucial paragraph of the whole chapter, bringing out its
main points and then retrace the steps by which Calvin arduously works his
way towards this paragraph.

> But in that obedience which we have shown to be due the authority of rul-
> ers, we are always to make this exception, indeed, to observe it as primary,
> that such obedience is never to lead us away from obedience to him, to
> whose will the desires of all kings ought to be subject, to whose decrees
> all their commands ought to yield, to whose majesty their scepters ought
> to be submitted. And how absurd would it be that in satisfying men you
> should incur the displeasure of him for whose sake you obey men them-
> selves! The Lord, therefore, is the King of Kings, who, when he has opened
> his sacred mouth, must alone be heard before all and above all men; next
> to him we are subject to those men who are in authority over us, but only
> in him. If they command anything against him, let it go unesteemed. And
> here let us not be concerned about all that dignity which the magistrates
> possess, for no harm is done to it when it is humbled before that singular
> and truly supreme power of God (*Inst.* 4.20.32; *OS* 5:501.28-502.3).

Clearly, if a ruler disobeys God's commands, then we should not obey the ruler.
We may be subject to those who rule over us, but 'subject only in the Lord'. So,
writes Calvin, 'if they command anything against him, let it go unesteemed'.
I will have more to say about this extraordinary paragraph at the end of my

---

made use of *Opera Selecta*, a five volume selection of Calvin's work in Latin. The third, fourth,
and fifth volumes contain the 1559 Latin edition of *Institutiones Christianae Religionis*, edited
by Petrus Barth and Guilelmus Niesel (Calvini 1559 [1957]). The format for references is to
cite *OS*, followed by volume, page, and line numbers. By and large I have followed the 2006
translation of the *Institutes* by Ford Lewis Battles in The Library of Christian Classics (Calvin
1559 [2006]).

discussion, so let us leave it for now, go back to the beginning of the last chapter of the *Institutes* and see how he comes to this conclusion.

1   Two Kingdoms or One

Through this long and complex chapter Calvin attempts to negotiate three main tensions: between temporal and the spiritual; between tyranny and anarchy; and then between obedience to evil rulers and obedience to God. The last one interests me most, but let us analyse the argument one point at a time. Earlier in the *Institutes* in the section called *De Libertate Christiana*, 'On Christian Freedom' (*Inst.* 3.19), we encounter Calvin's sharp distinction between the spiritual and the temporal domains. In a last-ditch effort to block the argument that Christian liberty – as liberty from the law through the grace of Christ – has radical political potential, Calvin deploys the distinction between spiritual and temporal. Liberty from the law and for Christ, he argues, applies only to the spiritual domain. Temporally one is subject to all the laws of the land. One is free only in the private inner life of faith.

The opening comments in the last chapter of the *Institutes* open on a similar note. Of the 'two governments' within us, Calvin admits that he has spent most of his energy exploring the inner one which relates directly to eternal life but that he does indeed need to say a few things about the other one, 'which pertains only to the establishment of justice and outward morality' (*Inst.* 4.20.1; *OS* 5:471.15-16). Here too he asserts the sharp difference between them for the same reasons as he did in his earlier discussion of 'Christian freedom' (he refers explicitly to *Inst.* 3.19): it is to forestall the mistaken souls who think that the promise of liberty from the law relates to this fleeting, temporal realm. They seek to overcome all that interferes with their freedom in this life – laws, courts, magistrates, government itself – until the revolution has been achieved, or, as he puts it, 'unless the whole world is reformed into a new form [*nisi totus in novam faciem orbis reformetur*]' (*Inst.* 4.20.1; *OS* 5:472.11-12). Not so, Calvin points out, since the spiritual and the temporal cannot be confused with one another.

Spiritual is spiritual and temporal is temporal with no intercourse between them. Or so it seems. As soon as he has re-asserted his earlier argument Calvin switches tack. Despite this very sharp separation between the realms, Calvin writes: 'We must know that they do not contend with each other [*ita nec quicquam pugnare sciendum est*]' (*Inst.* 4.20.2; *OS* 5:473.8-9). *Pugnare* is a strong word, meaning fight, struggle and contend. The spiritual and temporal realms do not battle with each other; they are distinct but – crucially – not opposed. Although this point appears first as a minor concession, it is extraordinarily important: now the spiritual and temporal, the internal and external are connected. Much turns on this concession, for once he admits that the spiritual and temporal are related, a mass of items begin to flow between them (Graham 1978, 158–59).

What is the role of a civil government in the life of faith? To begin with, it should ban idolatry, blasphemy and any slanders against the truth (*Inst.* 4.20.3; *OS* 5:473.30-474.24). Substantial enough, but Calvin goes further, suggesting that the government must also maintain public peace and quiet, as well as ensuring that private property remains intact. Now that he is on his way, Calvin adds the protection of commerce, as well as ways of maintaining honesty and modesty and even a decent form of public religion among Christians. This list has become somewhat comprehensive.[2] Here Calvin appears as a good conservative: everything must be done to ensure that order is maintained and any revolutionary threat negated. But he has also gone further, for the proper task of government is to protect and nurture 'the true religion [*vera religio*], which is contained in God's law' (*Inst.* 4.20.3; *OS* 5.474.13 see also 4.20.9; *OS* 5:479-81). If it does so, then the very earthly civil government actually plays a role like that of food and water, even light and air, albeit with greater dignity.

Thus far, I have been exegeting the third paragraph of Chapter 20 since it brings out how close the spiritual and the temporal realms have come to one another in the space of a few short sentences. But Calvin also seems to realise that his argument is a complete about-face, so he now attempts to show why his argument is consistent. But let me ask an initial question: why does Calvin make this move to connect the spiritual and temporal? The short answer is that he wants to prevent both tyranny and anarchy. The long answer is in what follows.

2   Anarchy or Tyranny

This opposition between tyranny and anarchy is one of the structuring features of the whole chapter. Initially Calvin deals with various forms of anarchy, whether spiritual escapism or political radicalism. Later he focuses on tyranny, working away at the problem of what Christians should do when faced with ungodly rulers. I analyse each one in turn.

The political radicals, whom we have already met in my earlier discussion and who we also keep meeting in the *Institutes*, connect the spiritual and the temporal very closely. Disdain for the existing political order, the law and other

---

2   One is reminded of the initial list of revolutionary elements in the prefatory letter to Francis I of France, where Calvin tries to reassure the king that he and his followers are not in the business of overthrowing the laws and the courts, disturbing the peace, tearing sceptres from the hand of kings or, to sum it up, turning society upside down.

matters of human society, translates into a radical and anarchistic agenda, for the social, economic and political life of this world is corrupt and depraved. However, instead of retreating from this world they seek to overthrow and replace it with a new society. In a rather good description of anarchism, Calvin writes: 'They ... think that nothing will be safe unless the whole world is reshaped to a new form, where there are neither courts, nor laws, nor magistrates, nor anything, which in their opinion restricts their freedom' (*Inst.* 4.20.1; 5:472.10-13). Faced with such a close connection between the spiritual and the temporal in the hands of these anarchists, Calvin opts for their separation – at least for the time being.

In the remainder of this last chapter of the *Institutes* Calvin keeps both forms of anarchy in mind. To counter the political anarchists, he constantly asserts the need to obey earthly rulers since they have been appointed by God. But he is also wary of spiritual escapism, which turns on the radical separation of spiritual and temporal. It may take two forms. On the one hand, it is a retreat within when faced with the troubling and complex matters of the world. One may find a quiet corner away from the cares and worries of life, block them out as best one can and live an inner life of faith in peaceful solitude. On the other hand, it may mean a complete disdain of the things of this world. Since we already have one foot in heaven and sit at the table of the Lord we really do not need to bother with the laws and sanctions of society. We are far above all those messy earthly matters and can therefore ignore the matters of politics and the legal system. We are a law unto ourselves; or rather, we already live out God's law and need no law of men. Both types of spiritual escapism are problematic for Calvin (see *Inst.* 4.20.2; *OS* 5:472.35-473.29). He knows full well that his argument for the purely spiritual and inner domain of Christian faith can lead in this direction, so in this case he switches and seeks to connect both spiritual and temporal. Against the spiritual escapists he harps on the point that civil government is there to protect and nurture the life of faith.

Nonetheless, spiritual escapism is less of a concern to Calvin, for tyranny draws more and more of his attention. Already in his opening statement Calvin lays out the threat of absolute power. Although he speaks of finding a way between the two extremes of anarchy and tyranny – between the 'insane and barbarous' people trying to overthrow God's order and the 'flatterers of princes' who oppose earthly power to God's government in order to enhance their own 'power without measure [*potentiam sine modo*]' (*Inst.* 4.20.1; *OS* 5:471. 21-23) – he is actually more interested in countering tyranny. The nub of the problem is that if an earthly ruler is opposed to God, what is a Christian or indeed a citizen to do?

The answer is not clear. For someone given to near obsessive precision and the careful arrangement of his arguments, this is curious indeed. Something must be bothering him. Calvin tries to deploy his usual efforts to categorize and organise. So we find that most of his attention in this last chapter is given over the respective roles of the king, magistrate, laws and people. This time his famed precision does not help him. One would imagine that the simple question – what to do with an ungodly ruler? – would be relatively easy to answer. But not so, and the reason is that Calvin is far too good a student of the Bible to find an easy answer to the question. Let us follow him as he twists and turns.

3   Ungodly Rulers

In section after section (from the fourth to the thirteenth of Chapter 20) we find various tasks of the rulers, both kings and magistrates. Calvin begins by emphasizing that they are appointed by God (*Inst.* 4.20.4-7; *OS* 5:474.25-478.10) but then already raises the problem of what to do when they tend towards tyranny. His preliminary response is to argue for a small aristocracy bordering on popular government (*Inst.* 4.20.8; *OS* 5:478.11-479.31) in order keep tyranny in check. Here his theology meshes with his politics very closely: analogous to the combination of his democracy of depravity (the doctrine of sin) and the aristocracy of salvation (predestination), Calvin argues for an aristocratic government with distinct popular elements. Since monarchy tends towards tyranny, aristocracy slips all too easily towards the faction of the few, and popular government has a tendency to be seditious, he seeks a system with the proverbial checks and balances: 'Therefore, men's fault or failing causes it to be safer and more bearable for a number to exercise government, so that they may help one another, teach and admonish one another; and, if one asserts himself unfairly, there may be a number of censors and masters to restrain his willfulness' (*Inst.* 4.20.8; *OS* 5:478.28-479.2). Calvin is no democrat, of whatever form. Instead, he is a careful conservative who feels that the Bible points in this direction. But he is also not interested in arguments for absolute monarchy, for this would be an open ticket to the exercise of 'power without measure [*potentiam sine modo*]' (*Inst.* 4.20.1; *OS* 5:471.23).

The next few sections cover matters such as the close relation between spiritual and temporal laws (*Inst.* 4.20.9; *OS* 5:479.32-481.26), an effort to find a moderate position between the command not to kill and the need for the death penalty (*Inst.* 4.20.10; *OS* 5:481.27-483.28) as well as the uses of war in light of the same argument, and the need to keep sedition in check (*Inst.* 4.20.11-12; *OS* 5:483.28-485.17). Taxes too should be necessary but not tyrannical (*Inst.* 4.20.13; *OS* 5:485.18-486.8). And then we enter a lengthy discussion of the law (*Inst.* 4.20.14-21; *OS* 5:486.9-493.15), where Calvin argues that the basis of civil law is and should be Moses's law and not common law. We are a long way indeed from the sharp division between temporal and spiritual realms on which Calvin was so keen not that long ago. In fact, here he goes so far as to argue that revelation is the basis of temporal law.

I have outlined all too briefly some features of Calvin's effort to give precise order to matters pertaining to civil government. Although the threat of anarchy turns up every now and then – especially in relation to the dangers of popular government – we gain the impression that it is not really the major issue. This impression is enhanced when we come to the closing sections of the chapter, for this is where Calvin really comes to grips with the issue of tyranny. And he is driven to do so by a series of problematic – for an innate conservative – biblical texts that deal with the overthrow of a ruler.

3.1   *Obey!*

Calvin begins the final stages of this chapter by asserting the importance of obedience to divinely appointed rulers. Starting with the flagship text of Romans 13:1-7 (see my Chapter 3), he engages with a string of biblical texts to show that this is as solid a biblical position as one will find: Titus 3:1 on obeying the powers, principalities and magistrates; 1 Peter 2:13 on submission to kings and governors; 1 Timothy 2:1-2 on prayers and intercessions for all in authority (*Inst.* 4.20.23; *OS* 5:494.6-26).[3] Clearly, the Bible has a good number of texts that give divine sanction to the ruler, whether king, dictator or despot. And over the last two millennia there have been more than enough rulers and small-minded churchmen who have been all too ready to use such texts for their own megalomaniac programs. So we face the next problem: if the Bible says we must obey our rulers, what do we do with the dreary run of ungodly and tyrannical ones? Calvin's initial answer is rather conservative:

> Indeed, he says that those who rule for the public benefit are true patterns and evidences of this beneficence of his; that they who rule unjustly and incompetently have been raised up by him to punish the wickedness of the people; that all equally have been endowed with that holy majesty with which he has invested lawful power (*Inst.* 4.20.25; *OS* 5:470.1-6).[4]

---

3   Stevenson (1999, 143–44, 2004) stresses this element in Calvin's political thought, drawing on letters that give direct advice on the matter. See also the commentaries on 1 Peter 2:13 (Calvin 1855, 79–80), 1 Timothy 2:1-2 (Calvin 1856, 51–53), and Titus 3:1 (Calvin 1856, 324).

4   So also: 'When we hear that a king has been ordained by God, let us at once call to mind those heavenly edicts with regard to honoring and fearing a king; then we shall not hesitate to hold a most wicked tyrant in the place where the Lord has deigned to set him' (*Inst.* 4.20.26; *OS* 5:497.10-13).

At this point he suggests that such a ruler is still to be obeyed, since he may be an agent of punishment in God's hands. The worst tyrant is still in a divinely appointed role, even if it is to remind us of our sinful state.[5] Calvin's first proposition is in place: the people must not disobey or even contemplate removing an ungodly ruler, no matter how rapacious or outrageous such a ruler might be. This would be an excellent place to close his argument, especially for a conservative like Calvin.

3.2 God's Agents

The problem is that Calvin is too good a student of the Bible. For in that troublesome collection of texts he finds at least two situations when one may remove a ruler from power. However, that 'one' is not anyone: only God may do so or someone specifically appointed by God for this purpose, whether this person knows they have been given the task or not. As for the first category, God's wrath has been and will be directed at any ruler who happens to disobey God. In language that comes close indeed to the Hebrew prophets and even Thomas Müntzer, Calvin writes: 'Before his face all kings shall fall and be crushed, and all the judges of the earth, that have not kissed his anointed [Ps. 2:10-11], and all those who have written unjust laws to oppress the poor in judgment and to do violence to the cause of the lowly, to prey upon widows and rob the fatherless [Isa. 10:1-2]' (*Inst.* 4.20.29; *OS* 5:500.7-13).

Obviously, this is an important text, for it is both saturated in biblical allusions and it marks the emergence of a different position on ungodly rulers.[6] The crucial principle here is as follows: rulers are no different from anyone else, so if they have done wrong they deserve to be punished. All have sinned and fallen short of the glory of God – including rulers. But if the occasional revolutionary might become eager, with fingers twitching at the scabbard, Calvin makes it perfectly clear that this task of removing an ungodly ruler is strictly God's, unless God happens to appoint someone to the task:

> Here are revealed his goodness, his power, and his providence. For sometimes he raises up open avengers [*vindices*] from among his servants, and

5   Although we may struggle in our time to find rulers explicitly arguing that they have been sent by God to punish us, Calvin's colourful description of such a ruler resonates at another, experiential level: 'If we are cruelly tormented by a savage prince, if we are greedily despoiled by one who is avaricious or wanton, if we are neglected by a slothful one, if finally we are vexed for piety's sake by one who is impious and sacrilegious, let us first be mindful of our own misdeeds, which without doubt are chastised by such whips of the Lord' (*Inst.* 4.20.29; *OS* 5:499.33-500.2).
6   The allusions are to Psalm 2:10 and Isaiah 10:1. We can see such a position espoused quite clearly in his commentaries on these passages (Calvin 1845, 22–24, 1850, 333–34).

arms them with his command to punish [*poenas sumant*] the accursed tyranny and deliver [*eximant*] his people, oppressed in unjust ways, from miserable calamity. Sometimes he directs to this end the rage of men with other intentions and other endeavors.... For the first kind of men, when they had been sent by God's lawful calling to carry out such acts, in taking up arms [*arma sumendo*] against kings, did not at all violate that majesty which is implanted in kings by God's ordination; but armed from heaven, they subdued [*coercebant*] the lesser power with the greater, just as it is lawful for kings to punish [*animadvertere*] their subordinates. But the latter kind of men, although they were directed by God's hand whither he pleased, and executed his work unwittingly, yet planned in their minds to do nothing but an evil act (*Inst.* 4.20.30; *OS* 5:500.14-19, 29-501.4).

Two types of agent appear in the divine (secret) service of doing away with sundry rulers, or at least delivering God's people from the iron fist of impious oppression. Perhaps the best way to distinguish them is in terms of the witting and the unwitting. Some are directly appointed for the task, fully aware of the role assigned to them (however unwilling they might be) and undertake this ministry with more or less enthusiasm. The examples are easy to call to mind (I cull a few from Calvin and add some others): Moses and the ungodly rule of Pharaoh; Gideon and freedom from Midianite oppression; Othniel the judge who overthrew the oppression of Cushanrishathaim, the king of Mesopotamia; Ehud the judge and assassin of Eglon king of Moab; Esther and Mordecai in response to the oppression of Haman.

Others are not aware of their divinely appointed roles, co-opted into the task without their knowledge. They may think that some minor affront needs to be avenged, they may be driven by fury and evil intent, but still they carry out the divine purpose (see also *Inst.* 1.18; *OS* 3:219-27). The biblical examples are not as numerous. The most notable is Cyrus, king of the Medes and Persians, who is named by Isaiah as Yahweh's anointed – 'messiah' no less in Isaiah 45:1 (Calvin 1852c, 394–95). Others include the use of one state to punish another – Tyre is punished by Egypt, but then Egypt is punished in turn by the Assyrians, who in their turn are chastised by the Babylonians and they find themselves at the receiving end from the Medes and Persians (Cyrus again). An intriguing way to read the processes of imperial rise and fall in ancient Southwest Asia, but then Calvin also points out that these empires punish Israel and Judah again and again.

Note carefully what has happened with this move by Calvin. Two fascinating twists have appeared in his argument, the first explicitly recognised, the second not. The first is one of the many moments when he sets out to reconcile what is really a contradiction: God appoints rulers (and so we must obey them) but then God also appoints agents to curb (*coerceo*), punish (*animadverto*), inflict recompense on (*poenas sumo*), take up arms against (*arma sumo*) and deliver from (*eximo*) ungodly rulers. How to make sense of this contradiction? Calvin asserts that such agents 'did not at all violate that majesty which is implanted in kings by God's ordination'. How so? Another order now comes into play. The people may be commanded to obey rulers appointed by God, but those rulers must obey the one who appointed them in the first place. They might be kings, but God is king of kings. Or, as Calvin puts it, they are his satraps. The catch with this argument, which was initially produced to deal with a biblical contradiction, is that it introduces a further problem for Calvin: rulers need to obey God. If they do not, they may well be punished. The emergence of this position will lead eventually to the explosive conclusion to Chapter 20.

The second argument concerning these divine agents of political vengeance – that God may use for his own good the evil intent of others – introduces an argument fraught with danger. It may go in either direction. For instance, one can see it being used by some for the argument that Hitler actually carried out a good and necessary task despite his evil intent, namely the belated bourgeois revolution in Germany. But then it may also be used to argue that Churchill's withholding of grain from India during the Second World War, leading to millions of deaths in the Bengal 'famine', ultimately benefitted the independence movement he sought to shut down through such an act, or that the theft of Hawaii by the United States has been good for the place in the long run. The list is endless, but it boils down to the old position that the end justifies the means. Adding the qualifier that the good in question must be good for God's people does not change the volatility of the original point. Obviously, this is a dangerous line to take.

We have reached the end of the second turn in Calvin's argument. At first we found him asserting, with the assistance of a long list of biblical texts, that the ruler must be obeyed even if he is an oppressive, evil and ungodly ruler. But then Calvin had to come to terms with the biblical accounts of punishing or removing ungodly rulers, so he allows that either God or one of God's agents may avenge or punish a wayward and tyrannical ruler.

3.3   *Magistrates*

Now we turn to third moment of his argument – the magistrate. This crucial figure actually fills a gap. In Calvin's text the magistrate is the contemporary form taken by the divinely appointed agent whose task (in part) is to curb the tyrannical excesses of the king. Thus, the magistrate occupies an intermediate position between king and people. Calvin sees such a magistrate embodied in figures such as Moses, who receives the law from God and appoints 70 judges to manage the judicial load in Exodus 18:13-27 (Calvin 1852b, 302–12), or like the judges in the book of the same name in the Hebrew Bible, or Samuel in the books of his name. Indeed, a little earlier Calvin is drawn to the texts of 1 Samuel, although he uses them to point out that the people should obey an unjust king (1 Samuel 8:11-17) and then to show how even David refrained from taking Saul's life when he had Saul in his power (1 Samuel 24). Yet Samuel the judge or magistrate functions at another level here, for he is the one who both anoints and removes kings from office. While Samuel anoints Saul as the first king of Israel, he later removes that divine sanction from Saul and transfers it to David. This king-making magistrate is one who seems to have played a role in Calvin's depiction of the relations between magistrate and king.

As far as the historical situation in Calvin's own time is concerned, the magistrate was not merely a bureaucrat or even a law clerk as we tend to think of magistrates now. Their task was to watch over public affairs, keep a watch on other public officials, collect taxes, lead armies into battle if need be, execute the odd criminal as a last resort, and, of course, see that the laws were followed and enforced. It should be no surprise, then, that Calvin covers these topics in this last chapter.

One of the tasks of the magistrate is that he has been 'appointed to restrain [ad moderandam] the wantonness [libidinem] of kings'. To make sure, Calvin repeats the comment in a slightly different way: magistrates are appointed 'to withstand [intercedere], in accordance with their duty, the fierce licentious-ness [licentiae] of kings' (Inst. 4.20.31; OS 5:501.17 and 23; translation modified). Here is a distinct echo of the curbing, punishing, inflicting recompense upon and taking up arms against tyrants that we found with the divinely appointed agents a little earlier. True, restraining and opposing is milder than curbing, punishing and taking up arms, but the difference is not so great. Precisely what this restraining and opposing may be is left unstated, but it is very clear that nei-ther absolute monarchs nor kings who act tyrannically have a place in Calvin's polity.

We seem to have an answer to our problem of what to do with ungodly rulers. If you are a member of the common people, all you can do is obey and bear an ungodly ruler as best you can. But if you happen to be a magistrate then you may do what is necessary to ensure that king does the right thing by the people. And if you are a king then you must put aside any pretension to absoluteness, for at the first sign of tyranny God may crush you or a magistrate may oppose you. So we have two propositions: the people must obey kings in all situations; and God and the magistrate are to keep a check on rapacious kings. It seems as though we have a cautious formula for political stability. Indeed, Calvin seems to have laid down a polity with some decent checks and balances in place: a kingship kept in check by a magistrate, who one assumes is appointed from within the aristocracy that Calvin so favours as the ruling body.

Calvin makes this careful argument by Section 31 of the last chapter of the *Institutes*. The problem is that it this is the penultimate section. Calvin knows full well that there are some final biblical texts with which he has not dealt. And they will undo all the careful work he has invested in this long final chapter.

3.4   *Let Princes Hear and Be Afraid!*

A little earlier I identified a move that would have profound consequences for Calvin's argument. At the point where he specifies the two ways in which a ruler might be resisted and removed – by God directly or by a designated agent – he introduces the following principle: since a ruler is subject to God, any ruler who does not obey and serve God will be dealt with severely. At that point, he is careful to stipulate that only God or his agent may undertake the task. But what happens when the people have to endure an ungodly or self-serving ruler? The answer with which we have become familiar is that the people should do nothing but endure. The last thing Calvin wants to do is give license to insurrection. So we find him asserting the following:

> But however these deeds of men are judged in themselves, still the Lord accomplished his work through them alike when *he broke the bloody scepters of arrogant kings and when he overturned intolerable governments. Let the princes hear and be afraid* [*Audiant principes, et terreantur*]. But we must, in the meantime, be very careful not to despise or violate that authority of magistrates, full of venerable majesty, which God has established by the weightiest of decrees, even though it may reside with the most unworthy of men, who defile it as much as they can with their own wickedness (Inst. 4.20.31; OS 5:501.5-13; emphasis added).

This is a fascinating and highly revealing passage. To begin with, the tension between reactionary and radical, between the conservative and revolutionary, comes to the fore. On the one hand, statements warn us not to violate the authority of magistrates which is 'full of venerable majesty', but on the other hand, we read of breaking 'the bloody scepters of arrogant kings' and overthrowing 'their intolerable governments'. The text is almost at war with itself, moving one way and then the next.

Further, I am particularly interested in the outburst against insolent and intolerable kings. For this passage is the second time Calvin has vented such political passion. We have already come across this slightly earlier one, but I cite it once again: '*Before his face all kings shall fall and be crushed, and all the judges of the earth*, that have not kissed his anointed [Ps. 2:10-11], and all those who have written unjust laws to oppress the poor in judgment and to do violence to the cause of the lowly, to prey upon widows and rob the fatherless

[Isa. 10:1-2]' (*Inst.* 4.20.29; *OS* 5:500.8-13; emphasis added). All kings and judges of the earth shall fall and be crushed; he will break the blood-soaked sceptres of insolent kings and intolerable tyrants – a theme is emerging here. This is nothing less than prophetic fury against oppressive and tyrannical rulers. However, up until this point Calvin must content himself with allowing God and his agents to do away with such tyrants – until we come to the extraordinary final section of the last chapter of the *Institutes*.

4 Subject Only in the Lord

I quote the passage again, this time with the Latin since I want to give it closer attention:

> But in that obedience which we have shown to be due the authority of rulers, we are always to make this exception, indeed, to observe it as primary, that such obedience is never to lead us away from obedience to him, to whose will the desires of all kings ought to be subject, to whose decrees all their commands ought to yield, to whose majesty their scepters ought to be submitted. And how absurd would it be that in satisfying men you should incur the displeasure of him for whose sake you obey men themselves! The Lord, therefore, is the King of Kings, who, when he has opened his sacred mouth, must alone be heard before all and above all men; next to him we are subject to those men who are in authority over us, but only in him. If they command anything against him, let it go unesteemed. And here let us not be concerned about all that dignity which the magistrates possess, for no harm is done to it when it is humbled before that singular and truly supreme power of God (*Inst.* 4.20.32).
>
> At vero in ea, quam praefectorum imperiis deberi constituimus, obedientia, id semper excipiendum est, imo in primus observandum, ne ab eius obedientia nos deducat, cuius voluntati Regum omnium vota subesse, cuius decretis iussa cedere, cuius maiestati fasces submitti par est. Et vero, ut hominibus satisfacias, in eius offensionem incurrere, propter quem hominibus ipsis obedias, quam praeposterum fuerit? Dominus ergo Rex est regum: qui ubi sacrum os aperuit, unus pro omnibus simul ac supra omnes est audiendus; iis deinde qui nobis praesunt hominibus subiecti sumus: sed nonnisi in ipso. Adversus ipsum siquid imperent, nullo sit nec loco nec numero; neque hic totam illam, qua magistratus pollent, dignitatem quicquam moremur: cui iniuria nulla fit dum in ordinem, prae singulari illa vereque summa Dei potestate, cogitur (*OS* 5:501. 28-502.3).

Finally, another impulse of Calvin's argument becomes clear. He begins by recalling the obedience due to rulers, a point that he has made before. But then he introduces an 'exception': *excipiendum est* – literally, an exception must be made. Any obedience should not be incompatible with obedience to God. Or, as Calvin puts it in his finely balanced writing, obedience to the one to whom rulers are in fact subject (*ne ab eius obedientia nos deducat*). So we find three balanced subordinate clauses that follow this central statement, each of them introduced by 'whose [*cuius*]': to whose will (*voluntati*), decrees (*decretis*) and majesty (*maiestati*) every king should be subject (*subesse*), must yield (*cedere*) and bow (*submitti*). Each item – will, decree, majesty, being subject, yielding and bowing – would be claimed by any garden-variety monarch. In response, Calvin points out that they all are attributes of God first and kings second. He reinforces the point a sentence or two later, asserting that God is King of kings and that God is the mouth we should listen to 'instead of all and above all [*simul ac supra omnes*]'. Much earlier in the *Institutes*, in the preface addressed to Francis, King of France – where Calvin is trying to assure the king that he means no seditious harm – we find exactly the same sentiment addressed directly to the king:

> Indeed, this consideration makes a true king: to recognize himself a minister of God in governing his kingdom. Now, that king who in ruling over his realm does not serve God's glory exercises not kingly rule but brigandage (Calvin 1559, 12).[7]

Let the princes hear indeed! This quotation also suggests that the point Calvin makes at the end of the *Institutes* is not really an exception at all. If we go back to the opening sentence of the text I quoted above, we find that what Calvin has to say must be observed above everything else: *in primus observandum* (the gerund of *observo* giving the sense of obligation). What Calvin writes here is simply the basic rule for all engagements by Christians with the state.

The remainder of the quotation turns around one point: when it comes to a choice between obeying God or obeying an ungodly ruler there is no choice.

---

7   See also his closing comment to the exposition of the fifth commandment: 'But we also ought in passing to note that we are bidden to obey our parents only "in the Lord"' [Eph. 6:1]. This is apparent from the principle already laid down. For they sit in that place to which they have been advanced by the Lord, who shares with them a part of his honor. Therefore, the submission paid to them ought to be a step toward honoring that highest Father. Hence, if they spur us to transgress the law, we have a perfect right to regard them not as parents, but as strangers who are trying to lead us away from obedience to our true Father. So should we act toward princes, lords, and every kind of superiors. It is unworthy and absurd for their eminence so to prevail as to pull down the loftiness of God. On the contrary, their eminence depends upon God's loftiness and ought to lead us to it' (*Inst.* 2.8.38; *OS* 3:379.16-27).

Three times he repeats what has become obvious. It would be simply 'prepos-terous [*praeposterum*]' to suggest that anyone would attempt to please men and thereby incur the wrath of God. Then again, we may be subject to our rul-ers, as Calvin has asserted again and again, but 'only in Him [*nonnisi in ipso*]'. And once again, bluntly, 'If they command anything against him, let it be worth absolutely nothing [*Adversus ipsum siquid imperent, nullo sit nec loco nec numero*]'. Or literally, 'let it be from nothing, in no place and with no number'.

I cannot emphasize enough the significance of the breakthrough in these last lines. This position may seem obvious now, but it was not so clear a little earlier where we were enjoined in no uncertain terms to obey even unjust, oppressive and wilful rulers for our own edification. I will return to this tension in a moment, but first an observation. When first reading this passage, I assumed Calvin was discussing magistrates. The word *magistratus* does appear towards the end and I had been told that Calvin did not endorse civil disobe-dience by the people. Only the magistrate can curb, check or even punish ungodly rulers. This would have the minimal benefit of maintaining some consistency within Calvin's own argument. The problem with such an argu-ment is twofold. First, this passage from Calvin mentions kings (*Regum*) and rulers (*praefectorum*) along with magistrates. *All* rulers come under the same principle. And that is the second problem with the superficial consistency that might have been maintained. To do so would betray a far deeper theological truth for Calvin: God is supreme and any obedience is due entirely to him. Rulers are no exception.

Often we come across efforts to solve the contradictions in Calvin's thought. I prefer to take the other path and push these contradictions as far as they will go. Here is the contradiction: either obey the rulers at all costs or obey God at all costs. Such a position works when there is no tension between the two, when the ruler's guidelines coincide with those of God. But when they clash, we have a problem. Calvin tries to mediate between the two, so he begins by arguing that the people should obey rulers in all situations, even when they are rapacious, oppressive and ungodly. Only God or his appointed avengers may punish such rulers, or indeed the magistrate, who is one such appointed agent.

But then he realizes that there is more at stake. It all turns on his theologi-cal position and his view of Scripture: if one's ultimate obedience is to God, there can be no compromise, and any ruler who decrees laws that contradict those of God must be shunned. Even more, if all of us are radically fallen and depraved, then that includes rulers as well. Thus, a ruler will more often than not tend to be oppressive and tyrannical since he or she is a fallen creature like everyone else. It is a radically democratic position, or what may be called the democracy of depravity. Further, Calvin is far too good a student of the Bible to let his earlier position stand. He knows well that the Bible has stories of civil disobedience, refusal to obey unjust laws and outright rebellion. He cites texts such as Daniel's refusal to bow to Nebuchadnezzar's decree to worship him (Daniel 6:22), or the edict of Peter in Acts 5:29 to obey God rather than men (see also Calvin 1844, 214–15), or indeed Paul's comment on not yielding to the depraved wishes of men (1 Cor. 7:23). In fact, Calvin glosses this text from Paul as the last statement of the *Institutes*: 'That we have been redeemed by Christ at so great a price as our redemption cost him, so that we should not enslave ourselves to the wicked desires of men – much less be subject to their impiety' (*Inst.* 4.20.32; *OS* 5:502.28-31). Or even more strongly in his commentary on Daniel 6:22 he writes:

> For earthly princes lay aside all their power when they rise up against God, and are unworthy of being reckoned in the number of mankind. *We ought rather to utterly defy than to obey them* whenever they are so restive and wish to spoil God of his rights, and, as it were, to seize upon his throne and draw him down from heaven.
>
> CALVIN 1852a, 382, emphasis mine

5   Conclusion

The outcome of Calvin's careful attention to the Bible is that he replicates the many-layered contradictions of that collection of texts. In closing, let me suggest that the tension I have been tracing may also be cast in terms of compromise over against principle. For much of this last chapter of the *Institutes* Calvin tries to find a compromise between obedience to rulers and obedience to God. We have seen the results of that compromise – the people must obey rulers at all costs, God and his agents may punish them – but in the end it cannot hold. The principled Calvin triumphs in the end and that principle is none other than obedience to God first and Scripture – a radical transcendence that was so characteristic of many revolutionary moments. That such a principle should lead to profound tensions between Calvin's innate conservatism and revolutionary possibilities makes his thought all the more intriguing. But it also had concrete political consequences in, for example, the English Revolution (1642–1651), where Calvin's radical strain was taken up with enthusiasm (Lyons 2016), let alone the fascinating development in the northern Netherlands where radical Anabaptism once flourished (flowing initially to Münster and then appearing in revolutionary cells such as those of Jan van Batenburg) only to turn decisively to Calvinism.

CHAPTER 6

From Luther to Marx and Engels

> In our own day we are approaching an era of revolution analogous to that
> of the sixteenth century.
>
> MARX 1847a, 312, 1847b, 331

From one magisterial reformer to another, from Calvin to Luther, thereby inverting the usual order. While the previous chapter analysed the internal dynamics of Calvin's thought through a careful reading of the final section of the *Institutes*, this chapter deals with Luther through another lens. Now I am concerned with the way Engels and Marx engage with Luther, an engagement with far more intriguing twists than one may at first expect. Indeed, the interactions between Luther and Marxism range from profound philosophical tensions to a positive, albeit critical, appreciation. In order to examine these engagements, I distinguish between three topics that illustrate the range of possibilities: the differences concerning human nature between Lutheranism and Marxism; the ambivalent depiction of Luther as the ideologue of the bourgeoisie in Engels's early study of the German Peasant Revolution of 1525; and Marx's dialectical appraisal of Luther as both the inaugurator of the first phase of the German revolution, thereby setting up the second stage which Marx saw beginning in his own time. As I am about to delve into this material, let me reiterate the point that the story of Christian communism since the nineteenth century cannot escape the complex interactions with Marxism.

1 Human Nature

On the matter of human nature, I need to set the scene more broadly. In societies shaped by Christianity, the understanding of human nature turns on the following question: can human beings do some good on their own initiative or are human beings unable to do good, relying completely on God? We may reframe the question in terms of evil and sin: is evil limited, thereby providing some possibility of good works, or is evil more powerful than human beings, which means that human effort is futile? The terms of these questions in Latin Christianity were set in the debate between Augustine and Pelagius in the fifth century. Although the disagreements were subtle and complex,[1] the names 'Augustine' and 'Pelagius' came to indicate two contrasting positions. While the former argued that only God's grace was able to overcome the inescapable evil of human existence, the latter argued that good works were possible since evil was more limited.[2]

Luther falls on the Augustinian side, which has implications for the understanding of human nature. The core question was the transformation of a fallen human nature, but the means for such a transformation were open to debate. Augustine argued that the new human nature could be achieved only through God's grace, for human beings were unable to do so on their own. Pelagius countered by arguing that human discipline and cultivation could achieve transformation, although not without divine assistance. His own much-admired asceticism was an indication as to how a person might become more holy. As his slogan would have it: if perfection is possible, then it is obligatory.

This early theological debate has also been seen in political terms, with – for some Marxists – Augustine coming to embody an aristocratic or ruling class perspective and Pelagius the perspective of those exploited. Thus, Augustine's argument becomes one for leaving the world as it is, a welcome message to the wealthy and powerful since they need not work to change the world, and solace to the poor and oppressed since they would find recompense in the afterlife. By contrast, Pelagius (and indeed other 'heretics') become champions for the downtrodden, urging that the only way to abolish poverty is to get rid of the rich (G.E.M. de Ste. Croix 1981, 436–47; Wood 2008, 160). Anti-socialists from Søren Kierkegaard to Eric Voegelin have agreed in their own ways, condemning socialism as a Pelagian heresy (Garff 2007, 486–90, 502–5; Voegelin 1989–2009, IV: 125; VI: 135, 145). If we consider a few examples from the Marxist tradition, then this assessment may seem to be justified, although it was mediated by the European Enlightenment's assertion of the inherent goodness of human beings. Thus, the proletariat and peasants have an inherent goodness, which will be released from the exploitation by their masters when the communists have taken hold of the reins of history. With this opportunity, workers and peasants will wholeheartedly engage in creating a new society and economy for mutual benefit. In other words, a Pelagian approach values the works that one can do now, especially by the exploited. This understanding can be seen in Marx's (1844a, 176, 1844b, 171) image of throwing off the chain and plucking the living flower, in the old slogan 'from each according to ability, to each according to

---

1 For a sense of the intricacy, see some of the key works (Augustine 1992; Pelagius 1993; Rees 1998; Mann 2001; Wetzel 2001).

2 I leave aside the Greek (Orthodox) effort to mediate: since salvation is a divine gift, one cannot earn salvation; yet, the gift can be accepted or refused, and so human activity is involved.

need';[3] or Anatoly Lunacharsky's (1981, 57, 165, 245, 247) notion of the ideal of human existence (represented by the gods of religion) to which one strives through revolution and education; or Lenin's sense (1917c, 272, 1917d, 350) that patient and logical argumentation, backed up by 'facts, facts, facts'; would persuade anyone who listened, or Stalin's (1906–1907a, 338, 1906–1907b, 336) early observation that 'it is obvious that free and comradely labour should result in an equally comradely, and complete, satisfaction of all needs in the future socialist society'; or indeed in the whole phenomenon of Stakhanovism and the new Soviet man and woman of the 1930s (Siegelbaum 1988).

2   Engels, Luther and Thomas Müntzer

The implications for Luther should be obvious. As an Augustinian, he stressed the power of sin and evil, the inability of human beings to do good works on their own (Luther and Erasmus 1969), and an utter reliance on God's grace through faith. As the Smalcald Articles put it:

> All have sinned and are justified freely, without their own works and merits, by His grace, through the redemption that is in Christ Jesus, in His blood (Romans 3:23-25). This is necessary to believe. This cannot be otherwise acquired or grasped by any work, law, or merit. Therefore, it is clear and certain that this faith alone justifies us … Nothing of this article can be yielded or surrendered, even though heaven and earth and everything else falls (Mark 13:31).
>
> MCCAIN 2005, 289

In the terms examined above, this would place Luther firmly with the ruling class, with the wealthy and powerful. Indeed, this is the assessment of Engels in *The Peasant War in Germany* (1850a, 1850b). Engels's effort at class analysis determines the structure of the essay, with princes, nobility, clergy, burghers, plebeians and peasants identified in the opening pages, to be followed by an assessment of the war's effects on these classes. As for Luther, he represents the wishes of a nascent ruling class, or burghers seeking reform and of princes with similar hopes. By contrast, Müntzer is the mouthpiece of radical peasants

---

3   Cited by every communist leader since Marx, the well-known slogan in its current form first appears with Louis Blanc (1851, 92), after the revolutions of 1848: '*de chacun selon ses facultés, à chacun selon ses besoins*', although it can be traced back through socialist circles in other forms (Bowie 1971, 82). The slogan is actually a gloss on the biblical text of Acts 4:35: 'They laid it at the apostles' feet, and it was distributed to each as any had need'.

and emerging proletarians. Thus, Luther infamously betrayed the Peasant Revolution, calling on all 'upright' citizens to eradicate the peasants, miners and others who had joined the movement.

Yet, despite the apparent symmetry in Engels's analysis between Luther and the first shoots of the bourgeoisie, he also hints at a greater complexity, if not ambivalence regarding Luther. Engels traces the way Luther's rhetoric and practice changed over time. Initially, this Augustinian monk of peasant background voiced staunch condemnations of the church and its cosy arrangement with the powerful. Luther's early statements evince a revolutionary zeal, which – according to Engels – brought together a united front of exploited peasants, plebeians, burghers, lesser nobility and even some princes. But when the situation became too heated, Luther opted for his real allies: burghers, nobility and princes. This entailed a watering down of his fervour, a preference for peaceful reform and condemnation of the radical extremes. This is, suggests Engels, the real Luther, who became a staunch advocate of the new burgher church. In this light, his earlier fiery statements and acts indicate that he had not yet clarified his true position.

Engels works hard to paint Luther into this corner, but he cannot quite do so. In distinguishing between the radical and moderately liberal Luther, Engels attempts a temporal progression from youthful radicalism to mature moderation. Yet, Engels's analysis betrays a more ambivalent approach, which comes to the fore in his observation on Luther's translation of the Bible:

> Luther had put a powerful tool into the hands of the plebeian movement by translating the Bible. Through the Bible he contrasted the feudalised Christianity of his day with the moderate Christianity of the first centuries, and the decaying feudal society with a picture of a society that knew nothing of the ramified and artificial feudal hierarchy. The peasants had made extensive use of this instrument against the princes, the nobility, and the clergy. Now Luther turned it against the peasants, extracting from the Bible such a veritable hymn to the God-ordained authorities as no bootlicker of absolute monarchy had ever been able to match.
>
> ENGELS 1850a, 419, 1850b, 386

The text seeks to reveal Luther's betrayal, but in attempting to do so, it identifies what may be called the political ambivalence, if not multivocality of Luther's own engagement with the Bible.[4] As should be clear from my analysis of

---

4 Already some years ago Arnal (1980–81) offered an insightful analysis of the tensions within Luther's own position in relation to the peasants.

quoted above and the criticism of religion is certainly older than Feuerbach. It makes more sense to propose that Marx actually sees the criticism of religion as beginning with none other than Luther. The first revolutionary stage is the criticism of religion. In this light we can understand the following statements:

> For Germany, the *criticism of religion* is in the main complete [*im wesentlichen beendigt*], and the criticism of religion is the premise of all criticism [*die Voraussetzung aller Kritik*].
>
> MARX 1844a, 175, 1844b, 170

> The evident proof of the radicalism of German theory, and hence of its practical energy, is that it proceeds from a resolute *positive* sublation of religion [*der entschiedenen* positiven *Aufhebung der Religion*]. The criticism of religion ends [*endet*] with the teaching that *man is the highest being for man*, hence with the *categorical imperative to overthrow all relations* [alle Verhältnisse umzuwerfen] in which man is a debased, enslaved, forsaken, despicable being.[7]
>
> MARX 1844a, 182, 1844b, 177

The relationship between the two revolutions is captured by the tension between two terms Marx uses to speak of the criticism of religion: *enden* or *beenden* (*beendigen*), with the sense of finishing or completing, and *Aufhebung*, the Hegelian sublation with the implication that it carries on into another level, albeit thoroughly transformed. The first indicates a distinct completion, an end beyond which nothing more can be done or said. The second suggests transition and transformation; what is transformed may continue but in a manner rather different from what we have seen thus far. As Marx puts it elsewhere, *Aufhebung* indicates a process in 'which denial and preservation, i.e., affirmation, are bound up together [*worin die Verneinung und die Aufbewahrung, die Bejahung verknüpft sind*]' (Marx 1844c, 340, 1844d, 299, 1844e, 412).

The terminological difference indicates the structure of both passages (even though *Aufhebung* appears only in the second). In the first passage, 'premise' or 'prerequisite [*Voraussetzung*]' signals the presence of a sense of *Aufhebung*. Thus, the criticism of religion is simultaneously 'complete [*beendigt*]' and functions as a 'premise [*Voraussetzung*]' for all criticism – but not as it was. The second passage makes a similar point: the radicalism of theory in Germany arises from the fact that it 'proceeds from a resolute *positive* sublation

---

7 Translation modified.

[*Aufhebung*] of religion'. At the same time, the criticism of religion ends (*endet*) with the teaching that human beings are the highest beings.

If the criticism of religion designates the Reformation and its legacy (the first revolutionary phase), then what are the implications for understanding its relation to the new revolutionary stage? We may argue that Marx is torn between a resolute effort to end the criticism of religion once and for all, if not to pronounce the end of religion as so many have done since the Enlightenment, and the need to appreciate its transformed presence (Van Leeuwen 2002, 184). But the two terms are actually related, as Marx's text reveals: one cannot have sublation and transformation (*Aufhebung*) without the former coming to an end (*beenden*). It cannot continue in its former state, so it must be completed, brought to an end, so that *Aufhebung* can take place and it can take on an entirely new form that has an indirect and dialectical connection with the former state. Thus, the first revolutionary stage, stemming from Luther, must come to an end so that it can be sublated by a second and more substantial revolution. At the same time, this later revolution could not have happened and cannot be understood without the former. So the criticism of religion may be complete, but it has been sublated so as to become the premise of all criticism that follows. The later revolution transforms the former.

3.2   *A Revolutionary Reformation?*

Thus far, I have dealt with the relationship between the two revolutions, but the question remains: for Marx, how was the Reformation itself revolutionary? Let us return to Marx's effort to identify this revolutionary nature in terms of the shift from external to internal religious expression.

> *Luther*, we grant, overcame the bondage of *devotion* by replacing it by the bondage of *conviction*. He shattered faith in authority because he restored the authority of faith. He turned priests into laymen because he turned laymen into priests. He freed man from outer religiosity because he made religiosity the inner man. He freed the body from chains because he enchained the heart.
>
> MARX 1844a, 182

> Luther hat allerdings die Knechtschaft aus *Devotion*[8] besiegt, weil er die Knechtschaft aus *Ueberzeugung* an ihre Stelle gesetzt hat. Er hat den

---

8   Marx uses 'Devotion' in his text, a loan-word that is not used so much in modern German. The English translation in MECW has 'piety', but this is misleading, since it gestures towards pietism, a very inner phenomenon. Marx seeks to indicate external and discernible acts of devotion, worship and ritual.

Glauben an die Autorität gebrochen, weil er die Autorität des Glaubens restaurirt hat. Er hat die Pfaffen in Laien verwandelt, weil er die Laien in Pfaffen verwandelt hat. Er hat den Menschen von der äußern Religiosität befreit, weil er die Religiosität zum innern Menschen gemacht hat. Er hat den Leib von der Kette emancipirt, weil er das Herz in Ketten gelegt.

MARX 1844 [1982]-d, 177

Given the dialectical balance of these sentences (deeply infused as Marx was at the time with Hegelian formulations), I have also given the full German text – with the spelling of the original manuscript. These sentences emphasise the profound shift brought about by Luther. All of the external forms of religious expression, such as devotion, authority, priests and the body, were internalised. Religion became a matter of conviction, faith, laity, the heart and the inner person. We may recast the distinction in terms of the shift from the public to the private, insofar as the private was not a given but invented in the process itself. Luther did operate with a given distinction, but in many respects reinvented the internal and the private – which is very much part of the first stage of radical revolutionary criticism. At the same time, the dialectical point is not that all of this was simply internalised, as though one had retreated into a cloister. No, this internalisation was a very public if not 'democratic' move. Private inwardness of religious expression was made available for all as a common experience. The monk and nun became a man and woman of the world.

I am not the first to note the anticipation of Max Weber's point that monastic discipline became universalised (Weber 1992; Sayer 1991). Indeed, elsewhere Marx makes the connection between Luther and Adam Smith – picking up Engels's point that Smith was the 'new Luther' (Engels 1844c, 422, 1844d, 474) – to suggest that Luther's internalisation of faith, the priesthood and religiosity has an analogous expression in Smith's proposal that private property is an internal reality rather than an external condition (Marx 1844c, 290–91, 1844d, 257–58, 1844e, 383–84). In *Capital*, this point becomes an undeveloped aside into which we should not read too much: Roman Catholicism is an externalised form of expression, suitable for a monetary system, while Protestantism is appropriate to the internalised realities of credit and commodities (Marx 1867a, 90, 1890, 78, 1894a, 587, 1894b, 583). Further, this point is less dialectical than Marx's observations on Luther, which I have been examining in some detail. Instead of homologies between Roman Catholicism and Protestantism, Marx's argument is that Luther universalises Christianity by internalising it, and in the process creating, as it were, a whole new category of religious and indeed human existence. This constitutes the first stage of revolution.

At the same time, this acknowledgement of Luther also identifies the limits of his revolution. To return to the earlier quotation: the first and last sentences indicate that the Lutheran revolution brought with it new types of servitude. Luther may have liberated people from external forms of religious expression, but he enabled a completely new way to be enslaved. This was through the heart, through conviction.[9]

3.3   The New Revolution

Luther's revolution may have been necessary, a first stage without which the second would not have been possible, but this revolution is by no means enough, falling short and leading to new forms of enslavement. What should the new revolution, the second stage, seek to achieve? It must focus on both internal and external dimensions. If internalisation has been universalised, so that laypeople have become priests, the struggle for liberation must deal with the internalised priest. Further, since Luther was a theologian, he focused on other-worldly matters, thereby missing the materialist basis. Or if there was some impact on the world of class and economics, then it was secondary to Luther's main agenda. Marx seeks to make this aspect primary.

An internal, if not personalised revolution? Is not Marx the great analyst of economics, of the forces and relations of production, and of the need for a socialist revolution? Yet here we find him arguing for precisely such an internal revolution in response to Luther. The new form of servitude is not merely one of economic exploitation, but also one of the heart due to Luther's internalisation of religious conviction and practice. Marx's point is far from petty-bourgeois urgings to change one's personal attitude as a key to changing the world. Instead, he identifies an internal alienation: Luther had internalised the earlier contradictions between layperson and priest, outer religiosity and internal devotion, so that they became contradictions embodied within each person – analogous to the tension between the private individual and citizen of a state that Marx credits to Hegel and seeks to overcome elsewhere (Marx 1843a, 1843b, 1844f, 1844g). The solution? On the one hand, this requires attention to the external conditions of existence, which need to be revolutionised so that the internal contradiction may be overcome. On the other hand, such a transformation requires a subjective intervention in the very conditions of existence. The conditions do not merely shape who we are, but we can reshape the conditions themselves so that we ourselves can be transformed.

In relation to Luther, Marx argues that the missing element of Luther and the Reformation as such was a popular, mass base. The revolution in Luther's hands was restricted to faith and knowledge, so much so that a common heart could not be found to match the theologian's head. For Marx, this common,

---

9   Here we find an anticipation of the point that would be developed by Foucault (1979).

popular basis will be found in the proletariat. In this respect, Marx's advocates for philosophy to 'grip' the masses, for the liberation of the proletariat from its radical chains in a way that will abolish its very status as a class.

Is this charge against Luther fair? To some extent it may be, but if we recall the earlier discussion of Engels it becomes clear that Luther too had – albeit unwittingly – a more radical edge, which set on their way the radical theologians and activists like Thomas Müntzer and indeed a host of revolutionary Anabaptists. These movements certainly found a way to grip the masses. And in another context – Italy – we find none other than Antonio Gramsci longing for an earlier revolution, like the Reformation, that had grasped the whole of society from bottom to top so that everything changed. As noted earlier, Gramsci observes, 'In Italy there has never been an intellectual and moral reform involving the popular masses' (Gramsci 1996, 243–44; Boer 2007a, 258–73). Like the Protestant Reformation, a communist revolution must shake up all levels of society.

The previous points question Marx's assertion that he is one of the first to discover a mass basis in the proletariat, albeit a discovery that he owed to Engels (Kouvelakis 2003, 167–231). Might it be the case that Marx not so much discovered but rediscovered the question of mass appeal? If the Reformation too had such an appeal, albeit on a different register, then the discovery of the proletariat by Engels and then Marx constitutes a rediscovery. Therefore, I suggest that 'the monk' is more present in 'the philosopher', a second Luther no less, in Marx's thought than he would care to admit. In other words, Marx's reflections on Luther constitute more of an *Aufhebung* of Luther's revolution. The theological nature of that first stage has been both brought to an end and transformed (*beenden* and *aufheben*). Marx's last sentence of the text I have been exegeting is full of implications: 'When all the inner requisites are fulfilled the *day of German resurrection* will be proclaimed by the *ringing of the Gallic cock*' (Marx 1844a, 187, 1844b, 183). That the German revolution is none other than a resurrection and the Gallic cock (an allusion to Mark 14:29-31; Matthew 26:33-35; Luke 22:33-34) signals the completion of the proletarian revolution that was tasted but stalled with the French Revolution. The resurrection and the crowing cock are of course biblical allusions: Luther would be present in a German revolution, albeit in a way that he would by no means have anticipated.

4   Conclusion

My analysis has moved from the significant differences between Luther and Marxism on the question of human nature, with the one following a more

Augustinian line and the other tending towards Pelagianism, to a greater interaction between them. Engels may still have kept his distance from Luther, whom he identifies as the ideologue of emergent bourgeoisie (in terms of burghers and progressive princes), but at the same time Engels recognises at some level the radical potential of Luther's message – to be taken up by Thomas Müntzer and other radicals. But it was Marx who provided the most significant engagement with Luther, in terms of the dialectical interaction with the champion of the first German revolution. This is not to say that Marxism is in some way a secularised form of Christian thought, or indeed eschatology – a question I examine in the next chapter – but that the history of Christian communism is perhaps more complex than it may at first have seemed.

CHAPTER 7

Heilsgeschichte, History and Marxism

By now it has become clear that Christian communism in a European context and Marxism are entwined in many ways: the identification and elaboration of a tradition of revolutionary Christian communism itself (Kautsky); the proposal that early Christianity was in some respects a communistic (Kautsky and Luxemburg) if not a revolutionary movement (Engels); the continued attention to and fascination with Thomas Müntzer and the Peasant Revolution, the Anabaptist revolution at Münster and the revolutionary nature of Europe's sixteenth century as a whole; the engagements with Luther by Engels and Marx; and even the possibility of identifying political tensions in the works of the Apostle Paul, Calvin and Luther. The question that arises from this continued interaction is whether Marxism shares with Christianity, if not Judaism, a deeper connection: are Marxist narratives of history secularised versions of Jewish or Christian ones, rendering Marxism as a version of secularised religion?

This chapter tackles the question directly, concluding that the common assertion is incorrect – at least in the way it is usually presented. That qualifier will eventually become extremely important, but let us examine in some detail the initial proposition. Usually propagated with a polemical edge (you may think you are atheistic, but you are really religious deep down), this assertion has gained the authority of countless repetitions.[1] Thus, proponents of this position argue that the theological *Heilsgeschichte* has influenced the Marxist narrative of history, which is but a pale copy of its original: the evils of the present age with its alienation and exploitation (sin) will be overcome by the proletariat (collective redeemer), which will usher in a glorious new age when sin is overcome, the unjust are punished and the righteous inherit the earth. The proposal, made without extended engagements with the texts of Marx and Engels, has been deployed for a wide range of purposes. In the hands of Nikolai Berdyaev (1937), early a Marxist but later a theologically inspired anti-communist, or indeed the equally apostate Leszek Kolakowski (1981), it has become the ammunition of anti-communist polemic. In the hands of historians

---

1 I have lost count of the number of times I have been asked this question when discussing Marxism and religion in many different parts of the world. This chapter is a distillation of the answers I have given to those questions.

such as Karl Löwith (1949), it becomes a way of negating the challenge of Marxism by including it within a wider sweep of historiographic analysis. In the hands of a philosopher like Alasdair MacIntyre (1971, 111), the assumption becomes an effort to find common ground between his two passions, Christianity and Marxism, for both offer a historical narrative that runs from weakness to strength, with human beings ultimately recovering the moral purity once lost so that we may live once again in a state of grace that transcends historical time. Or in the mind of a theologian like John Milbank (1990, 177–205), it is a means for leaping over Marxism by arguing that theology is the *fons et origo* of all modern thought and politics.[2]

My response has three steps. First, I focus on the crucial moments in the texts of Marx and Engels where a secularised version of eschatological Christian history is most likely to occur, especially Engels's complex engagements with the New Testament Apocalypse, Marx's study of Isaiah and close friendship with the biblical scholar, Bruno Bauer, and the influence of the apocalyptically minded Moses Hess, who first introduced communism to Marx and Engels. Second, we cannot leave unquestioned the assumed common *Heilsgeschichte*, passing via a redeemer that overcomes the fallen state of humanity in order to usher in the millennium of peace and joy. Is this really the historical narrative Marx and Engels construct? A consideration of the neglected treatment of Max Stirner in *The German Ideology* is necessary at this point. Third, the question remains as to whether Marx and Engels unwittingly used the form of theological history. A theological question requires a theological answer, now in terms of the absolute or relative status of theology and its claims.[3]

---

2   Concerning the wider issue of Marxism as a secularised religion, critics may point to the rituals of socialist states, without noting that ritual is a common feature of human activity and thereby not necessarily religious. Or they may suggest that the fervour, utopianism and capacity for martyrdom are drawn from religious commitment, without realising that commitment to any cause may produce such fervour (Bergman 1990, 221). Or they may opine that Marxism is an atheistic Gospel, a position that was first put forward by the left-leaning priest from the Russian Orthodox Church, Alexander Vvedensky (the Metropolitan of Moscow), in his debate with Anatoly Lunacharsky (Commissar for Enlightenment) in 1925 – without realising that atheism is a red herring within Marxism (Vvedensky 1925 [1985], 190–91). For a more recent example of this suggestion, see Gabel's superficial analysis (2005, 179–83).

3   I too once assumed the validity of this rapprochement between Marxist and Christian histories, but the more I read Marx and Engels as part of a much larger decade-long study of the relation between Marxism and theology, the more it became apparent that the connection fails (Boer 2012).

1   **Calculating the Day**

At a number of crucial junctures, one may be forgiven for seeing a connection
between the writings of Marx and Engels and sacred history, or what I prefer to
leave in the original German, *Heilsgeschichte*.[4]

1.1   *Bruno Bauer and Marx*
To begin with, Marx had occasion in 1839 to study the Bible's great prophetic
text of Isaiah – the Hebrew text read by many Christians as foretelling many
centuries earlier the birth of Christ – when he was a student at the Friedrich Wilhelm University in Berlin.[5] His teacher was the young Bruno Bauer,
who would become a close friend and collaborator before major differences
ended the collaboration, although not the friendship. Would not the study
of one of the great prophetic books of the Bible with one of Germany's leading, if somewhat radical, biblical scholars have provided Marx with a golden
opportunity to appropriate not only the critique of injustice found in that
biblical text but also to see the value of an eschatological view of history? The
problem is that Bauer would have been the last to explore the eschatological
dimensions of Isaiah and expound on them in glowing terms. For already at
this time, Bauer was developing his argument that religious dogmatism and
free self-consciousness were implacable antagonists. His constant target was
the obscene relationship between the ossified established church and the repressive state.
    What would Bauer have taught Marx? Here we may consider his book
on the Hebrew Bible published the year before. In *Die Religion des alten
Testaments* (1838), Bauer had begun to develop his argument that religion
is caught in a tension between a false and oppressive particularity and universal free self-consciousness. Apart from ensuring that Marx was up-to-date
on the rapid developments in the first wave of modern German biblical
criticism, Bauer had already come to hold that all religion was problematic.
By definition, religion was a hubristic effort by a certain particularism – be
that individual, group or institution – to lay claim to the abstract universal.
As soon as it did so, it became a crass sectarian monopoly that brooked no
opposition. One should not be surprised that the church had become close-
minded and authoritarian. Even Isaiah, who was far better than the priestly

---

4   This section creatively summarises a detailed investigation made elsewhere (Boer 2011c).
5   This fact is little known, for it can be easily missed unless one pays close attention to Marx's
    leaving certificate from the university. There we read, regarding the summer term of 1839:
    'Isaiah with Herr Licentiate Bauer, attended' (1839, 74).

material that lay (as scholarship held at the time) at the earliest layers of the Hebrew Bible, succumbed to this problem. Isaiah might have moved past the law-driven externality of the priests, he might even have expressed an ethical monotheism in which the universal was immanent in the community, but he still held to religion as such, and that was the problem. Bauer's teaching was a far cry from the idea that the prophets were harbingers of the eschaton.

1.2   *Engels and the Apocalypse*

Given that Marx had been divested any eschatological dimension of the biblical prophets, might it not have been Engels who gave Marxism a secularised and eschatological *Heilsgeschichte*? After all, Engels had a lifelong fascination with the biblical Apocalypse (also known as 'Revelation'). He had been brought up as a believing Reformed (Calvinist) Protestant, read the New Testament in the original Greek and generally kept abreast of recent developments in biblical criticism. In his early texts we find extensive discussions and treatments of the Bible, especially in letters to his close friends, the pastors Friedrich and Wilhelm Graeber,[6] and in the amusing and well-written poem, *The Insolently Threatened Yet Miraculously Rescued Bible* (Engels 1842a, 1842b).

In these texts, we find a number of creative engagements with the Apocalypse, yet it never appears in an eschatological sense. Thus, Engels may use its language playfully, to make fun of and attack those who would hold him back (Engels 1841a, 1841b, 1842a, 1842b), or to tease his friend Friedrich Graeber (Engels 1839a, 1839b), or to celebrate his own awakening (Engels 1842c, 238–40, 1842d, 312–14). In other words, Engels's use of the Apocalypse is quite idiosyncratic (Boer 2012, 284–91). He uses it for humour, polemic and to provide a language for his own self-discovery – not quite what one would expect in terms of historical expectations, especially as the glorious march of history to an eschatological moment. It is crucial to note that these types of engagements with the Apocalypse petered out by the time he was 25, with the satirical attack on Bruno Bauer and Max Stirner appearing in the final pages of *The Holy Family* (Marx and Engels 1845a, 210–11, 1845b, 222–23).[7]

---

6 These letters provide extraordinary insights into Engels's struggles concerning religious faith and critical scholarship. They are collected in volume 2 of MECW and volume III.1 of MEGA.

7 Similar examples appear in equally early pieces, such as an account of the struggle between the Hegelian Michelet and the Pious Leo (Engels 1839c, 1839d), the street fight between the supporters of the two ministers in Bremen, Krummacher and Paniel (Engels 1840a, 1840b), and his anticipation concerning the overcoming of Hegel (Engels 1844a, 1844b). He also makes use of the same language laced with biblical quotations and allusions to blast the

Nonetheless, this is not the last of the Apocalypse in Engels's writings, for many years later he would deploy it in a very different fashion. In the final pages of a text we have encountered on a number of occasions, 'On the History of Early Christianity' (Engels 1894–95a, 1894–95b),[8] Engels returns to the same biblical text but now in a very different fashion. It becomes a historical source for an unfamiliar earliest Christianity. Basing his work on Ferdinand Benary and Bruno Bauer, Engels argues that the Apocalypse is the oldest Christian document. Now he uses it as a purely historical source, mining it for information about the beliefs and practices of the early Christians. Above all, he seeks to decode the Apocalypse and show that all those who use it for speculation about the end of history are simply misguided. Assuming a date of composition between late 68 and early 69 CE, he argues that it presents a group of Jews (not Christians) who believed the end would come soon. This revolutionary group had none of the following: Trinity (for Jesus is subordinate to God), Holy Spirit, doctrine of original sin, baptism or sacrament of communion, justification by faith, or an elaborate story of the death and resurrection of Christ. And there is no religion of love, for the author preaches 'sound, honest revenge [*gesunde ehrliche Rache*]' on their persecutors (Engels 1894–95a, 462, 1894–95b, 292). Following Benary, Engels suggests that the infamous number 666 (or 616 in a textual variant) can easily be deciphered through some deft playing with numbers: given that Hebrew used letters of the alphabet for numbers, all we need do is add up the value of *Neron Kesar* (Greek *Neron Kaisar*) and we have 666. So the Apocalypse predicts the end of the 'beast', Nero, at the hand of God and ushers in the new age.

Engels's later engagement with the Apocalypse seems completely at odds with his earlier interest in this biblical book. Once he took up and often mocked the speculation concerning the Last Judgement, but now the book is useful as a window into the earliest form of Christianity. As for its influence on Marxist theories of history, Engels writes, 'All this has now lost its interest, except for

---

close ties between the German nobility and an arrogant Roman Catholic Church (Engels 1840c, 66–67, 1840d, 98–99).

8 Engels had the first hunch concerning this argument as far back as 1841, when he was 21. He writes to Karl Kautsky, on 28 July, 1894: 'There is no hurry about printing the article. Once I have seen to the proofs you can print it when you wish, in September, say, or even October. I have been mulling over the thing ever since 1841 when I read a lecture by F. Benary on *Revelation*. Since then I have been in no doubt that here we have the earliest and most important book in the New Testament. After a gestation period of fifty-three years there is no great need to hasten its emergence into the world at large' (Engels 1894e, 328–29, 1894f, 276). The precursors to this final text may be found in 'The Book of Revelation' (Engels 1883) and 'Bruno Bauer and Early Christianity' (Engels 1882a, 1882b).

ignorant persons who may still try to calculate the day of the last judgement'
(Engels 1883, 13).

1.3   Early Eschatological Communism

On two counts Marx or Engels have failed to appropriate a *Heilsgeschichte* for
their own historical narrative: while Marx found anything but an eschatological interpretation of the Hebrew prophets when he studied under Bruno Bauer,
Engels effectively diffused the apocalyptic effect of the Apocalypse through his
own extended engagement with that text. On a third occasion, they become
even more explicit, resolutely opposing the early form of communism that
leaked over the border from France. These socialists, especially Saint-Simon
and Fourier, sought to transform Christianity's teachings into codes of ethics,
of brotherly love without all the supernatural trappings. This moral vision and
sense of progress in human society towards brotherly love inspired thinkers
and activists like Heinrich Heine, August von Cieskowski and especially an
early collaborator with Marx and Engels, Moses Hess (Breckman 1999, 131–76).
It also influenced some of the early leaders of the German communist movement, such as Wilhelm Weitling, Hermann Kriege, Karl Grün and Gottfried
Kinkel. Marx and Engels worked tirelessly to excise this very Christian element
from the communist movement (Marx and Engels 1846a, 1846b, 1845–46a,
484–530, 1845–46b, 473–520, 1852a, 1852b). Marx, for one, was scornful of this
French-derived socialism, which 'sentimentally bewails the sufferings of mankind, or in Christian spirit prophesies the millennium and universal brotherly
love, or in humanistic style drivels on about mind, education and freedom'
(Marx 1852a, 142, 1852b, 135).

Most significantly, Marx and Engels consistently opposed the apocalyptic
tone of this early communism, especially as it entered Germany through Moses Hess.[9] In his *Die heilige Geschichte der Menschheit* and *Die europäische*

---

9   The wider political context is also worth noting. For a number of historical reasons Germany
    in the 1830s and 1840s dealt with a whole range of modern issues through theology and the
    Bible. While France had the radical atheistic criticism of Voltaire and company and while
    England had the deists, in Germany the debate was restricted to the nature of the Bible.
    So we find in the early part of the nineteenth century the bombshell of David Strauss' *Das
    Leben Jesu* (1902, 1835), where he argued that the accounts of Jesus in the Gospels are myth-
    ological, or the arguments of the biblical critic Bruno Bauer for an atheistic and free self-
    consciousness (1838, 1839, 1840, 1841, 1842, 1843), or those of Ludwig Feuerbach that religion
    is actually the projection of what is best in human beings, a projection that leads us to create
    an entity called 'God' (1841a, 1841b). Through these theological and biblical works, all of the
    central questions were debated, such as democracy, freedom (of the press), reason, republi-
    canism and parliamentary representation. It cannot be stressed enough that these debates
    took place above all on the territory of the Bible, so much so that it provided the enabling

Trierarchie, Hess both introduced communism to Germany and gave it a distinctly apocalyptic tone (Hess 1837, 1841, 2004; Kouvelakis 2003, 121–66). The popular *Die europäische Trierarchie* proposed that the fusion of the Young Hegelian criticism of theology, French socialist politics and English industrial materialism would bring about the total collapse of the existing order and usher in a new age. For Marx and Engels this approach to communism was seriously problematic, if not entirely unrealistic. I would suggest that those who charge Marx and Engels with a secularized eschatological framework have the wrong target in their sights. The charge applies not to Marx and Engels, but to Moses Hess and other early communists to whom Marx and Engels were opposed.

2   Moving Mountains: Concerning Narrative Structure

In response to the preceding argument – that Marx and Engels consciously set themselves against any version of Christian history, sacred or secularised – one may identify a ready objection: they still absorbed theology and produced a secularised *Heilsgeschichte*, but they did so unaware, sucking up the structure of that *Heilsgeschichte* as a plant absorbs sunshine and water. Their historical narrative is thereby one more example (to gloss Schmitt 2005, 36) of the suggestion that all theories of history are really varieties of secularised theology. That would mean they absorbed such a narrative structure in the very process of trying to resist it.

But what narrative structure is assumed by this suggestion? Is it a passage from a fall from the state of grace, through redemption and a return to grace? Or is it, as I suggested earlier, one that focuses on the redeemer, now a collective entity (the proletariat or perhaps its revolutionary vanguard), which will save us from our state of oppression and economic injustice (sin) and bring about the glorious era after the revolution when the meek shall inherit the earth and justice abound? Or is it perhaps a version of election, in which the proletariat (the righteous) will smash the bourgeoisie (the unrighteous) and thereby establish heaven on earth? The problem with each of these quasi-theological versions is twofold: they miss the crucial discovery made by Engels and (especially) Marx and thereby the actual Marxist historical narrative.

One of the signal problems of many assessments of Marxist historical narratives is that nearly everyone seems to know in advance precisely what they

---

conditions for the tide of German biblical criticism as a global force – a situation that lasted
for a century.

are, without having considered Marx and Engels's own arguments. So let us do precisely that and focus on a much neglected text that is really the engine-room of historical materialism, where the first breakthrough appears: the well-nigh endless pages on Max Stirner (a pseudonym for Kaspar Schmidt) in *The German Ideology*.

2.1   *Stirner's Ego and Christ*

Here Marx and Engels pull to pieces the ramshackle work by Stirner, *The Ego and His Own*. For Stirner the key to his fundamental recasting of history is that 'the individual [*Einzelne*] is of himself a world's history [*Weltgeschichte*], and possesses his property [*Eigentum*] in the rest of world history, goes beyond what is Christian' (Stirner 1845a, 365, 1845b, 428). In this light, he organises the work into a number of loose historical stages: child, youth and 'man'; Negro, Mongol and Caucasian; ancients (restricted to Greeks and Romans), moderns (Christianity and especially the Roman Catholic-Protestant struggles), and then the discovery of the ego in the present (German philosophy in his own time).

However, the most significant feature of Stirner's argument is its deeply theological nature. Although much of the text is given to pointing to yet another failing of Christianity, every now and then he seeks to appropriate an element for his own project. The pertinent example for our purposes is his appropriation of the incarnation as a model for the ego:

> Christ is the I of the world's history, even of the pre-Christian; in modern apprehension it is man, the figure of Christ has developed into the *figure of man*: man as such, man absolutely, is the 'central point' of history. In 'man' the imaginary beginning returns again; for 'man' is as imaginary as Christ is. 'Man' as the I of world history closes the cycle of Christian apprehensions.
>
> STIRNER 1845a, 365, 1845b, 427

Stirner has picked up the internal logic of Christology, for in Christ God becomes a human being. Note carefully: Christ is not a half-man, half-God, taking on a human body with a divine soul. Instead, in Christ God becomes a complete human being. This is where the logic also threatens to break down, for according to orthodox theology Christ is also fully divine. But Stirner focuses on the human dimension – Christ is a man, man as such, man absolutely. This human Christ is the key to the ego. Further, the complete man known as Jesus Christ is also the 'central point' of history, the pivot on which history turns. What is good enough for Christ is even better for the ego, for Christ is the paradigmatic ego.

A few lines later, Stirner tackles the other side of the Christological equation. Christ may have been fully human, but he is also completely God. Human and divine meet in the one person:

> They say of God, 'Names name thee not'. That holds good of me: no *concept* expresses me, nothing that is designated as my essence exhausts me; they are only names. Likewise they say of God that he is perfect and has no calling to strive after perfection. That too holds good of me alone.
>
>   STIRNER 1845a, 366, 1845b, 429

Christology opens up a two-way street: Christ may have become human, but that means human beings may also become divine. Stirner's ego joins the ride, but with a twist: it is not that the ego wishes to join God or attain God's status. The simple truth is that God has never existed, so when the ego arrives as wherever God is supposed to be, it finds that it is the only one there. That means that whenever we have been talking about God – perfection, the inability to name God and so on – we have, as Feuerbach had already pointed out (1841a, 1841b), been talking about nothing less than the individual human being all along.

It is not for nothing that Marx and Engels charge Stirner with being a theologian still. One crucial point remains, for now Stirner makes use of Jesus Christ as the paradigm of the lever of history:

> That the individual [*Einzelne*] is of himself a world's history [*Weltgeschichte*], and possesses his property [*Eigentum*] in the rest of world history, goes beyond what is Christian. To the Christian the world's history is the higher thing, because it is the history of Christ or 'man'; to the egoist only *his* history has value, because he wants to develop only *himself.*
>
>   STIRNER 1845a, 365, 1845b, 428

Not only is the egoist's history the only one that has value, not only is it the principle by which Stirner offers his reinterpretation of the ages of world history, but he does so in response to the Christian schema of that history whose lever is Christ. However much he may protest, he is playing the same game.

So Stirner's ego, the proud individual dismissing all collective and divine forces, is at a formal level a theological one. In reply, Marx and Engels level some of their strongest polemic at precisely this feature, pinpointing the fact that Stirner offers a reinterpretation of history through theology itself. Or, in more Hegelian language, the incomplete *Aufhebung* of Christology ends up being more deeply Christological, especially in the question of history. As Marx and Engels put it with reference to 1 Corinthians 17:20, Stirner's faith, specifically in the ego, 'moves all the mountains of world history' (Marx and Engels 1845–46a, 157, 1845–46b, 140).

This biblical allusion is not an isolated occurrence, for in *The German Ideology* a deluge of biblical quotations and allusions swamp the text (Engels is responsible for most of them). More distinctive still is the way the Stirner chapter is structured like the canonical sequence of the Bible. So we find that the first part is called 'The Old Testament: Man' and it includes chapters on 'The Book of Genesis' and 'The Economy of the Old Testament'. Not unexpectedly, the second part is entitled 'The New Testament: Ego' and contains chapters called 'The Economy of the New Testament' and 'The Revelation of John the Divine'. Or, as Marx and Engels put it, the division is between 'the unique history of man (the Law and the Prophets) and the inhuman history of the unique (the Gospel of the Kingdom of God)' (Marx and Engels 1845–46a, 120, 1845–46b, 103). It is of course a very effective way of connecting Stirner at a formal level with the canonical structure of the Bible, for that canonical ordering of a sacred text provides a structure of world history that turns around a crucial lever. That is, Marx and Engels want to make it perfectly clear that at this structural level Stirner is playing the same game, despite his assertions otherwise.

2.2   *Towards Contradiction*

Marx and Engels respond by producing an entirely different approach: a thoroughly non-theological and materialist theory of history, one that does not depend on a world spirit, or an infinite self-consciousness or an ego modelled on Christ. Thus, in the second half of this long study on Stirner, Marx and Engels move beyond destructive to constructive criticism, supplying ever more comments and alternative proposals to those of Stirner. A major reason is that Stirner begins to launch attacks against property, competition, labour, money, revolution, love and freedom of the press. Above all, he maintains a persistent critique of any form of the collective, whether the closed-in circle of the family, the collaborative hold on power by the aristocracy, the rise in his own time of the party, the state itself, or the fatherland, common weal, 'mankind' and especially the communists.[10] Released from all these constraints is the individual, the ego, which becomes the key to history, the fulcrum on which history turns.

---

10   The problem, argues Stirner, is that the various liberalisms really retain society and the state. One may argue for responsible citizenship, for the need to respect the rights of one another. Another may say that the state and society are undesirable, but then slips them in the back door. Why? Because the state is needed to ensure that liberal values are upheld. All of which gives Marx and Engels plenty of ammunition with which to charge Stirner with being a true liberal, defending the private individual even against state institutions that seek to protect that individual.

Marx and Engels disagree, for Stirner has mystified rather than clarified history. The problem is that he has not made a revolutionary break at all, following in the tradition of speculative, idealist German philosophy. Or, as Marx and Engels put it, Stirner is still beholden to Hegel, albeit with less finesse than his master. This argument is closely tied in with the criticism that Stirner merely expresses the particular world-view of the petty bourgeoisie. All Stirner does is provide an ideology of the individual with no sense of the social embeddedness of such an individual, who thereby is abstracted into a solipsistic world of his own, an abstract history of 'ghosts'. In other words, there is no break whatsoever with the tradition of speculative German philosophy or, most importantly, with a theological schema of history.

In reply, Marx and Engels begin to construct the various parts of their alternative history, inserting more and more sections that contain their own proposals. It may be in response to Stirner's comments on property, or money, or labour or competition, but we encounter increasingly complex and alternative presentations of a materialist version of these topics. The interventions are most persistent in the last hundred pages, where Marx and Engels begin to clarify matters for themselves. Thus, when they begin to tackle the topic of law, they weave in more and more materialist replies into their argument with Stirner. And then at certain moments there is need for a larger comment on law, which becomes a brief history concerning modes of production, class, economics and politics (Marx and Engels 1845–46a, 328–30, 335–36, 1845–46b, 311–13, 318–19). Soon, this becomes a standard approach, with ever more expansive explanations of topics such as crime, society, private property, competition, revolution, labour, money, exploitation, class, contradiction, as well as language, railways and food.

Rather than explore each topic in detail, I will focus on the issues of exploitation and class, for they lead us to the crucial category of contradiction. Stirner's treatment of 'usefulness' opens up the discussion of exploitation. For Stirner, 'usefulness' is the key to human interaction: an individual relates to another purely through the criterion of use. Marx and Engels point out that this theory of mutual exploitation has a long pedigree. But the theory does not appear in a vacuum, the product of pure speculation. Instead, it comes into its own with the growth of the bourgeoisie and commercial social relations. Particularly important is the connection between the theory of exploitation and class. In this situation, the theory becomes the necessary correlate to a rising bourgeoisie, for as the theory of exploitation became the central and overriding universal economic concept, thereby enabling political economy to become a distinct science, so also did the bourgeoisie no longer present itself as a particular class but as the universal class that determines all others. When it had achieved this status, the abstract and universalising theory became an explanation and apology for the capitalist relations which were spreading rapidly throughout Europe.

Marx and Engels show how the rise of this theory of exploitation could not happen without the assumption of class. Armed with this category, Marx and Engels examine how personal and distinctly individual interests develop into the common and general interests of a class (Marx and Engels 1845–46a, 245–46, 1845–46b, 227–29). It follows that Stirner too, despite his protests, finds himself located in a class situation. But Marx and Engels forestall his protests by pointing out that this class connection takes place against the will of individuals. In other words, we have a contradiction between individual and collective interests. Stirner may think he is a pure ego, independent of any class, but he cannot avoid the fact that his individual interests are characteristic of a whole class, the petty bourgeoisie. The explanation for the contradiction may be found in the nature of production, for the contradiction between individual and class is but an expression of a deeper contradiction in the mode of production, and that is nothing other than the division of labour.

Another example of the way the Marx and Engels move inevitably to matters of class and contradiction, specifically in their observations on class within a mode of production (Marx and Engels 1845–46a, 418–20, 1845–46b, 403–5). Distinguishing between the revolutionary 'vocation' of the oppressed class and the dominating vocation of the ruling class, which tries to impose its ideology on the proletarians, they identify a basic contradiction: between the bourgeoisie and the proletariat. In other words, class is inevitably a contradictory category, which arises from the conditions of production. How does this work? A little earlier (Marx and Engels 1845–46a, 289–90, 1845–46b, 270–71), they describe a proletarian who needs to work fourteen hours a day even to survive. This proletarian is thereby reduced to a beast of burden, or even to an article of trade or even a thing. Opposed to this proletarian is a bourgeois who believes that the particular task of domination of the proletarian is in fact a universal human task. In response, the proletarian has, given his circumstances, no option but to revolutionise his own conditions and overthrow the bourgeoisie. Or, as Marx and Engels put it, when 'the bourgeois tells the proletarian that his, the proletarian's, human task is to work fourteen hours a day, the proletarian is quite justified in replying in the same language that on the contrary his task is to overthrow the entire bourgeois system' (1845–46a, 290, 1845–46b, 271).

Thus, in this text on Stirner, Marx and Engels develop the first, albeit rough, outline of a historical materialist narrative. It follows a basic dynamic of class identity and conflict, one that operates according to a fundamental contradiction that leads to a revolutionary communist position. In other words, Marx and Engels seek to oust Stirner's lever of history, the ego, and produce a very different one indeed. But what is this lever? Or is it a lever at all? It is certainly not the proletariat as a secular saviour. Is it class and especially class conflict? None of these apply, although the latter comes closest, for the key is contradiction itself. Towards the close of the section of Stirner, Marx and Engels finally lay out the explanation (1845–46a, 431–32, 1845–46b, 417–18). Productive forces contain within themselves a contradiction, one that is based on the insufficiency of these forces. The insufficiency means that a few who are able to satisfy their needs gain control of the limited productive forces while the rest fall under their sway. Inevitably this tension, or the desire of the oppressed class to satisfy its needs, leads to the overthrow of a narrow-minded ruling class that cannot see the problem. 'Thus, society has hitherto always developed from within the framework of a contradiction – in antiquity the contradiction between free men and slaves, in the Middle Ages that between nobility and serfs, in modern times between the bourgeoisie and the proletariat' (Marx and Engels 1845–46a, 432, 1845–46b, 417). Here already is the position that will be stated succinctly in the opening lines of *The Manifesto of the Communist Party*.

Here is a new pivot of history and thereby a historical narrative that is qualitatively different from that of Stirner, or indeed Hegel or theology, for it is a contradiction within the mode of production.[11] Contradiction becomes the Archimedean point by which history shifts from one epoch to the other, specifically in the way contradiction between productive forces and relations of production reaches a crisis, namely, the moment of revolution. A crucial caveat applies: this analysis is focused largely on objective forces of history, which has the potential to lead to a somewhat imbalanced perception of a Marxist approach to history. Needed of course is the role of subjective intervention in revolution and the construction of socialism, which reshapes the objective conditions.

I have traced the development of Marx and Engels's argument in some detail, for in the Marxist-theological tussle over history it is vital to be clear concerning the nature of the Marxist narrative. That narrative turns out not to be one that moves from a state of sin to grace through a redeemer, or one that

---

11   A somewhat systematic account of the division of labour, class, class conflict and the contradiction at the heart of all modes of production appears in the first section on Feuerbach, but only because of the complex editorial history of the manuscripts, which gathered material from elsewhere and located them in the constructed chapter on Feuerbach (Marx and Engels 1845–46a, 59–93, 1845–46b, 46–77). They now form part of that famous first and somewhat rough statement of historical materialism. For a detailed treatment of the genesis, production and publication of Feuerbach chapter, see Carver and Blank (2014).

sees the elect vanquishing the damned and inheriting the earth; that is, it is not derived from and thereby 'secularised' from a theological *Heilsgeschichte*. Instead, the objective dimension of the Marxist historical narrative turns on contradiction between the forces and relations of production, a contradiction that then opens up the possibility of a new mode of production that attempts to overcome those contradictions. Would contradictions finally be resolved after such a revolution? In earlier rough works such as *The German Ideology*, Marx and Engels may have entertained such a possibility, but in later works they began to see the necessity of the development of new contradictions – a reality that would be examined in detail by those who actually engaged in the construction of socialism after a revolution, from Lenin onwards.

3   Relativising Theology

I have argued at some length that Marx and Engels do not offer a secularised form of *Heilsgeschichte*, either at the level of explicit content or of implicit form. Does this conclusion, then, exclude all dimensions of contact, all cross-overs between the two on the question of history?[12] Or is there a bridge between the two? The point of contact may well turn out to be the very abstract question of the pivot or lever of history. As we saw, the Marxist lever or turning point is contradiction, rather than Christ, the ego or even the Hegelian world spirit. The natures of these pivots seem to be qualitatively different. Yet, if we move to a higher level of abstraction, then a likeness does begin to emerge: the very effort to construct a world history in the first place, especially one that turns on a fulcrum, may be seen as analogous to the biblical and theological structure of history.

   On this matter, I am ready to admit that a possible connection exists, although one needs to be exceedingly careful – as the above argument shows – in identifying such a connection. Thus, while the very nature of the pivots is qualitatively different, it also indicates an abstract and formal analogy. The role of contradictions as both enabling for the rise of modes of productions and disabling, so much so that these contradictions become an objective mechanism for transition to other modes of production, is distinctly different from a biblical or theological narrative in which one moves from paradise, through sin and redemption to a state of grace. Yet the very existence of a pivot, if not the

---

12   Here I think not of the myriad and overlaid engagements with the Bible and theology that one finds throughout the work of Marx and Engels.

need for a grand historical narrative at all, is indeed a point of contact, even if we are now at a very general and abstract level.

Now at last, with a point of contact, is it time to deploy my last argument. All hitherto efforts to argue that Marxism involves a secularised *Heilsgeschichte* assume – in stronger or weaker versions – that theology or the Bible function as sources, as origins for Marxism. The problem is that such an argument absolutizes theology and gives the Bible almost divine power as the ultimate and absolute source of all conceptions of history. That is, such arguments themselves rely on a theological position. They also confuse temporal priority – in this case in regard to the Bible – with ontological priority. The latter is by no means a necessary correlate of the former, although theologians and biblical critics often seem to think so. Against such absolutizing, the need for relativising the claims for theology becomes apparent: theological language is not absolute, but rather one mode for speaking of history, or indeed of the human condition, suffering, subjectivity and collectives. Other modes have existed and exist, without any need to refer to theology or the category of transcendence itself,[13] thereby relegating theology to a viable place alongside many other discourses. As Lunacharsky points out (1911, 163), Christian theology is 'only a form, one of the many forms that social-economic progress can take'.

All of which makes it much easier to see how carefully and precisely identified contacts between Marxism and theology may be understood. In the context of this specific discussion concerning history, that contact is restricted to the abstract level of the pivot of history and the need for grand historical narratives. Yet those overlaps do not function in terms of origin and derivative, source and appropriation, but rather as two possible languages for speaking about history at all. Once we have this relativising move, the critiques of Marxism as a secularised *Heilsgeschichte* lose their bite. So also may we appreciate in a different way the myriad engagements with, citations of and allusions to the Bible and theology in the Marxist tradition (Boer 2007a, R. Boer 2009a, Boer 2011a, 2012, 2013a, 2017b). I would also extend this approach to the various efforts to introduce theological themes into Marxism, from Kautsky's 'new gospel [*ein neues Evangelium*]' (1892b, 231) to Lars Lih's 'great awakening' (2007), for they too trade on the translations between two different languages or codes for speaking of history, revolution and the future. Yet in neither case is the language ontologically absolute, for each is all too aware of its relative and limited status, with its own benefits and drawbacks.

---

13   For example, Chinese philosophy and culture does not operate with the distinction between ontological transcendence and immanence. This reality reveals the specific and contextual nature of the distinction and indicates a rather distinct approach to Marxism. This is the topic of another study.

CHAPTER 8

Revisiting the Marxist-Christian Dialogue

> My thirst does not prove the existence of the spring. For the Marxist, the
> infinite is absence and exigency, while for the Christian, it is promise and
> presence.
>
> GARAUDY, RAHNER, AND METZ 1967, 80

The Marxist-Christian dialogue of the 1960s and 1970s is the specific concern
of this chapter. But what counts as a 'dialogue' in this instance? More broadly,
it may refer to anyone – Marxist or Christian or both – who is engaged in
some way with the two terms. The logical outcome of this approach is that the
whole history of Marxism entails a Marxist-Christian dialogue.[1] Or, at least,
Marxism in its European, Russian and Latin American incarnations. Thus,
one may study – to keep the examples to the twentieth century – theologians
such as Karl Barth, Josef Hromádka, Christoph Blumhardt,[2] Reinhold Niebuhr,
Paul Tillich and Dorothy Sölle to see what they had to say about Marxism, or
Karl Kautsky, Ernst Bloch, Louis Althusser and other Marxists to inquire what
they have written concerning Christianity (West 1958; Machovec 1965; Bentley
1982).[3] My approach is more specific: it concerns those who actively engaged in
dialogue, through conferences and publications, in both Eastern and Western
Europe in the 1960s and 1970s.[4]

Some of the more notable gatherings included: the Christian Peace Conference in Prague (1959);[5] the two gatherings in Salzburg (1965) and Chiemsee
(1966), which were organised by *Paulusgesellschaft* and included Protestants

---

1 In this light, my earlier work on European and Russian Marxism may be regarded as a
comprehensive assessment of the Marxist-Christian dialogue from the side of most of the
leading Marxist thinkers in the tradition (Boer 2007–2014, 2013a, 2017b).
2 Blumhardt was the first member of the clergy to join the German Social-Democratic Party in
1899, leading to the church defrocking him (Bentley 1982, 23–35).
3 A similar referential wideness applies to the use of the term 'encounter', since this potentially
covers most areas of the world (Piediscalzi and Thobaben 1985).
4 This is a chapter I have wanted to write for more than 30 years. A substantial part of the
research entailed working through old photocopies from the 1980s, which constitute a
unique collection on the dialogue.
5 Organised by Josef Hromádka, collaborator with Karl Barth and leading Czech theologian at
the time who urged working with the communists (Bentley 1982, 137–40). Indeed, Czechoslovakia seemed to be particularly germane to the dialogue.

and Roman Catholics (Hebblethwaite 1977, 17); Marianbad in Czechoslovakia (1967),[6] organised by the Czech philosopher, Milan Machovec (1980); the Melbourne Pax Convention in 1967 (Garaudy et al. 1967); and gatherings in the United Kingdom (Dunman 1968) and in the United States (Schuler 1975).[7] Needless to say, publications around the issue multiplied, some of which I will discuss in more detail below (Aptheker 1970; Lobkowicz 1967a; Garaudy and Lauer 1968; Mojzes 1968; Oestreicher 1969; Kuczyński 1979). My aim is not so much to report on the conferences and debates as to engage critically with the issues raised, identifying what may have faded with time and what remains pertinent in the somewhat different situation today. The chapter is structured in four sections: the first deals with the limitations of the dialogue, while the second summarises the points that were important at the time but are not so today. The third devotes more attention to the questions of human nature, protest (Prometheus) and approaches to the future, while the final section reassesses the context of the dialogues.

1   Limitations

I begin with the limitations of the dialogue, which are now, some four decades or more later, much clearer: the desire for 'core' positions; relatively little engagement with actual texts; a tendency to romanticise communism in light of Marx's earlier texts; and its extraordinarily Euro-American focus. Again and again, one encounters efforts to identify the core of both Marxism and Christianity.[8] Marx's earlier 'humanistic' texts become the focus, especially the 'Economic and Philosophic Manuscripts of 1844' and *The German Ideology*, both collated and first published in the Soviet Union in 1932 (Marx 1844c, 1844d, 1844e, Marx and Engels 1845–46a, 1845–46b).[9] At the same time, there is surprisingly little detailed engagements with the texts of Marx and Engels.

---

6   The themes of these three conferences were, respectively: 'Ideological Co-existence', 'Christian Humanity and Marxist Humanism' and 'Creativity and Freedom in a Humane Society'. For a useful pre-history leading up to the dialogues, see Banks (1976).

7   The major impulse was from Protestant theologians, not least because of the encyclical *Divini Redemptoris* of 1937, which outlined a Roman Catholic refutation of both Marxist theory and practice and forbade engagement with communist parties. This meant that any rapprochement would have to be indirect for Roman Catholic theologians who at least toed the Vatican line (Curtis 1997; Krišto 1985). By contrast, in Italy radical clergy simply became involved in left-wing political action (Drake 2008).

8   Garaudy entitles his core chapters 'The Realization of What is Basic', by Marxists and Christians (Garaudy, Rahner, and Metz 1967, 31–108).

9   Garaudy (1970, 122–24) is a rare exception.

Perhaps the participants assumed a common ground in such knowledge, but the danger is that the 'canon within the canon' runs its usual course, with the effect that the rougher edges and more intriguing texts of the founders disappear. In this 'canon', we find concerns with *'praxis'*, 'alienation', 'species-essence' and idealised forms of primitive agrarian socialism that included anti-statism – the *de rigueur* position for all radicals. I will reinterpret this 'humanistic' concern in terms of human nature, since it enables me to lift the specific concerns of the time to another and more abiding level.

A comparable desire for the core of Christianity appears, which often turns out to be the radical tradition in Christianity with the attendant challenge of the status quo.[10] This Christian articulation reveals what was at stake for both Marxists and Christians: if one can identify the core message, then other forms become aberrations from the truth, if not heterodoxy. The pertinent form of this question was applied to Christianity (Machovec 1980) but more often to Marx's approach to religion. What precisely was Marx attacking? One answer was that Marx had in his sights the outward forms of Christianity, manifested in the institutions of the churches, the history of interaction with (so often reactionary) political structures, if not the whole dimension of the Christianity as a temporal reality – for which the name 'Christendom' functions as a shorthand (Lichtman 1968, 84–94; Forrester 1972). With this move, one can then point out that Marx's criticisms of such outward manifestations are indeed correct, but that he leaves relatively untouched the core truth of Christianity, which lies elsewhere. Or, one may suggest that Marx had a particular tradition of Christianity in mind, especially its Augustinian-Lutheran line with the idea of supposed absolute subservience to God in a type of master-slave relation (Girardi 1968, 26–27). One can then counter this position with, for instance, a Roman Catholic approach. In response to these moves, Marx's observation is rather relevant:

> Economists have a singular method of procedure. There are only two kinds of institutions for them, artificial and natural. The institutions of feudalism are artificial institutions, those of the bourgeoisie are natural institutions. In this they resemble the theologians, who likewise establish two kinds of religion. Every religion which is not theirs is an invention of men, while their own is an emanation from God.
>
> MARX 1847c, 174, 1847d, 139, 1867a, 92, n. 1, 1867b, 49, n. 28

---

10   Garaudy (1967, 9–10) is an exception, stressing the political ambivalence of Christianity (see Chapter 3).

Obviously, I am less interested in these features of the dialogue, but there is one that I will pick up later, albeit with a twist. This is the limitation to a European (and occasionally United States) context. Here 'east' and 'west' become Eastern and Western Europe, with the Soviet Union an outlier and China not even on the register. Of course, the policies in the Soviet Union had a bearing, with many identifying the turn from a 'Stalinist repression' to a 'thaw' under Khrushchev as a key development. How that situation actually worked out needs to be re-examined.

2   From Then …

The most serious and insightful contributors set out to seek some common ground, albeit not so much a Golden Mean, with the uncomfortable edges carefully filed away, but a dialectical approach in which either side did not give up their positions for the sake of a compromise (Zabłocki 1979, 94). The challenge of the dialogues was framed in various ways, although the best is expressed by Adams: 'On the one hand, the Christian cannot accept the secularism, the self-sufficient finitude (as Tillich called it), of Marx. On the other hand, the Marxist offers a vigorous challenge to the Christian, the challenge to give a cogent restatement of the "ground" or "object" of … faith' (Adams 1967, 374). Going a step further, Lauer observes not only that 'Philosophy today cannot even call itself Christian if it is unable to synthesize the insights and methods which Marxism has developed', but also that a 'Marxist could be even more consistent than Marx himself and not only recognize but even welcome the possibility' of a reconciliation between Marxism and Christianity (Lauer 1968, 47, 55).

As to how this challenge would work itself out is another question. At the time, many were vexed by the tension between theism and atheism, a problem that does not seem so pressing now. More specifically, the key question was whether atheism was an integral and inescapable feature of Marx's approach and therefore of Marxism itself (Girardi 1968, 18–21; Norris 1974, 27–34; Thiemann 1985), whether Marx may have seen religion as a secondary phenomenon but that after Marx religion was – through a conventional 'Western' narrative of betrayal – made into an essential feature of Marxism (McGovern 1985, 490–91; Lobkowicz 1967b, 303–7), whether it was a new development – 'humanist' atheism in contrast to earlier 'political' and 'scientist' forms – in the history of atheism (Garaudy 1970, 106–8), or whether it was always secondary and therefore not essential (Lichtman 1968, 79; Marković 1985). Or as Kerševan (1985, 501) puts it: 'Marxism cannot begin with "I do not believe in the only God," or "I believe in material unity of the world," and then continue with the general development and movement of the world and society, to reach the class struggle and the need for a socialist transformation of social relations'. Perhaps the Marxist philosopher, Machovec (1980, 6), offered the most in-depth analysis, arguing that the very understanding of God had changed from the time of Marx to a dynamic and future-oriented deity, so much so that Marxists would have to address the whole question again.

Another feature of the dialogue was an emphasis on *praxis*, with the term directly taken from the German. Normally translated simply as 'practice', including a professional office (such as a dentist or doctor), the term gained specific meaning from Marx's first thesis on Feuerbach: 'The chief defect of all previous materialism (that of Feuerbach included) is that things [*Gegenstand*], reality, sensuousness [*Sinnlichkeit*] are conceived only in the form of the *object, or of contemplation*, but not as *sensuous human activity, practice* [*sinnlich menschliche Tätigkeit, Praxis*], not subjectively' (Marx 1845a, 3, 1845b, 5). This 'sensuous human activity' is properly 'revolutionary' and 'practical-critical' activity. The obvious point here is that the insight is one of a number the young Marx discovered in his early to mid-twenties – philosophical discoveries as he worked his way through and past the Hegelian legacy and the positions of his Young Hegelian peers. But they are not the result of the long years of careful study, reflection and rewriting on political economy that characterised his later years (full of overwork, lack of sleep and endless smoking and caffeine).

Yet it was precisely this Marx – deeply Hegelian with a strong dash of anti-industrial socialism – with his focus on *praxis* that drew the attention of the dialogue partners. How did they understand this *praxis*? Thiemann (1985, 545) offers the clearest definition: '*praxis* is that "sensuous human activity" by which human beings create the world of culture and society and by doing so create themselves ... human beings *are* what they *do*'. The next step is to connect this point with Marx's analysis of labour in the 'Economic and Philosophic Manuscripts' of 1844. Labour becomes the action of producing products from the material of nature, products which are the extension and embodiment of human nature in the external world. In other words, '*praxis*, the sensuous labouring activity of human agents, is human self-creation, the externalization of human nature in external form' (Thiemann 1985, 545).[11] Or to quote Marx: 'The object of labour is, therefore, the objectification of man's species-life: for he duplicates himself not only, as in consciousness, intellectually, but also actively, in reality, and therefore he sees himself in a world that he has created' (Marx 1844c, 277, 1844d, 241, 1844e, 370).

---

11   Others offer variations on the same definition, occasionally connecting it with revolutionary activity by the proletariat (Girardi 1968, 13–14; Dean 1972; Banks 1974, 139; Lash 1981, 63).

The question is how this early statement by Marx becomes a core Marxist position. In his insightful intervention, Garaudy begins his definition of 'what is basic' for Marxists by quoting Marx's first thesis on Feuerbach – glossed as the 'creative act' of human beings, if not a 'methodology of historical initiative' (Garaudy, Rahner, and Metz 1967, 61, 64). Indeed, he stresses that of the eleven theses on Feuerbach, seven are devoted to this theme, which may be summarised in terms of the active dimension of knowledge, the criterion of collective practice (*praxis*) as the only source of truth and the role of philosophy in the transformation of the world. Marx may have begun with a basic understanding of human transformations of nature, but his interpreters take it much further, connecting it with labour, creativity, socialist revolution and the active effort to reshape society and economics after a revolution. The gains of such a position are obvious, although we would now speak more of subjective intervention than *praxis*. When the dialectic works well, objective and subjective factors interact with one another. Thus, careful scientific analysis of the objective conditions is absolutely necessary, but the danger of falling into a form of historical determination is overcome by the constant role of creative and subjective intervention, when the objective conditions themselves are transformed.[12] As Marx put it somewhat later, we may be subject to the given circumstances of the past, but we make our own history (Marx 1852a, 103, 1852b, 96–97). It also makes sense in the Soviet Union of the interchangeable usage of *politika* (policy) and *stroitel'stvo* (construction), such as language policy (*iazykovaia politika*) and language construction (*iazykovoe stroitel'stvo*). They clearly saw it as a deliberate intervention by socialists into the process of producing and developing a new society (Reznik 2003, 34; Slezkine 2000, 323–24; Martin 2001, 67).

Tellingly, the participants were keener to stress what they perceived (at times incorrectly) as the tendency in Marxism to an objectivised 'history is on our side' approach, alongside a version of 'vulgar' Marxism in which the base determines the superstructure. The cuplrits are many, whether Engels, Lenin, Stalin or indeed 'superficial disciples' and 'excessively hasty or ill-intentioned opponents' (Garaudy, Rahner, and Metz 1967, 63).[13] In the context, one can understand the desire of the participants to stress creativity, freedom, subjectivity and transcendence, not least because of a felt need to recover the

---

12   As Lenin found with his rediscovery of Hegel's dialectic in the library in Berne in 1914–1916, leading to the Russian Revolution, and as Mao found during the intense and creative engagement with Lenin's thoughts on Hegel in Yan'an in the mid-1930s (Boer 2017a).

13   Similarly, at the Melbourne Pax conference in 1967, Denis Kenny identifies the 'sub-rational and sub-Christian' response by many Roman Catholics to Marxism (Garaudy et al. 1967, 15).

energetic, history-changing dimension of Marxism, but also to open up the possibility of assessing religion more positively. How this was done entailed slipping in another and related feature of the Marxist tradition: the role of ideas. Let me put it this way: any materialist theory worthy of its name must be able to account dialectically for the role of theory and ideas. This entails not so much a deterministic base-superstructure model as a proposal put forward most clearly by Engels:

> If some younger writers attribute more importance to the economic as-pect than is its due, Marx and I are to some extent to blame. We had to stress this leading principle in the face of opponents who denied it, and we did not always have the time, space or opportunity to do justice to the other factors that interacted upon each other'.
>
> ENGELS 1890a, 36, 1890b, 465

I would add Stalin's observation from the *Short Course*: 'New social ideas and theories arise precisely because they are necessary to society, because it is *impossible* to carry out the urgent tasks of development of the material life of society without their organizing, mobilizing and transforming action' (Sta-lin 1938a, 116–17, 1938b, 111). With this in mind, it becomes possible to argue that religion involves a theory, a project or a model that seeks not only to interpret reality but to break away from and even transcend a given reality by protesting against and transforming this reality (Garaudy, Rahner, and Metz 1967, 66). From here, one can trace the history of religion, through myth and ritual to doctrine. It seeks out the realm of causes in relation to the realm of experienced phenomena. Obviously, this means that the initial motive force of religion is analogous to science, even if science moves a step beyond mythi-cal explanations.

Despite the gains of this renewed emphasis, we can identify at least two shortcomings. To begin with, little if any analysis is to be found concern-ing the realities of socialism in power,[14] with its many achievements and failures – and this despite the fact that the context in the 1960s and 1970s in Europe was very much socialism in power (I will have more to say on this point below). Second, in setting up the opposition so strongly – between subjective and objective, creative and scientific, *praxis* and 'vulgar' Marxism – the danger is that one loses the dialectical relation between these two terms. The point is that not only subjective and objective factors can be found in Marx's works, but also that there is a tension between creative

---

14   An exception is Lochman (1970b).

and 'vulgar' dialectics. To offer but a few examples, Marx could offer highly complex arguments concerning the fetishism of commodities, struggling to find a new level of analysis in which both real and unreal exist together in the commodity (Marx 1867, 81–94, 1890, 70–82;[15] Boer 2011b), but he could also observe that in the earlier stages of human existence the 'religious' was a reflection or 'reflex [*Wiederschein*] of the real world' (Marx 1867a, 90, 1867b, 48), indeed that the 'origin of history' is found in nothing less than 'vulgar *material* production [groß-*materiellen* Produktion]' (Marx and Engels 1845a, 150, 1845b, 159). The tension I am emphasising is expressed best by two quotations, the first from 1859: 'It is not the consciousness of men that determines their existence, but their social existence that determines their consciousness' (Marx 1859a, 263, 1859b, 9). The second is from none other than the famous introduction to his critique of Hegel in 1844: ' theory also becomes a material force as soon as it has gripped [*ergreift*] the masses' (Marx 1844a, 182, 1844b, 177).

The question arises whether Christianity can be understood in light of this particular dialectical tension. I think less of the pertinent criticisms of Christianity's more egregious moments of reaction and outright despotism, from internal persecution through to the recent revelations concerning systemic sexual abuse, nor even of the many moments of purely progressive and revolutionary action (more of this question later). Instead, is it possible to assess religion in terms of both a reflex or reflection of the real world and as a genuine material force that grips the masses? Perhaps it may be put in terms of so much of Christian thought and practice that does nothing more than manifest human constructions, while at one and the same time acknowledging a 'spiritual reserve'. Indeed, they would seem to be part of the same phenomenon, impossible to separate without destroying Christianity itself. And by 'spiritual reserve' I mean the radical transcendence that so often goes hand-in-hand with radical critique of the world as it is, unfolding in terms of alternative communities and revolutionary movements (as I have discussed in earlier chapters). But it also means material, historical effect, a 'gripping of the masses' that I proposed in my treatment of early Christian communism. The sheer uncertainty concerning historical verifiability of this communism, let alone the reality of texts with historical force, meant that this too would come to realisation in concrete terms time and again.

---

15   I have cited the third edition of *Capital* here, since it contains the fully revised argument concerning fetishism and is the basis of the English translation. The first edition of 1867 has a relatively undeveloped argument over fewer pages (1867b), 44–51.

3   To Now

As I mentioned earlier, the overwhelming focus of nearly all the participants in the dialogue was on the writings of the young or 'humanistic' Marx. Triggered by the 1932 publications of key texts, they felt they had found a version of Marx that offered more than the careful scientific investigations of political economy, let alone the grand overviews provided in the standard works by Engels read by all Marxists of subsequent generations – *Anti-Dühring* and the later published *Dialectics of Nature* (Engels 1877–78a, 1877–78b, 1873–82a, 1873–82b). This Marx also suited the existential tenor of the times (Gardavský 1973), with some even seeing the renewal of Marxism comparable to the renewals underway in many of the Christian churches (Raines and Dean 1970). My treatment of *praxis* was already part of this concern, but here I seek – after identifying some of the main features – to reinterpret the debate in terms of the more basic concern over human nature. In this light, the discussion over 'alienation' gains another purchase in terms of the need for a robust doctrine of evil.

3.1   *Human Nature*

Above all, the humanistic Marx seemed to provide significant possibilities for considering religious, if not metaphysical questions (Dean 1972). For instance, the perceived break with ontological materialism enabled a more 'regional materialism' that would see 'theology' as the hope that injustice will not have the last word (Siebert 1977a, 1977b). Others suggested that religion would be needed for any form of humanisation, which may be understood as the process of developing human beings from what they are to what they ought to be (Borchert 1971, 1131, 1133). While this form of Marxism may value the dignity of human beings,[16] its focus on humanity as an end in itself misses the foundation of humanism as the 'identity of being and love in God' (Girardi 1968, 81). Theologians were not the only ones making such points: For Machovec (1980, 14) Christianity and especially the Bible may offer something 'spiritual', in terms of the 'search for the meaning of life', that moves beyond the satisfaction of socio-economic needs.[17]

---

16   Although, as Garaudy warns (1970, 147), Marx 'does not postulate a subject who creates the world, in the Hegelian way, nor a subject who maintains the relations with the object which were conceived by Cartesian dualism. Marx, on the contrary, emphasises the constant reciprocal action' between human beings and beings found in nature.

17   Not all took this approach. For example, Kirk (1976a, 1976b) suggests that the very humanism of the early Marx provides the seeds of the 'titanic' or 'faustian' nature of Marxism, with its resolute focus on human endeavour, leading to hubris, domination, repression and the Soviet system. In reply, only an ideal Christianity offers the true answer.

The problem with this focus is not merely its time-bound nature, but also the character of the material from Marx that provided much of its basis. Specifically, the vision of communism was significantly romanticised (Garaudy, Rahner, and Metz 1967, 78–80; Girardi 1968, 24; Banks 1974, 140), with its overcoming of social and individual bifurcations in a vision of human wholeness, or what Marx called 'human emancipation [*menschliche Emanzipation*]' (Marx 1844f, 168, 1844g, 163, see also Marx 1844a, 187, 1844b, 182–83; Leopold 2007, 183–277). This early approach – well before the 'dictatorship of the proletariat' – is best captured in Marx's image of 'communist society', which 'regulates the general production and thus makes it possible for me to do one thing today and another tomorrow, to hunt in the morning, fish in the afternoon, rear cattle in the evening, criticise after dinner, just as I have a mind, without ever becoming hunter, fisherman, herdsman or critic' (Marx and Engels 1845–46a, 47, 1845–46b, 33). As Harding points out, this image – with touches of 'agrarian anti-industrial socialism' – does not present one working as a 'collier, fitter, assembly-worker and salesman' (Harding 1984, 4).

In reply, let me recast this 'humanistic' question as one of human nature, hinted at by Marx's widespread use at the time of *Gattungswesen* and *Gattungsleben*, or 'species-essence' and 'species-life'. The key was not to identify an eternal human nature, but rather the transformation of this nature (Marcuse 1970, 7–9).[18] Marx and subsequent Marxists were very much concerned with this transformation of human nature, which was integral to the thorough shift from one mode of production to another. To use the terminology I developed in Chapter 6, this may be called a Pelagian approach (Garaudy 1970, 112), mediated through the European Enlightenment's assertion of the inherent goodness of (some) human beings. Given the opportunity, workers and farmers would enthusiastically throw themselves into creating a new society. While Marx's use of 'species-being', 'species-life' and 'species-essence' often suggests that productive and collective labour is its true, non-alienated form, he also argues that the 'species-being' postulated by the political economists and based on the division of labour is actually an alienated 'species-being' that requires transformation (Marx 1844c, 317, 1844d, 309, 1844e, 429).[19] At this level, there is

---

18   In the 1970s, Stromberg (1979) observes that the search for a more robust Marxist theory of human nature remained rather thin and abstract, although it was one of most exciting frontiers that had opened. Had he considered some of the developments in the Soviet Union (see below), he may have found a more concrete and profound theoretical elaboration on this score.

19   Geras's argument (1983) misses the fact that Marx sought a transformation of human nature. It is worth noting that in his earlier writings Stalin too adhered to this position: 'it is obvious that free and comradely labour should result in an equally comradely, and

an obvious connection with theology. As I pointed out earlier, the Latin tradition turned on the debate between Augustine and Pelagius, but underlying this debate and the many variations since is the underlying assumption not that human nature is eternal, but that it seeks transformation.[20]

3.2   Alienation

With this recasting in mind, let me turn to the question of alienation, which vexed the dialogue partners. Based on Marx's 1844 manuscripts (Lash 1981, 170–76), most were quick to point out that Marx took Feuerbach's position a significant step further, arguing that religion arose as a response to alienating socio-economic conditions (fourth thesis on Feuerbach), but that at times religion too could be alienating.[21] Much of the debate over alienation feels very 1960s, with its existentialist concerns that made Marx's early and romanticised vision of non-alienated existence – as reuniting the broken and split parts of human existence as 'human emancipation' (see above) – rather appealing. That Marx was largely to dispense later with the terminology of alienation[22] for more concrete terms did not prevent the theological participants learning much in terms of reassessing Christian understandings of sin and evil, which had suffered under the individualising drive of liberalism and the restriction to 'purely' religious matters in terms of one's relationship with God (Garaudy 1970, 117–18). So we find a renewed awareness of structural and collective sin, embodied in institutions, politics and economic systems (Gutiérrez 1969; Metz 1977; Packull 1977b, 69; Lash 1981, 170–76). On occasion, we encounter an effort to connect Marx's deployment of fetishism – for his analyses of money, labour, capital, if not the whole socio-economic system – with the biblical critique of

---

complete, satisfaction of all needs in the future socialist society' (Stalin 1906–1907a, 338, 1906–1907b, 336).

20   The Greek speaking – or Eastern Orthodox – tradition has the same basic concern, although it seeks a mediation between what it saw as two extremes. On the one hand, one cannot do anything to earn salvation, for it is a gift from God; on the other hand, the gift needs to be accepted by a person, which is where human action comes into play. While it may be refused (God does not enforce salvation), the focus was on God and human beings working together – *synergeia* – to the end that the entire human being, in terms of will and act, conforms to the divine (Lossky 1978, 73, 86).

21   Except for Girardi (1968, 18–21), who insisted that Marx consistently saw religion itself as alienating. A couple of the more wayward proposals include Lischer's suggestion (1973) that Marx's approach – in terms of economic concupiscence, labour and community – owes certain analogies to a Lutheran approach to evil and sin, and Lobkowicz's hypothesis (1967b, 328) that Marxism (via Hegel and Feuerbach) owes its position to Luther's incarnational self-emptying.

22   Despite Israel's effort (1971) to see alienation as a continuing theme in Marx's work.

idolatry (Suda 1978; Lash 1981, 180–86). Later Latin American liberation theologians were also keen on the connection, stressing that the economic realities of foreign debt, as well as the worship of gross domestic product, growth and the need for national account balances were elements of a destructive cult with death-dealing idols – let alone the neo-classical economic theories that explain, justify and support such idols (Assmann and Hinkelammert 1989; Hinkelammert 1986; Dussell 1993, 2001). Despite the gains, the problem is that they revert Marx's approach, in which the older category of idolatry – with its dogma, institutions and clergy – was sublated within the newer idea of fetishism. That category could only become an entirely new tool of analysis through this *Aufhebung*, enabling Marx's analysis of capital itself as *Kapitalfetisch* (Boer 2011b).

More significant was the discussion over the continuation of alienation under socialism. If one assumes the early Marx's assumption that with the overcoming of socio-economic misery, alienation would disappear, then one is faced with this problem: how do we understand the continuation of alienation, if not exploitation, under socialism and indeed communism? Further, how does one understand the persistence of religion under socialism in power? One may take the position that the old forms had not yet fully been overcome and replaced, but this approach will hold only for a time. Or one may argue that education was the key to overcoming the residues of religion, as happened in the Soviet Union (Boer 2013a, 10–13). While the second approach was more successful than is often assumed, the more substantial question is whether some forms of alienation simply cannot be overcome through creative social reconstruction. It was precisely at the Salzburg conference in 1965 that Johann Baptist Metz first raised this question, proposing that core theological doctrines concerning sin, guilt and evil have a distinct place in understanding this condition (Norris 1974, 25–39). Indeed, can sinful and alienated human beings construct any form of fulfilled society? For a theologian, the obvious point is that human beings can never achieve this level of social existence without some outside assistance, but the argument risks assuming an eternal and 'fallen' human nature.

In contrast to Metz, I find that Lochman's insight goes further, for he was actually practicing theology in the context of socialism in power (Czechoslovakia). He points out that some of the most dehumanising conditions of life had indeed been overcome under socialism, with the elimination of poverty, the resultant minimal differences in economic status, the lifting up of the working class as leaders and thereby involvement in political and social life, and the free national healthcare and education available to all. He also observes that socialism is by no means perfect, indeed that it 'poses some new and rather serious questions' (Lochman 1970b, 15, 1970a), specifically elements of alienation that continue, if not new forms of dehumanisation. Here he focuses on the monopoly of power, embodied in the dictatorship of the proletariat. Tellingly, he does not condemn this reality, refusing to moralise, since it is a 'necessity of the post-revolutionary order in its first stage' (Lochman 1970b, 16). With the mention of this initial stage, Lochman deploys what had become a common position concerning the stages of socialism and communism,[23] arguing that the next stage required a move past the dictatorship of the proletariat into a mature socialism in which everyone had a say and greater democratisation would take place. Here a theological contribution can be made, with an emphasis on the prophetic tradition, the Exodus and the humanising and demythologising challenge of Jesus of Nazareth. For Lochman, theologians – even of his Reformed background – have a distinct contribution to make to constructing socialism. I find particular value in Lochman's approach, since it did so from within socialist construction, seeking to be part of its ongoing project – too rare a feature of the dialogue as a whole.

Closely related is the question of the doctrine of evil, a topic only touched upon by a few participants. As I mentioned, Marxism had tended to rely on an Enlightenment inspired assumption concerning the inherent goodness of human beings, with a distinct dose of Pelagian good works. Missing was a robust materialist doctrine of good and evil. What the dialogue participants missed was that the beginnings of such a doctrine appeared in the Soviet Union in the 1930s – a period off limits for the participants given their assumptions about the Soviet Union. If we consider this period more carefully, we find that it was one of the most creative and turbulent periods in the twentieth century. It was triggered by the socialist offensive, with its twin projects of rapid industrialisation and collectivisation that turned the Soviet Union into an economic superpower.[24] This decade was full of affirmative action projects with national minorities, massive gains in the provision of the first 'domestic' or socialist welfare state, an astonishingly progressive constitution, but it was also a time of plots, purges, violence and disruption. Many were its enthusiastic supporters, with the search for the first signs of the new Soviet man and woman (Stakhanovism) but many too were those who were unsettled, dragging their feet and

---

23   The argument for the stages of socialism and communism, with the possibility of further stages within socialism itself, was first developed by Lenin in his exegesis of Marx's brief comments on the initial and further stage of communism in 'Critique of the Gotha Programme' (Marx 1875a, 1875b; Lenin 1917a, 472–79, 1917b, 95–102). Notably, Marx does not specify that there would be only two stages.

24   The material here summarises a long and detailed argument I have made elsewhere (Boer 2017b, 65–114).

engaging in outright and often hostile opposition. In this situation, the question of human nature loomed large, with good and evil at the forefront. This was not merely in terms of the evil of outward opponents, but the slow and often painful awareness that each social body and each individual bore an intense opposition of good and evil within themselves. The two were inescapably present, entwined within the collective itself and within each individual. It meant that any policy of reconstruction needed to take this new awareness into account.

3.3   *Prometheus and the Future*

Two final features of the dialogue – Promethean protest and the future – may be considered together. The context of the 1960s was of social movement and protest, at least in the parts of the world that mattered most to the participants. Communist parties began to make statements acknowledging radical potentials within religion. For example, the Italian Communist Party acknowledged at its tenth congress in 1962 that the 'religious conscience' may provide a 'stimulus with regard to the dramatic problems of the contemporary world' (Girardi 1968, 49, 1988, 135). And Maurice Thorez, in extending the 'outstretched hand' of the French Communist Party to the church, observed: 'Christianity's progressive role appears in the effort to realize charity and solidarity, in the attempt to bring about fairer and more peaceable relationships ... in the concern of religious communities – communist groupings in intention, in fact, and in action – which assumed the mission of preserving, developing and transmitting to future ages the sum total of human knowledge and artistic treasures of the past' (Garaudy, Rahner, and Metz 1967, 74; see further Murphy 1974).

The question remained as to how this awareness might be developed theoretically. The key was provided by the Czech theologian Jan Lochman, in an essay (and lecture) published on a number of occasions (Lochman 1972, 1978, 1985).[25] For Lochman, Prometheus becomes the 'great saint' of the Marxist tradition, drawing initially from Marx's invocation of the Greek god in his earliest writings, especially his doctoral thesis: 'Prometheus is the most eminent saint and martyr in the philosophical calendar' (Marx 1841a, 31, 1841b, 15). The importance for Marx lay in Prometheus's rebellion against the other gods, bringing fire, houses and human settlements; in his martyrdom, suffering in chains for his rebellion; and in his unbroken spirit. But not only for Marx, since this became the symbol of the proletarian struggle itself. Yet, Lochman's real question is whether Prometheus also has a place in the Christian calendar, alongside not

---

25   Although others have commented on Prometheus, I focus on Lochman's statement (Bentley 1982, 108–14; Vereš 1985).

merely the other saints, but alongside Christ. Instead of an either/or, Lochman seeks a both/and situation.

Ostracised from the Greek tradition, Prometheus is more at home in the biblical tradition on three counts: the doctrines of God, evil, and grace and justification. To begin with, Lochman distinguishes (too sharply) between the oppressive Zeus-Prometheus relationship and the God-human relationship in the Bible. He would like to see an engaged God, making human beings in God's image to become the 'creative subject of history', involved in 'soteriological participation' and not 'ontological separation' (Lochman 1978, 245, 246). But he misses the fact that both elements also appear in the Bible and the Christian theological tradition. Too easy it is to offload all that is undesirable onto another. Fortunately, on the question of evil he acknowledges a 'Promethean' element within the Bible, in which hubris – the effort to intrude into the divine realm – appears (Tower of Babel). Here he prefers to identify a more neglected element of the tradition, which is the sin of omission, of failing to participate in the liberating project and remaining comfortable with the way the world is. For this a 'Marxist Promethean Christology' is a genuine correction. On the third question – grace and justification – Lochman's Reformed heritage comes to the fore. Indebted as it is to the Augustinian emphasis on God's primacy in salvation, he gives it a distinct Reformed reinterpretation. The risk of '*sola fide – sola gratia*' is that one may emphasise the '*sola*' and sit back waiting for God to act without bothering to act oneself (hence the Marxist suspicion of its use for reactionary purposes). By contrast, the emphasis of Luther and especially Calvin is that this radical primacy of grace leads not to quietism but to even greater engagement in works. On this score, Prometheus reminds the Reformed tradition of its own emphasis. I would add that the history of Christian communism, especially in its revolutionary dimensions, emphasises precisely the radical transcendence of the divine, so much so that one cannot avoid acting in response. From Thomas Müntzer to Karl Barth, from the Peasants revolution to Barth's lifelong socialism (so much so that he spoke out in support of the Soviet Union[26]), the emphasis on grace and transcendence led them to such positions.

---

26   Most sharply expressed in the following from 1949: 'It would be quite absurd to mention in the same breath the philosophy of Marxism and the "ideology" of the Third Reich, to mention a man of the stature of Joseph Stalin in the same breath as such charlatans as Hitler, Göring, Hess, Goebbels, Himmler, Ribbentrop, Rosenberg, Streicher, etc. What has been tackled in Soviet Russia – albeit with very dirty and bloody hands and in a way that rightly shocks us – is, after all, a constructive idea, the solution of a problem which is a serious and burning problem for us as well, and which we with our clean hands have not yet tackled anything like energetically enough: the social problem' (Barth 1954, 123).

Nonetheless, Lochman does not acquiesce to a full integration of Promethean Marxism within theology, seeking instead a dialectical tension between the traditions. While Christianity so often needs to be 'demythologised' due to its tendency to valorise reactionary and oppressive structures, so too does Promethean Marxism, which readily runs the danger of producing new mythologies of human labour, revolution and socialist construction. The answer for Lochman is ultimately a Reformed one, focusing on transcendence and grace as a way to unburden the Christian tradition of its counter-revolutionary predilection and to release human beings from the soteriological burden, thereby freeing them for creative action. Other theological traditions may quibble with this move, but the more interesting result is a dialectical tension: both Marxism and Christianity need to engage in mutual criticism and self-criticism, supporting each other and calling out the dangers to which each is prone (see also Garaudy 1970, 155).[27]

All of which brings me to the question of the future, a theme that runs through all of the material. They share the sense that such a future is not predetermined, but unfinished, open-ended and capable of the new (Dean 1972, 88).[28] Obviously, the emphasis on *praxis* as well as exploring the possibility of a common project entails that one is working towards such a project, if not that the project itself is incomplete. But I would like to take a slightly different line here and draw upon a number of the Protestant theologians who were at various times engaged in the dialogue. At this time, they began to develop a form of 'proleptic' theology, which entailed a sense of the future that is 'creatively present to all the temporal things that precede this future' (Pannenberg 1991–93, vol. 3, 531). It is neither pushed into a distant future, nor is it realised fully in the present. Instead, the present is understood in terms of prolepsis, in which events happen 'before their time' (Pannenberg 1991–93, vol. 3, 580–646;

Surprisingly, there are few recent works that deal with Barth's socialism (Rumscheidt 2001; Boer 2002). The classic statement is by Marquardt (1972).

27   In doing so, he focuses not so much on the marginal dimensions of theology – as much of the Christian communist tradition that I have explored – but on its core messages. The biblical God of creation, Exodus, Jesus Christ, grace and transcendence are liberating, albeit there is always the danger that they may side with reaction and oppression (see also D. Boer 2015).

28   Surprisingly, there are only a few efforts to suggest that Marx's historical schema relies on religion in some way, whether crude versions of secularised religion to the point of the Marxist-Leninist 'Church' (Fessard 1967), the standard line in terms of form (Girardi 1968, 21) or perhaps parallelism (Kirk 1976b, 85–86; Masani 1979). Only Comstock (1976) offers a more sophisticated approach based on an ambivalence in Marx's earlier and later methods. The reason for not dealing with this issue here is that I have dealt with it at length in Chapter 7.

Moltmann 1965, 1999). Or as Rahner puts it, if the very name of 'God' means the absolute future of the world and of human beings, then we already move 'within it' in a way that is neither fulfilled nor still outstanding (Garaudy, Rahner, and Metz 1967, 12). The eschatological future is 'the basis for the lasting essence of each creature that finds its manifestation already in the allotted duration of its life and yet will achieve its full manifestation only in the eschatological future'. Although we are still on the way to becoming ourselves, we are 'in some sense already the persons we shall be in the light of our eschatological future' (Pannenberg 1991–93, vol. 3, 603–4).

Interesting enough, but what is the source of this renewed emphasis on the constitutive eschatology of theology? The answer entails an inversion of a common narrative, in which Marxism in some sense 'secularises' the Christian narrative of 'salvation history', if not the 'messianism' of the Hebrew Bible (see Chapter 7). By contrast, as more than one participant observes clearly, the debt for this emphasis lies clearly with Ernst Bloch, especially his dual approach of a hermeneutics and philosophy of utopia as an extraordinary effort at the renewal of Marxism (Moltmann 1965, 1976; Lochman 1978; Bentley 1982, 79–97). Since I have written extensively on Bloch elsewhere (Boer 2007a, R. Boer 2009b, Boer 2013b, 2014d), I will not outline the details of his approach here. But it is clear that Bloch influenced these theological developments deeply indeed, so much so that they fed into the very fabric of the Marxist-Christian dialogue. We are faced with an intriguing situation, for the dialogue participants imply that the recovery of theological eschatology, with its resolute and definitive emphasis on God as a God of the future first and foremost, was actually the result of Marxism. In other words, this proleptic theology was clearly a theologising of and response to communism, as much in terms of its actual practice as its unrealised potential.

4   Conclusion: Reconsidering the Background

From time to time, I have hinted at the context of the Marxist-Christian dialogue, situated as it was in primarily a European context during the upheavals of the 1960s and 1970s. But I have held back in dealing with contextual issues more fully until now – for a distinct reason. Where the dialogue participants were explicit about the context, they mention the immediate events of Vatican II, the new developments in Protestant theology, anti-colonial struggles which were in many places coming to fruition (although the Chinese and Cuban revolutions barely rate a mention), as well as the threat of nuclear annihilation as a code for the Cold War (Garaudy, Rahner, and Metz 1967, 25–31, 72–74;

Garaudy et al. 1967, 7–8; Garaudy 1970, 21; Aptheker 1968, 95–97, 1970, 158). Missing from this list is the awareness that the anti-colonial struggles were so often fostered, in terms of logistics, education and arms, by the Soviet Union's anti-imperial struggles, if not the fact that the Russian Revolution itself had provided a longer impetus for the dialogues, leading to a situation where one third of the world was socialist (one can hardly imagine them taking place if Marx had remained an obscure thinker).

But my interest is drawn to a more immediate contextual matter, where the Soviet Union does have an obvious presence in the debates. The assumed narrative for many of the participants was that the dialogue's possibility from the Marxist side was enabled by the end of the Stalin era and the 'revelations' of Khrushchev's 'secret speech' of 1956.[29] With an end to the stifling repressions, openness ensued, leading to engagement, discussion and dialogue, only to come to an end when Brezhnev ordered tanks to end the 'Prague Spring' in 1968 (Bentley 1982, 151–55). This narrative may be supported by the fact that some of the Marxist participants in Czechoslovakia, such as Machovec and Gardavský, lost their teaching positions. Yet it makes little sense of actual developments. To the point, it was precisely Khrushchev who reinstated many of the repressions of earlier days in the Soviet Union. He did this in response to the last ten years of Stalin's period, which were the most open in the history of the Soviet Union. To understand this situation, we need to go back to the 1936 'Stalin' Constitution: article 124 makes it clear that citizens had freedom of religious worship and of anti-religious propaganda. This was not mere rhetoric, as the later patriarch, Sergei, knew well. He petitioned the government to hold to the constitution, having in 1927 already issued a statement seeking rapprochement between the communists and the church. Now he requested permission to reopen churches, admit openly religious people to regular jobs, even suggesting that religious candidates could run for elections (as they did in 1937). Stalin eventually responded to the church's persistence, not least because he knew the church very well given his years of theological training (1895–1899). On 5 September of 1943, Stalin met with church leaders and agreed to a historic compact (Miner 2003). In return for support in the Great Patriotic War that eventually defeated Hitler, Stalin allowed the reopening of thousands of churches, as well as theological colleges and monasteries, the release of imprisoned clergy, and the re-establishment of the church's leadership hierarchy. Three days later, Sergei was elected patriarch, with the official service taking place on 12 September. In light of his intimate knowledge of the church, Stalin

---

29   For an assessment of the political motivations of this speech, its errors and effects, see
      Losurdo (2008) and Furr (2011).

was fully aware of the benefits of the compact, which was much deeper than moral support and propaganda. Indeed, Sergei had already called on all citizens of the Soviet Union to support the fight against Hitler, providing funds for specific units in the Red Army. Notably, this agreement remained in place until Stalin's death in 1953. Only then did the old repressions return.[30]

So let me make the following proposal: the period of 1943–1953 in the Soviet Union marked the culmination of a rather different but even more intriguing form of the Marxist-Christian dialogue, with active and wily participation from both sides. Even more, this period may well have had a belated effect elsewhere, for the dialogue that emerged further west, in Europe, began little more than a decade later. That Stalin was mourned throughout the world on his death and that theologians like Karl Barth could find repulsive the early moves to demonise Stalin by the *reductio ad Hitlerum* indicate that the effect of this earlier period may not have been merely subconscious.

---

30   For a detailed analysis of these developments, in which the church leaders saw Stalin as 'divinely appointed', see Boer (2018).

CHAPTER 9

Althusser and the Possibility of Religious Revolution

An assumed position in the Marxist-Christian dialogue is that Marxists and Christians were two distinct groups. One was either a Marxist or a Christian, but not both.[1] While this is an understandable assumption given Cold War oppositions, it is also rather curious, especially since Marxist Christians were present and did engage in dialogue, even if it was at times an internal debate.[2] Engels is the most obvious example, but in this group we also find Terry Eagleton in his days with the magazine *Slant*, if not also more recently a good number of Cuban communists, Louis Althusser and a relatively unknown Australian, Farnham Maynard. In this and the next chapter, I focus on Althusser and Maynard.

In exploring the internal dialogue and tensions within Althusser, I focus on his effort – albeit not without some problems – to argue that a revolution in personal religious life is analogous to a socialist revolution. The key text is one written in 1948, 'A Matter of Fact', which I will exegete carefully in what follows. Here we find a young man simultaneously in the Roman Catholic Church and the French Communist Party.[3] While he had grown up in the former and would soon leave it, he had only recently joined the party. So the argument of 'A Matter of Fact' seeks to keep the two together, if only for a brief time. It was originally published in February 1949 as the lead article in the tenth *cahier* of the *Jeunesse de l'Église*, a complex group that sought renewal in the French Roman Catholic Church in the immediate post-war era. The theme of that issue was '*l'Évangile captif*', which sought to ask the question: Has the Good News been announced to the men of our day? Althusser reiterates the theme throughout the article, at times in the form of the 'Word', a word that is simultaneously the spoken word of the Gospel, the message it contains, and Jesus himself. As is already characteristic of Althusser's thought, his essay contains arresting proposals coupled with significant limitations. In what follows, I note the latter as

---

1 I have found only one acknowledgment that someone could be both a Christian and a Marxist (Raines and Dean 1970, xiv).
2 Although the very idea of 'believing' in Marxism is a distinctly European idea with obvious religious heritage.
3 For biographical detail, see Boutang (1992).

I work carefully through his text, but ultimately I am interested in the way he seeks to develop a viable and radical form of religion – as far as he understood it – within a Marxist framework.[4]

1   Trapped in the Past

Less time may be spent on Althusser's diagnosis – the medical analogy is his – of the condition of the Roman Catholic Church.[5] For Althusser, this sick church is a relic of a world that has passed, yet it continues to ground itself in this world. More specifically, it is caught in a time warp: it holds to a feudal ideological system in the context of a tottering capitalism. How can it manage to survive in such a situation? He offers three interrelated levels of analysis: it rests upon a hybrid and out-dated socio-economic base;[6] its ideology is trapped in the distant past; and its politics are overwhelmingly reactionary. His analysis here is still within a more orthodox Marxist framework, seeking to find the cause and origin of his church's malaise in its material and ideological conditions. (Later, of course, he would develop his argument for the semi-autonomy of each level or zone, in which the 'last instance' of the economic never comes (Althusser 1977, 113, 1996, 113).[7])

In a little more detail: the Roman Catholic Church's social and economic situation is mixed, with some still living in semi-feudal structures or at least limited capitalist industrialisation. His purview includes only those parts of the world that are majority Roman Catholic, such as South America, Canada, Ireland, Spain, Southern Italy and Central Europe. But why is Canada included in such a list? Is it perhaps because of Quebec, a significant pocket of Francophone Roman Catholicism in an otherwise largely Protestant country? Or it due to Althusser's characteristic rush during his manic periods, when the checking of facts fell victim to the theoretical push? We will never know, for

---

4 Critical work on Althusser's earlier theological writings is alarmingly thin, although this has been corrected somewhat by a volume edited by Agon Hamza (2016), which includes an early and brief piece by Breton (1997). See also my earlier study of Althusser (Boer 2007a, 107–62).
5 Although he writes of 'the church', his focus is clearly the Roman Catholic Church, especially in France.
6 Althusser does not raise the possibility that since the church was established before capitalism, it cannot be entirely absorbed by it – or indeed that it will outlive capitalism.
7 The crucial text reads: 'In History, these instances, the superstructures, etc. – are never seen to step respectfully aside when their work is done or, when the Time comes, as his pure phenomena, to scatter before His Majesty the Economy as he strides along the royal road of the Dialectic. From the first moment to the last, the lonely hour of the "last instance" never comes'.

he gives no reasons for such an inclusion. Yet, these semi-feudal structures sit cheek by jowl with the parts of the world that have undergone a thorough bourgeois revolution and where the bourgeoisie's initial opposition to the church has settled into a comfortable relation with the Roman Catholic Church. In other words, in France, Italy, Belgium and the United States this church has made its peace with bourgeois capitalism. The upshot is that this church as a whole functions within a mixed infrastructure, a feudal-capitalist hybrid that is both past and passing. With that note – that capitalism itself is crumbling – one cannot help being struck by an undercurrent of optimism in the way Althusser frames his argument. The argument has a whole may seem to cast a pessimistic note, yet a little beneath the surface a deeper optimism emerges. His hopefulness may be read as a signal of the time of writing – immediately after the devastation of Second World War. At that moment, the USSR under Stalin had defeated fascist Germany, socialist revolutions had swept through Eastern Europe, anti-colonial struggles were gaining momentum, and the Chinese revolution was on the verge of success. Althusser had every reason for this quiet optimism.

The Roman Catholic Church's social and economic base may have been an increasingly outmoded hybrid, but its ideological situation was even more backward. Its theology was decidedly feudal, with its Augustinian and Thomistic forms that rely upon Platonic and Aristotelian foundations. Its positions may have been adjusted opportunistically from time to time in the face of the more glaring challenges, but they are not to be questioned. Althusser's point is not merely that a system first developed in the thirteenth century is out-dated, but also that it is theologically suspect: it has replaced a God who addresses human beings with a mere concept. God has become an abstraction that leaves people cold.

All the same, abstractions and ideological systems cannot sustain themselves in thin air. So now we come back to a materialist argument that is simultaneously theological. Thus, Thomistic theology, mediated through Augustine, could survive because of the vestiges of feudalism that are embodied not only in the social and economic situation of some places on the globe, but above all in this church. Althusser is both astounded and fully aware that the Roman Catholic Church is able to keep its professionals and many members cocooned in an institution where their way of life and set of assumptions continues to have validity for them. Concepts such as natural law and Thomistic theoretical hierarchies justify, protect, and foster an institution that coddles them from the cradle to the grave. As so often happens with such an institution, its members have long forgotten the reason they are part of the church (if ever they knew). Faith in God has been replaced by faith in the institution itself, which must be maintained at all costs: 'the modern Church is no longer at home in our times, and the vast majority of the faithful are in the Church for reasons that are not really of the Church' (Althusser 1997, 186, 1994, 263).

This situation, with a hybrid, out-dated base and a conservative ideology, leads the church to an overwhelmingly reactionary political position. Althusser cites the examples of explicit arrangements with fascist governments – Italy, Spain, and Vichy France – as well as the tacit agreement with the Nazis in Germany. In the immediate hindsight of the late 1940s, these agreements are the most obvious. But he also mentions the papal encyclicals that formed Roman Catholic 'Social Teaching'.[8] Even before the spate of collegial encyclicals from the Second Vatican Council,[9] it was clear to Althusser that the encyclicals were craven accommodations to medieval corporatism and liberal reformism. Apart from mild reprimands for the 'excesses' and 'abuses' of economic exploitation, they firmly reject any form of socialism and liberation movements. In sum, the Roman Catholic Church maintains 'a deep, compromising commitment to world-wide reaction, and is struggling alongside international capitalism against the forces of the working class and the advent of socialism' (Althusser 1997, 191, 1994, 269). No wonder, then, that this church is no longer able to preach the 'good news' to people of 'our time'.

2   Sources of Hope

Despite the grim assessment of his beloved church, beneath Althusser's essay runs a deep current of hope. He still believes that this church may well be able to turn itself around and speak the good news once more. His proposed solution is a bravura attempt to connect socialist revolution with spiritual transformation, to link the collective with the personal. The church may soon face the objective realities of history, as socialist revolution sweeps even into France. In this wider context, the Roman Catholic Church cannot avoid being transformed – or so Althusser hopes. Concomitant with that social

---

8   At the time of Althusser's writing, only *Rerum Novarum* (1891) and *Quadragesimo Anno* (1931) had appeared, but it is already clear that they responded to periods of social unrest and the appeal of socialism.

9   Althusser would later see *Mater et Magistra* (1961), *Pacem in Terris* (1963), the conciliar encyclicals *Dignitatis Humanae* and *Gaudiem et Spes* (1965), *Populorum Progessio* (1967), *Octogesima Adveniens* (1971), *Laborem Exercens* (1981), and *Solicitudo Rei Socialis* (1987). After his death and in the context of the destruction of communist governments in Eastern Europe, there appeared *Centesimus Annus* (1991), *Evangelium Vitae* (1995) and *Deus Caritas Est* (2005). See further Boer (2014b).

and institutional upheaval, he proposes a personal spiritual revolution in which one may be able to reappropriate an authentic religious life. Althusser juxtaposes the two forms of revolution with one another, seeking by verbal connection to place them within the same process. Yet, it soon becomes clear that he is really proposing an analogy between social and spiritual revolution. Obviously, such an analogy faces a number of problems, which I broach in a moment, but it may also be read as an effort to extend Marxist approaches to revolution so that they include the religious and the spiritual.

2.1   *From Social Revolution ...*

'The social liberation of the church' – this subtitle of the first part of Althusser's proposed solution is a little misleading. What he really proposes is a socialist revolution in which the church is drawn into the larger dynamics of transformation. And the agents of such revolution should come from the working class movement, with whom the faithful of the church should join as part of a politics of alliance. Althusser already foreshadows this argument at an earlier moment in his essay, where he writes:

> We have to trace matters back to these concrete structures in order to understand the tenacity of obsolete concepts in religious ideology. More-over, we have to expose these structures in order to help bring them to their appointed end, and to help the men who are brought up in them overcome them and become contemporary with their times.
>
> ALTHUSSER 1997, 189, 1994, 266

Initially, an echo of Marx's fourth thesis on Feuerbach seems to bounce between the words of this passage (Marx 1845a, 4, 1845b, 6). For Marx, of course, Feuer-bach was still too concerned with religion, which lifts itself up from its secular basis and gains an independent existence in the heavens. In response, what is needed is an analysis of the causes of this alienated religious situation, and these causes may be found in the strife-ridden contradictions of the worldly basis of religion. 'The latter must', writes Marx, 'itself be both understood in its contradiction and revolutionised in practice'. Is this not Althusser's approach, one that he draws from Marx? Let us assume an affirmative answer to this question for a few moments, before drawing out a number of tensions with Marx's canonical approach.

At one level, the whole tenor of Althusser's argument has been mov-ing towards 'the real means required for the Church's social emancipation' (Althusser 1997, 193, 1994, 272). Any substantial liberation must take place at an infrastructural level, at the hands of the workers' movement. At the historical conjunction in which he writes, this movement is an objective force, opposed to capitalism and the vestiges of feudalism. Only in this way is real transformation possible; thus, the best option for anyone who cares about the church is to join this movement. Not only is Althusser clearly swayed by the optimism that comes from the sense that 'history is on our side', but he also proposes what may be called a politics of alliance. Progressive Christians should join the socialist movement, not for expedient or strategic reasons, but for the simple reason that they share the same political assumptions: 'the struggle for the social emancipation of the Church is inseparable from the proletariat's present struggle for human emancipation' (Althusser 1997, 194, 1994, 273). This argument is by no means new, although Althusser seems to feel that it is. At this point, we come across the first of a series of lapses in historical awareness. If he had cast a glance at the history of the socialist movement, Althusser would have found that Marx and Engels had urged that religious commitment is not a bar to membership of the First International.[10] Further, this approach to religion was consolidated in the freedom of conscience clause in the platform of the Second International. Indeed, they argued that even a priest may join the socialist movement.[11] As long as a believer agrees to the party platform, sharing the aims of the working class movement, then he or she is welcome to join. In fact, many had been doing so, especially during the period of the Second International.

Thus far, I have assumed for the sake of analysis that Althusser follows Marx's approach to social revolution, according to which the focus must be on analysing and transforming the base for any substantial results. Soon enough Althusser begins to move beyond – or rather, expand – Marx. The first hint is in his curious observation that the economic, social and even familial structures which need to be revolutionised in practice belong 'to worlds that our period has consigned irrevocably to the past' (Althusser 1997, 189, 1994, 266). Why propose a social revolution if history has consigned such structures to the past? Or rather, why revolution when evolution – the unfolding of history – would be sufficient? All one needs is a little more patience and the whole edifice will crumble into the dust of ages already gone. On this matter at least, Althusser is able to escape the tension he has created, for he has already shown that the Roman Catholic Church has a peculiar tenacity in terms of both its base and

---

10   Marx and Engels faced pressure, on one side, from the anarchists who wanted to make atheism part of the party platform, and, on the other, from opponents who stated that atheism was compulsory in the First International. Their response was to insist that atheism is not compulsory for party membership (Marx 1868, 208; Engels 1871a, 608, 1871b, 28).

11   The *Erfurt Program* of 1891 states: 'Declaration that religion is a private matter [*Erklärung der Religion zur Privatsache*]' (SPD 1891a, 3, 1891b, 3).

superstructure. Yet, his argument does raise the curious situation of a call for social revolution directed at an obsolete institution.

This hint of a tension with Marx's own approach becomes a full-blooded difference on the question of the continued validity of religion. Marx's main argument was that religion itself would dissipate when the alienating social and economic basis that led to religion had been revolutionised – hence the absence of any need for a direct opposition to religion, since religion is a secondary phenomenon. By contrast, Althusser seeks to hold onto the possibility that religion too may be transformed in a revolutionary process. Yet, he develops that possibility not through any direct confrontation with Marx, but through subtle modifications of what seem initially to be conventional Marxist statements. Let me focus on two such statements. The first reads:

> The 'theoretical reduction [*réduction théorique*]' of the present religious malaise has led us to identify religious alienation as its true origin. We need, then, to consider the means that can operate a practical 'reduction' of that origin by destroying it so as to transform it into its truth.
>
> ALTHUSSER 1997, 193, 1994, 272–73

Does this not read like a solid Marxist approach? Religious alienation requires a practical 'reduction' to its social and economic causes, so at to bring about both its destruction and its transformation (*Aufhebung*) into 'its truth'. But what is its truth? For Marx, truth entails a socialist revolution so that a new mode of production may be constructed in which alienation is no longer a reality. Given that alienation is the cause of religion, religion itself will disappear. For Althusser, the truth sought is quite different, for it is nothing less than the recovery of religious truth and authentic commitment. This argument will appear shortly, but already a signal appears with the crucial phrase, 'religious alienation as its true origin'. The crucial replacement of 'economic alienation' with 'religious alienation' alters the whole meaning of the passage I quoted above. This crucial shift becomes clearer a few sentences later, where Althusser writes: 'the reduction of collective religious alienation presupposes this political and social struggle as the condition without which no emancipation, not even religious emancipation, is conceivable' (Althusser 1997, 194, 1994, 273). On this occasion, the simple insertion of the phrase 'not even religious emancipation [*même religieuse*]' changes the whole sense of the sentence. Without that phrase, Althusser is in conventional Marxist territory; with it, emancipation is no longer emancipation from religion (among many other features), but emancipation of religion. He does not wish to abolish the church, but to save it.

These subtle shifts in Marxist approaches to religion and revolution set the scene for the final section of Althusser's essay – 'The Reconquest of Religious Life'. I turn to that section in a moment, but first I would like to note another dimension of the shifts I have identified. Here we find a prophetic anticipation of Althusser's own subsequent movement out of the church and away from his faith, or at least a movement from one faith to another. For this moment of prophecy, we need to backtrack a little in the essay, to the earlier discussion of philosophy and truth. Althusser asks: how does one find truth? The Roman Catholic Church may insist that it can appropriate truth by means of the contemplation of philosophy, but it is faced with the reality that truth is no longer found in such a fashion. Instead, the workers' movement has shown that truth is to be appropriated through action: 'our time has seen', writes Althusser, 'the advent of a new form of human existence in which humanity's appropriation of the truth ceases to be carried out in philosophical form [*la forme d'une philosophie*], that is, in the form of contemplation or reflection, in order to be carried out in the form of real activity' (Althusser 1997, 189, 1994, 267). The upshot is that philosophy becomes a collection of illusions, which fade once we have reclaimed integrated human action. Now Althusser is on slippery ground, which will eventually take him away from the church: the illusion is that one may find truth through contemplation, which is precisely how the church approaches truth. Or does he really mean that one may find *faith* through contemplation? The translation is easily made; indeed, it seems to me that Althusser is speaking as much about faith as he is about truth. In doing so, he entertains the possibility that faith itself is now open to question, precisely in the way that Marx argued for the abolition of philosophy in the face of action, which repossesses philosophy and turns it into something qualitatively different. Is Althusser laying the ground for a transition from one philosophy to another, from one faith to another? It seems so, particularly since he speaks of the form of philosophy rather than philosophy as such. Philosophy as contemplation (idealism) ceases to have validity, while philosophy as action (materialism) marks its distinct presence in his work. The transition from religious faith to Marxist faith – not without significant and contradictory traces of his earlier faith – would come later, signalled above all by the long 'Letter to Jean Lacroix' (Althusser 1997, 197–230, 1994, 277–326). However, since I have written on that dimension of these early writings elsewhere, and since my focus here is on Althusser's embryonic theology of liberation, I turn now to the final section of his essay.

2.2   ...to Spiritual Revolution

In the relatively few lines of this final section, Althusser outlines what is needed to reclaim the authentic spiritual life of the church. As I mentioned earlier, the revolution in question now focuses on personal spiritual life, in contrast to the distinctly political revolution he proposes in the previous section. Yet this spiritual life takes place within the church, so he cannot avoid speaking of the latter as well. In this respect, he hovers between reform and what may be called a 'foco theory' of revolution (with debts to the Cuban Revolution). Althusser is not always clear whether he is advocating reform per se of the church or whether he is able to keep his reform-oriented proposals under the rubric of revolution.

Earlier in his text, Althusser offers some small hints – forerunners perhaps – of what is to come. He speaks of a 'few active but isolated small groups', even of the 'most open-minded of the priests or the faithful' who oppose the church's passion for reactionary politics (Althusser 1997, 191, 192, 1994, 269, 271). These people return in the final proposal, now as 'small groups of activists' who are 'relatively small and terribly isolated' in the immensity of the Roman Catholic Church (Althusser 1997, 195, 1994, 274–75). Althusser does not shirk the reality that such groups exist on the margins, as 'pockets of humanity' that work hard at reducing the alienation of capitalism. With this phrase, it seems that Althusser is advocating a foco (*foquismo*) theory of revolution. This approach assumes that the dominant system is unable to be all-pervasive, that pockets exist in which one may create a new and unalienated life. If such enclaves are able to expand, providing models for others to follow and to which they will be attracted, then it may be possible to bring about a full-scale revolution. One example is the Cuban Revolution, with its small revolutionary groups in the jungle-covered mountains that eventually managed to take over the whole country (Guevara 1998). Yet, the Cuban Revolution itself drew from the more significant example of the Chinese revolution, which first established rural enclaves in the Jiangxi-Fujian Soviet and then – after the Long March – in Yan'an, only to succeed through struggle at conquering the cities and winning the revolution many years later (Snow 1937).

The problem is that the small progressive groups in Althusser's church are stricken with self-doubt. Their efforts at providing an alternative model for the Christian life, full of self-criticism, meets with silence and disinterest from those it seeks to persuade. They seem to have little hope of reforming the collective power of this church. For Althusser, the problem is that the objective conditions for a recovery of authentic religious life in this church do not yet exist. The social conditions for revolution, in which the church may be swept up, do exist, but not the spiritual conditions. However, between the lines of Althusser's text, another reason emerges. He hints at this reason with his comment that the groups in question fear that they may induce the church 'to threaten or repudiate them' (Althusser 1997, 195, 1994, 275). In other words, they are attempting to transform the church by example, by exhibiting a way of living the religious life that will show others what is possible. They are certainly not threatening to tear down the fabric of the church and construct a new church from the ruins of the old. This approach is clearly an option for reform from within, although it also reveals the internal logic of the claim to be 'catholic', to incorporate the whole of Christianity within this particular institution. If one assumes that there is no salvation outside the church, then one's only option is reform rather than revolution.

At this point, the historical thinness of Althusser's essay emerges once again. A wider view of the history of Christianity would have revealed to him a perpetual pattern of stagnation and efforts at reform, in the name of a return to the original form of Christianity (as it was constructed by the various groups attempting reform). From the monastic movement of the fourth century, through the Beguines and Beghards of the twelfth century, to the Reformation itself, each set out to reform an otiose institution. Some succeeded in reforming the church from within, as the many monastic orders of the Middle Ages illustrate; some were eventually closed down, as with the Beguines; and some found themselves leading a new movement and new church, as we find with the Reformation. Others, however, challenged the very structure of the church and sought revolutionary overthrow – Thomas Müntzer and the Peasants is the most well known example, but many other movements appear in the history of Christianity (as we saw in Chapter 1). At this moment, Althusser does not seem to suggest such an approach, preferring a transformation from within. Indeed, he unwittingly draws closer to the Reformation itself, seeming to express a suppressed longing that the Reformation had succeeded in France and that the Huguenots had not been crushed so brutally.[12] In the name of an authentic religious life, the reformers set out to transform the church from within, believing it had lost its way. Their movement had two clear consequences, neither of which they initially intended. The first was to reform the Roman Catholic Church itself, via a Counter-Reformation that set itself, paradoxically, against the Reformers; the second was to establish a new institution, or rather, a series of institutions.

I make this connection with the Reformation, since Althusser seems to wish for a transformation from within, even if it may lead to rebuilding of the church on a new foundation. But the connection is formal only, for Althusser goes much further. Just when we may begin to suspect that he is a reformer at heart, he turns around and offers a revolutionary approach. Since the Roman

---

12   Antonio Gramsci is explicit concerning this wish for a successful Reformation in Italy, pointing out that Italy was the worse for not undergoing such a thoroughgoing transformation of all levels of society (Gramsci 1996, 142, 213, 243–44; Boer 2007a, 255–73).

Catholic Church is unable to engage in the necessary task of transformation it-self, due to structures that will not tolerate any challenge, he states: 'It is neces-sary, then, to shatter these structures and struggle against the forces protecting them' (Althusser 1997, 195, 1994, 275).

But what, precisely, does this revolutionary shattering mean? For Althusser, the overthrow and reconstitution of his church – which may well be brought about through a wider social revolution – is but the condition for a transfor-mation of personal religious life. Here is the real revolution. In order to in-dicate what he means by a spiritual revolution, Althusser deploys the same language used earlier for speaking of social revolution: it requires a 'reduc-tion' of religious alienation so that one may reconquer religious life. Crucially, he does not mean a reduction to the social and economic causes of religious alienation – note that he uses quotation marks for this type of 'reduction', since is it analogous to but not the same as the reduction of social and collective alienation. Instead, he seeks to shift this conventional Marxist revolutionary approach to personal religious life. Thus, a reduction of religious alienation en-tails systematic criticism and even destruction of all that an individual believer has come to assume is constitutive of the religious life. The list of items to be so destroyed is intriguing: the conceptual universe of faith, theology, and the moral system; then the *theory* of the family, of education, of Catholic action, of the parish and so on. All of these operate at the level of beliefs and theory, of ideas and thereby of ideology. Althusser implicitly admits that religious life is different from collective social life. It belongs to the realm of ideology, of the superstructure – given that he assumes the Marxist metaphor of base and superstructure in this essay.

He seeks, then, a religious revolution at the personal level, by analogy with the collective dimension of social revolution. As with the latter, destruction is but the first step, for construction of the new must follow. Yet, all he can of-fer here is that every form of human existence – he writes of conduct, living and being – that are now alienated must be reconstructed 'in the truth'. As to what that truth might be (he uses variations on the word 'truth' four times in one sentence[13]), he can say only that is to be found in the 'revelation of their origins'. Are these Christian origins, as one reform movement after another has claimed in the history of the church? Or are they the events and facts that are to 'freely confront one another', with the merest allusion to the objective

---

13   'It truly leads, when one lets events and facts freely confront one another and produce
      their own truth, to the revelation of their origins and the production of that truth, to the
      constitution of new, concrete modes of behaviour – familial, moral, educational, etc. –
      that are the truth of the alienated modes' (Althusser 1997, 194, 1994, 274).

conditions of social revolution he has discussed earlier? Althusser is quite vague at this point, caught perhaps in the internal dynamics of the personal religious life. Or perhaps he has realised that he is proposing a reconstitution – now at an authentic level – of all the ideological features I mentioned earlier, which are features of the religious life constituted by the church.

Yet this moment of vagueness does not prevent Althusser from closing his essay with a reassertion of his analogy. He calls for both a politics of alliance between progressive believers and the forces of the proletariat in a social revolution, and for a transformation of the religious life of the individual believer. Once again, an unexpected Althusser emerges in the final sentence: 'The Church will give thanks to those who, through struggle and in struggle, are once again discovering that the Word was born among men and dwelt among them – and who are already preparing a humane place for it amongst men' (Althusser 1997, 195, 1994, 275).

3   Conclusion

The core of Althusser's argument is an effort to develop an analogy – filled with quiet hope – between social revolution and religious revolution, by means of the model of 'reduction', destruction and creation of a new mode of religious life. Such an argument obviously reveals his dual position at the time of writing, still in the Roman Catholic Church and yet a new member of the French Communist Party. The tensions and weaker points are thereby indications of the struggle involved in holding together the two sides of his life and thought at the time – Marxism and religious commitment. But I prefer to close by focusing on another matter, namely, the insight contained in two phrases. Althusser writes: 'We cannot affirm *a priori* that religion is reactionary'; and again, 'If religion is not, *a priori*, a form of alienation' (Althusser 1997, 190, 194–95, 1994, 268, 274). These express the core of a position that remains underdeveloped in his argument. The analogy between social and religious revolution is possible precisely because religion itself – he speaks of Christianity – may also be a revolutionary force. Against the weight of much of the Marxist tradition, he asserts that religion may be progressive, that it may offer an unalienated life. I for one would have liked Althusser to show greater awareness of the long tradition of revolutionary Christianity, on both its theological and Marxist sides, where this option has been pursued in many different ways – and as this book as a whole indicates. Even without such awareness, he does reveal a moment in this essay that he too sees himself as part of this tradition of Christian communism.

CHAPTER 10

By Science and Prayer: The Christian Communism of Farnham Maynard

> We are involved in the struggle of a dying order ... Is this change to be unguided by Christian insight, unredeemed by Christian love?
>
> GARNSEY 1947, 2

From one unknown corner of the Christian communist tradition to another, from France to Australia, from Althusser to Farnham Maynard (1882–1973), I present this analysis of Maynard as another case study of the personal Christian-Marxist dialogue, one that an individual sought to develop between two beliefs. But who is Farnham Maynard? In histories of socialism, he gains no more than a footnote (Macintyre 1998, 455). In histories of Christianity, he is offered a little more space, albeit in terms of his Anglo-Catholicism, liturgical practices, involvement with the Student Christian Movement, and especially his role as priest at St Peter's Eastern Hill (Melbourne), from 1926–1964 (Nicholls 1997; Howe 1997; Hilliard 1997).[1] I am interested in the intersection between the two, between Maynard's Christianity and his socialism. His approach may be stated in a sentence: he argued that socialism is the necessary expression of a Christian commitment, let alone of the incarnational theology of an Anglo-Catholic like himself.[2] Explaining what this approach meant for Maynard is the burden of what follows.

My presentation focuses not so much on the historical context of Maynard's work, except where necessary. Instead, I am concerned with Maynard's theoretical contribution. In doing so, I hope to shed light on a uniquely Australian contribution to the Christian communist tradition. Maynard took to heart the slogan, 'without theory, we are dead', and found that he could not engage in his parish, in society or in politics, without theoretical clarity. In the following, I begin with the methodological core of his position, which may be described in terms of a combination of science and prayer. He had trained as a scientist before joining the priesthood, and he valued the scientific method. But he was also a priest, of an Anglo-Catholic persuasion. In this respect, incarnational

---

1 He retired at the age of 82 due to ill health.
2 The few who deal with this central feature of Maynard's thought and practice do so warily, finding the conjunction somewhat odd, or perhaps that Maynard knew not quite what he did (Holden 1986, 1996, 200–4, 1997b; Howe 1997).

theology, devotion, commitment, mysticism and prayer were central, not only in his own life but also in the church he led for almost four decades. What interests me most about this approach is its inherently dialectical nature, which was a feature of his thought more generally. So in the second section I analyse this dialectic at various levels. The main topics deal with his threefold approach to religion and his understanding of the connections between Christianity and socialism. Here he addresses criticisms of religion by socialists and criticisms of socialism by Christians, with a view to producing a dialectic of translation between them. I close by considering what may be called his enthusiasm, for both Christianity and socialism. In terms of the former, the Anglo-Catholic tradition was known at the time for appealing to the senses and the emotions, evoking a sense of mystery, awe and intensity. In terms of socialism, Maynard's enthusiasm appears in light of his religious commitment, but also in his advocacy of the inevitability of socialism as a social and economic form. Both may be described in terms of the 'warm stream' of Marxism.

A word on the texts: I am concerned with three works by Maynard: the relatively early *Economics and the Kingdom of God* (1929) and the later texts, *A Fair Hearing for Socialism* (1944) and *Religion and Revolution* (1947). I spend less time with the first, since it is really a pre-socialist work. It offers sustained criticisms of capitalism,[3] as the manifestation of the profoundly anti-Christian principles of greed, selfishness and covetousness, but offers as solutions Christian social-democratic advice as to how we may ameliorate the worst effects capitalism. In other words, it constitutes a characteristic Anglo-Catholic incarnational concern with social justice. The remaining works are explicitly socialist, and therefore are the focus of more sustained attention. As for the conditions of their publication, *Economics and the Kingdom of God* was written as a sole-authored booklet, while the other two were initially given as lectures, along with other presenters. In *A Fair Hearing for Socialism*, Maynard offers the last lecture of three, called 'Christianity and Socialism'. This was preceded by lectures by Kurt Merz and Ralph Gibson, dealing respectively with 'Marx and Socialism' and 'Socialism in Australia'. They were delivered as a series at the Chapter House of St. Paul's Cathedral in Melbourne (1944), with large numbers in attendance and a lively discussion. Similarly, *Religion and Revolution* was originally a series of lectures, with two given each by Maynard

---

3   As Maynard wrote in *The Defender* magazine in 1935, no greatest danger for the church existed 'than an easy slipping into an association with the existing, but doomed, capitalistic system' (Maynard 1935, 8, quoted in Nicholls 1997, 65). This position was deeply influenced by his three months' working (in 1920) as a miner and truck-driver in the Mount Morgan goldmine in Queensland.

and Merz.[4] They were delivered on two occasions, at St. Paul's Cathedral (1936) and then at the annual conference of the Australian Student Christian Movement in Corio, near Geelong (1947).

Maynard was the driving force behind the public lectures and he did his best to include Marxists and Christians as authors of the lectures. Thus, the author of the second lecture in *A Fair Hearing for Socialism* was Ralph Gibson, at the time president of the Victorian state branch of the Communist Party of Australia. And in *Religion and Revolution* we find a foreword by Jack Blake, secretary of the same branch (Blake 1947). However, Maynard spoke and wrote primarily with Christians in mind. The locations of the lectures indicate as much, as do the majority of prefaces and forewords from church leaders.[5] His comrade, Kurt Merz, was a fellow student of Marxism but also a candidate for the priesthood in the Anglican Church. Maynard was also for many years the editor of *The Defender*, which in 1936 became the *Australian Church Quarterly*, the magazine of the Australian Church Union. Above all, the patient explanations of Marxism and socialism, as well as the desire to negate criticisms of socialism from other church leaders, indicate a desire to educate Christian audiences.

1   **Science and Prayer**

Maynard was a vigorous proponent of the importance of modern science in all dimensions, including economics (Maynard 1929, 9–12). He saw socialism too as a science, in terms of the science of history, economics and society. This was due in part to his initial training as an engineer at the University of London, graduating with a Bachelor of Science in 1904. Indeed, during his early ministry in Queensland (Gladstone and then Brisbane), he had invented and patented a machine that made blinds, and he established an orchard at Yeppoon (McPherson 2000). Yet, this background provides only the beginnings of his devotion to modern science. Maynard was deeply influenced by Charles Gore's revision of the Oxford movement, particularly by enabling it to embrace modern science and methods of biblical interpretation.[6] Maynard was also of

---

4   Maynard is the author of the first and fourth chapters, while Merz penned the second and third chapters on the French and Russian Revolutions.

5   Notably, the invitations for both series of lectures were extended by H.T. Langley, then dean of the cathedral. Langley was a known evangelical, but maintained a warm correspondence with Maynard. He also wrote the foreword to *A Fair Hearing for Socialism* (Holden 1997a, 7).

6   These positions were laid out in the – at the time – controversial edited work by Gore, called *Lux Mundi* (1889).

an era when scientific approaches, or rather 'historical critical' approaches, to the Bible and theology were widely championed and seen as a way forward from obscurantism. For those with an inquiring mind, the various myths of Christianity were neither the focus of belief in opposition to science, nor the embarrassment that some felt as marks of the primitive nature of such material. Rather, they too were the subject of careful, scientific and historical analysis. This predilection added weight to his preference for socialism, although the source of that identification was also due to his theological emphases.

I will speak more of those later, for I am interested here in the role of religious belief in relation to science. For Maynard and many of his ilk, this was the mystery of faith, or what I have designated prayer: 'By study men may be able to see the situation in an impersonal and scientific way, and by prayer they may gain the grace to act in loyalty to principles of truth and justice, in defiance, if need be, of self-interest' (Maynard and Merz 1947, 59). This mystery was one of the three pillars – institutional, intellectual and mystical – of his approach to and understanding of religion, by which he mostly meant Christianity. Religion touches and is able to address the core issues of human existence in a way that no other ideology and practice is able. It gives a deeper meaning to life, which Maynard sought to address through the symbolism and sensory invocation of the Anglo-Catholic tradition.

But how do the two dimensions relate to one another? Inspired by Gore, Maynard saw them as not so much in competition but rather as spheres that are at times distinct and at others complementary. Science deals with the world of matter, of history and society as well as technology and human ingenuity. By contrast, religion concerns the question of inner wellbeing, which he understood in both collective and individual terms. At the same time, religion is involved with science, albeit not as an opponent but as an advocate and comrade. It is the church's concern, if not that of all Christians, to 'see that the best science is made available for the remedy of human ills' (Maynard and Merz 1947, 57). Christians 'gladly join hands' with science 'to abolish ignorance poverty and disease', indeed to relieve those who are 'oppressed in mind, body or estate' (Merz, Gibson, and Maynard 1944, 41). He uses the common analogy of medicine to illustrate his approach: the Christian does not challenge the advances of modern medicine, for the Christian encourages its breakthroughs and achievements (Maynard and Merz 1947, 57–58). It matters not what the specific religion might be of the doctor in question, for medicine is of the domain of science. All a Christian can ask is that the best medicine and correct procedure be used for the illness in question. Prayer should be devoted, in the first instance, to asking that the doctors can perform their tasks to the best of their ability. But what happens after the procedure is completed? The doctor's task may be over, for the patient is physically healed. But the questions of death and life have not been addressed. Here religion has its crucial role.

At the time, Maynard's advocacy of both science and prayer was a progressive position, since significant parts of Christianity had been fighting a centuries-long rear-guard action against the challenges of science – despite the fact that science itself arose from the theological incentive to study the world God had created (Certeau and Domenach 1974; Certeau 1988, 179). In his own time, Maynard's main opponents were evangelicals within the Anglican Church, who dominated the diocese of Melbourne. The battle lines were many, including liturgy, vestments, church furniture and especially what was regarded as 'liberal' scholarship in relation to the Bible and theology (Holden 1997a; Frame 2002). Maynard identified closely with what was seen as a minority position in Melbourne, heavily influenced by the scholarship and practices of the Anglo-Catholic tradition, from the Oxford Tractarians to Charles Gore (Chadwick 1992),[7] and oriented to seeing the church as a 'force to be used to bring in the Kingdom of God on earth' (Bouma 2009, 132).

Yet, Maynard went a step or two further than most. To begin with, he was willing to argue that if any religion is not able to stand up to the investigations of science, it is not worth the devotion given to it. But he was confident that the form of Christianity he championed would be up to the challenge, for this Christianity speaks of issues crucial since the foundation of the world. But now he went beyond many of his contemporaries, for he was willing to issue the challenge to socialism itself, which he saw in terms of a rational, planned approach to social and economic transformation, in contrast to the haphazard nature of capitalism's booms and busts.[8] The challenge he had in mind was a dominant socialist position concerning religion: religion was the result of alienated social and economic conditions (Merz, Gibson, and Maynard 1944, 39–40; Maynard and Merz 1947, 37–41). With the removal of those conditions – through revolution or peaceful means – religions would in due course disappear. Maynard's answer is both direct and confident: 'Christians are not afraid of the test ... We are completely confident that nothing of the kind will happen' (Merz, Gibson, and Maynard 1944, 41). The reason is that the spring of religion lies elsewhere than in this particular interpretation of its material causes.

Delineation, cooperation, meeting challenges – so did Maynard conceive of science and prayer. But let me close this section by noting an unexpected

---

7 For an overview of Anglo-Catholicism in Melbourne, see Hilliard (1997).
8 On this matter, he was profoundly affected by the Great Depression in capitalist countries and was fully aware of the Soviet Union's massive economic growth – through industrialisation and collectivisation – during the same period.

outcome of his arguments: science and religion should know their limits. Maynard does not proclaim that one or the other has all the answers. If the 'province of science is a limited one' (Maynard and Merz 1947, 57),[9] so also with religion. This limitation relates to range, purpose and method. But does this also apply to socialism, which Maynard tended to see in scientific terms? Is it too limited, and, if so, what role does religion have in relation to socialism?

2 Modulations of an Anglo-Catholic Dialectic

Science and prayer may provide Maynard's method, but I am interested in how this method works itself out in a reasonably coherent position. This position may be called an 'Anglo-Catholic dialectic', which repeatedly reveals yet further modulations. I distinguish between two main topics in this dialectic: the three dimensions of religion – institutional, intellectual and mystical – and relations between Christianity and socialism.

2.1 Discerning the Tension between Revolution and Reaction

To begin with, Maynard provides a threefold definition of religion, which springs from an initial scientific effort to distinguish between false and true religion. The distinction was and remains a common one in theological circles,[10] and Maynard has no difficulty in recognising it as such, quoting from John Macmurray's *Creative Society* (Macmurray 1936, quoted in Merz, Gibson, and Maynard 1944, 44–45). False religion is nothing less than an 'illusion' and a 'sham', the type of institutional religion (identified by Marx and Engels) that is more concerned for its material wellbeing in the world and willing to provide ideological justification for any would-be despot. Now Maynard's understanding of this distinction becomes intriguing, for he does not follow conventional theological approaches and identify 'true religion' as the direct opposite to 'false religion'. Instead, he argues that the institutional dimension is but one feature of religion. The mistake, then, is to suggest that it is the core of religion.

In seeking to correct this mistake, Maynard proposes that the institutional cannot exist without intellectual and mystical dimensions (Merz, Gibson, and Maynard 1944, 45; Maynard and Merz 1947, 5–19). On the one hand, this

---

9   See also his observations on the 'frustrations' of science, in that many solutions to the world's problems are available from science and yet people refuse to take them up, and his criticisms of the tendency to explain current realties in light of origins, in which an original authentic core has become distorted (Merz, Gibson, and Maynard 1944, 31–32, 42–43).

10   For a relatively recent example, see Ward (2002).

definition follows a long tradition in modelling 'religion' after Christianity, if not also Islam and Judaism.[11] On the other hand, Maynard develops his position for a unique and specific purpose: he seeks to understand the internal political dynamic of Christianity, which constantly moves between reaction and revolution, between Constantine 'the Great'[12] and Thomas Müntzer, between Christian emperor and Christian revolution. But Maynard's real insight is not that one side provides the truth and the other an aberration, but that both are perfectly justifiable from within Christianity and especially its sacred texts.

In a little more detail: for Maynard, the institutional is in some respects connected with the early phases of religion, with reference to what was then Malinowski's ground-breaking work (1932). I am less interested in this resort to a type of evolutionary model common at the time, moving from 'humble' to 'full' and 'developed' forms, for Maynard's argument is not tied to such a schema. He does not need such a position – apart perhaps from indicating his constant use of the latest scientific research – to make his main point: the institutional is inherently conservative. This point relies partly on a functionalist explanation, in that institutions need to resist change not merely for their own wellbeing, but also for social wellbeing. Here we find moral codes, rules of conduct and laws.[13] More significant is Maynard's ability to read this feature dialectically. It may be easy to regard the church's inertia as reactionary, he writes, but this is to neglect the benefit of such inertia for revolutionaries themselves: 'if it tends to resist change, it also tends to secure change once it is effected' (Maynard and Merz 1947, 56). Revolutionaries too would agree from the perspective of power, for once they have seized power, they become interested not merely in carrying through the promises of the revolution, but also in preserving what they have gained. And if the church can play such a role, then so much the better (think of Stalin's famous compact with the Russian Orthodox Church in 1943 (Miner 2003; Boer 2018)).

---

11   This was a move fostered initially by European exploration and colonialism, which both provided immense data on diverse beliefs and practices and struggled to understand the diversity (Dubuisson 2007).

12   Alongside Constantine, Maynard mentions Peter I's turning the church into his tool in Russia and Napoleon's use of the papacy to consolidate his power (Merz, Gibson, and Maynard 1944, 41).

13   Merz – in chapters two and three of *Religion and Revolution* – makes much of this dimension of religion in order to understand of the roles of the Christian churches during the French and Russian Revolutions, in which they took a mostly counter-revolutionary position for the sake of preserving their own privileges and access to power (Maynard and Merz 1947, 20–52).

However, the more obvious revolutionary dimension of religion is to be found in its intellectual dimension, which is cast in terms of the individuality of the intellectual against the collective nature of the institution. The intellectual is concerned with 'knowledge of things unseen' (Maynard and Merz 1947, 6) and thereby speaks truth to power, challenging in a prophetic way the vested interests of church and state. For such prophetic figures, 'the essence of religion was social justice' (Maynard and Merz 1947, 12). The Hebrew prophets have been and remain champions for the religious left, so Maynard's identification of the prophets is not particularly new, even to the point of noting that such a radical tradition is intensified in the New Testament, especially with the Magnificat of the first chapter of the Gospel of Luke. But I am more interested in two features of his depiction of intellectuals. First, behind Maynard's depiction of radical intellectuals lies the socialist movement. As Kautsky's study (1892a, 1892b) of the Erfurt Program put it, the formation of socialist parties involved the merging of radical intellectuals (and thereby class traitors) with the working class movement. Here we find Marx and the First International, Lenin and the Bolsheviks and so on.

Second, Maynard (and Merz in the sections on the French and Russian Revolutions in *Religion and Revolution*) notes that intellectuals with alarming regularity find themselves pushed outside the institutions in question. Such banishment is through no desire of their own, for they usually begin by seeking to challenge the institutions in question to change them from within. However, when the institutional leaders and stake-holders reject the proposals of the intellectuals for change, the latter find themselves forced into an oppositional role. Luther and the Reformers, Müntzer and the Peasants, Voltaire and the philosophes – these and more did not necessarily begin with powerful anti-institutional positions and desires to break all ties and begin again. But the shifts of the powers that be to staunch counter-revolutionary positions forced the hands of the intellectuals towards more radical and often violent positions.

This conjoining of institutional and intellectual features of religion provides Maynard with the prime reason for the political ambivalence of a religion such as Christianity. If the institution is inherently conservative (albeit not without benefit), the intellectuals are the radicals. Maynard knows full well that many intellectuals are not radical, offering their good services to institutions for the sake of bolstering the ideological justification of the latter. For this reason, he stresses that proper intellectuals hoist the banner of truth and will search for that truth no matter what the obstacles. But even in this situation, religion finds itself in a tension between conservative and progressive, between reactionary and revolutionary. Despite his love for the radicals and their dynamite, he does not wish to jettison the institutional dimension. Instead, he would prefer to keep them in a creative, if not dialectical tension, not least because this situation helps keep each side aware of its own limitations: 'When we bear in mind the two elements of religion about which we have been thinking we can see how it was possible for acute minds to make two contradictory statements both containing the truth and neither exhaustively true, namely, that religion is the opium of the people and that "Christianity is a revolutionary force"' (Maynard and Merz 1947, 14).[14]

Thus far the opposition is a reasonably conventional one, although Maynard gives it a twist in terms of the creative tension between conservative and revolutionary forces. By contrast, the third feature of religion comes out of both his Anglo-Catholic sensibilities and his search for a counter-argument to what he perceives to be the Marxist criticism of religion. This is the mystical, 'the soul's aspiration towards God'. Outwardly, this aspiration is manifested in the 'surpassing beauty of the sacred music and religious poetry' (Maynard and Merz 1947, 7), while inwardly it concerns the beauty of the spirit's holiness. Unable to be expressed in the words of science and the intellectual, the mystical finds voice in analogy, metaphor, myth and parable.[15] Here the Anglo-Catholic urging for a devoted religious life and observance comes to the fore, as also the desire to stimulate all of the senses in worship – the taste of the Eucharist, the smell of incense, the sounds of music and bells, the touch of fabrics and the sights of symbolic art and architecture. In short, the intellectual dimension may stimulate the mind, but the mind cannot realise its full potential without feeling.

The viability or otherwise of Maynard's effort to define religion is not my concern, for I am interested in what insights the threefold approach enables and its function in other parts of his argument. The key insight I have already discussed, in terms of the dialectical tension between reaction and revolution that lies at the heart of Christianity: 'religion may crush and destroy values as much as preserve them' (Maynard and Merz 1947, 19). Earlier, I argued that this tension is embodied in the contradictions of the prime ideologue of Christianity, the Apostle Paul, but it also runs through the many streams of Christian history.

Yet this much we have seen – explicitly and implicitly – in the tensions between what Maynard calls the institutional and the intellectual. How does the mystical fare in the dialectic? Initially, it may seem to be an outlier, a deeply personal experience somewhat removed from the struggle between the other two. But in an intriguing paragraph, Maynard offers another perspective, in

---

14   The second quotation is placed in Otto von Bismarck's mouth.
15   Note the parables with which Maynard concludes two of his texts: one is the parable of the sick man and the other offers a retelling of the Good Samaritan (Merz, Gibson, and Maynard 1944, 47–48; Maynard and Merz 1947, 71–73).

which the dialectic shifts away from tensions between the different dimensions and applies to each:

> The noblest actions have been inspired by religion, but also the most dastardly deeds. Religion includes the faith of saints and bigotry of fanatics. Religion has produced a David Livingstone and a Caiaphas. It has inspired countless missionary martyrs and the Thugs of India.
>
> MAYNARD AND MERZ 1947, 8

In the sentences that surround this passage, Maynard veers towards the distinction between true and false religion, but I suggest that he also touches on the possibility that each of his dimensions faces the struggle between reaction and revolution.[16] This requires both an awareness of such a pattern, to the point where religion cannot be understood or appreciated without it, and a need for discernment as to what leads to human and natural flourishing and what does not.

The final use to which this threefold definition is put concerns Maynard's arguments with the socialists, so to the different facets of those arguments I now turn.

2.2   *Christianity and Socialism*

I move from the internal tensions of Christianity to those between socialism and Christianity. On this matter, I suggest that Maynard evinces a dialectic of translation between the two. In brief, while he argues that Christianity naturally flows into socialism, seeking to overcome misunderstandings between them, he is also aware of the resistance between the two. Their respective semantic fields may overlap, so much so that they enrich one another, but they also resist such translation since some meaning threatens to be lost in the process. Thus, a constant moving back and forth takes place, in which both Christianity and socialism seek common ground but at the same time insist on their own terms and perspectives. The terms translated are therefore temporary, continually open to re-translation (R. Boer 2015b).

The first point of resistance comes from socialism's conventional understanding of religion, against which Maynard deploys his threefold definition

---

16   See also his observations on the dangers of stressing one or the other element (Maynard and Merz 1947, 16). In the section written by Merz, he notes the ferment in the Russian Orthodox Church before and after the Revolution, with many progressive clergy ('The Living Church' or Renovationists) backing the Bolsheviks (Maynard and Merz 1947, 46–48; Roslov 2002).

of religion. This understanding was drawn from a 'canon within the canon' of the writings of Marx and Engels, a canon that was determined soon after their deaths and framed subsequent positions. In relation to religion, Marx's few pages in the Introduction to the *Contribution to the Critique of Hegel's Philosophy of Right* (1844a, 1844b) became determinative, as did Engels's observations in *Anti-Dühring* (1877–78a, 300–2, 1877–78b, 474–76).[17] Lenin too is drawn into service to bolster such a position, especially his explicit writings on religion and his letters to Maxim Gorky.[18] According to the representation of this position, religion is a secondary phenomenon, a product of alienated social and economic conditions. In such a situation, human beings seek solace in religion, finding there 'the heart of a heartless world' and 'the soul of soulless conditions'. For communists, the target should not be religion, but the conditions that produce religion. Overcoming oppression and exploitation is the key. The outcome is twofold. First, when a new mode of production has been established after a revolution, religion will fade away, for its conditions will no longer exist. This may take some time, since relics of the old order would remain, but eventually religion would become obsolete. Second, it is futile to attack religion directly, for this would make the socialist movement focus on a secondary issue, unnecessarily split workers, and side with bourgeois attacks against religion.

Before I deal with Maynard's response, it is worth noting that this canonical interpretation is quite one-sided. It neglects the many texts outside the canon, such as four decades of Marx's reflection on and reinterpretation of fetishism (Boer 2011b), so much so that it became a core motif in his understanding of capitalism, Marx's criticism of Hegel's theological categories (Marx 1843a, 1843b), and – as we have seen earlier – Engels's argument for the revolutionary nature of Christianity and indeed the first identification of the revolutionary tradition of what Karl Kautsky would call 'Christian communism'. These are but a few examples of a much richer collection of texts, let alone the many engagements with religion in Lenin's and Stalin's texts (Boer 2013a, 2017b). Even in the canon within the canon, the decision had been made quite early that Marx's famous opium metaphor meant that religion was a drug that dulls the senses, obscuring reality. This interpretation misses the profound ambivalence in Marx's image, which he saw not only as a curse but also as a blessed cure (McKinnon 2006).

---

17   Maynard quotes Engels at length (Merz, Gibson, and Maynard 1944, 40).
18   Maynard quotes from one of Lenin's letters to Maxim Gorky (Lenin 1913a, 1913b; Merz, Gibson, and Maynard 1944, 39). In his contribution, Merz quotes from a range of Lenin's texts (Lenin 1905e, 1905f, 1909a, 1909b, 1909c, 1909d).

Maynard does not make these points, although one cannot blame him for accepting the canonical position, since this was the standard position of communist parties throughout the world, including the one in Australia.[19] Instead, he criticises the limits of this position, arguing that it concerns only the institutional side of religion, with its inherent tendency to become reactionary and provide ideological and practical support for one despot after another. In this light, institutional religion was an obstacle that must be overcome for the sake of revolution. At times, Maynard suggests that religion in this form was a distortion of religion itself, used to stultify and control the masses. Without the influence of intellectual and mystical elements, religion does indeed have a 'deadening effect on the spiritual sensibilities' of human beings (Maynard and Merz 1947, 17).

In short, Marx, Engels and Lenin had misinterpreted Christianity, seeing it only in institutional terms. Or rather, the canonical reading of the Marxist position had distorted religion. I would go a step further and argue that such a canonical position actually distorts the work of Marx, Engels and Lenin by focusing on one dimension of their writings. But Maynard produces another argument: Marx was a scientist and was thereby open to new findings in scientific inquiry. Obviously, Maynard the scientist comes to the fore here, but he uses this point to argue that, as a scientist, Marx himself would have been the first to admit the limited nature of his inquiry into religion and would have been open to new research.[20] This is precisely what Maynard, with the assistance of scholars, sets out to do so with his argument not only for the intellectual and mystical dimensions of religion, but more significantly with his awareness of the ambivalent political nature of Christianity, between and even within each of these dimensions.

So the challenge to socialists on the issue of religion is that they may have misunderstood a religion like Christianity and, as scientists, that they should be open to more refined research. But I am intrigued by a final point in Maynard's engagement with Marxist criticisms of religion, in which he pushes further what I have called the dialectic of translation between socialism and

19   It appears in the Introduction to *Religion and Revolution*, by Jack Blake, secretary of the Victorian State Committee of the Communist Party of Australia, and in the presentation of the positions by Marx, Engels and Lenin in the sections of *Religion and Revolution* written by Kurt Merz (Blake 1947; Maynard and Merz 1947, 37–41). As Maynard notes, it was particularly Engels's formulations in *Anti-Dühring* that influenced such a position (Merz, Gibson, and Maynard 1944, 41).

20   Indeed, there is some evidence to suggest that Marx was fully aware of Engels's developing argument concerning the revolutionary side of Christianity – apart from the fact that they discussed their ideas almost daily (Marx 1871b, 633, 1872a, 255, 1872b, 160, 1881a, 67, 1881b, 161).

Christianity. In order to highlight the point, I offer two quotations, one concerning capitalism and the other socialism:

> Mammon is still the God of this world, and although we know his hands are dripping with the blood of the poor, it is exceedingly hard not to bow down in his temple.
>
> MAYNARD 1929, 43

A Christian understanding of capitalism sees in it the manifestation and exacerbation of anti-Christian greed, exploitation, dehumanisation and the extremes of wealth and poverty (Maynard 1929, 16–34). Christianity does not translate into capitalism, for the latter manifests much that is anti-Christian. By contrast, Christians see 'in socialism the political form of society most expressive of the principles of the Kingdom of God' (Maynard and Merz 1947, 71).[21] Even more:

> One would think it was the most Christian thing possible to try to bring God's good gifts right home to all the needy, and to organise society so that this can be done. Certainly one would think that it was the most Christian thing possible to develop God-given powers to the limit of their capacity, and to use the riches of the earth for the benefit of all mankind.
>
> MERZ, GIBSON, AND MAYNARD 1944, 32

In our time, we would want to widen the scope to include all of nature in such a description, but Maynard's point is Christianity leads naturally to a socialist position. In order to bolster his suggestion, he invokes the traditions of Christian socialism, the Christian leaders of socialist and labour parties in the United Kingdom as well as significant church leaders in that part of the world, and none less than the patriarch of the Russian Orthodox Church, Nikhon, who changed his tune and offered support for the Soviet government, condemning those who would speak ill against it. Following in his footsteps, Sergei, the Metropolitan of Nizhny Novgorod and Deputy Patriarchal Locum Tenens, provided in 1927 as full a statement as one could find of the church's accommodation to the communist government.[22] Sergei would later be elected patriarch after Stalin allowed the episcopal council to meet once again in 1943 (see Chapter 8).

---

21   Indeed, 'The economics of the Kingdom – the House Law of the Rule of God – is just the translation of the principles of Christ into laws which regulate human social relationships' (Maynard 1929, 12).

22   For the original texts, see Acton and Stableford (2005, 252–56).

For Maynard, Christians were not – or at least should not be – opposed to socialism, since they are comrades with a common goal. The problem was that not all Christians agreed, so he addresses the other side, the religious opponents of socialism. To these he felt the need to explain Marxism in some detail (Maynard and Merz 1947, 58–70). I need not replicate this detail here, except to note that he identifies the core of a Marxist analysis in terms of the multiple contradictions of capitalism, moving from class conflict to Lenin's (and even Stalin's) careful observations on the contradictions of imperialist capitalism (Lenin 1916a, 1916b). But I am particularly interested, as I noted earlier, in Maynard's identification of Marxism as a scientific theory of the laws of history. Thus, Marxism is not so much a philosophy or political ideology, but rather a method of scientific thought. This 'scientific socialism' enables one not only to understand the 'great impersonal forces within society', but also provides the ability to 'forecast in real measure the movements about to take place' (Maynard and Merz 1947, 60). Much like Newton or Darwin, Marx had discovered the scientific laws of history. We are perhaps now a little more wary about claiming laws for anything, for they are constantly undermined by exceptions that render the old laws less than secure. But for Maynard the scientist, the claim to scientific socialism had great appeal, for it removed Marxism from ideology and party politics.[23]

I will indicate a different approach in a moment, but let me first acknowledge the gains of such a position. The first is a unique argument concerning private property. Maynard's target is the tradition of Roman Catholic social teaching, dating from Leo XIII's *Rerum Novarum* of 1891 and followed up in 1941 by Pius IX's *Quadragesimo Anno*. As part of their trenchant rejection of socialism, they try to uphold the inviolability of private property. Maynard adroitly points out that the encyclicals have misinterpreted the Marxist position on property (Merz, Gibson, and Maynard 1944, 34–36). Instead of a blanket approach to property, Marxists distinguish between the ownership of the means of production and individual property. Socialists wish to do away with the latter, or rather, transfer that ownership from capitalists to workers and peasants. By contrast, individual property is encouraged by socialism, so much so that socialism will enable everyone to have the individual property that they were denied by the capitalist ownership of the means of production. In other words, the abolition of private ownership of the means of production will lead to the full realisation of individual property. He concludes: 'It is not too much to say that Socialism professes to the scientific way of establishing the conditions which St. Thomas demands for the achievement of man's true end' (Merz, Gib-

---

23   One might compare debates in our time concerning climate change, with 'science' invoked as the objective arbiter on both sides of the debate.

son, and Maynard 1944, 36). The key is the abolition of bourgeois private property for the sake of individual property.

Second, in response to the criticism that Marxists espouse violent class struggle and revolution, Maynard responds that Marx and Engels were observing the reality of class struggle in their own time. As scientists, they were describing the world as it was, especially in terms of the resistance to the appropriation of the means of production by the masses. But with proper scientific analysis, one may discern the moving forces of history rather than be subject to them. Thus, it becomes possible to bring about a peaceful transition to socialism (Merz, Gibson, and Maynard 1944, 26–27). It may be necessary to defend such a transition from attacks, but Maynard stresses again and again the possibility of peaceful means. The crucial factor here is the ability to persuade those who have most to lose in this transition, namely, the owners of the means of production and those with vested interests in that situation. On this matter, Maynard relies heavily on the objective, scientific nature of socialism. If it is a science, and if such change is inevitable (as many believed at the time), then it may well be possible that those who would initially lose out in the process may be persuaded that it is in their own interest to be part of the transition.

Here he risks the position advocated by Eduard Bernstein (1993, 1899) among the German Social Democrats. Bernstein's evolutionary approach held that socialism could be achieved gradually through parliamentary reform and within the framework of bourgeois democracy. With such changes, workers would benefit gradually and see the futility of revolution. As capitalism was gradually reshaped into socialism, the capitalists too would see the benefits. Nonetheless, too many differences arise for a close identification between the positions of Bernstein and Maynard. Bernstein argued that capitalism was not nearing a crisis, while Maynard clearly felt that capitalism, especially after the Second World War, was a dying order. Further, Bernstein held that reforms would ameliorate the conditions of workers and that the process could be undertaken within bourgeois democracy. By contrast, Maynard stressed the objective reality of a very new world order and was not apparently committed to any form of bourgeois democracy. His extensive visit to The German Democratic Republic, Czechoslovakia, the Soviet Union and the new People's Republic of China in 1952 confirmed this position.

However, Maynard firmly held to the position that it was the task of intelligent men and women, Christians among them, to discern the signs of the times and make the best preparation for such a change. With this approach, they could ensure that the churches at least did not fall into the reactionary camp, seeking to hold onto vested interests, but marched at the forefront of a new world order. He was fully aware of the risks and frustrations that might be encountered, but he was also committed to the idea that Christian leaders should and could undertake such a task, for 'intellectual probity is part of their loyalty to Christ' (Maynard and Merz 1947, 59). How should this be done? Maynard canvassed a number of possibilities. One was to leaven socialism with the insights of Christianity, so that the shortcomings of the anti-religious position of many socialists might be overcome. But he also suggested that, if need be, Christians should work with those opposed to religion, for they have a common goal. Another is to suggest that Christian involvement may make the crucial difference between a peaceful or violent transformation (Merz, Gibson, and Maynard 1944, 46). If the church chooses to resist, it may suffer extensively, but if it is at the forefront of change, it may well make all the difference. Finally, what happens after the transition? Maynard resorts to a distinction between the material and the spiritual. Socialism may provide much of what is needed in material terms, but it falls short of answering deeper human needs and the questions of existence and the purpose of life. Here Christianity has a crucial function (Merz, Gibson, and Maynard 1944, 46–47).

3   Conclusion: On Enthusiasm

Maynard has come at last to a position in which Marxism may provide materialist and indeed objective answers, but Christianity provides the crucial missing element of subjective answers. He tends to see the difference between science and religion in similar terms, with the one impersonal and the other very personal. But he seems to have missed a crucial dimension of Marxism itself. Maynard, as many socialists, stressed the objective side of Marxism. This is the Marxism of cold reason, science and planning, of the analysis of the objective forces of society, history and economics. The other side of this dialectic is subjective intervention in those objective conditions, for the conditions themselves are created and recreated by such intervention. Thus, Christianity is not alone in providing a subjective dimension, whether in terms of direction during the transition to socialism or in guidance regarding ultimate concerns. For Marxism too the subjective is crucial. This may be in the form of subjective intervention as the very possibility of revolution, but it may also be in what Ernst Bloch (1995, 209, 1985, 241) called the 'warm stream' of Marxism – the Marxism that excites political passions, that makes one enthusiastic for liberation, that causes us to hope and have faith in a cause, that rises again and again in the face of disappointment and disenchantment.

   This warm stream may seem a far cry from Maynard's emphasis on the scientific objectivity of Marxism, but I suggest that it suffuses his work in other ways. Much comes from his religious commitment, especially the commitment and devotion characteristic of an Anglo-Catholic.[24] But this enthusiasm also shows through clearly in the notes made during his 1952 visit – despite a ban by the Menzies government during the Korean War – to the Soviet Union and the People's Republic of China, ending with a peace conference in Beijing (Holden 1997b).[25] Further, I sense this enthusiasm in his oft-reiterated point that socialism is inevitable and that the church should do its best to be at the forefront of such change. In the supposedly sober period after the 'fall' of the Berlin Wall, some may smile wistfully at such optimism. But the realities of socialism – however they may be interpreted – in the rising powers of Asia, with China now the strongest socialist power in world history, suggest that our assumptions concerning the 'failure' of socialism are a little premature. Thus, I read 'inevitability' less as a sense of history being a process of impersonal forces, and more as enthusiasm and hope, for a world which Maynard earnestly anticipated. Indeed, if socialism is the true expression of 'the principles of the Kingdom of God', then that enthusiastic hope is as much Christian as it is socialist.

I close on a slightly different note. Maynard worked and wrote at a time when the ties with the United Kingdom were still very strong. He was born in England, and more than ninety percent of the relatively small Australian population claimed a heritage from the United Kingdom. His writings reveal close connections with developments in England, with the writings of the Charles Gore, the Anglo-Catholic theologian and Christian socialist, being the most influential (Waddell 2014). The situation now, with the majority of Australians of a background other than the United Kingdom, and with long-running debates about Australian identity in an Asian context, could not be more different. Yet the paradox is that in Maynard's time there was a stronger sense of setting out upon a very new path. Australia could be quite distinct from all that had gone before, and Maynard's socialist Christianity may be seen as one indication of such a desire. Indeed, he went much further than many of his contemporaries,[26] as an ardent socialist with profound sympathies for the Soviet Union and the People's Republic of China. That he did do on the basis of a deep Christian conviction and theoretical basis makes him so intriguing.

---

24   On the emotional appeal and experience of conversion within Anglo-Catholicism, see Holden (1997a, 14–15).

25   Holden is somewhat embarrassed by Maynard's enthusiasm, attempting to mitigate it by suggesting he saw what he wanted to see.

26   However, the fact that he was priest at St Peters Eastern Hill for almost four decades indicates that the parish was behind him. For an example of fellow socialist Christians, see the study of the correspondence between Helen Baillie and Maynard in Grimshaw and Sherlock (1997).

CHAPTER 11

Christian Communism and the Bolsheviks

> They would certainly think that such a man was either crazy or a 'Christian Socialist' who had found his way into the ranks of Social-Democracy by mistake.
>
> LENIN 1907c, 343, 1907d, 322–23

I have dwelt long with the West Asian and European tradition of Christian communism, not least because it took root in that part of the globe. But this is by no means the only region where we find such currents. In the previous chapter, I already engaged with the southeast Asian country of Australia, which long saw itself as an outpost of Western Europe but has since the time of Farnham Maynard begun to struggle with a somewhat different identity. Indeed, taking up Maynard's interest in the Soviet Union and China, which he visited in the early 1950s, the remainder of the book moves eastward – if one thinks of the Eurasian landmass – dealing with various dimensions of the Christian communist tradition in relation to the Russian and Chinese revolutions.

This chapter considers these currents in Russia, where the influence of peasant communes (*obshchina, mir* and *sel'skoe obshchestvo*) was widespread in the various socialist movements of the late nineteenth and early twentieth centuries. With their common ownership of the village lands, periodic reallocation of agricultural strips of land for cultivation and the communal allocation of produce, these village communes were a particular Russian variation on subsistence-survival agriculture (R. Boer 2015a, 53–81). This ancient, well-tried and remarkably persistent economic form produced much debate among the variety of communist groups in Russia. If we make use of these village communes, they thought, can we make a transition to socialism without passing through a full capitalist phase? The nineteenth century movement, *Narodnaia volia* (People's Will) or Narodniks, sought to do so, adding individual acts of terror, a preference followed by the later and larger Socialist-Revolutionaries (Offord 1986). They agitated for egalitarianism, the abolition of private property in land, and the equal division of the land (or of land tenure) as the means to destroy poverty, unemployment and exploitation. Largely urban intellectuals, they infamously decided to go to the countryside to bring their message to the peasants, only to meet bewildered looks and immediate calls to the police. Lenin and the Bolsheviks were not so enamoured, arguing like Plekhanov that the peasant commune had become an instrument of tsarist oppression and nascent capitalism (Lenin 1894a, 176, 494–95, 1894b, 176, 520–21, 1895a, 238–39,

245, 264–65, 1895b, 232–33, 240, 261–62, 1910a, 1910b). This did not prevent Vera Zasulich asking Marx whether the peasant commune would possibly enable communism in Russia (Marx 1881c, 1881d).[1] But I am interested in the religious, if not theological tenor of the persistent appeal of subsistence survival in its village communes, for it came to inform a number of Christian communist movements, often with an anarchist edge. My particular interest is peasant socialism and the deeply influential life work of Tolstoy – the focus of the first two sections below. This analysis is mediated through the eyes of Lenin, who evinces both criticism and appreciation, misunderstanding and insight in his engagements.[2] A third section brings to bear an intriguing alternative tradition, the God-Builders, especially through the important but under-appreciated Anatoly Lunacharsky. Here the tradition of Christian communism via Kautsky and others finds expression in a unique fashion in a Russian situation.

1 Peasant Socialism

'The land is God's' – this was the core slogan of peasant socialists, which they deployed again and again in Duma debates between 1905 and 1917. In these limited parliaments, reluctantly granted by the Tsar after the 1905 revolution, peasant socialist positions began to be represented by independent peasant representatives, as well as the Socialist-Revolutionaries in the Duma. Lenin and the Bolsheviks were less interested in the Socialist-Revolutionaries, seeking at times coalitions with them and at others opposing their undeveloped agrarian socialism. But the independents were far more intriguing, especially the radical rather than conservative ones (as embodied in the Doukhobor movement). Let me give a few examples, which provide a good sense of their positions and how the Bolsheviks responded to them.

The first concerns a certain priest, Tikhvinsky, who was an independent left-wing Duma representative. Lenin quotes the priest:

This is the way the peasants, the way the working people look at the land: the land is God's, and the labouring peasant has as much right to it as each one of us has the right to water and air. It would be strange if anyone

---

1 Marx begrudgingly allowed the possibility, with qualifications, but the greater significance of this piece, among other late works, is Marx's growing realisation that the universal prescriptions he had so assiduously developed earlier were '*expressly* limited to the *countries of Western Europe*' (Marx 1881c, 71, 1881d, 166).

2 I draw on earlier research undertaken for *Lenin, Religion, and Theology* (Boer 2013a), albeit adapted and reworked for the present study.

were to start selling, buying or trading in water and air – and it seems just as strange to us that anyone should trade in, sell or buy land.

LENIN 1907a, 297, 1907b, 157

We cannot miss the basic theological justification for this claim: the land is God's. The widespread assumption of an original state of common property had already vexed the early theorists of capitalism such as Hugo Grotius and John Locke, who sought to retell and reinterpret the biblical text of Genesis 1–3 and find a theological justification for private property (Boer and Petterson 2014). But the Russian peasants found the very idea of trading in land, let alone air and water, as passing strange. Tikhvinsky for his part was speaking in favour of a Trudovik land bill. As a breakaway group from the Socialist-Revolutionaries, the Trudoviks too supported the project of land reform, in which the land would be taken from the landlords and returned to the peasants.

Lenin found all of this both admirable but somewhat simplistic. The underlying reality of capitalism would render any land reform futile, for capitalism was already putting land and water up for sale in the large industrial centres, mines and factories, apart from the sale of labour power and its consequent wage slavery. Indeed, as with his other reflections on religion, Lenin is often caught between two positions, condemning religion – in traditional Marxist fashion – as reactionary and yet appreciating the sharp insights generated by the peasant Christian socialists. For example, he refers in 1907 to a Duma speech by the peasant Moroz, who said, 'The land must be taken away from the clergy and the landlords'. Moroz goes on to quote Matthew 7:7: 'Ask and it shall be given you; knock and it will be opened unto you'. But, observes Moroz, 'We ask and ask, but it is not given us; and we knock, but still it is not given us. Must we break down the door and take it?' Lenin is less than impressed: 'this is not the first time in history that bourgeois revolutionaries have taken their slogans from the Gospel' (Lenin 1907c, 385, 1907d, 365). At the same time, Lenin also admires such a position for other reasons. A proponent like Tikhvinsky 'deserves all respect for his sincere loyalty to the interests of the peasants, the interests of the people, which he defends fearlessly and with determination'. Further, Tikhvinsky and others – like the 'kindly village priest', Poyarkov (a member of the first Duma in 1906), who knew very well how the liberal landlords acquired land by whatever foul means were available – share instinctively socialist ideals: 'I am well aware that this viewpoint springs from the most noble motives, from an ardent protest against monopoly, against the privileges of rich idlers, against the exploitation of man by man, that it arises out of the aspiration to achieve the liberation of all working people from every kind of oppression and exploitation' (Lenin 1907a, 297, 1907b, 158).[3]

The second example concerns the continued contribution, after the October Revolution, from sectarian groups with communist tendencies (Etkind 1998, 631–74). Already in the early years of the twentieth century, Lenin wrote that the Social-Democrats 'demand ... an amnesty for all "political prisoners" and members of religious sects'. Until this is done, he continues, 'all talk about tolerance and freedom of worship will remain a miserable pretence and discreditable lie' (Lenin 1903a, 348, 1903b, 125). Lenin's later informant and collaborator on such matters was Vladimir Bonch-Bruevich, who had a deep interest in sectarian groups such as the Old Believers, Doukhobors, Molokans, Khlysty and Mennonites. His 1903 work, 'Schism and Sectarianism in Russia', drew Lenin's attention, to the extent that the latter read it to the delegates at the second party congress of that year. It was agreed by the congress that one way to enlist the anti-tsarist sentiment among the sectarians was to publish a newspaper called *Among Sectarians*, under the editorship of Bonch-Bruevich. Six issues of what was called eventually *Dawn (Rassvet)* were published (Etkind 1998, 636).

What is the reason for this interest? It was precisely their Christian communism, especially in the strong form that entailed devotion to an authoritarian leader with consequent commitment to the collective. This communism was clearly a tougher version of Christian communism than what was found in the universal love and peaceful living of Tolstoy, or the rural village commune so beloved by the Narodniks and Socialist-Revolutionaries. After the October revolution and during the life-and-death struggle with counter-revolution and the first steps in constructing socialism, these groups became even more interesting. In the Kremlin, Lenin took every opportunity to escape for a time and browse through Bonch-Bruevich's extensive ethnographic archive. He was particularly taken with the philosophical pamphlets written by the sectarians. According to Bonch-Bruevich:

> On one occasion he was particularly drawn into this reading ... and he told me: How interesting! This was created by simple folk ... whereas our Private-Docents have authored a huge amount of talentless papers on all

---

3 Note also: 'The peasant Narodniks in both of the early Dumas were full of fire and passion. They were eager for direct and resolute action. They were ignorant, uneducated and unsophisticated, but they rose against their class enemy so straightforwardly, uncompromisingly and implacably that one sensed what an impressive social force they were' (Lenin 1913c, 555, 1913d, 363).

> kinds of philosophical bullshit [*drebeden'*] .... These manuscripts are a
> hundred times more important than all their scribble.
>
> ETKIND 1998, 649

This enthusiasm was not only theoretical, for Lenin also saw their practical possibilities. Bonch-Bruevich had invited some Old Believers to establish a commune on abandoned land in Lesnye Poliany, located close to Gorki, where Lenin would retreat for a few moments of peace. The blessing for this venture appears in a proclamation addressed to 'Members of the Sect of Old Believers' (Marie 2008, 392–93).[4] The proclamation quotes a text we have already met, Acts 4:32, 'No one said any of the things which he possessed was his own, but they had everything in common', but Lenin was very interested since the commune indicated a potential alternative to the compromise of the New Economic Policy.

The third example comes from around the same time. In a letter to Nikolai Osinsky (Valerian Obolensky), chair of the State Bank and of the Supreme Economic Council, Lenin mentions a certain Ivan Afanasyevich Chekunov, an activist peasant keen on improving the lot of toiling peasants. Having improved his own farm, he had toured other areas (around Novgorod and Simbirsk) and tells Lenin that the peasants have lost confidence in Soviet power. Realising the crucial role of peasants in building a new society and sensing Chekunov's enthusiasm, Lenin urges Osinsky to appoint Chekunov to the role of representative of the People's Commissariat of Agriculture, with a view to establishing a non-Party Peasant Council. For my purposes, the vital point is that Chekunov 'sympathises with the Communists, but will not join the Party, because he goes to church and is a Christian (he says he rejects the ritual but is a believer)' (Lenin 1921a, 91, 1921b, 85). Before Lenin stands a communist-leaning Christian peasant, whom Lenin is eager to enlist in process of communist reconstruction. He sees an opportunity to go much further, for in developing the basis for a Non-Party Peasant Council, Lenin suggests that it should begin with an old farmer who favours the peasants and workers, along with another person from an area not producing grain. Crucially, not only should they be experienced, but 'it would be good for all of them to be *both* non-Party men *and* Christians' (Lenin 1921a, 91, 1921b, 86). Only such an organization would gain the confidence of peasants, showing both support for the communist government from

---

4   The Old Believers had broken away from the Orthodox Church in the seventeenth century and had by this time between three and four million members. Earlier, Lenin had written to Inessa Armand of an Old Believer, a peasant from Voronezh, a 'man of the earth' and a 'breath from the Black Earth', who had spent a year in a German prison camp. Lenin notes that 'he sympathises with socialism' and yearns to return to the land (Lenin 1917e, 279–80, 1917f, 377).

outside its own ranks and revealing that Christians may not be so much of a
threat to the success of the revolution.

The examples I have given are occasional and often marginal. But they begin to reveal a picture in which Lenin and Bolsheviks would occasionally stop
and pay attention to radical peasants. They had much to criticise, but they
could not help feeling a deep affinity. While the peasants' revolutionary organisation was still woeful, its actions scattered, its allegiances with liberals
fateful, its resolute focus on land redistribution too monarchist, and its slogans
concerning 'God-given land' too theological, the Bolsheviks were still enthused
by their innate revolutionary spirit, especially their refusal to be cowed by the
landlords and their fearless ability to speak truth to power. Yet, Lenin and the
Bolsheviks cannot avoid the fact that the peasants' unrelenting attacks against
the landlords and against unjust land distribution drew their inspiration from
theological and biblical sources.

2   Twisting over Tolstoy

If the occasional peasant encountered by Lenin and the other Bolsheviks have
passed through and out of history, the same cannot be said of Tolstoy – a
towering proponent of a version of peasant Christian communism. Indeed,
Tolstoy had become so influential on his death on 20 November 1910, that
many indeed tried to claim him for their own cause. His spiritual awakening,
call for a return to simple Christianity (Sermon on the Mount), vegetarian-
ism, peasant values (even his wearing peasant clothes), nonviolent resistance
and trenchant criticism of the state and modern society, lent him a moral
authority on par with his literary achievements. Many indeed were those who
laid a claim to him (Sorokin 1979). Here we find Slavophiles such as Grigor'ev,
Strakhov and Dostoyevsky, aesthetes like Turgenev and Symbolists such as
Merezhkovsky, but also radicals from as far back as the 1850s: Chernyshevsky
and Pisarev, and Narodniks like Mikhailovsky. The appeal for the radicals
arose from Tolstoy's advocacy of peasant values, enabling a romanticising of
peasant life and the village commune for a distinctly Russian path to socialism. As for the Mensheviks, especially Neviadomsky and Bazarov (in *Nasha
Zaria*), they argued that Tolstoy represented the misdirected aspirations of
the Russian intelligentsia, focused on the principle of non-resistance to evil
(Morawski 1965, 8). As if these efforts were not enough, government news-
papers at the time – both liberal and conservative (*Russkoe Znamia, Novoe
Vremia* and *Rech'*) – sought to claim Tolstoy as one of their own. He was
a great seeker of God, they opined, a prophet expressing the Russian soul
(Morawski 1965, 8).

My specific interest is how Tolstoy and the loose movement he inspired – with its anarchist tendencies – encountered and influenced the Russian communist movement. Plekhanov (1974, 559–61, 572–89) had already suggested that Tolstoy was an extreme representative of idealist individualism, even siding with the oppressors (Tolstoy was an aristocrat and landlord by birth), but that he was at least able to reveal from time to time the undesirability of the present situation, without understanding at all the struggle for transformation of social conditions. This reading would long influence subsequent assessments, such as that of Lukács (1972, 126–205), who flattens his analysis in seeking to bolster his preference for realism. For Lukács, Tolstoy is much like Balzac, a reactionary who is brilliant enough to provide insights into the decay of the ruling class. Later still, Rubenstein (1995, 379–82) attempts to follow Lukács, suggesting that Tolstoy's confusion reflects those of the peasants themselves with the result that his solution is a thin veil over his insights into social chaos. By contrast, Lenin's approach is more sophisticated, appearing in half a dozen articles that sought to counter other assessments of the time in the desire to identify potential contributions to socialism (Lenin 1908c, 1908d, 1910e, 1910f, 1910g, 1910h, 1910i, 1910j, 1910c, 1910d, 1911a, 1911b).

Lenin's analysis reveals significant insight while missing a crucial dimension of the nature of Christian communism. His main argument is that Tolstoy's criticism of Russian economics and society are largely correct, but that his biblically inspired solutions are wayward, if not regressive. Communists must therefore listen to and make the most of Tolstoy's insightful criticisms but offer more thoroughgoing and forward-looking answers. In more detail: Tolstoy's insights uncannily pinpointed the ever-increasing destitution of the peasantry, whether through government repression, legal corruption or adroit exploitation of post-serfdom conditions by landlords (demanding labour and produce in exchange for access to 'cut-off' lands with water and fodder). The outcome was ruined peasants flocking to towns seeking work in railway construction, mills and factories, thereby feeding a growing working class. With the rapid spread of capitalist relations that were simultaneously enmeshed with so many feudal assumptions and practices (Alexinsky 1913, 114–61; Olgin 1917, 3–36; Lenin 1899a, 1899b), exploitation, destitution, hunger and want were everywhere. For Lenin, it is a mark of Tolstoy's genius that he managed to depict these processes and express the 'mountains of hatred' that had arisen against the landlord system and the ravages of capitalism.

The solution – for Tolstoy – was to draw upon two traditions. The first was the perpetual dynamic of reform in the Christian tradition, especially in response to an otiose and corrupt church, enmeshed with a derailed socio-economic and political system. The reform in question sought an authentic original Christianity, cutting away the accretions of institutional time. Thus, Tolstoy challenged the dirty contract between church and ruling class, in which the church provides the theological bulwark of feudal and capitalist economic depredations. In claiming a return to original Christianity, Tolstoy sought a simple spirituality, ascetic life, withdrawal from politics, eschewing violence and seeking inner peace. Or, as Lunacharsky puts it, Tolstoy sought out the man 'born of God', the 'quiet, meek little angel' who divides the land up into little gardens: 'he can grow cabbages there, eat them, fertilise his garden and plant more cabbage, and thus, sustaining himself self-sufficiently and ever so sweetly, he will have no need for his neighbour, except for soul-saving talks or mutual prayer' (Lunacharsky 1973, 180). The second resource for Tolstoy came from the rapidly disappearing village commune, where he found living Christian moral values. Here one may follow the commandments of an anarchist Christ: do not be angry; do not lust; do not bind yourself by oaths; resist not him who is evil; be good to the just and the unjust (Tolstoy 2009, 45–71). Indeed, for Tolstoy these are the '"eternal" principles of morality, the eternal truths of religion' (Lenin 1911a, 50, 1911b, 101) found in many of his works (Tolstoy 1857, 1885, 1887, 1889, 1900).

As I mentioned earlier, Lenin praises Tolstoy's artistic power in identifying exploitation at the heart of feudal and capitalist economics, but he finds the proposed solution highly problematic, focused as it was on a simplified and ascetic Christian spirituality disengaged from politics. At this point, Lenin's response echoes that of Plekhanov, at least when the latter left room open for Tolstoy. But Lenin goes further: Tolstoy's approach itself manifests a series of inherent contradictions that are due to the context in which he was writing and living. These contradictions include: the class contradictions of Tolstoy's own situation as an aristocrat identifying with the peasants; peasant political aspirations, which Tolstoy's genius has identified and expressed very clearly; the contradictions of the Russian Revolution of 1905; and the troubled and drawn-out transition from feudal economic relations to capitalist ones, signalled by the abolition of serfdom in 1861 and the revolution of 1905.

I will not dwell long on the first contradiction, based on Tolstoy's class situation, particularly since Lenin does not make much of it (in contrast to Plekhanov). Thus, although 'Tolstoy belonged to the highest landed nobility in Russia' (Lenin 1910g, 331, 1910h, 39–40) through birth and education, he sought to break with all of these class assumptions. Often he managed to do so, but at times Lenin suggests that the contradictions in Tolstoy's art may be influenced by the tensions inherent in his class context: 'Despair is typical of the classes which are perishing' (Lenin 1910g, 332, 1910h, 41).

The second contradiction is more substantial, for Tolstoy expresses both the economic despair and the political aspirations of the peasants: 'The ancient foundations of peasant economy and peasant life, foundations that had really held for centuries, were broken up for scrap with extraordinary rapidity' (Lenin 1908c, 206, 1908d, 210). Tolstoy's greatness is to register the disruptive changes experienced by the peasants, voicing their collective anger that blends centuries of hatred of landlords, priests and Tsar with a newer hatred of capitalist bosses and tax collectors. The protest may be genuine, but the peasants still struggle to find a political answer: 'Through his lips there spoke that multitudinous mass of the Russian people who *already* detest the masters of modern life but have not *yet* advanced to the point of intelligent, consistent, thoroughgoing, implacable struggle against them' (Lenin 1910i, 353, 1910j, 70). The reason: as a class, the peasants are situated somewhere between the old regime and a class-conscious proletariat. In their anger at the old regime, they may be spontaneously revolutionary, but they are not yet politically conscious enough for a full revolution.

In this light may we understand the third contradiction, expressed in the 1905 revolution, which was led initially by the ambivalent priest Gapon.[5] For Lenin, at this moment the peasantry emerged as a political force, seeking to abolish old and new forms of oppression and replace them with communities of free and equal citizens (Lenin 1910e, 324, 1910f, 20).[6] The catch is that the imagined new society is actually old and patriarchal. Here the village commune's equality is reinforced by a deeply moral Christianity, precisely where Tolstoy seeks to find inspiration. But it is a backward looking reactionary utopia, longing for a mythical past for which one weeps and prays, moralises and dreams, and writes petitions to the authorities to grant one's wishes. For Lenin and the Bolsheviks, violence almost always comes from the political right (witness the Black Hundreds), but one must be practical and prepared to respond

---

5   I leave aside the ongoing debates over the priest Gapon (1905), who led the protest of 200,000 workers with their petition to the Tsar (Harding 1983, 309–12) that resulted in 'Bloody Sunday' on 9 January, 1905 (old calendar) and sparked the revolution of that year. While many are ready to condemn Gapon's role as a police agent (Krupskaya 1930, 111–19; Cliff 2002, 133–37; Le Blanc 1990, 110–13), Lenin was far more open to seeing the developments in a dialectical manner and giving Gapon credit for his revolutionary credentials, even if Gapon did not know quite what he did (Lenin 1905c, 1905d, 1905a, 1905b; Lunacharsky 1905). It is worth noting that Lenin held in his personal library in the Kremlin a copy of Gapon's book, *A Proclamation to the Entire Peasant Folk*, which Gapon presented to Lenin in 1905 with the following autograph: 'To the most honoured comrade Lenin by way of good memory from the author. Georgy Gapon April 14, 1905'.

6   Macherey (1992, 120–34) follows Lenin here, drawing out the implications of Tolstoy as a 'mirror' and 'expression' of peasant aspirations and those of the 1905 revolution.

to violence. Thus, non-resistance to evil resulted in 'a most serious cause of the defeat of the first revolutionary campaign' (Lenin 1908c, 208, 1908d, 213), to which the autocracy responded with even harsher conditions for the peasantry.

All of this leads to Lenin's final point concerning the deep contradictions arising from the transition between modes of production, with the attendant dislocation, violence and exploitation, as well as release from encrusted and apparently unassailable ways of life of the system now falling to pieces (Lenin 1910e, 1910f, 1911a, 1911b). Tolstoy's art registers this transition and all its tensions, where the relics of feudalism still appear in the autocratic state, church monopoly, landlord tyranny and robbery. At the same time, capitalism leaps ahead, expressed best in a statement made in the novel, *Anna Karenina*. Here the character Levin talks about harvest arrangements, pointing out that 'Here in Russia everything has now been turned upside down and is only just taking shape' (Lenin 1911a, 49, 1911b, 100; Tolstoy 1877, 870). Tolstoy registers this shift at the most profound level, but for Lenin at least the solution is woefully inadequate.

By now it should be clear that – for Lenin – Tolstoy should not be dismissed, for his incisive criticisms of both crumbling feudalism and rampant capitalism provide immense possibilities for communists. But Lenin goes even further, pointing out that these possibilities appear in the midst of and even through the reactionary elements of Tolstoy's work. Precisely because Tolstoy expressed the pain and desire of a class being replaced by the bourgeoisie, he thereby provided insights for the class that will replace the bourgeoisie. Feudal agrarian socialism may be passing, finding a great voice in Tolstoy, but it is the dialectical harbinger of proletarian socialism. Tolstoy contributed, however unwittingly, to the 'epoch of preparation' (Lenin 1910e, 323, 1910f, 19).

I have taken some time with Lenin's assessment of Tolstoy since it is his most sustained engagement with a form of Christian communism. Although Tolstoy is often identified as a Christian anarchist (largely due to his anti-statism), much also derives from the Christian communist tradition. By now, Lenin's approach should be clear: he attempts to quarantine the religious dimensions of Tolstoy's thought and practice to a regressive form of communalism. At the same time, Lenin seeks to detach the insightful criticisms from any religious features so they might be appropriated for the communist movement. The problem with this move is twofold, despite the insights generated by his dialectical engagement. First, as we have already seen (Chapter 1), revolutionary criticism is also inspired by the tradition of Christian communism. If a society does not live up the prescriptions found in the Scriptures, then it must be criticised in the name of a better world. But this is to separate too sharply revolutionary criticism from communal life. The catch is that these two dimensions are so often entwined in the Christian communist tradition, where the alternative communistic life entails within itself critique of the world as it is, leading at times to the necessity of revolutionary action. True, Tolstoy may have owed much to the peasant rural commune of Russia, if not the millennia-long practices of subsistence-survival agriculture, but if we pick up my earlier argument concerning the complex intersections between subsistence-survival agriculture and early Christian communism (Chapter 2), we may see that Tolstoy's inspirations are actually linked. This point leads to Lenin's second problem: all he sees in Tolstoy's religious heritage is nostalgia rather than hope, quietism rather than action, retreat rather than advance. Yet these prescriptions are not necessarily regressive, for they are able to look forward as well as backward. So many of the Christian communist organisations that emerged throughout European history also looked to the future by drawing on the past, advocating a simplicity of life, hard work and eschewing political power for the sake of providing alternative models of cooperative existence. In this light, perhaps Lunacharsky was correct after all, arguing that Tolstoy in his own way offers a variation on Christian communism (Lunacharsky 1985, 183–85).

3   God-Builders

The mention of Lunacharsky brings me to the third and most unique stream of Christian communism in relation to the Russian Revolution. Unlike the peasants and Tolstoy, Lunacharsky and the God-Builders were not inspired by the Russian tradition of peasant communalism. Instead, Lunacharsky was deeply influenced by work that had been done on European Christian communism (especially Kautsky). But who were the God-Builders? They did not follow the line of the 'God-Seekers', pursuing links between Orthodoxy and Marxism, for they were atheists who wished to increase the emotional power – the 'warm stream' – of Marxism by drawing upon positive elements from religion, especially Christianity. The key statement of God-building is Lunacharsky's two-volume *Religion and Socialism*.[7] The first volume concerns definitions of religion, socialist positions on religion (including Engels, Plekhanov, Feuerbach and Dietzgen) and an evolutionary theory of religion that ends with Brahmanism, Judaism and Hellenism. The second volume focuses on the New Testament, the historical Jesus and the Apostle Paul, moves through the millenarianism of early Christianity, Gnosticism, orthodoxy (Augustine), and then

---

7   A brief statement of Lunacharsky's position appears in 'Atiezm' (Lunacharsky 1908a).

to Christian socialism (with a Russian focus), liberal theology and contemporary European (German) religious philosophy. A discussion of utopian socialism precedes the final treatment of Marx and Engels.

The primary motivation for the work was twofold. To begin with, it seeks a dimension that goes beyond the cold, '"dry" economic theory' (Lunacharsky 1908b, 9) characteristic of Second International Marxism and especially the 'father' of Russian Marxism, Plekhanov. Instead, it emphasizes what Ernst Bloch later called the 'warm stream' of Marxism, its enthusiastic, emotional, and ethical elements, the Marxism that inspires 'conversion' and offers a 'deeply emotional impulse of the soul' (1908b, 9). Second, *Religion and Socialism* explores the 'place of socialism among other religious systems' (1908b, 8). By 'religion' he means not belief in divine beings in a supernatural world (the standard Marxist position at the time), but rather the emotive, collective, utopian and very human elements of religion. Religion offers hope, in the sense that the 'dreams of humanity' are expressed in nothing less than 'religious myths and dogmas' (1908b, 7). Lunacharsky seeks the working core of religion, focusing not 'so much on the external socio-economic fate of institutions' (Lunacharsky 1911, 126), but on the analysis of the main religious ideas and sentiments – even including matters such as Christology, justification by faith, salvation and eschatology.

From this investigation some key ideas emerge: myth and poetry, the crucial role of revolution and revolutionary history, deep awareness of the political ambivalence of religion, and the value of Christian communism. To begin with the question of myth and poetry, Lunacharsky is not interested in worshipping human beings (contra Fitzpatrick 1970, 1; Bergman 1990). Rather, it is God-*building*, in which the 'ideal is the image of man, of man like a god, in relation to whom we are all raw material only, merely ingots waiting to be given shape, living ingots that bear their own ideal within themselves' (Lunacharsky 1981, 57). In such statements, the poetic image-laden language characteristic of all his writing shows forth. But he also reads texts with the same sensibility, especially the Bible. The Gospel narratives of Jesus are full of drama, linguistic power, tragedy and triumph (Lunacharsky 1911, 18–22). He finds the Apostle Paul a writer of remarkable skill – the bright and sparkling poet of early Christianity, the internationalist democrat who at the same time spiritualizes Christian thought (1911, 27–60). It comes as no surprise, then, that he sees the political importance of myth (anticipating Ernst Bloch by many decades). Religion itself may be characterized as myth, a 'wonderful, graceful interweaving of tales' (1908b, 191), for in such language do the artists of tomorrow reach out to the new, or rather bind the gold of the past with the art of the future.

The second feature is Lunacharsky's resolute focus on revolution, with a twist: 'In a religious society one cannot make a revolution or a broader reform that is not a revolution in the field of the relationship with God' (1908b, 70). And when the October revolution happened, he saw it as 'the greatest, most definitive act of "God-building"' (Lunacharsky 1919, 31), seeking to share with his comrades a form of spiritual ecstasy and proclaiming 'These events are epoch-making! Our children's children will bow their heads before their grandeur!' (Fitzpatrick 1970, 1). Caught up in these immense, strongly felt experiences, he was not afraid to speak of God, albeit a God that has now been given to the world. In this way may human beings take a leap forward in the process of shaping the 'living ingots'.

Third, Lunacharsky reveals a sustained awareness of religion's political ambivalence (see Chapter 3), which requires a strategy of discernment. Christianity may be both a 'creed of democracy' and a justification for 'meekly bearing the yoke' of oppression (Lunacharsky 1985, 92). Thus, the gods may embody democracy, aspirations of the poor and resolute hatred for the rich and powerful; yet the gods may also sit very snugly in the seat of power (Lunacharsky 1908b, 64). This dialectical tension appears with Hebrew prophets like Isaiah. Echoing Lenin's analysis of Tolstoy, Lunacharsky argues that the revolutionary impulse of the prophets is itself enabled by a backward-looking, small-proprietor and anti-progress perspective. Without the latter, they would not have been revolutionary, yet that reactionary element ultimately hobbles the unleashing of a full revolutionary approach (Lunacharsky 1908b, 165, 169). But the most astute dialectical interpretation focuses on the Apostle Paul (Lunacharsky 1911, 41–45, 53, 58–60). The dialectic here has many twists, so let us pay attention to each step. In response to the delay of Christ's return, Paul constructs an idealised and other-worldly theology that spiritualises an earthly and political movement, so much so that the heavenly face of Christ overshadows the worldly person (Lunacharsky 1911, 53). Yet, by means of this spiritualisation Paul breaks through to a more international and democratic form of Christianity. No longer ethnically and nationally limited, it belongs to all. The dialectic takes another turn: by internationalising Christianity, Paul overcomes yet another tension, now within early Christianity. That form may have been resolutely communistic, yet it was trapped within a fierce nationalism and hatred of foreign oppressors. Paul's response both moves away from that early communism and negates its nationalistic focus. Indeed, he was able to do so only through an anti-communist spiritualisation. Even more, at this higher level (*Aufhebung*) Paul offers a new revolutionary doctrine: justification by faith is itself deeply revolutionary, for it destroys the privilege of the rich and powerful (Lunacharsky 1911, 55). Finally, it is precisely this mystical theology that makes of Paul the great myth-maker, producing a reshaped myth of the dying and rising Christ, a myth that Lunacharsky admires for its sparkling poetic power.

Let me dwell a little longer with on Lunacharsky's reflections on the Christian communist tradition, given the emphasis of this book as a whole.[8] A consistent motif throughout *Religion and Socialism* is that early Christianity was characterized by comradeship, equality and honesty, with the early communities 'permeated by a spirit of collectivism', sharing what little property they had (Lunacharsky 1911, 211). The early message was a 'Gospel of the poor', of slaves, artisans and proletarians – as Engels had argued only a few years earlier. At the level of definition, Lunacharsky finds this collective dimension by drawing on the Latin etymology of the term: 'religion is a "bond" [*religiia* – "*sviaz*"]' (Lunacharsky 1908b, 14). Historically and textually, he draws upon all of the key texts in the Acts of the Apostles and the Gospels concerning such communism and the resolute opposition to acquiring private property (Lunacharsky 1911, 65). He adds further evidence from this dual tradition, including: the democratic virtues of the God of the Hebrew Bible, offering a sense of justice and aversion to power, luxury and the associated vices and crimes (Lunacharsky 1911, 7); the importance of the Essenes and their monastic communism, as well as the Ebionites or 'the poor' (Lunacharsky 1911, 11, 23–26, 35–36, 61); and the subsequent history of Christian socialism, with all its continuities and breaks (Lunacharsky 1911, 139–82). For Lunacharsky this tradition is nothing less than 'democratic, egalitarian socialism' – terminology he uses throughout *Religion and Socialism*.[9]

At the same time, he was too good a student of Engels and Kautsky[10] not to identify the problems: the communist dimension was often other-worldly; it did not address the question of production, remaining within the realm of consumption; and the democratic element lasted only as long as the early church was made up of the lower classes. All of which means that he must, like Kautsky, deploy a version of the betrayal narrative. Lunacharsky suggests that in a relatively short time, Christianity became a religion of power and hierarchy, ready to argue that God justifies the rich and mighty as they exercise their influence over the masses by promising reward in heaven in exchange for

---

8   The following material is drawn more directly from my earlier study of Lunacharsky (Boer 2014c). I have decided to include this material here for obvious reasons.

9   See also his later *Religiia i prosveshchenie* [*Religion and Enlightenment*] (Lunacharsky 1985, 76, 84–85, 92, 120–21, 173–76).

10   When called upon to make socio-economic points, Lunacharsky relies even more heavily on Kautsky. The references are drawn from Kautsky's *Foundations of Christianity*, 'Social Democracy and the Catholic Church', and his *Ethics* (Kautsky 1908a, 1908b, 1903, 1910).

subservience on earth. While we have met a version of this 'Fall' narrative with Kautsky, Lunacharsky offers an alternative approach. He focuses on Gnosticism, which he argues is the aristocratic answer to the democratic and revolutionary forms of Christianity (Lunacharsky 1911, 69–101). From the amorphous movement of Gnosticism[11] come the doctrine of the Logos, crucial to Orthodox Christianity, and of individualism and thereby of individual power (which he is clear does not derive from Paul).[12] But the motifs of Gnosticism were not merely ideas, for they were integral to a class dynamic in which the morally bereft aristocracy and propertied classes found an ideology that would justify marginalising the revolutionary communist side of Christianity in the name of becoming a religion of empire (Lunacharsky 1911, 104–39). In other words, Gnosticism did not fail, as the conventional narratives of the early ecumenical councils would have us believe, but succeeded in gaining control at structural and doctrinal levels. The last chance for an alternative lay with the ambiguous work of Clement and Origen, especially in their efforts to produce syntheses of communist and aristocratic elements, but they failed, as may be seen in the full statement of orthodox Christianity in Augustine and the clear class identification of the clergy with the ruling class (Lunacharsky 1911, 106–22). As Lunacharsky sums up in the later debates with Vvedensky, a transformation took place from a 'chaotic primitive church into a strong, cunning, subtle instrument of oppression' (Lunacharsky 1985, 92).

I have already indicated the problems with narratives of betrayal (Chapter 1), which are deeply indebted to biblical narrative patterns from Genesis 2–3. Apart from the need for an initial, original impulse that one must seek to restore (characteristic of Christian reform movements), it substitutes a linear narrative for what may potentially be a subtler analysis that recognizes the tensions at the heart of a religion such as Christianity. As I have already indicated, this subtlety emerges in Lunacharsky's concern with the theological and political ambivalence of Christianity. In this light, Lunacharsky introduces a crucial distinction into his treatment of Christian communism: communal, democratic and radically equal living constitutes only one dimension, for the other is revolution itself – precisely what Lenin missed in his engagement with Tolstoy. Christianity may have exhibited elements that qualify it as communist in the first sense, but what about revolution? Here Lunacharsky is unequivocal:

---

11   For a useful review of approaches to Gnosticism in the last 50 years, see the study by Dillon (2016).

12   He also describes it as a wonderful doctrine for the bourgeoisie, which 'seeks mystery and faith. Gnosticism is deep, beautiful and flexible' (Lunacharsky 1911, 104).

Christianity was also revolutionary, since it included a rough justice for the wealthy and ruling class:

> The communist spirit of early, popular Christianity is not in doubt. But was it revolutionary? Yes, of course. In its negation, the radical, merciless negation of the civilized world of the time, in posing in its place a completely new way of life, it was revolutionary. Any ideology that truly reflects the mood of the oppressed masses can only be revolutionary in its depth.[13]
>
> LUNACHARSKY 1911, 139

Lunacharsky invokes this dual nature of early Christianity, including both communist living and revolution, in a number of ways. At times he sees their close connection and at others he explores their contradictions, but he also espies enough similarity on both counts between Marxism and Christianity to call them communist, for their 'their ideals are partly congruent' (1911, 159).

But how exactly do the two traditions relate to one another, in light of the historical gap between early Christianity and modern Marxism? Here Lunacharsky draws upon an old motif, distinguishing between false and true forms of Christianity, or, in this case, of Christian communism. The false tradition is represented by the relatively recent – for Lunacharsky – form of Christian socialism that appealed to so many, whether in England, Germany or Russia. This form, he argues, is an aberration, given its tendency to adopt secularist and free-thinking approaches so that it is hardly Christian at all, if not counter-revolutionary. Further, Lunacharsky faces a problem that we have already seen with Kautsky and Luxemburg: if contemporary Christian socialism had too much legitimacy, then the question arises as to the need for modern socialism at all. So Lunacharsky finds himself arguing that the authentic tradition of revolutionary religious communism is an ancient one, going as far back as the biblical prophets, who gave voice to a radical dimension of the Hebrew God, Yahweh. Intriguingly, he is not content to rest with this argument, for he also traces a marginal tradition (like Ernst Bloch) that owes its debts to the ancient prophets, identifying the 'everlasting Gospel' of Joachim of Fiore, as well as Francis of Assisi, Fra Dolcino, Thomas Müntzer and the Peasant Revolution, the Münster Revolution of 1534–1535 and even the Puritans of the English Revolution (Lunacharsky 1911, 55, 141, 145–55, 1908b, 183–84). It is precisely this

---

13   See also his later statements in the same vein in *Religiia i prosveshchenie* (Lunacharsky 1985, 177–78).

tradition that leads to 'the greatest of the prophets – Karl Marx' (Lunacharsky 1908b, 188).

4   Conclusion

I have traced some of the manifestations – expected and unexpected – of Christian communism at the margins of the Russian Revolution, if not on the edges of the Bolsheviks who were given the opportunity to construct socialism in Russia. Peasant socialism, mediated through the village commune (which hung on in Russia into the twentieth century), would also come to play a significant role in Tolstoy's efforts to recover a form of early Christianity. As we have seen, Lenin and the Bolsheviks were intrigued from time to time and even interested where it might benefit their project. But the religious dimension always remained suspect in an extraordinarily complex way (Lenin 1905e, 1905f, 1909a, 1909b, 1909c, 1909d). Within the Russian Orthodox Church, the Bolsheviks may have worked with the Renovationists (Roslov 2002) until the death of Metropolitan Vvedensky in 1946. But already from 1927, Sergei – who would become patriarch some eighteen years later – had begun to express support for the new government, agitating for religious freedom after the Constitution of 1936 and eventually managing the famous compact with Stalin in 1943 (Miner 2003; Boer 2018). All of this meant that the strands of Christian communism would remain on the edges of revolutionary tendencies in Russia. This was also true of the extraordinary contribution of Lunacharsky and the God-Builders, who evoked the European tradition of Christian communism more directly. Lunacharsky's first volume was, of course, subjected to scathing criticism by Lenin (Lenin 1908a, 1908b), so much so that it virtually disappeared. Lunacharsky may have responded obliquely to Lenin in the second volume of 1911, but both volumes were left out of his collected works (Lunacharsky 1963–1967). At the same time, Lunacharsky maintained his core position concerning God-building, basing his educational theory on this foundation while Commissar for Enlightenment after the October Revolution. Might it be said that this is where the tradition of Christian communism came to influence socialism in the Soviet Union in an unexpected and mediated manner? Perhaps, but it was modulated and mediated through the idea that the image of the gods in religion was really an ideal to which human beings should strive (Lunacharsky 1981, 45–46, 57). The trap is to read such an approach as individualistic, but Lunacharsky had a more collective emphasis in mind, so much so that it also expressed the striving for communism itself.

CHAPTER 12

The Taiping Revolution: Christian Communism Comes to China

> The Chinese revolution will throw the spark into the overloaded mine of the present industrial system and cause the explosion of the long-prepared general crisis.
>
> MARX 1853, 98

The story of Christian communism continues, running along unexpected historical paths. One such path was to China in the nineteenth century, when revolutionary Christianity – in the shape of the Taiping Revolution – first appeared in this part of the world. The reason for making this claim will become clear as my analysis unfolds, but here it is necessary to make a disclaimer. The movement itself was incredibly complex, offering many currents and possible interpretations. Depending upon what aspect one emphasises, one's interpretation will differ. Was it the first modern revolutionary movement in China or was it merely another peasant revolution seeking to install a new emperor? Was it part of the anti-colonial struggle or was it yet another signal of the chaos into which China was descending? Was it actually another feature of nineteenth century colonialism, inspired by a 'foreign teaching' with its strange notion of transcendence? Was its leader, Hong Xiuquan, simply a bandit with megalomaniac pretentions who fostered immense violence and destruction, or was he a genuine visionary who offered hope to millions of oppressed peasants? Was Hong Xiuquan the hero or was it Zeng Guofan, the Qing general and Confucian who ultimately destroyed the revolution? Was it progressive for the time or was it largely reactionary? Was religion really important, especially for the many peasants who joined the movement, or was it a peripheral feature in which politics and economics were at the forefront? The questions and perspectives could be multiplied. In this light, my modest proposal is that a few aspects have perhaps not been given due attention. The first is the crucial question as to why the Taiping movement placed so much emphasis on the Bible, reprinting it even to the last days, interpreting it, even modifying some sections that they found objectionable. The second is the way some aspects of the revolution show distinct connections with the longer tradition of Christian communism that I have tracked thus far, so much so that one can speak in some respects of the arrival of the Christian communist tradition in China. In what follows, I emphasise these particular aspects, but I do not suggest that this is the only way to understand the Taiping Revolution. Instead, they are aspects that must seriously be considered in the broader range of possible interpretations.

1   The Dream

The account begins in early 1837. In that year, Hong Xiuquan sank into a delirium and had a vision in the small southern Chinese village of Guanlubu.[1] The vision seems to have been full of the characters one may expect from Chinese mythology. Equally so, some were not so conventional. Taken up into heaven, he was greeted by children dressed in yellow, as well as a cock, a tiger, a dragon and men playing music. Placing him in a sedan chair, they took him to a high gate bathed in light, surrounded by musicians. Here men in dragon robes and horned hats cut his body open and replaced his old and dirty earthly organs with clean new ones. The incision was healed and disappeared, as seems to happen in such places. But now his suspicions that he was on his way to death seemed to be confirmed, for a woman who looked like the goddess Meng appeared, ready to give him the memory-destroying drink on the edge of a blood-coloured stream. Instead, she washed him in the stream and called him 'son'. Alongside his mother, he became aware of a man, who seemed to be a brother. Inside the gates, he was led to his father, a tall erect man sitting on a throne, wearing a high hat and a black dragon robe, with a golden beard that flowed down to his waist.

Hong's father spoke of his grief at the way people on earth had forgotten him, offering the father's gifts of food and clothes and the products of their hands to none other than the demon devils. These devils pretended that they were the source of all that the father had given them, producing immense frustration, rage and pity in the father. Yet, the father waited to punish them, even when the demons had infiltrated the 33 levels of heaven. Eventually, Hong persuaded his father to let him act. With the gift of a powerful sword called 'Snow-in-the-Clouds', Hong attacked the demons throughout the heavens, while his brother held up a heavenly seal which blinded the demons by its fierce light. They managed to chase the demons out of heaven and onto earth, where Hong captured the demon king, Yan Luo. But his father told him not to kill the demon king yet, for he may pollute heaven. After this battle, Hong stayed for a

---

1   Hong Xiuquan's own account may be found in *Taiping Heavenly Chronicle* (*Taiping tianri*), written in 1848 (Michael and Chang 1966, vol. 2, 51–76).

time in heaven, with a wife who had born him a son. He studied mysterious texts, guided by his patient father, for they took some effort to understand. His elder brother was not so patient with Hong, so he had to be soothed by Hong's sister-in-law. Yet Hong's father would not let him forget the demons, for they still roamed on the earth below and did much damage. To earth Hong must return, albeit with a new name (Xiuquan), two mysterious poems and a title, 'Heavenly King, Lord of the Kingly Way, *Quan* [Completeness]'. So Hong set out, with his father's words of blessing and protection singing in his ears.

What did Hong's family and friends do as he ranted and raved while they kept watch at his bed in the village of Guanlubu? They thought he had gone mad. At times during his delirium, he would call out, argue with those around, get up and run around the room while making sword thrusts, only to collapse back on his bed. At one point, he wrote out the two poems his father in heaven had bequeathed him, at another he wrote his new title in red ink and posted it on the door. That door was kept firmly locked, since the family would have been held to account should he have done harm to anyone else. They certainly did not understand what was happening. But did Hong? Upon waking and calming down, he was unable to make sense of it all. So he gradually settled back into village life, began teaching children again and studying the Confucian texts in preparation for his next attempt at the civil service examinations, at which he had thus far failed.

2 Hong and the Bible

Let me fill in some context (Spence 1996, 23–65; Kilcourse 2016, 46–49). Hong Xiuquan (born Renkun, with the courtesy name of Huoxiu in 1814) was a young Hakka man, a minority group in China.[2] He was part of a large family that had moved more than a century earlier to the village of Fuyuanshui and then later to Guanlubu, in the mountainous county of Hua (in those times Huadu, 50 kilometres north of Guangzhou). The rugged area was a favourite haunt of secret societies, bandits and rebels (the distinction is artificial), for the mountains offered plenty of protection (Cai 1988). Young Hong was widely regarded as the scholar of the family, so he studied hard for the civil service examinations based on the Confucian texts. On two earlier occasions, he had passed the local examination, which entitled him to travel to Guangzhou (Canton) for the major examination. The stakes were high, for success enabled one to enter the imperial service and gain prestige for oneself and one's family. To finance

---

2 On the broader context of Hakka rebellion and revolution, see Erbaugh (1992).

his study, he taught in his village, being paid in food and the basics of life. But on the two previous occasions, he had failed the examinations in Guangzhou. By 1837 the pressure was even higher and he arrived with high expectations. Again he failed the examinations, which brought on his nervous breakdown and the extraordinary vision with which I began.

On this occasion there was one crucial difference: Hong had in passing accepted from a missionary (and his assistant) a collection of biblical tracts known as *Quanshi liangyan*, or *Good Words to Admonish the Age* (Liang 1965). They were written in Chinese by an evangelical convert, Liang Fa.[3] The tracts and then the Bible itself (which he acquired a few years later) would become the catalyst for the Taiping Revolution. But at the time, Hong paid little attention to the collection of tracts, tossing them in his bag and ignoring them as the vision descended upon him. Indeed, he ignored them for some years afterwards, as he returned to what resembled normal life.

Six years later, in 1843, he made one last attempt at the civil service examination. The fourth failure reminded him painfully of his vivid dream, but now he turned to the biblical literature that lay gathering dust in a corner. Soon enough, the biblical tracts and then the whole Bible gave him the key to his visions. He had been in heaven and had met none other than God the Heavenly Father (*tianfu*) in physical form, with a long beard and wearing a black dragon robe, who vouched for the authenticity of the Bible (these were the mysterious moral texts that had taken considerable effort to understand) and had entrusted him with slaying demons. He also learned that the heavenly elder brother (*tianxiong*) he had met was none other than Jesus himself. This of course meant that he was Jesus's 'natural younger brother' (*baodi*) and therefore that he, Hong Xiuquan, was a human but non-divine 'son' of God. At this point, many have suggested that Hong was indeed somewhat mad. But to do so would be to miss a vital feature of religious revolutionary movements: visions and dreams function as powerful sources of inspiration, along with the Bible. Both are perfectly authentic forms of divine revelation, one from the past and the other in the present. In Hong's case, the biblical material provided the interpretive key for the dreams.[4] Even more, his initial visions and interpretive insight provided the ideological basis of the Taiping movement.

---

3 See the detailed study by Kim (2011), although he overplays the role of the tracts in Taiping thought and practice.

4 But when his dreams ceased, the movement turned to other visionaries – especially Yang Xiuqing – and to detailed interpretation of the Bible, although they inevitably used such visions in the factional struggles that threatened the movement (Spence 1996, 210–45; Kilcourse 2016, 149–53).

Hong Xiuquan learnt much, much more from the Bible, which became central for the movement and to which considerable resources were devoted for reprinting and even making corrections. In Hong Xiuquan's own words, from the *Taiping Heavenly Chronicle* (*Taiping tianri*):

> The Heavenly Father, the Supreme Lord and Great God, ordered that three classes of books be put out and indicated this to the Sovereign, saying, 'This class of books consists of the records which have been transmitted from that former time when I descended into the world, performing miracles and instituting the commandments. These books are pure and without error. And the books of the second class are the accounts which have been transmitted from the time when your Elder Brother, Christ, descended into the world, performing miracles, sacrificing his life for the remission of sins, and doing other deeds. These books also are pure and without error. But the books of the other class are those transmitted from Confucius .... These books contain extremely numerous errors and faults, so that you were harmed by studying them'.
>
> MICHAEL AND CHANG 1966, vol. 2, 56–57

He studied the Bible in detail in 1847, when he spent some time in Hong Kong with a Baptist missionary from the United States, Issachar Jacox Roberts, who had the Chinese name of Luo Xiaoquan (Rapp 2008; Yuan 1963; Durham 2013). This study gradually led Hong to realise the political dimensions of his religious visions, with a focus on founding a heavenly kingdom on earth, which entailed punishing the idol worshippers and evil ones (Reilly 2004, 104–15; Kilcourse 2014, 131, 2016, 49–53). The Bible in question had been translated by the missionaries Karl Gützlaff and Walter Medhurst, who had translated – respectively – both the Old and New Testaments (Zhao 2010). Significantly, this translation rendered the name for God into Chinese as *Shangdi*, Sovereign on High, or at times *Huang Shangdi*, Supreme Sovereign on High (Reilly 2004, 19–53, 78–100).[5] Crucially, *Shangdi* was the original name given to the Lord of Heaven by the Chinese classics. This translation for the Bible had first been suggested in the sixteenth century by the Roman Catholic missionary, Matteo Ricci. It had suffered under a papal decree that banned it in 1715, but was resurrected in the nineteenth century in the midst of immense debate among the idiosyncratic circle of missionaries based in Hong Kong. Thus, in

---

5   By contrast, the official Union translation, dating from 1904 and updated frequently (most recently 2003), uses the generic *shen*. At the same time, popular spoken usage today prefers *Shangdi* when speaking of the biblical God.

their translation of the Old and New Testaments, Medhurst and Gützlaff used *Shangdi* for the name of God.

The choice of *Shangdi* had profound implications for Hong Xiuquan and those who followed him. From the first imperial Chinese dynasty (the Qin in 221–206 BCE) the term *Huangdi* (supreme *di*) had been used to designate the emperor. By claiming the title of *di*, the emperor ever since – in the eyes of the Taiping – was laying claim to a name that should be reserved for none other than God. Absolutely no one was to use either *Shangdi* or *di* (Hong insisted that he be called nothing more than *zhu*, 'lord').[6] In other words, from the first moment and throughout the Chinese imperial system, God (the most high *Shangdi*) had been blasphemed. The key for the Taiping was in the first three of the Ten Commandments, which concern the worship of one god and the ban on graven images. These commandments, they believed, were applicable to the Chinese imperial system, and particularly the Qing dynasty of their own time. The emperors and all who supported them had created false gods in place of the High God, *Shangdi*. In the words of the *Taiping Imperial Declaration* of 1844–45:

> By referring to the Old Testament [*Jiuyizhao shengshu*] we learn that in early ages the Supreme God [*Huang Shangdi*] descended on Mount Sinai and in his own hand he wrote the Ten Commandments on tablets of stone, which he gave to Moses, saying, 'I am the High Lord [*Shangzhu*], the Supreme God; you men of the world must on no account set up images resembling anything in heaven above or on earth below, and bow down and worship them'. Now you people of the world who set up images and bow down and worship them are in absolute defiance of the Supreme God's expressed will. ... How extremely foolish you are to let your minds be so deceived by the demon!'[7]
>
> MICHAEL AND CHANG 1966, vol. 2, 41

And not only was the emperor himself a self-proclaimed imposter, but so also were the myriad symbols and representations of imperial rule through the length and breadth of China, along with the pervasive Buddhist 'idols', Daoist immortals and the many minor deities of popular religion. The whole imperial system and its religious bulwarks had to be destroyed.

---

6   This also included Jesus, for if the Taiping had claimed that Jesus or indeed Hong was also divine, they would have contradicted this position (Kilcourse 2014, 134–36).

7   See also the detailed discussion of the strongly monotheistic nature of Taiping theology in Kilcourse (2014, 129–33, 2016, 79–108).

3   Revolution and Community

The Taiping movement found many other revolutionary texts in the Bible, all the way from Exodus to the Book of Revelation. But let me outline the main features of the revolution,[8] which was the most important and largest movement anywhere in the world in the nineteenth century. The revolutionary sparks in Europe of 1848 were a sideshow by comparison. It began as a small movement with a few local followers in the villages around Hong Xiuquan's home in Guanlubu, in Guangdong province. Forced to move into more remote areas, they established their base in the mountainous regions of Guangxi province. Yet the message of resistance found fertile soil among any who were oppressed and exploited. These included peasants, miners, ethnic minorities and organised 'bandit' groups who had for long carried out their own forms of resistance. Memories of oppression run deep and the opportunities for genuine release are few. This seemed to be one such occasion, when all of the bottled-up revolutionary will could explode against systemic economic exploitation, colonial depredations, political suppression by the ethnically foreign dynasty of the Qing, and the ideological straightjacket of Confucianism. Within a few short years, the revolution swept northwards, capturing swathes of territory, cities and major Qing garrisons. By the time the old imperial Ming capital of Nanjing was captured in 1853 and renamed Tianjing (heavenly capital), the Taiping Revolution controlled the 'cradle' of Chinese civilisation, the most populous and prosperous part of China in the central planes around the Yellow River. Here a new state was established.

The scale of the revolution was staggering. At their peak, the Taiping armed forces numbered up to a million. They developed innovative and complex military tactics with spectacular coordination against largely enervated Qing forces (Luo 1991), engaged in massive pitched battles, instituted strict discipline, and reorganised the social and economic fabric of the new state. Their eventual destruction left anywhere from ten to twenty million dead and far more devastated. Left to their own devices, the Taiping revolutionaries would have overthrown the otiose Qing imperial rule itself. They key to the collapse of the revolution was not so much a Qing revival, but the intervention of British forces at a crucial juncture (Platt 2012). The British were clearly concerned

---

8   It was indeed a revolution, as the Chinese term 'Taiping Heavenly Kingdom Movement' (*Taiping tianguo yundong*) implies. A useful survey of earlier debates over its revolutionary nature may be found in Kroeber (1996, 32–33). The efforts by some recent US-based scholars (Li 1998; Meyer-Fong 2003; Platt 2012) to rebadge it a 'civil war' may be well-intentioned (to give the Taiping movement more credibility), but the unfortunate effect is to equate it with the American Civil War, with which it has little in common.

at losing both their North American and Chinese markets within the space of a few years. The imposition of opium on the Chinese had turned the balance of accounts into the British empire's favour and it was loath to lose such a lucrative venture as the drug market. Of course, the British forces had their own agenda, quite different from the Qing imperial court, but the result was the same: to strangle the Taiping Revolution. As a result, the tide of war turned against the Taiping revolutionaries. Nanjing fell barely more than a decade after being captured, in 1864. Anyone associated with the revolutionaries was slaughtered *en masse*, including extensive examples of 'ethnic cleansing' in the south, and the last holdouts were 'mopped up' in the 1870s and 1880s. Neither the Qing nor the British could erase the profound effect on Chinese society, so much so that it heralded the end of more than two millennia of imperial rule only a few decades later.

In the hands of the Taiping revolutionaries, the Bible had become a potent source of inspiration for revolution. But it also provided the basic guidelines for a very different organisation of society. As for economic factors, the basic principle was stated in *The Land System of the Heavenly Divinity*:

> The whole empire is the universal family of our Heavenly Father, the Supreme Lord and Great God. When all the people in the empire will not take anything as their own but submit all things to the Supreme Lord, then the Lord will make use of them, and in the universal family of the empire, every place will be equal and every individual well-fed and clothed. This is the intent of our Heavenly Father, the Supreme Lord and Great God, in specially commanding the true Sovereign of Taiping to save the world.
>
> MICHAEL AND CHANG 1966, vol. 2, 314

Not only had *Shangdi* created all the richness of the earth, but he also desired that his children should partake of it equally. In a practice established early in the movement, this meant that all goods were stored in a communal or 'holy' treasury (*shengku*) and redistributed to the people as they had need. Initially, the common treasury was filled with the ill-gotten gains of the Qing ruling class in the cities conquered, but it also entailed relieving landlords of their stores, if not their heads and sumptuous dwellings, much to the appreciation of the large peasant base of the movement. When the Taiping movement had achieved relatively stable power, it continued to fill the common treasury with plunder, but it also set out to institute land reform, according to which the land too was held in common and allocated to each man and woman over sixteen years old in equal shares, albeit in light of the land's productivity. They were given animals and the responsibility for growing crops.[9] They would be able to keep that which was sufficient for their needs, but the rest would go into the common stores. From here special needs were met, whether for illness, birth, death, or indeed surpluses for times of warfare, which was an ever-present reality for the Taiping movement. Often, the organisation was left up to the local villagers, without the pest of landlords, and after the process was completed, each dwelling had a plaque attached to it to indicate that the dwelling in question was now part of the new economic order. This approach did not remove specialisation, for those skilled in various tasks – such as carpenters, bricklayers, ironsmiths, potters, firefighters, medical workers, bakers, tailors, soy sauce and bean curd makers, and especially printers (for the Bible, which was a major project in Nanjing) – were to contribute their skills to common projects, such as the building and then, after a fire, the rebuilding of Hong Xiuquan's residence in Nanjing. Ideally, all would contribute their skills and then receive what they needed from the local common stores. It also became clear that one common treasury was impractical. So they instituted a system of local common stores, based upon collective units of 25 families. This system required both the removal of speculative trade, especially in the military bases where defensive preparations were paramount, and detailed accounting methods (Zhu 1991), so that an accurate record of people, stores and relevant needs were recorded – down to matters such as cooking oil, salt and drinking water. We can see here the principle of Acts 4:42–35 being implemented, according to which everyone laid all they had at the feet of the apostles and it was distributed to all according to need.

As for social organisation, the Taiping movement banned what would one expect in nineteenth century China: opium, gambling and slavery, on pain of death. But they added to their list alcohol and tobacco. They also did away with some of the inescapable hierarchies of Confucian-inspired Chinese society, with complex levels of respect for emperor, parents, elder siblings and nearly everyone else in the social pecking order.[10] Apart from the leaders and ranks in the army, each one was to call each other 'brother' and 'sister', as the early Christians did. While this may seem innocuous, in a Chinese situation with its deeply ingrained practices of social deference and respect, embodied in everyday terms of address, this move was more radical than an outsider may suspect. Gender did not escape the Taiping, especially in light of the typical

---

9   They did not prevent stalls at the city gates of the various fortresses, where farmers could exchange vegetables, grain, meat, fish and even tea.

10   However, Kilcourse (2016, 109–32) argues that despite the Taiping demotion of Confucius (which he describes as 'rhetoric') in the *Chronicle*, their localised version of Christianity was heavily influenced by Confucian ethics.

Confucian denigration of women, according to which the role of women was to be illiterate child-bearers and home-keepers, so much so that social and political disaster was believed to ensue when a woman did not fulfil her allotted role.[11] By contrast, the Taiping abolished not only foot-binding, but they also replaced the centuries-old Confucian examinations with a system open to both women and men and based on the Bible. Women often took senior roles of management and administration, especially in the large household of Hong Xiuquan. As a forerunner of communist practice in the twentieth century, women and men served in the armies, in which service was expected.[12] At the same time, the relative equalisation of gender also entailed strict separation of the sexes, with no sexual intercourse (this was later practically relaxed) – a practice that was common among other radical religious movements.[13] All of these practices – however compromised, partial and imperfect they might have been – were bound together with religious observance.[14] Groups of five families, under the leadership of a corporal, were to gather weekly for worship at a local church, while every seventh Sabbath they would gather with twenty other families at a larger church. Here, women and men sat on each side, partaking of a liturgy of Scripture readings, sermons, prayer, singing and one sacrament, that of baptism for new converts (the Eucharist seems not to have been practiced). At communal meals, prayer was said and the Ten Commandments recited. The telltale signal of the new order already emerging was the promulgation of a new calendar in 1851, drawing upon traditional Chinese and Christian features, with a focus on the seventh day for worship and prayer. Years now began from the inauguration of the Taiping Heavenly Kingdom.

4   Interpreting the Taiping Revolution

Interpretations of the Taiping Revolution are myriad, focusing on every aspect from economic reorganisation to its linguistic innovations. As indicated at the

---

11   The worst outcome for this social ethic was for a woman to become an emperor, for this was a recipe for disaster. Thus, the empress Wu Zetian (624–705) was viewed with particular disfavour.

12   A strain of scholarship has sought to downplay the innovations in terms of gender, suggesting that the Taiping movement did little for women (Wang and Xiao 1989; Xia 2003, 2004; Liao and Wang 2004; Kilcourse 2016, 157–67). I stress here that such moves were relative and often ambiguous, but that they constitute a significant challenge at the time.

13   Such segregation appears in not a few radical European movements, such as the Moravian Brethren (Petterson 2015, 2016).

14   Buddhist and Daoist temples and features were mercilessly destroyed in the process, but Muslims and Roman Catholics were often spared.

beginning of the chapter, the movement was very complex with many currents that can give rise to contrary interpretations. Given that my focus is on religion, I suggest that we group the interpretations in the following terms. First, all of the missionaries at the time and even those with a modicum of theological sensibilities dismissed the Taiping movement as a heresy. For example, Issachar Roberts, Hong Xiuquan's erstwhile theological teacher, called his former student 'a crazy man ... making himself equal with Jesus Christ'.[15] The paths to the charge of heresy differed. Some argued that Hong claimed to be divine, like Jesus, while others argued that the Taiping revolutionaries saw both Jesus and Hong as divinely appointed human messengers, with the result that Jesus's divinity was denied.[16] However, a longer historical view soon reveals that the charge of heresy was a standard way in which 'mainstream' theological traditions dealt with revolutionary religious movements. Second, modern, mostly non-Chinese critics have equally marginalised the movement, albeit with a range of assessments. These include it being a 'spiritualised' Confucianism that had little to do with equality, a form of local popular religion, a distortion of Christianity in light of traditional Chinese folk religion, a new form of Chinese religion, another type of millenarianism, fanatical totalitarianism, theocracy or a somewhat ignorant revision of Protestantism (Boardman 1952; Gregory 1963; Michael and Chang 1966; Shih 1967; Franz-Willing 1972; Jen 1973; Russell 1977; Wagner 1982; Spence 1996; Reilly 2004; Moffett 2005, 293, 299; Saucier et al. 2009; Foster 2011; Kim 2011; Cook 2012).

Third, the richest resource for research is Chinese scholarship.[17] Although every aspect of the movement has been analysed in detail, and although positions have shifted and been contested over the years,[18] the core religious dimension has not often been given the attention it deserves, with a preference for dealing with class, economics, land redistribution, colonialism, social structure and, more recently, the drive to modernisation.[19] When Chinese

---

15   See the useful survey of missionary attitudes in Kilcourse (2014, 126–29).
16   See the careful reassessment of Taiping theology by Kilcourse (2016, 79–108), who argues that they held to one divine being, God the Father, and that Jesus was his human but non-divine offspring. Hong Xiuquan too was given such a role, albeit in a position inferior to Jesus.
17   For relatively insightful, albeit dated, surveys of Chinese scholarship until the more recent period, see Volkoff and Wickberg (1979), Liu (1981) and Weller (1987).
18   For example, the earlier scholarship of Luo Ergang (1951) stressed the egalitarian and revolutionary nature of the movement, while more recent scholars have either seen this as peasant utopianism or challenged its progressiveness.
19   When presenting occasional lectures on the Taiping Revolution in China, I have been made acutely aware of how the changing perspectives on the movement respond to wider social questions in China. For example, the emphasis on peace and stability in the last few

Marxist scholarship has faced the question of religion, it has often resorted
to Engels's methodological assumption in interpreting the sixteenth-century
Peasant Revolution in Germany: theological language was a cloak for political and economic factors, an approach that is indebted to an application of
the base-superstructure model (Engels 1850a, 1850b).[20] Thus, studies seek the
infrastructural 'reality' behind the unstable superstructural Christianity of the
Taiping movement, whether in terms of its bourgeois or 'Western' nature, or
indeed psychological factors (Wei 1987; Yin 1989; Zhu 1990; An and Bai 1991; Xia
1992; Zheng 2000; Liao 2005). Two approaches have more promise: either religion is inherently reactionary and must be separated from the revolutionary
dimensions, or religion itself may express the longings of the peasants, if not
the Chinese people, against exploitation and oppression (Qin 2010; Xie 1989;
Chen 1996). By drawing on different aspects of Marx and Engels's observations
concerning religion, they go further than the cloak metaphor. Not only does the
possibility arise that religion itself may provide the sources for revolutionary
action, thereby indicating that it is not by default reactionary, but that religion
becomes a material force. This may take place either in terms of the historical consequences of its ideological framework and scriptural injunctions (as I
argued in Chapter 2) or in terms of the material dimensions of religion itself.

A fourth approach is possible, although it has not been explored in research
thus far: the Taiping Revolution marks the moment when the revolutionary tradition of Christian communism arrives in China. I have of course structured the
preceding account of the movement and its revolution with this position in
mind, but this has been done to bring to the fore a dimension that has thus far
been quite neglected. It is by no means the only explanation, to the exclusion
of all others, but it does offer a new perspective. Let me summarise the main
features as follows:

(1)   Most obviously, the Taiping movement manifests clearly the revolution-
       ary dimension of Christianity in China. This is in contrast to Christi-
       anity's long prior history in this part of the world, beginning with the
       Church of the East (Nestorians or *Jingjiao*) from the seventh to the tenth
       centuries and then again in the thirteenth to the fourteenth centuries,
       moving through the Roman Catholics from the sixteenth century, to
       the Protestants of the eighteenth and nineteenth centuries. They had
       preferred to seek imperial favour for their work. By contrast, the Taiping

---

        decades shows up in assessments that are critical of the violence and disruption of the
        movement and its time.
20   Weller (1987, 740–45) points out that the 'outer garment' theory was particularly strong
        during the Cultural Revolution, but Volkoff and Wickberg (1979, 485) observe that it was
        also a key position afterwards.

revolutionaries challenged the imperial system to its foundations. This impulse arises from a sense of radical transcendence (a category thoroughly foreign to Chinese culture), with a high sense of the divine, the centrality of the Scriptures, and the need for all to obey divine laws – including the ruling class. In light of a current situation in which exploitation exists in economic relations, injustice in social relations, corruption in institutions such as religious bodies, and oppression in political forms, it becomes clear time and again that the status quo does not measure up to the transcendent requirements. The emphasis on transcendence leads not to acquiescence to oppression, but to human agency in responding to such oppression. This response may take a revolutionary path, as has happened frequently in the histories of Christianity, but it may also lead to a withdrawal from the society in question in order to establish a new collective that models an alternative believed to be divinely sanctioned. The two are by no means incommensurable.

(2) This brings me to a feature of the Christian communist tradition that we have already met on a number of occasions: forms of communal life, with some type of property in common and the principle of distributing to any who have need. For the Taiping, this entailed a thoroughgoing reorganisation of economic and social life, based on well-organised patterns of allocation and re-allocation, if not an initial effort at a relative, albeit limited, reorganisation of gender relations.

(3) Further, it was based on what is so often seen as an unorthodox or 'heterodox' reading of the Bible, determined by original and detailed interpretations by Hong Xiuquan. The Bible was clearly central, as indicated by the Taiping devoting immense energies to publishing and studying (edited) versions, even up to the last days. Biblical texts shaped their understanding of experiences in the revolution as it swept northward, in organising social and economic life, worship and worldview. While the details may differ – such as the focus on the idolatry of the Qing emperors or the place of Hong Xiuquan in the context of radical monotheism – the centrality of new interpretations of the Bible links the Taiping Revolution with European and even Russian forms of Christian communism.

(4) The role of immediate inspiration through visions and dreams is also a feature of the Taiping movement that appears in earlier moments of Christian communism. While one may point to the consistent charismatic tendencies within 'mainstream' Christianity (although they tend so often to be marginalised), the most notable connection is with the well-documented role visions played in the theology of Thomas Müntzer and the leaders of the Münster Revolution.

(5)   Even more, it was deeply 'indigenised' or 'contextualised', producing a new form of religious expression in China that transformed both Chinese traditions and Christian interpretations of the Bible into what may be called the sinification (*Zhongguohua*) of Christian communism. Indeed, the argument for 'indigenisation' or 'glocalisation' is the main thesis proposed by Kilcourse (2014, 2016), in which the Taiping movement rediscovered and laid claim to the authentic Chinese traditions concerning the high god, *Shangdi*, in light of the deep and contradictory patterns of Confucianism in Chinese culture.

(6)   Finally, its appeal was to peasants and disaffected workers (miners) – precisely what Engels had argued in relation to early Christianity (with the addition of slaves). With nothing left to lose, these classes in particular were drawn to the movement, along with the rebel groups that are often described as 'criminal gangs'. But China had peasant revolutions before, so what was different? In the past, they had sought to restore the 'mandate of heaven', which an imperial system had corrupted. By contrast, the Taiping Revolution challenged the age-old justification for imperial rule and set the scene for the demise not only of the Qing dynasty but of the imperial system as such. Taiping revolutionaries were themselves conscious of a distinct rupture with a millennia-old imperial order. As Samir Amin has argued, it was the first modern revolution in China, as well as the first revolutionary struggle by peoples on the periphery of capitalism. It thereby became the 'ancestor of the "anti-feudal, anti-imperialist popular revolution" as formulated later by Mao' (Amin 2013, 159).[21] It is not for nothing that the Taiping Revolution was consciously invoked in the republican revolution of 1911. Sun Yat-sen explicitly claimed the revolution as a forerunner of his own, so much so that he was known by the nickname of Hong Xiuquan. All of this was enabled by the first manifestation in China of the Christian communist tradition.

5   Mao Zedong and the Taiping Revolution

I would like to close on a slightly different note, especially in light of Amin's observation that the Taiping Revolution was the first modern revolution in Chinese history, opening up a path to the communist revolution a century later.

---

21   The revolution also influenced changes in the social patterns of those who opposed them, challenging the assumed frameworks of traditional Chinese society in the Qing era (Zheng 2009; Hou 2014).

The question is how Mao Zedong understood the Taiping movement. Most of his references to the movement appear in lists. Although the function of these lists varies, nearly all of them express a sense that the movement formed part of older tradition of revolutionary upheaval in Chinese history. For example, the Taiping Revolution sometimes appears as part of a long list of peasant uprisings that began in the distant past and culminated with the Taiping Revolution (Mao 1939a, 282, 1939b, 625). More often, the Taiping come at the beginning of a more recent list of movements from the middle of the nineteenth century, at the earliest moments of Chinese struggles against foreign colonial powers, such as the Anti-Opium Wars (1839–42), the Sino-Japanese War (1894), the Boxer Rebellion (1899–1901), the Revolutionary War of 1911, the war of the Northern Expedition in 1926–1927, the May Fourth Movement (1919), the struggle against the Japanese occupation and then the agrarian communist revolution of which he was a part. The function of these more recent lists varies: as an example of a 'just' war against foreign capitalist aggression occupation (Mao 1935a, 101, 1935b, 161, 1939e, 71–72, 1939f, 563–64, 1939a, 288–89, 1939b, 632–33); as part of the long bourgeois-democratic revolution that would eventually pass to a socialist revolution (Mao 1939c, 1939d, 1939e, 1939f, 1940a, 333, 1940b, 666); as an indiscriminate anti-colonial struggle (Mao 1937c, 607); and as yet another failure, however noble, that will not be repeated with the communist struggle (Mao 1938a, 328, 1938b, 449, 1939g, 47, 1939h, 170). For these lists, Mao does not always distinguish between imperial resistance to foreign invasion (Anti-Opium Wars), the activities of the Guomindang (Northern Expedition), anti-colonial struggles and peasant revolutionary movements.

On a couple of occasions, the assessment of the Taiping Revolution becomes more focused. The first appears in a critical engagement with the Paris Commune (Mao 1926a, 1926b), in which Mao situates the commune and the Russian Revolution – the 'bright flower' of defeat and the 'happy fruit' of victory – in the context of class struggle and the international situation. Crucially, he goes beyond Marx's observation that while international wars are the preserve of capitalist imperialism, only internal class war is able to liberate humanity. Instead, suggests Mao, international struggles that overthrow capitalism are significant, as also are civil wars in which the oppressed classes overthrow their oppressors. How does this position influence his approach to the Taiping Revolution? Now he still situates it in the tradition of peasant revolutions against emperors, which may be assessed in terms of the history of class struggle. He gives the examples of the uprising of Chen Sheng and Wu Guang (*Dazexiang Qiyi*) in 209 BCE at the time of the Qin dynasty, and the uprising Liu Bang (256–195 BCE), who was a peasant and known as a *liumang*, or vagabond, and yet established the Han dynasty. However, the class conditions were not developed, so leaders like Liu Bang could fall back only onto existing patterns and become aristocrats. The Taiping Revolution is the next example, but unlike his comments elsewhere, Mao does not see it merely as a continuation of an old pattern, nor indeed of an 'ethnic' war between Han and Manchu. By contrast, he emphasises its clear class nature, with Hong Xiuquan calling on a 'broad group of unemployed peasants' only to be opposed by Zeng Guofan, who often appears as a Qing general steeped in the Confucian tradition. However, Zeng was originally a leader of the *tuanlian*, the local militias organised by landlords for oppressing peasants in the nineteenth century.[22] To Zeng and the landlords, the very nature of the Taiping Revolution was a challenge and affront, not only to traditional Confucian values, but also to Chinese society as a whole (Zeng 1854). Thus, it required the utmost energy and brutality to suppress. For Mao, all of this meant that Taiping Revolution constituted nothing less than a social revolution, a class war 'between the peasants and landlords' that was of 'great significance' (Mao 1926a, 367, 1926b, 35).

At this point, Mao leaves open what this significance might be, but a dozen years later he clarifies it (Mao 1938a, 1938b). Once again, he situates developments of his time in terms of international revolutionary movements, mentioning the 1905 and 1917 revolutions in Russia in relation to the War of Resistance against Japan, as well as the supporting role that the Soviet Union played in international anti-imperialist and communist movements. The Taiping Revolution itself appears in the context of a discussion of progressiveness: this revolution and the Republican Revolution of 1911 were progressive, albeit in terms of challenging and then abolishing 'feudal' society (Mao 1938a, 331, 1938b, 451–52). Note what has happened: as Mao's analysis proceeds, the position of the Taiping Revolution has shifted. In the accounts I mentioned earlier, it was one of a longer list of revolutionary and anti-colonial movements, or one of a number of peasant revolutions that should be analysed in terms of class conflict. Now the Taiping Revolution is first in the list of progressive revolutions in a Chinese context. Implicit here is the sense that the 'great significance' of this revolution is that it opens up a new phase in revolutionary history.

Yet even when he acknowledges the importance of the Taiping Revolution, Mao is wary. Part of his wariness arises from the need to retain some form of innovation for the communists.[23] This problem of old and new had bedevilled

---

22   For more detail on the *tuanlian*, see Kuhn (1967) and Zhang (2000, 716–17). Although some assess the role of other elements of the ruling class in opposing the Taiping (Liu 2009), the point is still so often missed by those who focus on Qing efforts to deal with the revolution (Yeung 2005).

23   This reticence does not prevent him from suggesting that the communists learn from the Taiping revolutionaries in terms of military organisation. Thus, instead of mercenary

the efforts of Kautsky, Luxemburg and Lunacharsky in relation to the Christian and Marxist forms of communism in Europe and Russia. So also with Mao in his own way. Thus, while the Taiping were 'progressive', they were progressive in the sense that they were seeking to overthrow what was still a feudal society under foreign oppression (Mao 1938a, 331, 1938b, 451–52). By contrast, the communists offer a different type of progressiveness, in the context of capitalism, class conflict and the parties that represent classes, politically conscious people, and a politically progressive Red Army. Another part of his wariness was due to the fact that the Taiping Revolution was deeply formed by foreign influences. Indeed, this was part of the troubled engagement with foreign influences on China, the subject of so much debate at the time. Aware of all that was negative of the Chinese imperial system, Mao tried to work through to a way of appropriating foreign influences while constantly transforming them in light of Chinese conditions (Mao 1917a, 130–32, 1917b, 84–86, 1938c, 538–39, 1938c, 658–59).

What are we to make of Mao's engagement? Were the Taiping revolutionaries yet another group of peasants revolting and challenging the imperial order, or were they harbingers of a new order, in response to foreign oppression, capitalism and colonialism? Were they the first signal of modern revolutions by oppressed peasants, which would finally come to fruition with the communist revolution? Many of these tensions appear in Mao's efforts to come to terms with the Taiping revolutionaries. On the one hand, they were part of the old revolutionary tradition, an ancient pattern of peasant revolutions; on the other hand, they signal a more recent development, a movement of the oppressed against the ruling class and in response to foreign influences on China. Here lies the new dimension of the Taiping revolution, for its innovation is signalled by the uprising of the poor and oppressed classes against their exploiting overlords. When he does acknowledge such innovation, the Taiping Revolution stands at the head of the modern revolutionary process – precisely a movement that arose under the inspiration of a foreign, revolutionary Christian influence. The reality is that the Marxism Mao embraced also had a 'Western' provenance analogous to the revolutionary religious tradition that appeared with the Taiping revolutionaries. It too was the result of foreign influence that was transformed in and shook up China.

---

armies, the communists ought to the follow the example of using militias, in which everyone in the movement is involved (Mao 1926a, 367, 1926b, 35, 1928a, 127, 1928b, 204, 1944a, 657, 1944b, 241).

CHAPTER 13

Chinese Christian Communism in the Early Twentieth Century

> In the future, when we deal with Christianity, we need to have a keen awareness and understanding of it, so that there will be no more confusions. What is more, we need to have a rather deep understanding, so that we can cultivate in our veins the lofty and great character of Jesus, as well as his affectionate and profound compassion, so that we may be saved from falling into the horrible, dark and dirty pit.[1]
>
> CHEN 2009, 70

Chen Duxiu, from whom this quotation is taken, was along with Li Dazhao one of the founders of the Communist Party of China (Tang 2012). Here he expresses an appreciation of Christianity, especially in terms of the revolutionary credentials of Jesus Christ, which was not an exception in the early years of the twentieth century in China. Indeed, he would have found such an interpretation of a revolutionary Jesus, with variations, among a number of Chinese Christian thinkers. These include Wu Leichuan, Shen Sizhuang (J. Wesley Shen), Wu Yaozong (Y.T. Wu), Zhu Weizhi (W.T. Chu), and Zhao Zizhen (T.C. Chao), who were part of a new phase in the history of Christian communism in China, which arose in response to the communist revolution of the twentieth century.[2] These Christians thought, wrote and acted in a turbulent and creative time. Not only did the imperial system come to an end with the republican revolution of 1911, and not only was it the time of the hugely influential May Fourth Movement (*wusi*), but it was also the period when the Communist Party of China was formed, developed and then led the Chinese revolution. In this chapter, I focus on three of the main thinkers who shaped Chinese Christian communism in the twentieth century: Wu Leichuan (1870–1944), Wu Yaozong (1893–1979) and Zhu Weizhi (1905–1999). I seek to identify their responses to the challenges of communism and the genuine breakthroughs they produced.[3]

---

1 Unless indicated otherwise, all translations are provided.
2 Although Kwok Pui-lan (2016) attempts to stress these developments (she mentions Wu Yaozong) in contrast to the Euro-American context, her description as 'postcolonial political theology' still operates within such a framework.
3 The archival work at the basis of the chapter was done by Chin Kenpa, who was co-author of the original article from which this chapter is drawn. See also his earlier article on Zhu Weizhi (Chin 2013).

1   Revolutionary Times and Influences

Before proceeding, a few comments on background are needed in order to highlight the specifics of the Chinese situation relevant to my study. Three factors are important. First, Christianity had been undergoing a long process of sinification at least since the time of Matteo Ricci in the sixteenth century, the 'rites controversy' and struggles over the choice for the name of God (Reilly 2004, 19–53).[4] This history was subsequently sidelined with Protestant missionary activity in the nineteenth century. Based in Hong Kong and enmeshed with the opium 'trade' in an ever-shifting and complex fashion, Christianity was seen by many Chinese as a colonial project and a foreign ideology (*yangjiao*), thereby being a significant part of the humiliation of China by European imperialism. The Opium Wars, the destruction of the summer palace in Beijing, the imposition of unfavourable economic conditions and the religious ideology of a foreign empire – these and more became signals of that humiliation.

Second, and in contrast to the connection with European colonialism, Christianity in China had already been associated with revolutionary activity through the Taiping Revolution of 1850–1864. The legacy of this revolution was ambiguous, to say the least. On the one hand, the dynamic of class meant that the revolution gave voice to a deep and long-held hatred of oppression at the hands of landlords under the old system. Further, its resolutely anti-imperial and anti-colonial tenor combined with class conflict to make it the first modern revolution in Chinese history, so much so that those involved in the Republican Revolution of 1911 saw themselves as its heirs and brought to completion what their forebears had begun.[5] On the other hand, the disruption and dislocation of the old order brought about by the revolution meant that many – and not only some among the ruling class – saw Christianity itself in this light. This 'foreign teaching' was – they felt – not merely colonial but could also tear down Chinese society through revolutionary action.[6] Thus, in the latter half

---

4   Ricci had sought to indigenise Christianity (in its Roman Catholic form) in terms of liturgy, vestments and language, proposing – as mentioned in the previous chapter – that 'God' (*Yahweh* in Hebrew and *theos* in Greek) be translated with *Shangdi* (Sovereign on High), the name of the ancient Chinese High God. The Pope took a dim view of such proceedings, mandating by papal decree in 1715 that *Tianzhu* (Lord of Heaven) should be used. The rift has led to two Roman Catholic churches in China, one recognised by the state but not by Rome, and the other recognised by Rome but not by the state. In 2018, a long overdue agreement was reached between the Vatican and the Chinese government that finally resolved the core issue of the appointment of bishops.

5   Not only was Sun Yat-sen known by the nickname of Hong Qiuquan, but also many of the later revolutionaries wore their hair long in the manner of the Taiping revolutionaries.

6   For a sense of the social impact, see the memoirs of Zhang Daye (2013), who experienced the events as a child.

of the nineteenth century, missionaries worked hard to dissociate themselves from the Taiping movement, particularly by painting it as an aberration and a heresy (Moffett 2005, 129). That their efforts were not often successful is revealed by the Boxer (Yihetuan) Rebellion of 1899–1901, which vented its rage against Chinese Christians. Therefore, Christianity already had a rather ambivalent presence in China by the early twentieth century. Thus far we have a submerged history of the two sides of Christianity in China (from above), between the connections with Protestant missions and European colonialism, and the outburst of the revolutionary religious tradition (which includes sinification from below).

Now a third factor comes into play, which was the immediate trigger for the theological developments of Wu Leichuan, Wu Yaozong and Zhu Weizhi. This was the 'anti-Christian movement' between 1922 and 1928. It responded primarily to the perception that Christianity was wedded to European colonialism. Thus, it sought government control of the Christian schools throughout China and questioned the loyalty of Chinese Christians. Were they really covert agents of the imperialism and colonialism which had so humiliated China? Indeed, was Christianity part of the problem? Christian thinkers and leaders found themselves called upon to make a clear identification of their allegiance: for the Chinese revolution or for foreign imperialism and its values (Zhang 1929). A number of Christian thinkers made it clear that they did indeed support the revolution and were opposed to foreign imperialism.[7] They did so in a novel way, holding onto their Christianity and identifying with the revolution.

But they faced a dilemma: on which of the threads should they draw? Obviously, the connection with European colonialism was not an option, but should they claim the heritage of Matteo Ricci or of the Taiping revolutionaries? Both could be seen as forms of the sinification of Christianity, from above and from below. They chose neither. Instead, they opted for an approach that drew together Christianity and Marxism, within a Chinese situation and in response to Chinese social, political and ideological issues. They were able to draw upon a precedent, which came from none other than Karl Kautsky's *Foundations of Christianity* (1908a, 1908b), the immense impact of which in different parts of the world we still have not assessed adequately. Since I have discussed Kautsky's work at length earlier, I am interested here in its impact on the Chinese Christian socialists. Here we see a process in which international debates concerning the rich intersections of Marxism and Christianity – fostered by the works

---

7   The twist is that later they would be criticised for 'accommodating' to the Communist Party of China or abandoning the specifically theological nature of Christianity (Gao 1996, 338–39; Liu 2016).

of Engels and Kautsky – were drawn into a Chinese situation for the reasons outlined above.[8] Kautsky's book was translated into Chinese in 1932 and, as one of the few books on Christianity available in China at the time, it became a must-read work for both Christians and Marxists (Kautsky 1932).[9] Its impact was almost immediately felt in the work of Wu Leichuan and Zhu Weizhi. For Wu Leichuan, a key idea drawn from Kautsky is the early Christian communist practice of having 'everything in common' (from Acts 2 and 4), which means a provision of the basic necessities of life for all through a just distribution of wealth (Wu 1936, 104–5). In such a society, taxation would be unnecessary, a position he found in the sayings of Jesus and Peter concerning taxes (Luke 20:25; Acts 3:1–10).[10] In the Gospels he found parables aplenty which criticised acquisitiveness and love of private property, although he focused on the parables of the lost sheep, the lost coin and the prodigal son (Luke 15:1–32). And when the crowds following John the Baptist asked him what they should do, he replied as follows: 'Whoever has two coats must share with anyone who has none; and whoever has food must do likewise' (Luke 3:11). In short, the application of these teachings meant a just and fair society, which was coterminous with socialism.

Zhu Weizhi's deployment of Kautsky was even more extensive, especially in a work to which we will return, *Jesus the Proletarian* (Zhu 1950). He is quite explicit about the way Kautsky's work enabled him to understand not only the nature of the proletariat but also who Jesus was (Zhu 1950, 3).[11] Zhu reiterates Kautsky's main points concerning early Christianity, while also taking up Kautsky's analysis of the Hebrew Bible to argue that the Exodus from Egypt

---

8   It was not so much a process of the Marxification of Christianity, or indeed the Christianising of Marxism that was at stake, but rather the complex intersections between the two.

9   Engels's 'On the History of Early Christianity' was translated in 1929 and was also read, but it seems to have had less impact than Kautsky's study (Engels 1929).

10   In the Gospel of Luke, Jesus's opponents seek to trap him on the question of taxes, asking whether it was lawful to pay them to the Roman emperor or not. Jesus asks for a coin (denarius) and asks whose image is on it. When they say, 'the emperor's', Jesus replies: 'Then give to the emperor the things that are the emperor's, and to God the things that are God's' (Luke 20:25). In the Book of Acts story, the first apostles or leaders of the early Christians, Peter and Paul, are asked by a lame man for alms. Peter replies: 'I have no silver or gold, but what I have I give you; in the name of Jesus Christ of Nazareth, stand up and walk' (Acts 3:6).

11   For example: 'Why did Engels say that the contemporary proletarian movement had much in common with early Christianity? Why did Kautsky have such great respect for Christianity? Why did he see it as one of the most significant movements in human history?' (Zhu 1950, 3). Note also: 'Jesus was a leader of great integrity who led the proletarian masses in the struggle against Roman imperialism. Indeed, Engels himself acknowledges that Christianity began as a revolutionary social movement' (Zhu 1950, 2).

was a revolutionary movement: 'The God they believed in helped them gain emancipation from oppression at the hands of their Egyptian masters' (Zhu 1950, 28). This history began with the Exodus, includes the Hebrew prophets (30) and Jesus, only to be manifested in Marx and Lenin. All of this was captured in the parable of the Good Samaritan (Luke 10:25–37). The act of self-sacrificing assistance from an ethnically despised person – a Samaritan – given to a man who has been attacked on the road and left for dead indicates that the 'true mark of internationalism' is found in the idea that 'class solidarity overcomes ethnic chauvinism' (Zhu 1950, 85). In other words, Christianity was an international movement, of the same type as the international proletarian movement, which would achieve its goal of the Kingdom of Heaven on earth (Zhu 1950, 27). The proletariat – as Kautsky and Engels argued – has a natural connection with Christianity, so much so that one of the epithets for Jesus, Emmanuel ('God with us') means 'God stands with the proletariat' (Zhu 1950, 3).

2   Christianity and Communism

The engagement with Kautsky has already introduced some initial connections between Christianity and communism, so let us examine this topic more extensively in the work of the three theologians. Three related areas are of interest: the various methods used, namely a proletarian perspective, historical materialism and a comparative approach (via Mozi); the reconstructions of Jesus and early Christianity; and the question of identity and difference between communism and Christianity.

2.1   *Method*
The approaches used by Zhu Weizhi, Wu Yaozong and Wu Leichuan are broadly similar, but they have their own emphases. Thus, Zhu Weizhi deploys what he calls a proletarian perspective in order to understand the Jesus movement and early Christianity. This is coupled with a common Christian practice of arguing that the subsequent developments entailed many accretions which ran counter to the original impulse. These additions have distorted Christianity, forcing it to deviate and even betray its original form. To judge Christianity on the basis of its current shape entails misunderstanding its nature, much as one would misinterpret capitalism if one were to assess its nature on the basis of its present shape. Zhu uses the image of a tree: 'On a huge flourishing tree there inevitably can be found a few withered leaves and branches, but it would be incorrect to take them as evidence that the tree is dead' (Zhu 1950, 2). While this approach is familiar in the long history of the church, with one reform or

revolutionary movement after another claiming to return to the original form of Christianity, Zhu gives it a distinct twist in a Chinese context. Against those who sought to dismiss Christianity as foreign teaching, a tool, and indeed a basis of European culture and its imperialism, Zhu argues that such an assessment is misguided. It understands Christianity only in its European, capitalist form, which is a distortion. By contrast, a proletarian perspective – drawn from Kautsky – enables the interpreter to remove the distorting accretions and recover the original, proletarian nature of Christianity. In this light, Zhu seeks to recover the proletarian revolutionary credentials of Jesus, which have been divorced from his religious role and quietly dismissed. This means that Jesus's criticisms of his own situation were not merely religious but also targeted the social and economic conditions which produced such problems. In other words, Jesus clearly identified with the oppressed, urging them to seek liberation not only from the local ruling class but also from the foreign ruling class that oppressed them. Zhu's argument contains an implicit dialectic, in which one removes the specific form of Christianity (its European accretions) for the sake of a more universal core (religious and socio-economic criticisms of oppression), which can then be seen as relevant for a Chinese situation, for there too oppression exists in the form of landlords over peasants and international colonial capital over China itself. So also with Marxism, which is based on a universal principle of liberation from oppression, but was transformed in a Chinese situation.

The approach of Wu Yaozong, founder of the Three-Self Patriotic Movement (TSPM),[12] was slightly different, drawing upon historical materialism in three respects.[13] To begin with, he saw it as a valuable tool to analyse social and economic conditions. Further, he sought to develop a materialist epistemology in order to appreciate the freedom and equality at the core of Christianity. In this way, class conflict would be eliminated and the value of human beings respected. Finally, he described materialism as a holistic approach, which enabled one to understand reality in all its diversity so that one might know how to transform the world. On this matter, Christianity had

---

12   The TSPM was established in 1951, after working closely with the new communist government, especially Zhou Enlai. The 'three-self' refers to self-government, self-support and self-propagation. The best work on TSPM remains Wickeri's careful study (1988). Needless to say, it has generated significant international controversy, of which Tee (2012, 73–118) provides a useful summary. The successor of Wu Yaozong as chair of the movement was Ding Guangxun or K.H. Ting (Wickeri 2007).

13   One can find a tendency to focus on Wu Yaozong's 'contextual' approach, spiced with an American 'social gospel' (Chen 2011), but this approach significantly plays down the importance of Marxism. By contrast, some recognise the importance of Marxism in his theology (Ting 1990; Kan 1997, 163–64).

a crucial role to play: it is concerned with the individual *and* society, with the love of God *and* human beings, with the Gospel *and* social conditions (Wu 1934, 27, 29, 32).

By contrast, Wu Leichuan approached his interpretation of Jesus through the figure of the lower class artisan, Mozi (470–391 BCE).[14] Towards the end of the Qing Dynasty, the revival of Mohism offered a challenge to the dominant Confucianism. In doing so, the revival had to overcome the earlier efforts – by Mencius and other Confucians – to align Mozi's thought with that of Confucius, although the alignment required a sidelining of Mozi's attacks on Confucius. The early Chinese communists also found Mohism appealing, since it challenged Confucian nostalgia and the embrace of harmony and universal love (*boai*) within the existing – and thereby hierarchical – forms of human relations. For Mozi, universal love (*jian'ai*) was non-differentiated and community oriented, rather than being focused narrowly on family and clan.

Wu Leichuan's *Mozi and Jesus* (1940) arose from this context, in which it was not uncommon to find close connections between the two. He sees both movements as materialist and socialist, so much so that Mozi was a minor Christ and a Marxist before his time. The deployment of Mozi evinces a dialectic similar to that used by Zhu Weizhi. Mozi was a universalist who sought to transcend the specificity of a Chinese cultural and political context, saturated as it was with Confucian ethics. So was the form of Christianity Wu sought to recover, for the mission of a just society championed by Jesus transcended the specific form it had taken as it was adapted to a European situation. In other words, Christianity was not indelibly 'Western', but was able to be indigenised in each situation where injustice and oppression existed. Like Mohism, Christianity was all the more relevant to the Chinese situation precisely because of its universal mission. Thus, through Mozi, Wu Leichuan found a way of representing Jesus as a revolutionary on a mission from God to bring about the Kingdom on earth.[15] This meant that Christianity had to play a central role in bringing about a just Chinese society. Since economic relations formed the basis of social structures and since political systems arise from that combination (as part of the superstructure), he argued that economic reforms were the key (Wu 1940, 159).

---

14   A complete translation of the surviving works of Mozi is now available in Johnston (2010). For the most comprehensive assessment of Wu Leichuan's work in terms of the connections between Jesus and Mozi, see Malek (2004).

15   Unfortunately, many works on Wu Leichuan attempt to efface his clear socialist perspective and suggest that his approach is 'Confucian-Christian' and liberal (Chu 1995; Liang 2008; Yieh 2009).

2.2 Reconstruction

Despite the variations in method, the results were strikingly similar. Jesus becomes a revolutionary, keen to bring about the Kingdom of God, which would be one of communistic life, economic justice, equality and social wellbeing. For Zhu Weizhi, Jesus's leadership was simultaneously spiritual and material, seeking to throw off the yoke of foreign powers (Rome), in order to establish a new socio-political order. The focus of the movement was Galilee, where Jesus spent most of his ministry, living among the proletariat and becoming deeply familiar with their suffering and aspirations (Zhu 1950, 35, 43). In this way, Galilee became the basis of the revolution, although at a crucial point Jesus decided to lead the movement to Jerusalem, the centre of economic power, religious oppression and imperial authority:

> Jesus hailed from Galilee, a region where the proletariat eked out a subsistence-level livelihood; Jerusalem was the centre of the privileged classes, one of whose favourite terms of abuse was 'Galilean pig!' Add to this the fact that he had received no formal religious training whatsoever, and it's easy to see why in the eyes of the social elite he was regarded as uncouth and uneducated.
>
> ZHU 1950, 33

If Jerusalem was the centre of political, economic and religious power, then the temple was the centre of Jerusalem. Zhu focuses on the two visits by Jesus to the temple, described as 'The First Disturbance' and 'The Final Battle' (Zhu 1950, 36–37). The temple was simultaneously the key to religion and economic activities, having become an instrument of oppression. Thus, Jesus's focus on the temple sought to highlight the need to overcome economic exploitation, class conflict and foster a religious revival. The fact that Jesus came to grief through his stern criticisms and indeed disruptive acts (for instance, when he overturned the tables of the money changers) in the temple in Jerusalem indicates not the failure of the movement but the need for perseverance and sacrifice. When all seems lost, the revolution lives on, as the sayings concerning the mustard seed and the wheat indicate (Matthew 17:20; John 12:24–25).[16] Indeed, they show the power of faith and sacrifice (Zhu 1950, 28, 71, 76).

---

16 Concerning the mustard seed, Jesus says: 'if you have faith the size of a mustard seed, you will say to this mountain, "Move from here to there," and it will move; and nothing will be impossible for you' (Matthew 17:20). The saying concerning wheat is as follows: 'Very truly, I tell you, unless a grain of wheat falls into the earth and dies, it remains just a single grain; but if it dies, it bears much fruit. Those who love their life lose it, and those who hate their life in this world will keep it for eternal life' (John 12:24–25).

A significant feature of Zhu's reconstruction is the anti-imperialist nature of Jesus's revolutionary work. Obviously he has in mind China's humiliation at the hands of imperialist European powers, as well as the criticisms of Christianity as an imperialist ideology by many in China. Like Pontius Pilate (who appears at the opening and closing of *Jesus the Proletarian*), many have misunderstood Jesus. He was far from the champion of any form of imperial power. Instead, he was resolutely opposed to foreign economic and military oppression, leading the proletariat of the time in resisting the Roman Empire. The skill of the Romans was to enlist the ruling classes of its colonial possessions in order to carry out Roman policies (Zhu 1950, 5), much as the European powers had done in China. In this light, Zhu interprets key accounts, such as the three temptations of Jesus by the devil (Matthew 4:1–11) and Caesar's coin (Mark 12:13–17). Concerning the latter, Jesus's answer – 'Give to the emperor the things which are the emperor's, and to God the things which are God's' – should be understood in terms of power: 'Money represents the colonial oppression and exploitation of the Roman Empire. God represents justice, truth, human rights and benevolence; he stands in solidarity with the oppressed!' (Zhu 1950, 36). Given that the prosperity of Rome was enabled by enslaving the proletariat (Zhu 1950, 23–24), the things which were due to the emperor would be very little, if anything at all.

To sum up:

> Once the workers of the world were united and of one heart and mind, they would struggle together to establish the Kingdom of Heaven. Whereas the Romans used military force to unite the world, Jesus used the power of the people. In addition to reviving the people's faith in God, he also introduced them to the ideas of justice, human rights, freedom and universal love. In this way, Jesus strove to liberate all humanity and establish the Kingdom of Heaven.
>
> ZHU 1950, 27

Wu Yaozong's concerns are much broader, attempting to embrace the whole historical reality of Christianity. Yet, his approach to Jesus provides a window into the rest of his thought. For Wu Yaozong, the Sermon on the Mount is the key, especially since it featured in his first conversion   the other was to historical materialism (Wu 1948a, 95).[17] This Jesus is shorn of any mystical or

---

17   The most frequently published account appears in the opening paragraphs of 'Christianity and Materialism: Confessions of a Christian'. First published in 1947 in the 7 July issue of *Daxue yuekan* (*University Monthly*), it was republished on four occasions, including as an afterword in the fifth edition of *Meiyouren kanjianguo shangdi*, published in 1948. This is the version used here.

miraculous elements; instead, he is entirely realistic and approachable, speaking of crucial human and material issues. Even more, Jesus provides a model not only for this-worldly concerns, but also gives us a glimpse into heaven's grandeur. For Wu, this brings him close to none other than Karl Marx, especially in *Manifesto of the Communist Party*:

> I find the personalities of Marx and Jesus alive on the paper. I can also find their similarities and differences. Both are enthusiastic with the vision of a prophet, calling for social justice and the creation of a new heaven and earth for humanity. Both have unsurpassable love and compassion; this is why they see injustice everywhere and do not put up with it. Both are faithful to their belief and died for it.
>
> WU 1934, 127

The implications for the remainder of Wu Yaozong's thoughts on Christianity and Marxism are far-reaching. Thus, love is revolutionary, so much so that love 'without a revolutionary spirit is not love' (Wu 1948a, 77), although this also means that such love includes a hatred of sin (Wu 1934, 15). Here we can see the reason for his support of class struggle, not so much against Christian reconciliation, but as a necessary and dialectical dimension of reconciliation (Wu 1934, 154–55).[18] Reconciliation entails not the melding of antagonisms in a grand liberal project, but struggle against oppressors through class struggle and a new level of reconciliation in which the oppressed determine how such reconciliation will be effected. The implication for the struggle against imperialist capitalism should be obvious. The first step is liberation from such oppression, especially in China, for only then would a new world order focused on reconciliation be possible (Wu 1947).

As for Wu Leichuan, this former imperial administrator developed a revolutionary interpretation of Jesus in a manner which – somewhat paradoxically – echoed the traditional Confucian focus on pithy sayings. The core of Jesus's position may be found in the Lord's Prayer, which, he argued, contained the essential truth of Christianity and should be recited and, most importantly, contemplated daily (Wu 1940, 302–4). This would enable people to follow in the footsteps of Jesus's mission, which he saw as an expression of God's love for humanity. It entailed working for God's glory, serving the people and bearing witness to truth. In a little more detail and in relation to the Lord's

---

18   Note also: 'We love peace, but we love justice more. We love people, but we hate sin. We have fiery wrath, but also sincere compassion. We are strict and severe, but also tolerant and open minded' (Wu 1934, 25).

Prayer, 'Our father in heaven' indicates that human beings should love one another, for we are brothers and sisters; 'Hallowed be your name' suggests the significance of a universally acknowledged truth; 'Your kingdom come' urges all people to work for the improvement of society so that it approaches the Kingdom of God; 'Your will be done, on earth as in heaven' instructs human beings to be truthful in all relations; 'Give us this day our daily bread' is not a demand but a reminder of the need for contentment; 'Forgive us our debts, as we also have forgiven our debtors' tells us to judge others as we would like to be judged by others; 'Lead us not into temptation, but deliver us from evil' instructs all people to avoid activities which may divert our path from righteousness and justice. If carried out, these principles would bring about the Kingdom of Heaven on earth, principles which also would reform China into a socialist 'kingdom' of freedom, justice and equality (Wu 1925, 1936, 90–92).

Wu Leichuan argued that social reform is not opposed to revolution, for when one follows Jesus's teachings on reform, the ultimate effect is to bring about social revolution. Incremental change will eventually bring about qualitative change. He worked through this position by arguing that the reform program proposed by Jesus has much in common with socialism, all of which meant that Jesus, like Mozi, was less of a wise sage than a revolutionary. Indeed, other texts from the Gospels reinforce such a position: the fair distribution of material goods to meet people's daily needs (Mathew 6:32–33); the abolition of private property so that all property is held in common (Mathew 19:24; Mathew 25: 14–30); the radical abolition of family ties, which was a profound challenge in China where such ties remain crucial (Mark 10:29; 3:35; Luke 9:60; 12:51–53; John 16:20–21) – all of which required a qualitative change of one's heart (Wu 1936, 66–72, 1940, 294, 299–300). These biblical texts indicate that Jesus had a clear plan for transforming society.

However, if we think that Wu Leichuan's Jesus was no more than a social revolutionary, then we are mistaken. For Wu, the key was precisely Jesus's understanding of God as compassionate and his own clear awareness of a divine mission as messiah. His death on the cross indicates that he was far more than a political leader, for not only did he have a divine mission but he refused – unlike Confucius – to seek the favour of worldly politicians (Wu 1936, 47–56). In short, Jesus was a great revolutionary precisely because he was a spiritual leader. Yet, he sought not to establish a new religion but to transform society, beginning with religious transformation. Wu Leichuan was bold enough to argue that Christianity provided the only way to do so, not only for all humanity but particularly for China. Thus, any church should make revolution its ideal and goal.

2.3   Identity and Difference

In their different ways, Zhu Weizhi, Wu Yaozong and Wu Leichuan identified closely with what was a longer tradition of Christian communism. The
times suited such a development, particularly in response to the strong anti-
Christian and anti-imperial sentiment in China at the time. But did this mean
that Christianity and socialism were essentially the same? For Zhu Weizhi, this
does seem to be the case. For Zhu, they express the same agenda for qualitative
social and economic transformation, becoming comrades in the process. Wu
Leichuan took a different approach, aligning reform and revolution. In contrast
to the tendency to oppose the two, with one tinkering with the current system
and the other seeking to overthrow it and begin again, Wu Leichuan saw, like
Lenin, that reform should be understood in terms of revolution. However, unlike Lenin, he felt that a series of reforms would eventually lead to qualitative
and thereby revolutionary change.

Yet, Wu Yaozong is arguably the most interesting, for he maintained two dialectical positions. The first concerns the difference between Christianity and
communism. While they both aim to create a society based on freedom and
equality (Wu 1949, 17),[19] Christianity holds dear the existence of God[20] and the
preference for love over violence, even if the latter becomes necessary at times.
Indeed, Christianity and communism arrive at the same conclusion for social
transformation but from very different premises. Materialist communism may
do so on the basis of the analysis of capitalism and the need for class struggle
and revolution, but Christian communism does so from the core doctrines of
Christianity and the practice of prayer:

> I have realised that Christianity and materialism do not conflict with
> each other. Moreover, they can complement each other. The reason why
> I came to this conclusion is based on the basic doctrines of Christianity,
> especially on God and prayer. I have had a long and deep reflection upon
> them, offering poignant criticisms as well.
>
> WU 1948a, 98

---

19   'What Christianity advocates is freedom, equality and democracy in the purest form.
     Therefore, it should be progressive and revolutionary, which truly embodies the spirit of
     Jesus. The mission of Christianity today is to transform society where people are treated
     as slaves and tools into one where the dignity of man is fully upheld, so that human beings
     will no longer form cliques and fight against each other because of economic interests
     and class opposition' (Wu 1949, 17).

20   In the 1960s he could still say, 'I can accept 99% of Marxism-Leninism, but when it comes
     to the question of whether there is a God or not, I keep my own counsel' (quoted in Cao
     2011, 139).

The mention of 'poignant criticisms' brings us to the second dimension of the dialectic: Christianity may be revolutionary, but it can also be profoundly re-actionary. It may have the resources to struggle with the communists for a new society, but it tends all too often to act as a religion of 'personal spiritual stimu-lation', becoming an 'opiate for the people, which is subject to judgment and punishment in due time' (Wu 1949, 183, 1948b, 4). This religion is idealistic, emo-tional, individualistic and anaesthetising (Wu 1934, 100), all too easily providing the 'enslaving toxicants of imperialism' (Wu 1949, 228). But this is only part of the reality of Christianity. Indeed, it embodies this dialectic from within, a polit-ical ambivalence which must be recognised and yet turned towards revolution:

> We believe that Christianity has a potential, a great potential. It is true that in the past, Christianity has been superstitious, narrow-minded, hypocritical and murderous in various cases, but it is also true that it is a great religion. Its form of organisation dates all the way back. Its congre-gation is huge. It has the spirit of fellowship. As for personal cultivation, it promotes integrity, innocence, righteousness and selflessness. As a faith, it has always been evolving, renewing and recreating itself. It has seen nu-merous persecutions and crises, but it always triumphs over failure, pain and death. If it has a clear goal and correct direction, then it has limitless possibility to turn its potentials into reality.
>
> WU 1934, 19

This is far from any apologetic defence of Christianity, for Wu Yaozong is will-ing to offer sustained criticisms of the ease with which Christianity sides with and enthusiastically supports one aspiring despot after another. Yet, he does not rest at this point, thereby siding with the many critics of Christianity in China. He also invokes the other side of the dialectic, insisting that Christianity has been and still can be a revolutionary movement. It does so not by subsum-ing itself under communism, but by coming from a different perspective.

3   Conclusion: Christianity and Marxism with Chinese Characteristics?

The positions of Zhu Weizhi, Wu Yaozong and Wu Leichuan have been present-ed in a way which highlights their main contributions to what may be called a Chinese Christian Marxist tradition,[21] which was itself part of a much longer

---

21   Kwan's effort (2014, 92–123) to interpret Wu Yaozong and Wu Leichuan under the rubric of post-colonialism has the effect of softening their revolutionary socialist positions.

Christian revolutionary tradition. Their positions had a number of outcomes, apart from the immediate one of aligning their proponents with the communists, if not with the wider revolutionary forces in China. In the context of significant criticisms of Christianity, they attempted to show that their own faith should not be understood merely as an ideology of European imperialism, for Christianity's history was much richer than that small slice of history. In fact, European Christianity had in many respects either distorted the message (Zhu Weizhi and Wu Leichuan), turning it into spiritual support of empire, or emphasised the despotic dimension of a dialectic (Wu Yaozong).

A further outcome concerns how their work may be seen in terms of the sinification of Christianity. Instead of arguing for the direct indigenisation or contextualisation of Christianity, in light of Chinese culture and tradition – a process that had been happening since Matteo Ricci in the sixteenth century – it actually takes place in a more indirect way. The initial move is to argue for the universal and transcendent credentials of Christianity. It is much more than the European or 'Western' form it had taken and which many in China had experienced in the nineteenth century. Crucially, this universal perspective has not been reduced to other-worldly and spiritual concerns, but is very much concerned with this-worldly problems of oppression and subjugation. The Jesus of their reconstructions is in many respects a revolutionary, challenging the status quo wherever there is injustice and oppression. Once this universalising move is made, it becomes possible to show how Christianity is exceedingly relevant for a Chinese situation, where internal and international patterns of socio-economic and cultural oppression were urgent matters. In this respect, Christianity had much in common with Marxism, not merely in terms of its revolutionary credentials, but also in terms of its universal appeal that could then be particularised in each location. In this way, Christianity could develop Chinese characteristics, much like Mao first claimed for Marxism.[22] Thus, these radical theologians attempted a recontextualisation of Christianity in much the same way that was happening with Marxism. We can see this process at work in Wu Yaozong's central role in establishing the TSPM and in Wu Leichuan's advocacy from his influential position as vice-president and chancellor at Yenching University (1926–1934). Above all, it took

---

22   'There is no such thing as abstract Marxism, but only concrete Marxism. What we call concrete Marxism is Marxism that has taken on a national form, that is, Marxism applied to the concrete struggle in the concrete conditions prevailing in China, and not Marxism abstractly used. Consequently, the sinification of Marxism – that is to say, making certain that in all its manifestations it is imbued with Chinese characteristics, using it according to Chinese peculiarities – becomes a problem that must be understood and solved by the whole Party without delay' (Mao 1938c, 538–39, 1938d, 658–59).

place through their religious commitment and the theological developments we have examined.

But the work of Wu Leichuan, Wu Yaozong and Zhu Weizhi has another implicit, and perhaps unexpected, outcome. In assuming that the Christian revolutionary tradition predates Marxism, let alone the revolutionary movements in China, they also placed Christianity in a more all-embracing position. Marxism and Chinese communism were, therefore, the latest manifestations of a longer tradition, for which Christianity had set and continues to set the agenda. Although they may have argued that Christianity and communism were unique phenomena, alternating between aligning them closely and keeping some dialectical distance between them, the implicit possibility remained that communism would be subsumed by Christianity.

CHAPTER 14

Religion and Revolution in Korea

There is no law preventing religious believers from making the revolution.
KIM 1994, I, 238

Christian communism has appeared elsewhere in Asia, most notably Minjung theology in South Korea (Kim and Ho 2013). But I am more interested in a part of Asia about which there is much speculation, misinformation and precious little realistic and reliable information: The Democratic People's Republic of Korea (DPRK), or 'North Korea' as it is unofficially called. Some have hypothesised that religion does not exist in the DPRK, since the state is atheistic and religious people have been suppressed and eliminated (Kong 1974; Worden 2008, 115–16; Havet and Gaudreau 2010). These accounts usually rely on the unverified hearsay of 'defectors', even though anyone who leaves the north and is willing to condemn the government is offered one billion won (USD $870,000) for doing so, as long as they provide information that is helpful to the United States and South Korean forces.[1] As was already found with research on the Soviet Union, the use of émigré hearsay is a highly unreliable and suspect historical source.[2] Others have suggested that Korean communism, with its 'cult of personality' and its philosophy of Juche (that human beings are masters of their own destiny) – is a form of 'religion', thereby deploying an overused trope in efforts to misunderstand communism (Cornell 2002, 5, 100, 112; Buswell 2006; Martin 2006; Worden 2008, 115; Cha 2013, 32–38). Serious studies are thin on the ground,[3] so in this chapter I delve into three aspects of the intersections between religion and Korean communism: the indigenous religion, Chondoism, which opens up my analysis to the extensive deliberations of Kim Il Sung; the latter's thoughtful experiences and assessments of Christianity, especially

---

1   For a timely caution against the nature and use of such 'evidence' as well as motivations by the United States and other countries, see Beal's careful study (2005, 129–66).

2   The case in point were the 'studies' by Robert Conquest (1968, 1986, 1992; Conquest and White 1984), erstwhile intelligence agent and employee of the Information Research Department (IRD), tasked with developing anti-communist propaganda. Historians have made it clear that Conquest's method entailed the use of 'lousy evidence' (Getty 1985; Thurston 1986).

3   A similar situation applies to economic studies of the DPRK. If one is to believe media speculation and guesses, one may gain the impression that the country has been teetering on the edge of economic collapse for decades. However, a careful albeit rare assessment indicates a rather different situation, with growth rates around 10 percent per annum (Feron 2014).

of the Reformed tradition in which he grew up; and the current situation in the DPRK, which is somewhat different from the opinions I have noted above.[4]

1   Chondoism

Article 68 of the socialist constitution of the DPRK (1948 and 1972, with revisions from 1992 to 2016) guarantees freedom of religion as a consequence of the Juche idea, although religion should not be used as an excuse to introduce foreign forces or harm the state (see also J.H. Kim 2017, 54–55).[5] If one holds that religion has been eradicated, then one must argue that the constitutions are not worth the paper on which they are written. The actual situation is quite different. To begin with, the local Chondoism (*Ch'ŏndogyo*) – or 'Religion of the Heavenly Way' – is recognised and favoured by the government. The reason: it is seen as a very Korean form of revolutionary religion. Christianity obviously does not have a monopoly on the combination of religious aspirations and revolutionary movements. The movement goes back to the teachings of Choe Je U, or Su Un (1824–1864), which were systematised by subsequent leaders, Choe Si Hyong, or Haewol (1827–1898), and Son Pyong Hui (1861–1922).[6] Based on an ecstatic experience by its founder in meeting the 'Lord of Heaven', the reappropriation and interpretation of traditional Korean symbols, subsequent organisation and publication of scriptures written in the popular *Kasa* poetry style (first developed by women) and regular worship, the movement offered the most oppressed and downtrodden of Korean society a sense of their intrinsic worth. The divine could be lived out on earth, with immense socio-economic implications. Obviously, this approach offering religious and material elevation to peasants was not viewed favourably by local landlords and foreign powers, who ensured Choe's trial and execution in 1864, along with outlawing the movement and trying to eradicate it. Its subsequent success was largely due to the indefatigable organiser and publisher of the scriptures, Choe Si Hyong, although he met a similar fate in 1898 after being drawn into supporting the 1894–1895 Tonghak revolution, or Kabo Peasant War as it is known in the DPRK. He was the one responsible for establishing the core principles

---

4   My interest in this topic was sparked by visits to the DPRK in 2015 and 2018, when I saw a number of church buildings in Pyongyang and attended worship. I was quite surprised, for I too shared the assumption that religion had been completely suppressed.

5   Article 68 concerns religion.

6   Given the focus of this chapter, I use the transliteration system used in the DPRK. Unlike other works studied in their original languages in this book, I am unable to read Korean, so I rely on translations.

of the unity of all things, based on the innate presence of the divine or heaven in all – 'humans are heaven [*in si chon*]', with the sense that 'to serve a person is to serve Heaven' (Beirne 2009, 158). The ruling class may have thought of themselves in such a manner, but for peasants to believe and act so was a revolutionary proposition.

Chondoism is usually described as somewhat 'syncretistic', melding Daoist, Confucian, Buddhist and Roman Catholic influences with local religious traditions, but this is to reduce a unique movement to an assembly of parts. I am more interested in whether it was primarily religious or political. In light of the previous chapters, it should be obvious by now that the dichotomy is an artificial one, especially at a time that also saw the Taiping Revolutionary movement, although this still does not prevent scholars favouring one or the other (Weems 1964; Beirne 2009; Kallander 2013). Notably, it gained wide and rapid acceptance in the countryside, coming to fruition in the peasant or Tonghak Revolution (the initial name for the movement was Tonghak, or 'Eastern teaching'). In the north, this enmeshment with the Tonghak revolution means that the social movement and its religious forms is seen as a precursor to the communist movement. Indeed, it is characterised as *minjung* or 'popular' (Lee 1996, 105–28), although its history has not always been smooth. Given the connections with the movement in southern Korea, it has at times been under suspicion, but the situation changed after Ryu Mi Yong (1921–2016) moved north with her husband in 1986. Since Chondoism is primarily a northern Korean movement (with almost three million adherents in the north and about 800 places of worship), and since Ryu was to take up leadership positions, her move was a natural one. And lead she did: chair of the Central Guidance Committee of the Chondoist Association of Korea, chair of the Chondoist Chongu Party (The Party of the Young Friends of the Heavenly Way, formed in 1946), chair of the Council for the Reunification of Tangun's Nation and member of the Presidium of the Supreme People's Assembly. In light of her achievements, she was awarded the orders of Kim Il Sung and Kim Jong Il, as well as the National Reunification Prize.

Chondoism bequeathed to Korean culture a number of principles, with an explicit drive to social and religious equality. These include: 'my heart is your heart', with reference both to others and to 'heaven'; 'treat humans as God' in a challenge to Confucian hierarchies; 'protect the nation, secure peace for the people' with clear reference to Korea in relation to foreign powers; 'all people evolve to unity' which has gained even more traction with the split between north and south; and 'the Kingdom of heaven on earth'. But I am most interested in three phrases, attributed to the first three leaders. Choe Je U initially proposed 'bearing the Lord of Heaven', focusing on the close relation of all with 'heaven [*chon*]'; Choe Si Hyong developed this saying by modifying a character or two, to 'humans are heaven [*in si chon*]'; while Son Pyong Hui took it one step further with 'humans are God [*in nae chon*]'. The Chinese-Korean character in this case is 天 (*tian-chon*), with a distinctly less personal dimension and more locational aspect to it than European Christian assumptions. So it means both 'heaven' and 'God', although the use of the latter term – in English translation – is a way of indicating to Christian-influenced audiences the close relationship between humans and divinity.

Why stress this particular principle and its development? At a particular point in his memoirs, *With the Century*, Kim Il Sung writes:

> Of course there is something I believe in like God: the people. I have been worshipping the people as Heaven, and respecting them as if they were God. My God is none other than the people. Only the popular masses are omniscient and omnipotent and almighty on earth. Therefore, my lifetime motto is 'The people are my God'.
>
> KIM 1994, V, 326; see also I, xxx

The invocation of Chondoism is obvious, although it may be better to see the effort to connect Chondoism and Kim's articulation of communism in terms of their common source in Korean cultural-religious traditions. The statement appears in a much longer engagement with Chondoism,[7] which is initially triggered – as is Kim's approach in his memoirs – by his encounter with a Chondoist who wished to join the united front fighting the Japanese (Kim 1994, V, 305–31). As a young peasant from the local area, he was a prime recruit, except for his religion. For some in the revolutionary forces, this was a step too far. The occasion enables Kim to highlight his own efforts to persuade his comrades to accept the young man, while acknowledging that it took some time and effort for all involved – the young man included.

The experience opens a door – slowly at first – to the whole Chondoist movement in Korea. At first, the young man introduces Kim to a certain Pak In Jin, a local Togong or leader who had risen high in the leadership structures of the religion. A poor peasant in origins, Kim's narrative establishes his revolutionary credentials by relating Pak's father's involvement in the Tonghak Revolution, as well as his own leadership in the March First Uprising of 1919 and subsequent suffering in prison. The eventual meeting between Kim and Pak – narrated at some length – leads to an agreement to join forces based on

---

7   The statement is actually an answer given to a question from Pak In Jin: 'I would like to ask you one thing. General, do you worship anything, like we believe in the "Heaven"? If you have, what is it?' (Kim 1994, V, 325).

the 'Ten Point Program' (Kim 1936a, 1936b), albeit not without differences of opinion and struggles among the leadership (Kim 1994, VI, 374). The pact is symbolised by Kim's insistence that Pak offer clean water, a core Chondoist ritual that goes back to its founder and symbolises the foundation of heaven and earth.

At last, the scene is set for an assessment, which is competent and extensive.[8] It includes the history of its founders in a Korean context, mention of the 'five commandments',[9] articulation of its core doctrines or principles and the complex history of the movement in relation to Korean struggles, both revolutionary (Tonghak rebellion against feudal overlords) and anti-colonial (March First uprising against Japanese colonialism).[10] This history includes occasional tensions between radicals and reformers, as well as between the senior leadership and grassroots members. When he comes to the details, Kim must – as a good communist – indicate where he differs from this Korean faith. The sticking point is the persistence of and infusion with theism, especially the central doctrine that God-heaven and human beings are one. How theism influences this doctrine emerges in two key elements: the *jigi* theory, in which human and divine share a 'spirit' that is the foundation of the universe and entails a version of predestination or 'fatalism'; and the idea that a future paradise will arise through non-violent struggle and by propagating key virtues. Obviously, any form of predestination runs counter to Kim's Juche theory (human beings are masters of their own destiny). And the idea of non-violent struggle is a little too reformist for the Marxist-Leninist tradition that was so important for Kim and the Korean revolution. In theory, it would be preferable if one did not have to resort to violent struggle, but it was inescapable in light of the inherent violence of right-wing and imperialist forces.

The criticisms are actually rather mild, for Kim is keen to stress how Chondoism draws nigh to his particular Korean form of communism.[11] His argument

---

8   Kim provides some detail as to how he has come to know Chondoism so well: study at the Hwasong Uisuk School in China, where the principal was a Chondoist who taught Kim much about the religion (Kim 1994, I, 141; V, 334–35); avid reading of the Chondoist journal *Kaebyok*; arguments with Kang Pyong Son, a Chondoist who was also a communist; and discussions with later leaders of Chondoism.

9   *Jumun* (a 21–word formula), *Chongsu* (offering of clean water), *Siil* (church worship on Sundays), *Songmi* (rice donation) and *Kido* (prayers) (Kim 1994, V, 321).

10   The following analysis is based on the key chapter from volume 5 of *With the Century* (Kim 1994, V, 332–56). Where relevant, additional references from other volumes in the memoirs appear.

11   Note also: 'Many of the nationalists in Korea also espoused, supported or sympathized with the idea of communism. Authoritative Christians, Chondoists and other religious believers were among them' (Kim 1994, III, 126; see also VI, 67, 75).

may be distilled into five points. First, he interprets the doctrine that human beings are God or heaven as meaning that Chondoism focuses on the need to believe in human beings rather than offer blind worship to 'Heaven', which so often has entailed providing the ideological bulwark for feudal class systems (Confucianism) or those of caste (Buddhism). With this emphasis, Chondoism draws nigh to Juche, particularly if we recall Kim's statement that the people are God-heaven. Second, he makes much of the doctrine to 'protect the nation, secure peace for the people', or in his own formulation, 'defending the country and providing of welfare for the people'. Obviously, he finds this doctrine particularly attractive, for it emphasises the rejection of foreign influence, the people's sovereignty and a consequent focus on public welfare. This principle had also been part of the ten-point program for a united front between all the anti-colonial forces working for Korean independence (Kim 1936a). But it also reflects the reality of the Korean peninsula, which has historically been strategically crucial for neighbouring large powers and has perpetually sought its freedom from foreign interference.

Third, Kim emphasises a feature of Chondoism I have already noted: the intrinsic worth of all, especially the poor and lowly. This entailed – in Kim's reading – the abolition of class differences. But it also concerned not merely the peasants who had suffered for centuries at the hands of landlords, but also all who had suffered, whether they were workers, simple shopkeepers or day labourers. It is not for nothing, notes Kim, that the first two leaders were executed, or that Chondoism became a broad mass movement. Fourth and obviously related to the previous point, Kim stresses the close integration with the Kabo Peasant War or Tonghak revolution, although he also notes that it did not come from the Chondoist leadership (with its tensions between radicals and moderates), but arose from the people under Jon Pong Jun, the military leader from the south. Only later did the Chondoist leadership come into the revolution. In typical fashion, Kim suggests that the Kabo Peasant War had a lasting effect in Korea, feeding into the independence and communist struggles of the twentieth century, but also that it had world historical significance in terms of global anti-colonial struggles. While the Chondoist leadership may have been somewhat tardy in supporting the Kabo Peasant War, it was at the forefront of the March First Uprising of 1919, which for Kim cements the revolutionary credentials of significant sections of Chondoism (Kim 1994, VI, 75). Finally, Kim appreciates the organisational ability of the Chondoists, with its various chapters throughout Korea and in the diaspora, its efforts to seek alignment with the Comintern, its more militant groups such as the Young Chondoist Party, the Koryo Revolutionary Committee and the Extraordinary Supreme Revolutionary Chondoist Commission, and its desire to work together with other organisations for Korean independence, especially the Association for the Restoration of the Fatherland (see also Kim 1945, 421, 425, 1994, I, 117; III, 128; IV, 470, 476; VI, 67–68, 76, 79, 362).

It should be no surprise that he finds it a 'progressive religion', by which he means that it was a distinctly Korean religion, characterised by the novelty of its ideas and doctrines, its spirit of strong resistance, the simplicity of its rites and practices and its inherently popular nature (Kim 1994, V, 344, 347). To be sure, Kim also notes other and minor Korean religions, such as Chonbulgyo, Taejong and Chonbul (Kim 1994, I, 262–64; V, 74), but Chondoism has a special place in his pantheon. Given that he was writing the memoirs in the early 1990s, not long before his death, he has an eye on the situation then, with the Chondoist political party involved in the DPRK parliament (see above) and a long-standing agenda for reunification that dates back some twenty years earlier, if not longer (Kim 1972, 1992, 1993).[12]

I would like to conclude this engagement with Chondoism on a different note, concerning Kim's understanding of Marx's most well-known statement that religion is the opium of the people. On two occasions, Kim has an opportunity to reflect on this statement, both in reply to comrades who object to working with a religious group, one of them the Chonbulgyo and the other Chondoism. On the first occasion, Kim argues that one is 'mistaken' if one thinks that the proposition concerning opium 'can be applied in all cases'. If a religion 'prays for dealing out divine punishment to Japan and blessing the Korean nation', then it is a 'patriotic religion' and 'all the believers in this religion' are 'patriots' (Kim 1994, I, 264). On the second occasion, he offers a slightly different interpretation. Now Marx's definition 'must not be construed radically and unilaterally'. For Kim, Marx was warning against the 'temptation of a religious mirage and was not opposing believers in general'. The upshot is that the communist movement should welcome and 'join hands with any patriotic religionist'. Given that the communist army is a people's army fighting with and for workers and peasants, its primary mission is 'national salvation against Japan', so anyone who has a similar agenda can join the struggle. 'Even a religionist', Kim argues, 'must be enrolled in our ranks without hesitation' (Kim 1994, V, 307).

The question in all this is how he understands opium. Given the history of China in relation to opium (Kim 1994, V, 26–27), with the British Empire forcing opium onto the Chinese context so as to empty the latter's coffers, one

---

12   The three basic principles iterated by Kim Il Sung outline a peaceful process without outside interference for the sake of establishing a federal system, socialist in the north and capitalist in the south.

may expect that the opium metaphor would be a negative one – in contrast to the ambivalence of the image when Marx deployed it (McKinnon 2006). The key for Kim is yet another encounter, this time with two peasant brothers who were opium addicts. Opium, he observes, was even used as money, and the 'more misruled the country is, the more prevalent are drugs like opium'. So why did they engage in this 'terrible habit' that 'sapped their strength in both body and mind' (Kim 1994, VII, 193). The brothers' reply is telling: how can we live in this world when there is nothing for which one may live? They would prefer to die, but if they have to live, they need to escape. Drinking is no good, since one needs friends in order to drink and the Japanese have forbidden gatherings. All they have left is opium. In response, Kim opines that a human being 'without dreams is as good as dead'. Dreams mean a purpose in life and thereby pride and a worthwhile life. The brothers were existing, not living (Kim 1994, VII, 194). Clearly, in this context under Japanese occupation, opium meant a futile escape from a life not worth living. So also with religion in a negative dimension, which explains why Kim seeks to reinterpret Marx's metaphor in terms of the specific situation in Korea. It is not, he argues, a universal formula that should be applied everywhere, but rather a guide for action that should be sensitive to the specific conditions and traditions of a situation. Chondoism was certainly not an opium in this sense of the term.

2   Protestant Christians

Kim Il Sung may have championed Chondoism as a distinctly Korean religion focused on the good of the Korean people, but his personal background was Christian, or more specifically the Reformed tradition embodied in Presbyterianism. In the late nineteenth century, Presbyterian and Methodist missionaries – largely from the United States – had been remarkably successful in converting significant numbers, although the converts tended to come from the various echelons of the ruling class. Pyongyang became a notable centre of Protestant Christianity and a range of hospitals, orphanages, schools and universities were established (Grayson 2002, 157–58). Why were these missions so successful here and not in China or Japan, countries with similar cultural histories? The situation is mixed. On a negative register, Protestant missionaries (especially from the United States) exploited a loophole in Korean law that made it difficult indeed for foreigners to be constrained (Ryu 2003). They found a ready audience among the elite, who were keen to 'modernise' and break with what was deemed a corrupt and decadent Buddhist culture. At the same time, a good number of the converts came to advocate Korean independence from domination by larger powers, especially those who were progressive Christians. These are precisely the Christians that Kim highlights in his memoirs.

As with my treatment of Chondoism, my interest is in Kim's written works. I leave aside any debates over their historical reliability or their political function, or indeed their skilful deployment of story techniques and cultural themes, since I am interested in the nature of his presentation and the engagements with Christianity that emerge. His style is to work through personal incidents or experiences and develop theoretical points from them, so I will structure my assessment in a similar manner. Three incidents are crucial, with each giving rise to a related but distinct theoretical elaboration, which leads me finally to consider a particular Methodist minister who deeply influenced the young Kim.

The first concerns his family's religious practices. Kim is quite willing to admit that his parents worshipped at a Presbyterian Church, although he asserts that his father was an atheist and his mother went to church only to relax. He writes that at first he, too, 'was interested in the church' and worshipped with his friends, but he began to find the ceremony 'tedious' and the preaching 'monotonous' so he stopped attending with the approval of his father (Kim 1994, I, 102). He claims that at the missionary school he attended in Chilgol,[13] he was one of the few students who ceased attending church. But just as he has established his non-religious (but not anti-religious) credentials, suitable for a revolutionary, he offers enough suggestions that his involvement in the church was greater than he initially admits. The admissions begin with his mother, who – as is so often the case in religious families – was the more devout of his parents. She clearly worshipped more than his father, and when she went to church at Chilgol, her son went with her.[14] He would wake her up from her doze, weary as she was from domestic labour and responsibilities, at the end of the prayers. At the same time, his father and his maternal grandfather, who was a teacher and elder at Chilgol church, 'knew much about Jesus Christ' (Kim 1994, V, 332). Further, as a teenager in Jilin, he indicates that he 'frequented the chapel' of the Reverend Son Jong Do, 'to play the organ there' as well as use the church as a base for a range of organisational and educational activities (Kim 1994, II, 7). Later, he sums up that the environment in which he grew up 'benefitted' his 'understanding of Christianity' (Kim 1994, V, 332).

---

13   Later, when he attended Changdok School, he mentions that 'there were many believers in Christianity' (Kim 1994, V, 332).

14   As Kim writes, 'I often went to church with my mother during my childhood' (Kim 1994, V, 332).

I am less interested in which of the two representations – between a very youthful son who refused to worship and admissions that he continued to be involved for many years – is more accurate, but rather in the emergence of a slight tension. At a theoretical level, this tension is captured in two sentences:

> Some people ask me if I was much influenced by Christianity while I grew up. I was not affected by religion, but I received a great deal of humanitarian assistance from Christians, and in return I had an ideological influence on them.
>
>   KIM 1994, I, 102–3

The difference is cast as one of personal influence and humanitarian assistance. We are left to fill in the gaps slightly in light of the earlier account, so 'influence' and 'affect' seem to concern religious commitment and assumptions about the existence of the divine. At the same time, Kim is clearly not opposed to Christian 'humanitarian' assistance, not least because it enables him to engage with Christians. Indeed, he can observe: the 'spirit of Christianity that preaches universal peace and harmony' does not contradict his idea of advocating an 'independent life' for human beings (Kim 1994, I, 103). Other examples of this humanitarian assistance are not difficult to find in the memoirs, whether the observation that the school attended by his father – Sungsil Middle School – was a Presbyterian mission school, or that a missionary assisted the family in having to move yet again due to harassment by the police, or even that Christians would gather daily to pray for his father's release from prison (Kim 1994, I, 19–20, 30, 64). Let me add that in one respect Kim draws near to the young Marx, who gained a systematic gymnasium-level education in theology, church history and biblical languages, but never seems to have had any religious commitment. In another respect, he is closer to Engels (who was deeply committed), not merely in terms of the Reformed background of the two, but also in the continuing interest in religion and religious history. Indeed, the path from Reformed Christianity to communism is not as uncommon as it may seem.

The second incident concerns an organisation for children while his family was in exile in Jilin province (China). Kim begins by noting that there were many children of Christians, believing in God and not initially prepared to change their belief due to the strong influence of their parents. No matter what the communist activists tried, the children would not give up their belief. On a particular Sunday, the children had gone to church and – hungry – had prayed for rice-cakes and bread. None were forthcoming, so the teacher in charge instructed the children to glean grain from the wheat fields, which was subsequently threshed and made into bread. The initial point seems to be the uselessness of religious commitment and belief in God for solving practical matters such as food. But this is not really the point: the aim was not to do away with religion, but religion without action. Or in Reformed theological terms, God's grace should lead one to a more intense response to that grace. Kim writes: 'We wanted to prevent them from becoming weak-minded and enervated and so useless to the revolution if they were to fall prey to religion and hold the Christian creed supreme'.[15] He seems to frame the point in terms of what is primary, religious belief or revolutionary action, but the next sentence clarifies this: 'There is no law preventing religious believers from making the revolution', but it was the lack of action leading to 'non-resistance' that was the problem (Kim 1994, I, 238). Or as he observes, psalms alone would not block the enemies' guns, for 'decisive battles' were needed.

The theoretical point that arises from this incident concerns the difference or tension between quietism and action, between sitting back and assuming that God would do all the work and the need for resolute action on the part of believers – a very Reformed tension. In this story, the labour is revolutionary, captured in the observation that there is 'no law preventing religious believers from making the revolution'.[16] To be added here is a resolute focus on nationalism, embodied in Korean independence from foreign powers, especially the Japanese, who had dominated Korea in the late nineteenth century and occupied it from 1910 to 1945 (Kim 1994, VI, 75).[17] A casual reader may gain the impression that nationalism rather than Marxism is Kim's overriding emphasis, but this is to miss the close connection between communism and anti-colonial movements – an insight that first emerged out of the logic of the affirmative action program with minority nationalities in the Soviet Union. What applied to the many nationalities within a diverse country also applied to those struggling to gain independence from colonial overlords (Boer 2017b, 168–72).

---

15   Elsewhere Kim is even more direct, mentioning that the brutality of the Japanese occupiers surpassed the earlier benchmark set by fascists and the tortures inflicted on victims by the churches during the European Middle Ages (Kim 1994, IV, 23, 347).

16   Note also the March First Uprising in 1919, at which independence was proclaimed and which was organised and led by Christians, but also by Buddhists and Chondoists (Kim 1994, I, 37, 251–52; VI, 75).

17   See also the 'Appeal to All Korean Compatriots': 'Religious believers, the enslaved nation's suffering and sorrow are no exception for you. Without driving out the Japanese imperialist aggressors from the country, you can neither save our suffering nation nor improve your position as the religious people of a colony. Take the sacred road of patriotism, the road of national liberation, for the country and nation, against the cunning, reactionary religious policy of the Japanese imperialists!' (Kim 1937, 349).

The third incident concerns a certain Reverend Kim Song Rak, who visited the DPRK in 1981. Kim Il Sung relates that at a luncheon to welcome the minister to the country, he advised him to pray before his meal (Kim 1994, V, 323).[18] The reverend was surprised, to say the least, for he had not expected a communist leader to be concerned about prayer, which he duly offered (Kim, Pak, and Han 2013, 18–20). The account provides Kim with an opportunity to elaborate on the religious policies of the DPRK after its founding. He is clearly aware of the suggestion that the DPRK had attempted to abolish religion in all its forms (see below), given that it is supposed to be an atheist communist state. In the case of the visiting reverend he had, he says, simply wanted to be a good host, especially since – as I noted earlier – the DPRK constitution stipulates freedom of religion. But he also keen to mention how the DPRK recognises religion: the state constructs churches for believers and provides housing for them; a religious department was recently established in Kim Il Sung University (as part of the philosophy program); and the affinity between some Christians in the south and communism, based on a desire for reunification.

The question arises as to how one accounts for the decline in religious observance in the north. The initial cause, he suggests, may be found in the Fatherland Liberation War (Korean War). After United States bombers had obliterated most of the north, few if any churches and temples were left standing. Commanders of United States forces have admitted this point. For instance, General Curtis LeMay, head of the U.S. Strategic Air Force Command, openly admitted in an interview in 1984:

> So we went over there and fought the war and eventually burned down every town in North Korea anyway, some way or another, and some in South Korea, too .... Over a period of three years or so, we killed off – what – twenty percent of the population of Korea as direct casualties of war, or from starvation and exposure.
>
> KOHN AND HARAHAN 1988, 88

Or as Dean Rusk, later United States secretary of state put it: the United States bombed 'everything that moved in North Korea, every brick standing on top of another' (Shorrock 2015). After running low on urban targets, United States

---

18   Comparable were the visits by Billy Graham in 1992 and 1994, when he was personally welcomed by Kim Il Sung, preached in the Bongsu and Chilgol Protestant churches and Jangchung Roman Catholic church in Pyongyang, gave lectures at Kim Il Sung University and the Great People's Study House, and was interviewed on radio (Graham 2007, 616–33).

bombers destroyed hydroelectric and irrigation dams in the later stages of the war, flooding farmland and destroying crops. To do so, the United States dropped 650,000 tons of bombs, including 43,000 tons of napalm bombs (more napalm than they subsequently dropped on Vietnam). Churches, temples, monasteries, crucifixes, icons and Bibles were all destroyed, and the 'believers were killed and passed on to the world beyond' (Kim 1994, V, 324).[19] On this basis, Kim recounts that religious believers came to see that God had not saved them or their places of worship, indeed that it was proclaimed Christians who had perpetrated such destruction. Not only was prayer to God useless, but they found that their faith was 'powerless in shaping the destiny of human beings'. As a result, they did not hurry to rebuild churches, preferring to focus on rebuilding the country. Further, due to education and culture, the younger generation simply do not believe that paradise will be attained by worshipping God, Heaven or Buddha, so they do not embrace religion (Kim 1994, V, 324).

Kim is fully aware of the international representation that religion has been supressed in the DPRK, so much so that its apparent 'reappearance' in the 1980s was a propaganda move by the government and thereby 'fake'. His answer is both theoretical and empirical. Theoretically, he simply states that it was and is not a 'conciliatory trick' seeking to inveigle religious believers into some form of a united front (Kim 1994, V, 325). Instead, he asserts that he has no intention of turning religious believers into followers of Marx or of communism, for the basic criterion is love of country and nation (as we have already seen). But he also has a second move, which is to point out that those who were punished were 'criminals and traitors to the nation', selling out the country and people. These occasions were 'deviations' in local areas and certainly not a standard policy by the central government (Kim 1994, V, 323–24). And if this is not enough, Kim refers to his personal relationships with religious figures, whether Chondoist or Christian, if not criticisms of the more doctrinaire comrades in the Red peasant unions, who smashed windows of churches, tore down crosses and destroyed Bibles in their misdirected revolutionary zeal (Kim 1994, VI, 320).

In all this, the greatest appreciation is reserved for the Methodist minister, Reverend Son Jong Do (also spelled Sohn Jeong Do), who appears frequently throughout the memoirs, particularly in a whole chapter from the second volume (Kim 1994, II, 2–17). In the select collection of photographs that typically appear in the opening pages to each volume, Son and his family are given significant space. The reason soon becomes obvious: Kim speaks of Son providing

19   A point confirmed by none other than Billy Graham (2007, 623) on his visit to the DPRK in 1992.

'active support just as he would his own relative', indeed that Son treated Kim as his own son and that Kim regarded him like a father (Kim 1994, I, 350; II, 7). Materially, this meant financial assistance to Kim's family, payment of school fees and regular meals at the Son home (Kim 1994, I, 350). A significant part of this relationship involved Kim attending Son's church in Jilin, but also the ability to use the church as a location for organisational work, meetings and rallies of independence groups, for which Son provided guidance (Kim 1994, I, 191, 199, 235, 294, 303, 308, 310). Above all, Son and his family provided crucial support while Kim was in prison in the late 1920s, showing 'unceasing concern', providing food and supplies through the wardens and even bribing the warlord in question so that Kim would be released and not handed over to the Japanese (Kim 1994, I, 350; II, 4, 7).

But who was Son Jong Do? According to the biographical sketches provided (Kim 1994, I, 20, 350–51; II, 3–11; IV, 189), Son had attended the same missionary school as Kim's father, Sungsil Middle School, which eschewed traditional Confucian education in favour of modern methods and produced many independence fighters and revolutionaries. Son had become a Methodist minister, a signal of the remarkable success of Korean missionary work in the nineteenth century, but had also become in his own way a tireless promoter of Korean independence. Like so many, he had been forced to flee Korea and find a new home in China. At first, he became involved with the Korean Provisional Government based in Shanghai, but internal struggles between reactionary and radical elements (the later anti-communist hitman, Syngman Rhee, was an erstwhile head of the organisation) led to Son withdrawing his involvement and setting up a church in Jilin. The church became a centre for a range of independence groups and their activities, even though Son's approach seems to have been more reformist than revolutionary. At the same time, Son had acquired some land around Lake Jingbo in Korea, running a small agricultural company that sought to model an alternative and 'ideal society'. By 1930, after Kim was released from prison, he notes a change in Son's tone, for the latter had become somewhat melancholy. The gramophone had ceased to play, the independence fighters who used to frequent the home had gone into hiding and the various movements were overcome by infighting. The pious congregation had dissipated, as had the children's choir and its songs. Kim records that after a futile trip to Beijing to renew connections with independence figures, Son had found them arrested. When he returned to Jilin, the gastric ulcer that had plagued him for years flared up and he died soon after being admitted to the Oriental Hospital in Jilin (with the ensuing speculation that he had been murdered by the Japanese who ran the hospital and had kept a close watch on Son for many years). At the simple funeral, Kim writes that he 'looked up to the sky above Jilin and wept without cease, praying for the soul of the deceased minister' (Kim 1994, II, 11). But that is by no means all, for on Kim's telling it was a revolutionary's prayer: it included a vow to liberate the country, take vengeance on the enemy, break the people's shackles, repay his benefactor's kindness, relieve the people of their suffering and 'safeguard their souls'.

In light of this biographical sketch, Kim is willing to admit that Son was a very 'devout Christian', being a 'man of consequence among the Christians and independence fighters in Jilin'. Indeed, like Son, many Korean Christians were 'respectable patriots', devoting 'their whole lives to the independence movement' even if they held differing views.[20] Not only did they pray for Korea and appeal to 'God to relieve the unhappy Korean people of their stateless plight', but their faith was 'always associated with patriotism', by which Kim means a 'peaceful, harmonious and free paradise' (Kim 1994, I, 350–51).[21] So important was the connection between Kim and Son, that one of the latter's offspring, Son Won Thae (also spelled Sohn Won Tai, who became a doctor in the United States), records that in 1991, Kim told him, 'Rev. Son Jong Do was the savior of my life' (Sohn 2003, 134). How so? In Kim's own detailed recounting of this reunion in Pyongyang, he relates that just as the Japanese were about to manufacture the excuse of the Mukden (Shenyang) incident, on 18 September, 1931, in order to invade Manchuria, Son Jong Do had advised him to leave Jilin (Kim 1994, II, 16; IV, 440). In this way he became the 'saviour' of Kim's life.

3   The DPRK Today

All of this material raises the question as to the situation in the DPRK today. Given the scarcity of scholarly material, I rely here primarily on two articles, one by Ryu Dae Young, 'Fresh Wineskins for New Wine: A New Perspective on North Korean Christianity' (2006) and the other by Kim Heung Soo, 'Recent

---

20   References to 'patriotic-minded' religious figures continue in subsequent volumes, at times in terms of a united front (Kim 1994, II, 45, 169, 179; III, 73, 126; IV, 447, 469; V, 96, 171, 211; VI, 59, 66–67, 78, 82; VII, 46; VIII, 334, 347, 355–56, 1975, 38, 47).

21   Later, Kim mentions other ministers, such as Hyun Song, the third minister of the Jong-dong Methodist Church in Seoul who represented the 'Faith in Jesus' organisation – bearing a letter of support of communism by other leading ministers – at the Far Eastern People's Congress in Moscow in 1922 (Kim 1994, III, 126–27). This dimension of revolutionary patriotism leads Kim at one point to argue that one should not judge people on the basis of party affiliation, religion or even class. His example is the landlord Zhang Wei-Hua, who provided material support and arms to the movement – leading Kim to argue that the basis of 'scientific' assessment should be virtues, ideas and practice, by which he means love of fellow human beings and their country (Kim 1994, IV, 399–401).

Changes in North Korean Christianity' (2009).[22] The main purpose of the studies is to offer an alternative historical model or periodisation of Christianity in the DPRK, especially in trying to account for the renewed religious vitality from the 1980s onwards – with new churches built, a Protestant theological college in Pyongyang, an increase in worshippers in both official and house churches, and international engagement by church leaders. We have already seen Kim Il Sung offer his own particular interpretation of this development, to which I will return.

Two models have thus far been proposed for understanding the relatively recent reinvigoration of Christianity. The first is a resolutely anti-communist (and Cold War) model: persecution (1945–1950); eradication and vacuum (1950s and 1960s); and fake reappearance as 'propaganda religion' (from 1970s or 1980s). The dates may vary slightly, but the overall shape of the narrative is similar.[23] The construction of this narrative relies on theoretical assumptions concerning the supposed incompatibility between Marxism-Leninism, if not a Korean approach to communism, and any form of religion. The evidence deployed in these reconstructions varies: anti-religious themes in literature, film and performing arts; items critical of religion in DPRK school materials and dictionaries; and reliance on unconfirmed personal testimonies by 'defectors'. Ryu points out that the material used as 'evidence' is quite untrustworthy, with misleading citations, unconfirmed quotations that are repeated time and again and a misreading of material from the DPRK. There is a particular fondness for quoting from Kim Il Sung as 'proof' that the DPRK is inherently hostile to religion.[24] It should be clear by now that a careful study of Kim Il Sung's works reveals a very different picture. Underlying this approach is not merely an anti-communist bias, but an assumption that 'capitalist-Christian conquest' of the north will provide the only genuine form of Christianity (Ryu 2006, 662).

The second model offers a variation: instead of a fake or propaganda form of Christianity in the final period, it regards this period as one of genuine recovery or resurrection. This model differs from the preceding one by arguing for a 'remnant' that survived persecution, which could then re-emerge from the 1970s onwards after a 'religious vacuum'. Ryu finds this approach an improvement on the preceding one, not least because it enables engagement with

22   Both authors have published a co-written book in Korean, upon which these articles are in part based (Kim and Ryu 2002).

23   Apart from the Korean sources cited by Ryu and Kim, a surprising number of foreign observers follow this narrative (Martin 2006, 349–51; Lankov 2007, 189–93; Worden 2008, 116–17; Cha 2013, 57, 120; French 2014, 33, 100, 112).

24   One may, of course, find negative observations on the futility of religion in less insightful works (Jo 1999, 10, 130, 143–44, 160).

Christians in the DPRK. It also raises the point that many of the Christians who fled from the north before and during the Korean War were of the upper or ruling class, but that they downplayed this dimension and tried to emphasise ideological differences. At the same time, this 'Remnant Model' is fundamentally flawed due to its acceptance of the earlier model's first two periods of persecution and eradication.

In order to develop a different approach, Ryu and Kim begin by attempting to shed a South Korean capitalist-liberal perspective by drawing on the work of the South Korean dissident Song Du Yul. Now a German citizen and retired professor at the University of Münster, Song has been a frequent visitor to the DPRK and has written extensively on the topic. His influential 'imminent approach', predicated on finding an alternative path to reunification (Song 1995), argues that one must seek to understand the very different values, norms and orientation of DPRK society. In other words, any research must seek to adopt a northern perspective. While Song overemphasises the differences, the result has been to shake up many of the assumed positions. What is a valid DPRK perspective and how can it assist in understanding Christianity in this part of the world? Initially, it may be possible to follow a stages model based on Juche-history, with anywhere between three and five stages based on the democratic revolution, socialisation of the economy and the construction of socialism. But the model undergoes continued modification, especially in light of the 'Arduous March' of the 1990s and – I would add – the DPRK's own version of the 'reform and opening up' that began in the late 1970s in China (M.C. Kim 2003). For these authors, this model still faces a problem, for it attempts to explain the situation in terms of politico-economic factors and not those intrinsic to Christianity in the north.

The solution is an even more radical 'imminent model', which pays careful attention to what has happened to Christians in the DPRK. It has four stages: encounter with socialism (1945–1953); endeavouring to survive (1953–1972); creating a socialist Christianity (1972–1988); transformation (1988–). One may immediately wonder why the longer revolutionary period before 1945 is not also featured here, especially given the material from Kim Il Sung that I analysed earlier. But Ryu and Kim mention a crucial class factor in this earlier period: the Koreans who became Christian as a result of missionary work from the United States tended to be professionals, business people and landlords, easily adopting the underlying capitalist spirit of the mission endeavours. This depiction of the missions emphasises their negative dimensions (Ryu 1997, 2003), in contrast to the progressives that Kim Il Sung favours in his memoirs. But his emphasis explains why a large number fled to the south before and during the Korean War, for their class affiliation meant they would obviously find their assumed privileges severely curtailed.

The Korean War did Christianity no favours. The widespread destruction and suffering inflicted on the north not only ensured a burning hatred of the United States, but also – in people's minds – connected Christianity and its missions with United States imperialism.[25] After the war, everyone's energy was focused on the reconstruction of society and economy, while many began to see their former faith as obsolete, giving away any commitment and formal observance. A careful reader will note how close this analysis is to that of Kim Il Sung (see above). Ryu and Kim add that those Christians who remained found themselves alone, meeting in unorganised 'house churches' or small congregations (Kim 2009, 11–12). This is the crucial period, one that many pundits have sought to depict as an 'eradication' or 'vacuum' for Christians. Ryu is keen to point out that evidence indicates that the government permitted approximately two hundred informal congregations in former centres of Christianity during the 1960s. Let me quote a crucial section:

> Contrary to the common western view, it appears that North Korean leaders exhibited toleration to Christians who were supportive of Kim Il Sung and his version of socialism. Presbyterian minister Gang Ryang Uk served as vice president of the DPRK from 1972 until his death in 1982,[26] and Kim Chang Jun, an ordained Methodist minister, became vice chairman of the Supreme People's Assembly. They were buried in the exalted Patriots' Cemetery, and many other church leaders received national honors and medals. It appears that the government allowed the house churches in recognition of Christians' contribution to the building of the socialist nation.
>
>   RYU 2006, 673

From this background, the role of the Korean Christian Federation (a DPRK organisation) makes some sense.[27] Dating from 1948, the Federation became active again in the 1970s, reopening the Pyongyang theological college in 1972, publishing Bible translations and a hymnal in 1983, and overseeing the

---

25   As one would expect in this situation, a significant strain of Protestant Christianity in the south has become virulently anti-communist and pro-USA, perpetuating this reactionary position through internal patterns of education and preaching (Ryu 2004, 2017).

26   Gang was Kim Il Sung's mother's cousin and erstwhile leader of the Korean Christian Federation.

27   The other organisations are the Korean Buddhists Federation, the Korean Catholics Association, the Chondoist Association of Korea and the Korean Council of Religionists, now known as the Religious Believers Council of Korea (J.H. Kim 2017, 55).

building of two new church buildings in 1988 with state funds.[28] One of these was Chilgol church, which had been destroyed in 1950 during the war and had previously been attended by Kim Il Sung's mother and a young Kim. In all, five churches now exist in Pyongyang: three Protestant, one Roman Catholic and one Russian Orthodox (completed with state funds in 2006).[29] A further signal of the increased activity and making the most of opportunities was the invitation to none other than Billy Graham to visit and preach in three of the churches in 1992 and 1994. We should also note the increase in numbers of Christian church members, rising from approximately 5,000 in the early 1980s to more than 12,000 at the beginning of the 2000s, with 30 ministers and 300 church officials (I.J. Kim 2003, 26; Borrie 2004; Beal 2005, 146).[30] But these numbers did not come from proselytising, which is restricted due to concerns over foreign influences, but from an active search for Christians, who may earlier have worshipped privately or in small house churches but could now worship openly.

Obviously, this presents a rather different picture from the one usually pedalled concerning Christianity in the DPRK. It is also a rather unique form of what I have been calling Christian communism. While Ryu and Kim openly admit that the context is somewhat hostile for Christianity, at least in the forms to which many have become accustomed, they stress the way Christians in the DPRK have been actively involved in the construction of socialism and support the government in what it is trying to do. This support appears in deed as much as in word. For example, the Korean Christian Federation has come to play a major role in international relations through their connections and dialogue with Christian organisations in South Korea and further abroad, especially for a country that has been so systematically demonised and isolated. This development enabled the Federation, through its channels, to secure massive amounts of foreign aid during the economic difficulties of the 1990s, brought on by the loss of economic connections with the USSR and Eastern Europe, as well as devastating hail storms and floods. The Federation called on the World Council of Churches, which organised Action by Churches Together to direct relief to the DPRK (Kim 2009, 14). The Federation and the other religious organisations also opened up many channels with the south in order to secure aid. It is no wonder that the 'Federation has successfully established itself as a

---

28 As one would expect, efforts are made to describe such activities as 'fake' or 'camouflage', geared for international consumption in time for the Seoul Olympics in 1988 and the World Festival of Youth and Students in 1989 in Pyongyang (Kim 2009, 10).
29 See the personal accounts of foreigners visiting the Bongsu Protestant Church and the Jangchung Roman Catholic Church (Borrie 2004; Beal 2005, 146–47).
30 One occasionally encounters misleading 'information' that Koreans are not permitted to attend such churches (Abt 2012, 215).

valuable organization that works for the greater good of North Korean society'
(Ryu 2006, 674). Or as Reverend Don Borrie (2004), long-time chair of the New
Zealand DPRK Society, put it:

> With great caution and sensitivity the North Korean Christian commu-
> nity, Protestant, Catholic and Orthodox, have been able to show by exam-
> ple that they are fully committed to the well being of their nation. They
> strongly identify with the ideals of the DPRK and sincerely believe that
> their Christian Faith strengthens and deepens their role as loyal citizens.

A second example, which now goes beyond the articles I have been following,
is the active work undertaken with the south for Korean reunification. Given
that this position has been a consistent state policy in the north from its early
days,[31] it should be no surprise that the Federation's activities have been seen
in a positive light. As a more recent signal, a combined worship service focused
on peace and reunification was held on 15 August 2014 at Bongsu Protestant
Church in Pyongyang.[32] It was organised by the Korean Christian Federation
and the National Council of Churches of Korea (from the south). The day itself
was auspicious, for it was Liberation Day over the whole of Korea, which cel-
ebrates the end of Japanese colonisation.

4   Juche Theology?

I finish on a more speculative note. Kim Heung Soo develops a particular point
beyond his joint work with Ryu: the possibility of a Juche theology. To understand this development, we need to put aside the simplistic trope that Juche is
a quasi-religion or replacement for religion (the trope derives from the speculative thought bubble that Marxism is a form of secularised religion) and trace
the development and elaboration of Juche thought over the last ninety years.
In a piece that would provide a preliminary framework, Kim Il Sung (1930)
speaks of the need for Koreans to avoid worshipping great powers, that the
masters of the revolution are the masses of the people and the need for correct
leadership on the road to victory. Although each of these points continues to

---

31   As Billy Graham (2007, 629) observed after his meetings with Kim Il Sung: 'I could not
      help but feel that in his heart he wanted peace with his adversaries before he died'. For
      recent comprehensive statements, with historical overviews and key developments from
      a DPRK perspective, see Ma Tong Hui (2010) and Kim Il Bong (2017).
32   For a report on this meeting, see http://www.pcusa.org/news/2014/8/22/worship-service
      -pyongyang-focuses-peace-and-reunif.

appear, one of them would be emphasised more during different phases. Thus, by the 1950s the emphasis was on the Korean revolution developing its own path and not falling into the pattern of – to use a wonderful term – 'flunkeyism [*sadaejuui*], or 'serving the great-ism' (1955).[33] Crucially, Kim Il Sung has in mind not the older lackeys of Japan or even the United States, but those communists who tend to worship and copy either the Soviet Union or the People's Republic of China in developing the revolution, while ignoring the specific history and context of Korea. By the 1970s and early 1980s, the emphasis became more philosophical and socio-political. The philosophical principle was that a human being, with creativity and consciousness, is the 'master of everything and decides everything' (Kim 1982, 14). Not an individual human being, but a collective one, meaning that the masses of the people as the masters of revolution and construction are the subject of history (Kim 1982, 18–36). In many respects, this emphasis develops further the Marxist emphasis on subjective intervention to change the objective conditions of history (Juche was initially a translation of the German *Subjekt*). On the preceding point, I have cited Kim Jong Il, for he in particular developed Juche into a full system of thought and worldview. Notably, already in this key essay from 1982, we begin to see a line of argument that would soon be enhanced in the 1980s and into the 1990s. While still mentioning the other themes, Kim Jong Il increasingly emphasises the role of the Workers' Party in guiding the construction of socialism, which then enables him to emphasise the need to adhere to the central role of the leadership. Obviously, he still means his father during this time, but this emphasis would also come to focus on his own leadership when he took over the helm (Kim 1983, 1987, 1991).

With these developments in mind (which I have elaborated somewhat), Kim Heung Soo traces the way a rapprochement has begun between Juche thought and theology, a connection – I emphasise – that has happened after the development of Juche and not because it in some way is a quasi-religious entity. Moves came from both sides, with those involved in elaborating Juche philosophy indicating an interest in the theological and philosophical understandings of human nature in Christianity and Buddhism, while the Korean Christian Federation already in 1981 began observing that Juche and theological approaches shared mutual concerns, such as charity, liberation for the oppressed, opposition to 'flunkeyism', a focus on national problems and a human-centred perspective. More specifically, Kim Heung Soo cites Park Seung Duk, from the Institute of Juche Philosophy of the Academy of Social Sciences,

---

33   Derived originally from Mencius, it means 'serving the great-ism' or 'loving and admiring the great and powerful' (Armstrong 2006, 57–58).

who has stressed the earlier collaboration between Kim Il Sung and progressive Christians in the communist movement, the need for Juche theorists to understand religious approaches to human aspirations and how Juche proponents and Christians can find a way to work together for 'human liberation and salvation' (Kim 2009, 17). From the Christian side, there have been efforts to interpret the human-centred focus of Juche as not excluding the role of God, for the incarnation itself is the clearest indication of such an approach from a theological perspective. Kim Heung Soo quotes Reverend Ko Gi Jun, general secretary of the Korean Christian Federation at a meeting in Canada: 'Christians in North Korea believe in almighty God who is the Creator, but they do not entrust everything to God ... We human beings must strive to accomplish what we must do by using all the God-given gifts and wisdom and talents' (Kim 2009, 17–18).

The strands of this development are admittedly rather thin and they may not go anywhere further. It may turn out that official Juche thought moves in a way that rules out such an engagement, especially if it emphasises further the unrivalled leadership of the Kims and downplays the two other elements noted earlier – the resistance to 'flunkeyism' and the focus on the masses as the subject of history. The latter two are obviously more amenable to theological emphases, although we should not rule out the possibility of adherence to the leader in a Christian context, as can be seen in the memoirs of Son Won Thae (2003). Or a theological engagement may take a direction seen elsewhere, in which Christian theology accepts many of the positions from a Marxist-inspired position but also maintains a certain ontological reserve for the role of God in liberation. If this rapprochement does proceed further, it would certainly be a new chapter in the story of Christian communism.

Conclusion

There is no need to revisit some of the key themes of the book, whether the tensions in the Christian communist tradition between communal and revolutionary concerns or the internal dynamic of reactionary and radical tendencies that is constantly at play in theology as such. Instead, I would like to address two issues: the nature of actual historical communist movements; and the role of 'protest' after one has achieved power.

On the first point, the best way to understand communism, Christian or otherwise, is to study historical examples. Too often the tendency is to view communism as an ideal world that may be found in the mists of a distant future. Perhaps human beings will get there someday, but meanwhile we need to get on with the messy business of life. This romanticised view I find not only wayward but historically ignorant. Why? There have been many concrete examples of communism in practice, some of which I have analysed in this book. That they have most often been of a Christian variety should be obvious by now. But there is a catch: they have been overwhelmingly small affairs. The long history of efforts to establish such communities, however short or long they have lasted, typically involves relatively few people living in circumscribed areas. At times, they have had to fight for the space to do so, and if the area in question was sufficiently remote or rugged, they may have been successful over a longer period of time (and I do not regard the temporal closure of an effort as a necessary 'failure', as if success can be measured simply in terms of longevity).

Perhaps this smallness of size is related to the apparent marginality of the movements in question. Time and again, my analysis found that the communist dimension in Christianity emerged on the edges, whether in thought or deed. Kautsky's extraordinary reconstruction had to look to the sidelines to identify and claim the various strands of Christian or 'heretical' communism. Luther and Calvin had to struggle with the more radical implications of their thought, so much so that it took Marx and Engels to espy the former's implicitly revolutionary dimensions. Or the Christian communism that interests me has also found itself on the margins of modern communism, most notably with the Russian Revolution – in terms of peasant communism, Tolstoy and the God-builders. Indeed, I have mentioned elsewhere that it is one of the great missed opportunities of the Russian Revolution that – despite its many stunning achievements – it did not find the means to appreciate and work with the strong elements of Christian communism in Russia. In other cases, I have had to look elsewhere, especially with material that scholars for varying reasons have passed over due to preconceptions, whether Farnham Maynard in

Australia, Chinese Christian communism in the early twentieth century, or the thoroughly demonised DPRK in our own time. I have argued that the dynamic of radical and reactionary elements is a constitutive feature of Christianity, indeed that one should not try to identify one as the core and the other as its perversion or aberration. And yet, so often the historical reality is that the radical, more communist element appears on the edges of thought and practice, having to challenge the powers that be.

At the same time, these movements have so often managed to establish some concrete form of communist practice. As I mentioned, the exercises have tended to be with relatively small groups in specific areas, even if they were and indeed are today linked to other groups of like-minded people or groups of the same organisation. So what can be learned from these historical examples? The first may seem somewhat paradoxical: the principle of 'all things in common', if not 'from each according to ability and to each according to need' requires a high level of organisation, even for a small group. Allocation and reallocation of labour, production, resources and products requires careful deliberation and continual reassessment. Second, the group in question requires a strong ideological justification for what it does, especially as it sets itself over against the world as it is. Given that I have focused on Christian communism, the ideological framework is invariably Christian, if not biblical. The obvious texts play a role (Acts 2 and 4), but so also do many others that are discussed and interpreted for the sake of the group's identity. Third, most groups desire peace – to be left alone to get on with the collective life they have chosen. This usually entails a certain level of retreat from the world as it is, to a quiet corner far from the madding crowd. And yet, fourth, the very act of doing so is based on a profound criticism of the world. At this point, a potential bifurcation opens up, for the criticism may be based on a conservative or a progressive agenda. Obviously, I am interested in the Christian communist formulation of this challenge, for it is based not on the return to some mythical Golden Age that never was, but a vision of a future world that gradually adopts – it is hoped – the project undertaken by the small community in the present.

Fifth, the problem is that the powers that be are not always happy with the explicit and implicit challenge to their own understanding and organisation of the world. The historical examples indicate so often the policy, 'if we cannot absorb them, crush them'. The communities in question find themselves harassed, expelled, persecuted, if not simply annihilated if the rulers have had enough. Retreat may be a possibility, if at all possible, but at other times there is no other option but to take up force of arms. The Taborites and the Taiping were relatively successful for a while, the Dulcinians lasted only a short while, while the peasants with Müntzer and the Anabaptists at Münster came to a rapid and martyr-like end. An alternative opens up with the Chinese Christian communists of the early twentieth century, if not the radical believers during the long struggle for the Korean Revolution. In these cases, they opted to join a united front with other forces, especially the communists. We also find this approach in Latin America, which I have not discussed in the book. But the lesson learned is that any communist movement, Christian or otherwise, must learn the arts of war to defend itself, since those who would destroy are often legion.

The final point is – given the more recent direction of my interests – the most pertinent of all. It seems to me that the type of organisation character-istic of Christian communism is possible only within relatively small groups. Having all things in common, a commitment to a significant level of equality in terms of labour and produce, a form of communist democracy in which all decisions are made by the group – much as Marx saw in his idealised version of the Paris Commune (1871a) – are possible only with small organisations. Every-thing changes when the effort at communism moves to state level, especially in a large country like Russia and China. The catch is that Christian commu-nists have never been in such a situation, so we need to consider the histori-cal examples of other types of state organisation, such as the Soviet Union or the People's Republic of China today. As Lenin and Mao said on numerous occasions, gaining power through a revolution is relatively easy; exponentially more complicated is the effort to construct socialism when one has power.

This point leads to the second matter I wish to discuss: the role of (prophetic) protest. Christian communism is predicated on a profound criticism of the world, often with a strong sense of transcendence. Yet, it is all very well – and at times relatively comfortable – to criticise the status quo from the margins, so much so that one does not wish to change the current situation too much. Let me dwell on this point for a few moments, focusing on the most succinct ar-ticulation of this position in the work of Max Horkheimer, especially his essay 'Theism and Atheism' (1996, 34–50, 1963). In Horkheimer's dialectical reading, either theism or atheism may form the basis of protest or the means of oppres-sion. Thus, when atheism offers resistance to a religion that has supped with the devil of an oppressive state, it is a profound form of protest and resistance: 'Atheism was once a sign of inner independence and incredible courage, and it continues to be one in authoritarian and semi-authoritarian countries where it is regarded as a symptom of the hated liberal spirit' (1996, 49, 1963, 185). The key is resistance. A political or social structure that has become oppressive should be challenged. Religion may indeed offer this path through its radical transcendence, or, as Horkheimer puts it, in the name of allegiance to a totally other. But so also may atheism, particularly if it challenges cathedrals, priests offering prayers for sundry tyrants, or the clergy comfortable with the benefits of allegiance to the ruling class and its monopoly on property.

Horkheimer notes that modern atheism is a late arrival and has struggled to grip the masses (1996, 41–45, 1963, 178–82). Thus, the Enlightenment's metaphysical atheism, the replacement of God with nature, or indeed the strain of English deism, belonged to the realm of salons and armchair intellectuals – Kautsky's 'Salonkommunismus'. Soon enough the situation changed, with European nation-states, science and technology, population explosions, world wars and multi-national capitalism. Only then could atheism begin to produce a historical narrative and gain institutional power. Horkheimer's prescience is rather remarkable, especially if we consider the movement of 'new atheists', who are now able to reclaim the narrative of nineteenth century atheism in order to proclaim their message (R. Boer 2009c). The problem – in Horkheimer's narrative – is that after atheism managed to gain its much-desired status, it betrayed its critical position. His basic position is that any compromise with state power is a problem, so when atheism becomes a state ideology, it is institutionalised and used to exercise that power. Horkheimer's core example is fascism, which he experienced at first hand, but implicit in his analysis is a certain perception of the Soviet Union under Stalin. In this light, he suggests that atheism too may become an authoritarian power.

Horkheimer's point is that theism and atheism do not constitute the real opposition. Instead, it lies between betrayal and resistance, or oppression and protest. Thus, both theism and atheism may, depending on the circumstances, find themselves on either side of this line. His own position is clear: 'The idea of a better world has not only been given shape in theological treatises, but often just as well in the so-called "nihilistic" works – the critique of political economy, the theory of Marx and Engels, psychoanalysis – works which have been blacklisted, whether in the east or in the west, and provoked the wrath of the mighty as the inflammatory speeches of Christ did among his contemporaries' (1996, 48–49, 1963, 185).[1] For Horkheimer, this position entails reading the specific situation carefully: when religion becomes the ideology of power, as happened with medieval European states or during the transitional absolute monarchies, and when it pursues, condemns, expels and executes those who protest too much, then atheism becomes a resolute stand in opposition, along with those marginal religious movement which have been proscribed.

---

1   See also: 'Those who professed themselves to be atheists at a time when religion was still in power tended to identify themselves more deeply with the theistic commandment to love one's neighbour and indeed all created things than most adherents and fellow-travellers of the various denominations' (Horkheimer 1996, 49–50, 1963, 185–86).

However, if atheism succeeds in ousting all religion and is transformed into the dominant ideology of a repressive state apparatus, then religion may once again become take on a position of protest and opposition.

The gains of Horkheimer's position are obvious: theism or atheism is not the key to the problem, as so many have thought. Instead, critique and protest is the heart of the issue. If atheism is an expression of protest, then it draws nigh to what might be called protest theism, a central feature of the Christian communism. At the same time, there is a problem in Horkheimer's approach: he views with deep suspicion any seizure of state power. This can be a relatively comfortable position to take, since one can always sit on the sidelines, criticising any form of state power and eschewing any opportunity to exercise power. But it begs the question: what happens if one does gain power, through a revolution? To be sure, this has never been the situation for Christian communism and may well never be the case, given its predilection for small communities. Or rather, it is only the case if Christian communists become part of a larger united front where the state is socialist. In this case, there are number of examples, whether in Latin America, China with the TSPM or indeed the DPRK and the Korean Christian Federation.

I have asked this question since it is increasingly at the centre of my thought, particularly with a project called 'Socialism in Power'. So I cannot help pondering how Christian communism might work within this framework. Since I have already analysed the situations in China (earlier in the twentieth century) and the DPRK, let me draw on two other sources for some insights. The first comes from Jan Lochman (1922–2004), the Reformed theologian working in Czechoslovakia in the 1960s and 1970s, although he later moved to Basel and continued working into the 1980s and beyond. For some strange reason, I have a longing for someone like Lochman, with his deep indebtedness to the Hussite Reformation and involvement in the socialist project of Czechoslovakia, although I also need to remind myself that the era has passed in that part of world and that it now exists in a state of post-communism. As we saw in my chapter on the Marxist-Christian dialogue, Lochman (1970a, 1970b) openly acknowledges that the socialism that had developed in Czechoslovakia at the time had indeed eliminated poverty and ensured relatively minimal differences in wealth and economic status. With national healthcare and free education – modelled on the Soviet Union's breakthroughs of the 1930s – those who had been downtrodden were now valued, so much so that workers and farmers took an active part in debates concerning the development of socialism. I am particularly drawn to Lochman's admission that the dictatorship of the proletariat is absolutely necessary in the first or even preliminary stage of socialism, with its attendant restrictions and alienations. But this is by no means all, for one longs for the next stages of socialism, without specifying how many there might be. It is precisely at this point that Christian theology may have a positive contribution to make in the process of developing socialist democracy. As a Reformed theologian, Lochman invokes the Exodus tradition and Jesus of Nazareth, who embodies in this context both a humanising and – to use the language of the time (Bultmann 1951) – demythologising effect, challenging the powers not to produce new mythologies.

Lochman's position is of a critic within, attempting to remind the socialists in power not to lose sight of their initial empowering vision. Let me now turn to my second example of a theologian under socialism, Dick Boer. I begin with some biography to set the scene: in 1984, Dick Boer was called to East Berlin to be a minister in the Dutch Ecumenical Congregation in the DDR (*Niederländische Ökumenische Gemeinde in der DDR*). He was minister for six years, until 1990, after the fall of the wall and the end of the DDR. Why did this congregation call Dick Boer? He was at the time a professor of theology in the University of Amsterdam, but he was also a member of the communist party. In short, he was a minister of the church, a professor and communist. As for the congregation, it was a small (100 members) communion of left-wing Christians in the DDR. It was established in October of 1949, when the DDR was itself founded in response to the establishment of West Germany. At that time, the church was made up of Dutch citizens who had come to Germany as foreign workers (*Fremdarbeiter*) during the Second World War and who lived in what became both East Berlin and West Berlin. After the construction of the wall in August of 1961, the part of the congregation in the DDR grew into a community of left-wing Christians. They became deeply committed to political readings of the Bible, especially the Hebrew Bible (Old Testament). They also developed a liturgy that included elements one may describe as 'secular' or 'non-religious'. Or rather, the liturgy saw the work of God in the world outside the walls of the church, outside what had become the acceptable zones of Christianity. For example, the hymn book contained not only the best examples of church music, but also the 'Internationale' and '*Vorwärts und nicht vergessen*'. All of which meant that the Dutch Ecumenical Congregation took a step further than the Federation of Evangelical Churches of the DDR, which defined itself as 'not against and not outside but within socialism [*nicht gegen, nicht neben, sondern im Sozialismus*]'. By contrast, the Dutch Ecumenical Congregation saw itself as a communion of 'Christians for socialism'. That is, they were both 'within socialism and for the DDR'.

The challenge for Dick Boer, as the minister and as a theologian, was to find ways to preach within the context of actually existing socialism. In the liberation and political theologies that arose in Western and Southern contexts – Latin America, North America, Europe – a key biblical narrative is the Exodus out of slavery, as is the Gospel promise of the 'Kingdom of God' that will provide healing, release from hunger and freedom from exploitation. In these cases, the moment of the Exodus or the new world is yet to come at a hoped-for future moment. But what does a minister do when the Exodus has, so to speak, already happened? How does one go about the difficult task of constructing the new society? To preach the Exodus in the DDR would mean to speak of liberation from slavery in the DDR. So Boer became interested in the time after liberation, after the Exodus. He discovered the importance of the 'historical' books (or 'former prophets' as the Jewish canon calls them) of the Hebrew Bible, such as Joshua, Judges, and the books of Samuel and Kings. He also re-discovered Ezra and Nehemiah, with their accounts of rebuilding a 'Torah Republic', when the exile to Babylon (sixth century BCE) was over. This was the problem of the 'travails of the plains', as Brecht put it. The task of climbing the mountain is now past and we are on the plateau where the real task begins. The experience led Dick Boer to develop his theory of 'actually existing' or 'real' Israel.

Further, since the government of the DDR recognised the congregation as an organisation with a special relationship to the Netherlands, the church was allowed to organise seminars with Dutch speakers who entered into discussion with Marxists from the DDR. The topics of these seminars included: 'The alliance of Communists and Christians'; 'Faith and Atheism'; 'Socialism and the Third World'; 'The New Economic World-Order'; 'Media'; and 'Gay Theology'. The Marxists who took part in these seminars actually felt free to engage in a robust critique of the official communist positions of the state – in the spirit of the tradition and theory of Marxism itself. Further, even though the government of the DDR officially forbade a 'Christian-Marxist dialogue', here that dialogue took place, regularly.

Since it was Boer's task to find and invite Marxist speakers for these seminars, he also had the opportunity to meet and speak with them in private. He became friends with many of them, a friendship enhanced by their common experience of being members of communist parties. They shared their hopes for a renewal of socialism and their frustrations in seeking such a renewal. These contacts also encouraged Boer to undertake an initiative to 'save' the DDR in the time of the 'Wende' (turn). He was inspired by the Dutch peace movement's project to 'Stop the N-bomb': one starts with a manifesto, which is signed by prominent figures without explicit political commitments. In the Netherlands, this action led to the largest mass-movement since the Second World War. So he proposed a similar action in the DDR: organise a manifesto, signed by well-known people from the new civic movements (Bürgerbewegungen: Neues

Forum, Demokratischer Aufbruch), the Church and the party (the section working for renewal and not related to the state and the ossified party apparatus).
This initiative, beginning with the manifesto *For Our Country* (*Für unser Land*)
which was written by Christa Wolf and Volker Braun, became the largest mass-
action in the period of the *Wende* in the DDR. They obtained no less than
1,167,048 signatures. Sadly, the initiative for renewal itself failed, not least because the Soviet Union was no longer able to protect the DDR from the unending efforts of the West to 'overthrow' communism. Yet, as Boer points out, the
sheer size of the movement (one among many) shows that, contrary to much
propaganda, the DDR was supported by many of its citizens until the end.

The result of this extraordinary experience was a biblical theology from a
Reformed perspective, published in German, Dutch and English (Boer 2008,
D. Boer 2009, 2015). The most significant feature of this study is the effort to
think theologically in the period after the revolution, after the gaining of power
when one needs to put into action one's hopes and plans. This is the time of
the 'real Israel' or 'actually existing Israel' – with an obvious play on 'actually
existing socialism'. It is the time of the 'travails of the plain' that I mentioned
earlier, when one has climbed the mountain and must put into action one's
plans. It is also a period of many mistakes, steps backward, reshaping the approach in light of changing and unexpected circumstances. So also the 'real
Israel' made many mistakes and certainly did not live up to the project as it
was outlined in the Torah (the first five and really core books of the Bible). As
a result, many would argue that it 'failed', especially when the project came to
an end. Too soon did this project succumb to imperial powers of the first millennium BCE, becoming a province (called 'Yehud') under the Persians and
Greeks and Romans. But 'failure' is a harsh term, beloved of right-wing critics
who deploy an impossible benchmark for what counts as success: perfect realisation and eternity. Anything less than eternally perfect is a failure. Of course,
in their eyes this applies only to the Left (for they conveniently ignore the disaster of their own project). In reply, we need to resist such a verdict, insisting
that any liberating project which achieves power and which is able to begin
the process of construction is a success, especially if it is able to overcome the
counter-revolution. It may come to an end before its time, leading to profound
disappointment. But the experience is enough to foster hope and energy for
yet another effort.

Thus, Boer too sees a critical role for a Marxist Christian, a communist theologian involved in the complex project of socialism itself, which should really
be seen as a long work in progress. By focusing on the Bible and interpreting
it in this light, he identifies the many problems that face such a project, if not
its temporary erasure and absorption by its enemies. By now, the very idea of

critique has taken on a whole new meaning, well beyond Horkheimer's protest against corrupt powers. Now it is criticism of a project that is not living up to its ideals, even if these change in the light of reality. I must admit that I continue to be inspired by the projects of Lochman and Boer, even if they were involved in 'actually existing socialisms' that were colonised – for a time – by Western European capitalism. But I am also inspired by the projects further east, especially by the Chinese Christian communists whom I discussed earlier – Wu Leichuan, Wu Yaozong and Zhu Weizhi – or indeed by the North Korean Christians who have developed – through great hardship – an approach that works with rather than opposes the arduous construction of socialism. In their cases, the reality of socialism in power continues.

Bibliography

NOTE: Since the references include a significant number of historically important original language texts, I cite the original date of composition and publication in the text. This provides accuracy for my arguments. Where appropriate, the bibliography includes in square parentheses the later date of publication.

1839 [1975]. 'Leaving Certificate from Berlin University'. In *Marx and Engels Collected Works*, Vol. 1, 703–4. Moscow: Progress Publishers.

1967. *The October Storm and After*. Moscow: Progress Publishers.

Abt, Felix. 2012. *A Capitalist in North Korea: My Seven Years in the Hermit Kingdom*. North Clarendon: Tuttle.

Acton, Edward, and Tom Stableford, eds. 2005. *The Soviet Union: A Documentary History. Volume 1: 1917–1940*. Exeter: University of Exeter Press.

Adams, James. 1967. 'Is Marx's Thought Relevant to the Christian? A Protestant View'. In *Marx and the Western World*, edited by Nicholas Lobkowicz, 371–88. Notre Dame: Indiana University Press.

Alexinsky, Gregor. 1913. *Modern Russia*. Translated by Bernard Miall. London: T. Fisher Unwin.

Althusser, Louis. 1971. *Lenin and Philosophy and Other Essays*. Translated by Ben Brewster. New York: Monthly Review Press.

Althusser, Louis. 1977. *For Marx*. Translated by Ben Brewster. London: NLB.

Althusser, Louis. 1994. *Écrits philosophiques et politiques. Tome 1*. Paris: Éditions Stock/IMEC.

Althusser, Louis. 1996. *Pour Marx*. Paris: La Découverte.

Althusser, Louis. 1997. *The Spectre of Hegel: Early Writings*. Translated by G.M. Goshgarian. London: Verso.

Amin, Samir. 2013. 'Forerunners of the Contemporary World: The Paris Commune (1871) and the Taiping Revolution (1851–1864)'. *International Critical Thought* 3 (2):159–64.

An Yu and Bai Shui. 1991. 'Shilun taiping tianguo he rujia wenhua de guanxi'. *Fuyin baokan ziliao: Zhongguo jindai shi* 2:66–70.

Anderson, Perry. 1974. *Passages from Antiquity to Feudalism*. London: New Left Books.

Aptheker, Herbert. 1968. 'Marxism and Religion'. *Religion in Life* 37 (1):89–98.

Aptheker, Herbert. 1970. *The Urgency of Marxist-Christian Dialogue*. New York: Harper and Row.

Armstrong, Charles. 2006. *The Koreas*. London: Routledge.

Arnal, Oscar. 1980–81. 'Luther and the Peasants: A Lutheran Reassessment'. *Science and Society* 44 (4):443–65.

Arthur, Anthony. 1999. *The Tailor King: The Rise and Fall of the Anabaptist Kingdom of Münster*. New York: St Martins Press.

Assmann, Hugo, and Franz Hinkelammert. 1989. *A idolatria do Mercado*. Petrópolis: Vozes.

Augustine. 1992. *Four Anti-Pelagian Writings*. Translated by John Mourant. Washington: Catholic University of America.

Baird, Robert. 2006. 'Stories Are Not All Equal: An Interview with Wu Ming'. *Chicago Review* 52 (2-4):250–59.

Bak, Janos, Rainer Wohlfeil, Ernst Engelberg, Günter Vogler, Edward Friedman, Kurt Greussing, and Hans Kippenberg. 2013. '"The Peasant War in Germany" by Friedrich Engels – 125 Years After'. In *The German Peasant War of 1525*, edited by Janos Bak, 89–99. London: Routledge.

Bakhtin, Mikhail. 1984. *Rabelais and His World*. Translated by Helene Iswolsky. Bloomington: Indiana University Press.

Banks, Robert. 1974. 'The Search for Man in Christian-Marxist Dialogue'. *Theology* 77:135–47.

Banks, Robert. 1976. 'The Intellectual Encounter between Christianity and Marxism: A Contribution to the Pre-History of a Dialogue'. *Journal of Contemporary History* 11 (2-3):309–31.

Barrett, Charles Kingsley. 1994. *A Criticial and Exegetical Commentary on the Acts of the Apostles*. Vol. 1. Edinburgh: T & T Clark.

Bartchy, Scott. 1991. 'Community of Goods in Acts: Idealization or Social Reality?' In *The Future of Early Christianity: Essays in Honor of Helmut Koester*, edited by Birger Pearson, 309–18. Minneapolis: Fortress.

Barth, Karl. 1954. *Against the Stream: Shorter Post-War Writings, 1946–1952*. London: SCM.

Bartlett, Roger, ed. 1990. *Land Commune and Peasant Community in Russia: Communal Forms in Imperial and Early Soviet Society*. London: Palgrave Macmillan.

Bauckham, Richard. 2007. 'James and the Jerusalem Community'. In *Jewish Believers in Jesus*, edited by Oskar Skarsaune and Reider Hvalvik, 55–95. Peabody: Hendrickson.

Bauer, Bruno. 1838. *Kritik der Geschichte der Offenbarung: Die Religion des alten Testaments in der geschichtlichen Entwicklung ihrer Prinzipien dargestellt*. Berlin: Ferdinand Dümmler.

Bauer, Bruno. 1839. *Herr Dr. Hengstenberg: Ein Beitrag zur Kritik der religiösen Bewußtseins. Kritische Briefe über den Gegensatz des Gesetzes und des Evangeliums*. Berlin: Ferdinand Dümmler.

Bauer, Bruno. 1840. *Kritik der evangelischen Geschichte des Johannes*. Bremen: Karl Schünemann.

Bauer, Bruno. 1841. *Kritik der evangelischen Geschichte der Synoptiker*. 2 vols. Leipzig: Otto Wigand.

Bauer, Bruno. 1842. *Kritik der evangelischen Geschichte der Synoptiker und des Johannes, Dritter und letzter Band*. Braunschweig: Fr. Otto.

Bauer, Bruno. 1843. *Das entdeckte Christenthum. Eine Erinnerung an das 18. Jahrhundert und ein Beitrag zur Krisis des 19. Jahrhundert*. Zürich und Winterthur: Verlag des literarischen Comptoirs.

Beal, Tim. 2005. *North Korea: The Struggle Against American Power*. London: Pluto.

Bebel, August. 1876. *Der Deutsche Bauernkrieg mit Berücksichtigung der hauptsächlichsten sozialen Bewegungen des Mittelalters*. Braunschweig: W. Bracke jr.

Beirne, Paul. 2009. *Su-un and His World of Symbols: The Founder of Korea's First Indigenous Religion*. Farnham: Ashgate.

Bender, Harold. 1944. 'The Anabaptist Vision'. *Church History* 13:3–24.

Bentley, James. 1982. *Between Marx and Christ: The Dialogue in German-Speaking Europe, 1870–1970*. London: Verso.

Berdyaev, Nikolai. 1937. *The Origin of Russian Communism*. Translated by R.M. French. London: G. Bles.

Bergman, Jay. 1990. 'The Image of Jesus in the Russian Revolutionary Movement: The Case of Russian Marxism'. *International Review of Social History* 35: 220–48.

Bernstein, Eduard. 1899. *Die Voraussetzungen des Sozialismus und die Aufgaben der Sozialdemokratie*. Stuttgart: Dietz Nachfolger.

Bernstein, Eduard. 1993. *The Preconditions of Socialism*. Cambridge: Cambridge University Press.

Biasini, Rosalba. 2010. 'Reconsidering Epic: Wu Ming's *54* and Fenoglio'. *Journal of Romance Studies* 10 (1):69–81.

Biéler, André. 2006. *Calvin's Economic and Social Thought*. Translated by James Greig. Geneva: World Alliance of Reformed Churches.

Blake, Jack. 1947. 'Foreword'. In *Religion and Revolution*, edited by Farnham Maynard and Kurt Merz, 3. Melbourne: Fraser & Morphet.

Blanc, Louis. 1851. *Plus de Girondins*. Paris: Charles Joubert.

Blanton, Ward. 2007. *Displacing Christian Origins: Philosophy, Secularity, and the New Testament*. Chicago: University of Chicago Press.

Blissett, Luther. 2004. *Q*. London: Arrow.

Bloch, Ernst. 1968. *Atheismus im Christentum: Zur Religion des Exodus und des Reichs*. Vol. 14, *Ernst Bloch Werkausgabe*. Frankfurt am Main: Suhrkamp.

Bloch, Ernst. 1969. *Thomas Münzer als Theologe der Revolution*. Vol. 2, *Ernst Bloch Werkausgabe*. Frankfurt am Main: Suhrkamp.

Bloch, Ernst. 1985. *Das Prinzip Hoffnung*. Vol. 5, In *Ernst Bloch Werkausgabe*. Frankfurt am Main: Suhrkamp Verlag.

Bloch, Ernst. 1995. *The Principle of Hope*. Translated by Neville Plaice, Stephen Plaice and Paul Knight. Cambridge: MIT Press.

Bloch, Ernst. 1968 [2009]. *Atheism in Christianity: The Religion of the Exodus and the Kingdom*. Translated by J.T. Swann. London: Verso.

Boardman, Eugene. 1952. *Christian Influence upon the Ideology of the Taiping Rebellion, 1851–1864*. Madison: University of Wisconsin Press.

Boer, Dick. 2002. *Een Heel Andere God: Het Levenswerk van Karl Barth (1886–1968)*. Amsterdam: Narratio.

Boer, Dick. 2008. *Erlösung aus der Sklaverei: Versuch einer biblischen Theologie im Dienst der Befreiung*. Münster: Edition ITP-Kompass.

Boer, Dick. 2009. *Verlossing uit de Slavernij: Bijbelse Theologie in Dient van Bevrijding*. Amsterdam: Skandalon.

Boer, Dick. 2015. *Delivery from Slavery: Attempting a Biblical Theology in the Service of Liberation*. Translated by Rebecca Pohl, *Historical Materialism Book Series*. Leiden: Brill.

Boer, Roland. 2007a. *Criticism of Heaven: On Marxism and Theology*. Leiden: Brill.

Boer, Roland. 2007b. 'Introduction: Bakhtin, Genre and Biblical Studies'. In *Bakhtin and Genre Theory in Biblical Studies*, edited by Roland Boer, 1–7. Atlanta: SBL Publications.

Boer, Roland. 2007c. *Political Myth: On the Use and Abuse of Biblical Themes*. Durham: Duke University Press.

Boer, Roland. 2007–2014. *The Criticism of Heaven and Earth*. 5 vols. Leiden and Chicago: Brill and Haymarket.

Boer, Roland. 2009a. *Criticism of Religion: On Marxism and Theology II*. Leiden and Chicago: Brill and Haymarket.

Boer, Roland. 2009b. 'Folly to the Rich: Ernst Bloch's *Atheism in Christianity*'. In *Caught Reading Again*, edited by R.S. Sugirtharajah, 30–40. London: SCM.

Boer, Roland. 2009c. 'The New Old Atheists'. *Australian Marxist Review* 50:10–19.

Boer, Roland. 2009d. *Political Myth: On the Use and Abuse of Biblical Themes*. Durham: Duke University Press.

Boer, Roland. 2011a. *Criticism of Theology: On Marxism and Theology III*. Leiden and Chicago: Brill and Haymarket.

Boer, Roland. 2011b. 'Kapitalfetisch: "The Religion of Everyday Life"'. *International Critical Thought* 1 (4):416–26.

Boer, Roland. 2011c. 'Marxism and Eschatology Reconsidered'. *Mediations* 25 (1):39–60.

Boer, Roland. 2012. *Criticism of Earth: On Marx, Engels and Theology*. Leiden: Brill.

Boer, Roland. 2013a. *Lenin, Religion, and Theology*. New York: Palgrave Macmillan.

Boer, Roland. 2013b. 'The Privatisation of Eschatology and Myth: Ernst Bloch Versus Rudolf Bultmann'. In *The Privatisation of Hope: Ernst Bloch and the Future of Utopia*, edited by Peter Thompson and Slavoj Žižek, 106–20. Durham: Duke University Press.

Boer, Roland. 2014a. *In The Vale of Tears: On Marxism and Theology v*. Leiden and Chicago: Brill and Haymarket.

Boer, Roland. 2014b. 'Ontology, Plurality and Roman Catholic Social Teaching: An Engagement with Liberation Theology'. In *Politics in Theology. Religion and Public Life*, edited by Gabriel Ricci, 93–120. Edison: Transaction.

Boer, Roland. 2014c. 'Religion and Socialism: A.V. Lunacharsky and the God-Builders'. *Political Theology* 15 (2):188–209.

Boer, Roland. 2014d. 'Theo-Utopian Hearing: Ernst Bloch on Music'. In *The Dialectics of the Religious and the Secular: Studies on the Future of Religion*, edited by Michael Ott, 100–33. Leiden: Brill.

Boer, Roland. 2015a. *The Sacred Economy of Ancient Israel, Library of Ancient Israel*. Louisville: Westminster John Knox.

Boer, Roland. 2015b. 'Translating Politics and Religion: A New Model'. *Stasis* 3 (2):10–28.

Boer, Roland. 2017a. 'From Berne to Yan'an: The Theoretical Breakthroughs of Lenin and Mao'. *Crisis and Critique* 4 (2):60–84.

Boer, Roland. 2017b. *Stalin: From Theology to the Philosophy of Socialism in Power*. Beijing: Springer.

Boer, Roland. 2018. 'Sergei and the "Divinely Appointed" Stalin: Theology and Ecclesiology in Church-State Relations in the Soviet Union in the Lead-up to the Cold War'. *Social Sciences* 7.4: 1–19.

Boer, Roland, and Christina Petterson. 2014. *Idols of Nations: Biblical Myth at the Origins of Capitalism*. Minneapolis: Fortress.

Boer, Roland, and Christina Petterson. 2017. *Time of Troubles: A New Economic Framework for Early Christianity*. Minneapolis: Fortress.

Borchert, Donald. 1971. 'The Future of Religion in a Marxist Society'. *Christian Century* 88:1129–33.

Borrie, Don. 2004. "Reflections on a Visit to the DPRK, April, 2004". *Scoop*, 18 May. Available from http://www.scoop.co.nz/stories/HL0405/S00177.htm.

Bouma, Gary. 2009. *Australian Soul: Religion and Spirituality in the Twenty-first Century*. Cambridge: Cambridge University Press.

Bousma, William. 1988. *John Calvin: A Sixteenth-Century Portrait*. New York: Oxford University Press.

Boutang, Yann Moulier. 1992. *Louis Althusser: Une biographie, Volume 1: La formation du mythe, 1918–1956*. Paris: Grasset.

Bowie, Norman. 1971. *Towards a New Theory of Distributive Justice*. Amherst: University of Massachusetts Press.

Boyarin, Daniel. 1994. *A Radical Jew: Paul and the Politics of Identity*. Berkeley: University of California Press.

Boyarin, Daniel. 2004. 'Paul and Genealogy of Gender'. In *A Feminist Companion to Paul*, edited by Amy-Jill Levine and Marianne Blickenstaff, 1–12. London: T & T Clark International.

Breckman, Warren. 1999. *Marx, the Young Hegelians, and the Origins of Radical Social Theory*. Cambridge: Cambridge University Press.

Brendler, Gerhard. 1989. *Thomas Müntzer – Geist und Faust*. Berlin: VEB Deutscher Verlag der Wissenschaft.

Breton, Stanislas. 1997. 'Althusser et la religion'. In *Althusser Philosophe*, edited by Pierre Raymond, 155–66. Paris: Presses Universitaires de France.

Bruce, F.F. 1990. *The Acts of the Apostles*. 3 ed. Grand Rapids: Eerdmans.

Bubenheimer, Ulrich. 1989. *Thomas Muntzer: Herkunft und Bildung*. Leiden: Brill.

Bultmann, Rudolf. 1951. 'Neues Testament und Mythologie: Das Problem der Entmythologisiering der neutestamentlichen Verkündigung'. In *Kerygma und Mythos*, Vol. 1, edited by H.W. Bartsch, 15–48. Hamburg: Herbert Reich-Evangelischer Verlag. Original edition, 1941.

Buswell, Robert, ed. 2006. *Religions of Korea in Practice*. Princeton: Princeton University Press.

Cai Shaoqing. 1988. 'An Overview of the Secret Societies of China During the Late Qing Period'. *Cina* 21:39–47.

Calvin, John. 1559 [2006]. *Institutes of the Christian Religion*. Translated by Ford Lewis Battles. Louisville: Westminster John Knox.

Calvin, John. 1844. *Commentary upon the Acts of the Apostles*. Translated by Christopher Fetherstone and Henry Beveridge. Vol. 1. Edinburgh: Calvin Translation Society.

Calvin, John. 1845. *Commentary on the Book of Psalms*. Translated by James Anderson. Vol. 1. Edinburgh: Calvin Translation Society.

Calvin, John. 1850. *Commentary on the Book of the Prophet Isaiah*. Translated by William Pringle. Vol. 1. Edinburgh: Calvin Translation Society.

Calvin, John. 1852a. *Commentaries on the Book of the Prophet Daniel*. Translated by Christopher Rosdell and Henry Beveridge. Vol. 1. Edinburgh: Calvin Translation Society.

Calvin, John. 1852b. *Commentaries on the Last Four Books of Moses Arranged in the Form of a Harmony*. Translated by Charles William Bingham. Vol. 1. Edinburgh: Calvin Translation Society.

Calvin, John. 1852c. *Commentary on the Book of the Prophet Isaiah*. Translated by William Pringle. Vol. 3. Edinburgh: Calvin Translation Society.

Calvin, John. 1855. *Commentaries on the Catholic Epistles*. Translated by John Owen. Edinburgh: Calvin Translation Society.

Calvin, John. 1856. *Commentaries on the Epistles to Timothy, Titus, and Philemon*. Translated by William Pringle. Edinburgh: Calvin Translation Society.

Calvini, Johannes. 1559 [1957]. *Institutiones Christianae Religionis*. Edited by Petrus Barth and Guilelmus Niesel. 3 vols, *Opera Selecta*. Monachii in Aedibus: Chr. Kaiser.

Cao Shengjie. 2011. 'Recalling the Later Years of Mr. Y.T. Wu'. *Chinese Theological Review* 23:128–45.

Capper, Brian. 1995. 'The Palestinian Cultural Context of Earliest Christian Community of Goods'. In *The Book of Acts in its Palestinian Setting*, edited by Richard Bauckham, 323–56. Grand Rapids: Eerdmans.

Capper, Brian. 1996. 'Community of Goods in the Early Jerusalem Church'. *Aufstieg und Niedergang der römischen Welt* 2 (26.3):1730–74.

Carter, Warren. 2004. 'The Irony of Romans 13'. *Novum Testamentum* 46 (3):209–28.

Carter, Warren. 2006. *The Roman Empire and the New Testament: An Essential Guide*. Nashville: Abingdon.

Carver, Terrell, and Daniel Blank. 2014. *Marx and Engels's 'German Ideology' Manuscripts: Presentation and Analysis of the 'Feuerbach Chapter'*. New York: Palgrave Macmillan.

Casana, Jesse. 2007. 'Structural Transformations in Settlement Systems of the Northern Levant'. *American Journal of Archaeology* 112:195–222.

Certeau, Michel de. 1988. *The Writing of History*. New York: Columbia University Press.

Certeau, Michel de, and Jean-Marie Domenach. 1974. *Le Christianisme éclaté*. Paris: Éditions Du Seuil.

Cha, Victor. 2013. *The Impossible State: North Korea, Past and Future*. New York: HarperCollins.

Chadwick, Owen. 1992. *The Spirit of the Oxford Movement: Tractarian Essays*. Cambridge: Cambridge University Press.

Chan, Adrian. 2003. *Chinese Marxism*. London: Continuum.

Chen Duxiu. 2009. *Chen Duxiu wenxuan*. Chengdu: Sichuan wenyi chubanshe.

Chen Hua. 1996. 'Lun hong xiuquan de lishi yishi: jiqi yu zongjiao xinyang ji xianshi kaoliang de guanxi'. *Qinghua Xuebao* 26 (1): 71–120.

Chen Yongtao. 2011. 'Y.T. Wu's Contextual Theological Method'. *Chinese Theological Review* 23:38–68.

Chin Kenpa. 2013. 'Wuchanzhe shiren: Zhu Weizhi de Yesu zhuan'. *Dao feng: Jidujiao wenhua pinglun* 39:157–86.

Choi, Agnes. 2014. 'Never the Two Shall Meet? Urban-Rural Interaction in Lower Galilee'. In *Galilee in the Late Second Temple and Mishnaic Period, Volume 1: Life, Culture, and Society*, edited by David Fiensy and James Strange, 297–311. Minneapolis: Fortress.

Chu Sinjan. 1995. *Wu Leichuan: A Confucian-Christian in Republican China*. New York: Peter Lang.

Cliff, Tony. 2002. *Building the Party: Lenin 1893–1914*. Chicago: Haymarket.

Comstock, Richard. 1976. 'The Marxist Critique of Religion: A Persisting Ambiguity'. *Journal of the American Academy of Religion* 44 (2):327–42.

Conquest, Robert. 1968 [2015]. *The Great Terror: A Reassessment*. Oxford: Oxford University Press.

Conquest, Robert. 1986. *The Harvest of Sorrow: Soviet Collectivization and the Terror-Famine*. Edmonton: University of Alberta Press.

Conquest, Robert. 1992. *Stalin: Breaker of Nations*. Harmondsworth: Penguin.

Conquest, Robert, and Jon White. 1984. *What to Do When the Russians Come: A Survivor's Handbook*. New York: Stein and Day.

Cook, Richard. 2012. 'Overcoming Missions Guilt: Robert Morrison, Liang Fa, and the Opium Wars'. In *After Imperialism: Christian Identity in China and the Global Evangelical Movement*, edited by Richard Cook and David Pao, 35–45. Cambridge: Lutterworth.

Cornell, Erik. 2002. *North Korea Under Communism: Report of an Envoy to Paradise*. Translated by Rodney Bradbury. London: Routledge Curzon.

Crossley, James. 2008. *Jesus in an Age of Terror: Scholarly Projects for a New American Century*. London: Equinox.

Curtis, David. 1997. *The French Popular Front and the Catholic Discovery of Marx*. Hull: University of Hull Press.

De Donno, Fabrizio. 2013. 'Müntzer's "Theology of Revolution" and Literary Activism in Luther Blissett's *Q*'. *Toronto Journal of Theology* 29 (1):37–54.

Dean, Thomas. 1972. *Post-Theistic Thinking: The Marxist-Christian Dialogue in Radical Perspective*. Philadelphia: Temple University Press.

Deissmann, Adolf. 1908 [1922]. *Light From the Ancient East*. Translated by Lionel Strachan. New York: Harper and Brothers.

Deissmann, Adolf. 1929. *The New Testament in the Light of Modern Research*. Garden City, New York: Doubleday, Doran and Company.

Diakonoff, Igor. 1974. 'The Commune in the Ancient East as Treated in the Works of Soviet Researchers'. In *Introduction to Soviet Ethnography, Volume II*, edited by Stephen Dunn and Ethel Dunn, 519–48. Berkeley: Highgate Road Social Science Research Station.

Diakonoff, Igor. 1975. 'The Rural Community in the Ancient Near East'. *Journal of the Economic and Social History of the Orient* 18 (2):121–33.

Diakonoff, Igor. 1976. 'Slaves, Helots and Serfs in Early Antiquity'. In *Wirtschaft und Gesellschaft im alten Vorderasien*, edited by János Harmatta and Geörgy Komoróczy, 45–78. Budapest: Akadémiai Kiadó.

Diakonoff, Igor. 1991. 'General Outline of the First Period of the History of the Ancient World and the Problem of the Ways of Development'. In *Early Antiquity*, edited by Igor. Diakonoff and Philip Kohl, 27–66. Chicago: University of Chicago Press.

Diehl, Judy. 2011. 'Anti-Imperial Rhetoric in the New Testament'. *Currents in Biblical Research* 10 (1):9–52.

Diehl, Judy. 2012. 'Empire and Epistles: Anti-Roman Rhetoric in the New Testament Epistles'. *Currents in Biblical Research* 10 (2):217–63.

Diehl, Judy. 2013. '"Babylon": Then, Now and "Not Yet": Anti-Roman Rhetoric in the Book of Revelation'. *Currents in Biblical Research* 11 (2):168–95.

Dillon, Matthew. 2016. 'Gnosticism Theorized: Major Trends and Approaches to the Study of Gnosticism'. In *Religion: Secret Religion*, edited by April DeConick, 23–38. Farmington Hills: Gale Cengage.

Dommen, Edward, and James Bratt, eds. 2007. *John Calvin Rediscovered: The Impact of His Social and Economic Thought*. Louisville: Westminster John Knox.

Drake, Richard. 2008. 'Catholics and the Italian Revolutionary Left of the 1960s'. *The Catholic Historical Review* 94 (3):450–75.

Dubuisson, Daniel. 2007. *The Western Construction of Religion: Myths, Knowledge, and Ideology*. Baltimore: Johns Hopkins University Press.

Dunman, Jack. 1968. 'The Marxist and Christian Concept of Man'. *Science and Society* 32 (3):278–87.

Durham, Walter. 2013. 'A Tennessee Baptist Missionary in China: Issachar Jacox Roberts and the Taiping Rebellion, 1837–1866'. *Tennessee Historical Quarterly* 72 (2):92–105.

Dussell, Enrique. 1993. *Las metáforas teológicas de Marx*. Estella (Navarra): Editorial Verbo Divino.

Dussell, Enrique. 2001. 'From Ethics and Community'. In *The Postmodern Bible Reader*, edited by David Jobling, Tina Pippin and Ronald Schleifer, 296–318. Oxford: Blackwell.

Ehrensperger, Kathy. 2007. *Paul and the Dynamics of Power: Communication and Interaction in the Early Christ-Movement*. London: T & T Clark.

Elliott, Neil. 1997. 'Romans 13:1-7 in the Context of Imperial Propaganda'. In *Paul and Empire: Religion and Power in Roman Imperial Society*, edited by Richard Horsley, 184–204. Harrisburg, Pennsylvania: Trinity Press International.

Elliott, Neil. 2008. *The Arrogance of Nations: Reading Romans in the Shadow of Empire*. Minneapolis: Fortress.

Engberg-Pedersen, Troels. 2000. *Paul and the Stoics*. Louisville: Westminster John Knox.

Engels, Friedrich. 1839a [1975]. 'To Friedrich Graeber, Bremen, February 19, 1839'. In *Marx and Engels Collected Works*, Vol. 2, 414–17. Moscow: Progress Publishers.

Engels, Friedrich. 1839b [1975]. 'An Friedrich Graeber, 19. Februar 1839'. In *Marx Engels Gesamtausgabe*, Vol. III:1, 101–4. Berlin: Dietz.

Engels, Friedrich. 1839c [1975]. 'To Friedrich Graeber in Berlin, Bremen, about April 23–May 1, 1839'. In *Marx and Engels Collected Works*, Vol. 2, 425–37. Moscow: Progress Publishers.

Engels, Friedrich. 1839d [1975]. 'An Friedrich Graeber, vor dem 24. April bis 1. Mai 1839'. In *Marx Engels Gesamtausgabe*, Vol. III:1, 114–26. Berlin: Dietz.

Engels, Friedrich. 1840a [1975]. 'To Wilhelm Graeber in Barmen, Bremen, November 20, 1840'. In *Marx and Engels Collected Works*, Vol. 2, 513–16. Moscow: Progress Publishers.

Engels, Friedrich. 1840b [1975]. 'An Wilhelm Graeber, 20. November 1840'. In *Marx Engels Gesamtausgabe*, Vol. III:1, 202–4. Berlin: Dietz.

Engels, Friedrich. 1840c [1975]. 'Requiem for the German *Adelszeitung*'. In *Marx and Engels Collected Works*, Vol. 2, 66–70. Moscow: Progress Publishers.

Engels, Friedrich. 1840d [1985]. 'Requiem für die deutsche Adelzeitung'. In *Marx Engels Gesamtausgabe*, Vol. I:3, 98–102. Berlin: Dietz.

Engels, Friedrich. 1841a [1975]. 'To Friedrich Graeber, February 22, 1841'. In *Marx and Engels Collected Works*, Vol. 2, 525–28. Moscow: Progress Publishers.

Engels, Friedrich. 1841b [1975]. 'An Friedrich Graeber, 22. Februar 1841'. In *Marx Engels Gesamtausgabe*, Vol. III:1, 214–16. Berlin: Dietz.

Engels, Friedrich. 1842a [1975]. 'The Insolently Threatened Yet Miraculously Rescued Bible or: The Triumph of Faith, To Wit, the Terrible, Yet True and Salutary History of the Erstwhile Licentiate Bruno Bauer; How the Same, Seduced by the Devil, Fallen from the True Faith, Became Chief Devil, and Was Well and Truly Ousted in the End: A Christian Epic in Four Cantos'. In *Marx and Engels Collected Works*, Vol. 2, 313–51. Moscow: Progress Publishers.

Engels, Friedrich. 1842b [1985]. 'Die frech bedräute, jedoch wunderbar befreite Bibel. Oder: Der Triumph des Glaubens. Unter Mitwirkung von Edgar Bauer'. In *Marx Engels Gesamtausgabe*, Vol. I:3, 387–422. Berlin: Dietz.

Engels, Friedrich. 1842c [1975]. 'Schelling and Revelation: Critique of the Latest Attempt of Reaction Against the Free Philosophy'. In *Marx and Engels Collected Works*, Vol. 2, 189–240. Moscow: Progress Publishers.

Engels, Friedrich. 1842d [1985]. 'Schelling und die Offenbarung. Kritik des neuesten Reaktionsversuchs gegen die freie Philosophie'. In *Marx Engels Gesamtausgabe*, Vol. I:3, 265–314. Berlin: Dietz.

Engels, Friedrich. 1843a [1975]. 'Letters from London'. In *Marx and Engels Collected Works*, Vol. 3, 380–91. Moscow: Progress Publishers.

Engels, Friedrich. 1843b [1985]. 'Briefe aus London'. In *Marx Engels Gesamtausgabe*, Vol. I:3, 451–66. Berlin: Dietz.

Engels, Friedrich. 1843c [1975]. 'Progress of Social Reform on the Continent'. In *Marx and Engels Collected Works*, Vol. 3, 392–408. Moscow: Progress Publishers.

Engels, Friedrich. 1844a [1982]. 'Engels to Marx in Paris, Barmen, 19 November 1844'. In *Marx and Engels Collected Works*, Vol. 38, 9–14. Moscow: Progress Publishers.

Engels, Friedrich. 1844b [1975]. 'An Karl Marx, 19. November 1844'. In *Marx Engels Gesamtausgabe*, Vol. III:1, 250–56. Berlin: Dietz.

Engels, Friedrich. 1844c [1975]. 'Outlines of a Critique of Political Economy'. In *Marx and Engels Collected Works*, Vol. 3, 418–43. Moscow: Progress Publishers.

Engels, Friedrich. 1844d [1985]. 'Umrisse zu einer Kritik der Nationalökonomie'. In *Marx Engels Gesamtausgabe*, Vol. I:3, 467–94. Berlin: Dietz.

Engels, Friedrich. 1850a [1978]. 'The Peasant War in Germany'. In *Marx and Engels Collected Works*, Vol. 10, 397–482. Moscow: Progress Publishers.

Engels, Friedrich. 1850b [1977]. 'Der deutsche Bauernkrieg'. In *Marx Engels Gesamtausgabe*, Vol. I:10, 367–443. Berlin: Dietz.

Engels, Friedrich. 1871a [1986]. 'Account of Engels' Speech on Mazzini's Attitude Towards the International'. In *Marx and Engels Collected Works*, Vol. 22, 607–8. Moscow: Progress Publishers.

Engels, Friedrich. 1871b [1988]. 'On the Progress of the International Working Men's Association in Italy and Spain'. In *Marx and Engels Collected Works*, Vol. 23, 28–29. Moscow: Progress Publishers.

Engels, Friedrich. 1873–82a [1987a]. *Dialectics of Nature*. In *Marx and Engels Collected Works*, Vol. 25, 313–588. Moscow: Progress Publishers.

Engels, Friedrich. 1873–82b [1973]. *Dialektik der Natur*. In *Marx Engels Werke*, Vol. 20. Berlin: Dietz.

Engels, Friedrich. 1877–78a [1987b]. *Anti-Dühring: Herr Eugen Dühring's Revolution in Science*. In *Marx and Engels Collected Works*, Vol. 25. Moscow: Progress Publishers.

Engels, Friedrich. 1877–78b [1988]. *Herrn Eugen Dührings Umwälzung der Wissenschaft (Anti-Dühring)*. In *Marx Engels Gesamtausgabe*, Vol. I:27, 217–483. Berlin: Dietz.

Engels, Friedrich. 1882a [1989]. 'Bruno Bauer and Early Christianity'. In *Marx and Engels Collected Works*, Vol. 24, 427–35. Moscow: Progress Publishers.

Engels, Friedrich. 1882b [1985]. 'Bruno Bauer und das Urchristentum'. In *Marx Engels Gesamtausgabe*, Vol. I:25, 299–306. Berlin: Dietz.

Engels, Friedrich. 1883 [2011]. 'The Book of Revelation'. In *Marx Engels Gesamtausgabe*, Vol. I:30, 8–13. Berlin: Akademie Verlag.

Engels, Friedrich. 1890a [2001]. 'Engels to Joseph Bloch in Königsberg, London, 21–22 September, 1890'. In *Marx and Engels Collected Works*, Vol. 49, 33–37. Moscow: Progress Publishers.

Engels, Friedrich. 1890b [1968a]. 'Engels an Joseph Bloch in Königsberg. London, 21. Sept. 1890'. In *Marx Engels Werke*, Vol. 37, 462–65. Berlin: Dietz.

Engels, Friedrich. 1891a [2001]. 'Engels to Kark Kautsky in Stuttgart, London, 30 April, 1891'. In *Marx and Engels Collected Works*, Vol. 49, 172–5. Moscow: Progress Publishers.

Engels, Friedrich. 1891b [1968b]. 'Engels an Karl Kautsky 30.April 1891'. In *Marx Engels Werke*, Vol. 38, 86–9. Berlin: Dietz.

Engels, Friedrich. 1891c [2001]. 'Engels to Karl Kautsky in Stuttgart, London, 13 June 1891'. In *Marx and Engels Collected Works*, Vol. 49, 198–201. Moscow: Progress Publishers.

Engels, Friedrich. 1891d [1968c]. 'Engels an Karl Kautsky 13.Juni 1891'. In *Marx Engels Werke*, Vol. 38, 112–15. Berlin: Dietz.

Engels, Friedrich. 1892a [2001]. 'Engels to Karl Kautsky in Stuttgart, London, 1 February 1892'. In *Marx and Engels Collected Works*, Vol. 49, 342–43. Moscow: Progress Publishers.

Engels, Friedrich. 1892b [1968d]. 'Engels an Karl Kautsky 1.Februar 1892'. In *Marx Engels Werke*, Vol. 38, 260. Berlin: Dietz.

Engels, Friedrich. 1892c [2001]. 'Engels to Karl Kautsky in Stuttgart, Ryde, 12 August 1892'. In *Marx and Engels Collected Works*, Vol. 49, 493–95. Moscow: Progress Publishers.

Engels, Friedrich. 1892d [1968e]. 'Engels an Karl Kautsky 12.August 1892'. In *Marx Engels Werke*, Vol. 38, 422–24. Berlin: Dietz.

Engels, Friedrich. 1894a [2004]. 'Engels to Karl Kautsky in Stuttgart, London, 26 June 1894'. In *Marx and Engels Collected Works*, Vol. 50, 314–15. Moscow: Progress Publishers.

Engels, Friedrich. 1894b [1973b]. 'Engels an Karl Kautsky 26./27.Juni 1894'. In *Marx Engels Werke*, Vol. 39, 260–61. Berlin: Dietz.

Engels, Friedrich. 1894c [2004]. 'Engels to Karl Kautsky in Stuttgart, London, 16 July 1894'. In *Marx and Engels Collected Works*, Vol. 50, 321–22. Moscow: Progress Publishers.

Engels, Friedrich. 1894d [1973c]. 'Engels an Karl Kautsky 16.Juli 1894'. In *Marx Engels Werke*, Vol. 39, 268–69. Berlin: Dietz.

Engels, Friedrich. 1894e [2004]. 'Engels to Karl Kautsky in Stuttgart, London, 28 July 1894'. In *Marx and Engels Collected Works*, Vol. 50, 328–30. Moscow: Progress Publishers.

Engels, Friedrich. 1894f [1973d]. 'Engels an Karl Kautsky 28.Juli 1894'. In *Marx Engels Werke*, Vol. 39, 276–78. Berlin: Dietz.

Engels, Friedrich. 1894–95a [1990]. 'On the History of Early Christianity'. In *Marx and Engels Collected Works*, Vol. 27, 445–69. Moscow: Progress Publishers.

Engels, Friedrich. 1894–95b [2010]. 'Zur Geschichte des Urchristentums'. In *Marx Engels Gesamtausgabe*, Vol. I:32, 277–99. Berlin: Akademie Verlag.

Engels, Friedrich. 1895a [2004]. 'Engels to Karl Kautsky in Stuttgart, London, 21 May 1895'. In *Marx and Engels Collected Works*, Vol. 50, 510–14. Moscow: Progress Publishers.

Engels, Friedrich. 1895b [1973e]. 'Engels an Karl Kautsky 21.Mai 1895'. In *Marx Engels Werke*, Vol. 39, 481–84. Berlin: Dietz.

Engels, Friedrich. 1929. 'Lun zaoqi jidujiao de lishi'. In *Zongjiao, zhexue, shehuizhuyi*. Wuhan: Hubin shuju chuban.

Erbaugh, Mary. 1992. 'The Secret History of the Hakkas: The Chinese Revolution as a Hakka Enterprise'. *The China Quarterly* 132:937–68.

Esler, Philip. 1987. *Community and Gospel in Luke-Acts: The Social and Political Motivations of Lukan Theology*. Cambridge: Cambridge University Press.

Estep, William. 1995. *The Anabaptist Story: An Introduction to Sixteenth-Century Anabaptism*. 3 ed. Grand Rapids: Eerdmans.

Etkind, Aleksandr. 1998. *Khlyst (Sekty, literatura i revoliutsiia)*. Moscow: Novoe literaturnoe obozrenie.

Feron, Henri. 2014. 'Doom and Gloom or Economic Boom? The Myth of the "North Korean Collapse"'. *The Asia-Pacific Journal (Japan Focus)* 12 (18). apjjf.org/2014/12/18/Henri-Feron/4113/article.html.

Fessard, Gaston. 1967. 'Is Marx's Thought Relevant to the Christian?' In *Marx and the Western World*, edited by Nicholas Lobkowicz, 337–70. Notre Dame: Indiana University Press.

Feuerbach, Ludwig. 1841a [1986]. *Das Wesen des Christentums*. Stuttgart: Reclam, Ditzingen.

Feuerbach, Ludwig. 1841b [1989]. *The Essence of Christianity*. Translated by George Eliot. Amherst: Prometheus Books.

Finger, Reta Halteman. 2007. *Of Widows and Meals: Communal Meals in the Book of Acts*. Grand Rapids: Eerdmans.

Firestone, Ya'akov. 1990. 'The Land-equalizing Mushâ' Village'. In *Ottoman Palestine*, edited by Gad Gilbar, 91–130. Leiden: Brill.

Fitzmyer, Joseph. 2008. *First Corinthians*. New Haven: Yale University Press.

Fitzpatrick, Sheila. 1970. *The Commissariat of Enlightenment: Soviet Organization of Education and the Arts Under Lunacharsky, October 1917–1921*. Cambridge: Cambridge University Press.

Forrester, Duncan. 1972. 'The Attack on Christendom in Marx and Kierkegaard'. *Scottish Journal of Theology* 25 (2):181–96.

Foster, Lawrence. 2011. 'When Do Millennial Religious Movements Become Politically Revolutionary? A Comparative Analysis of the Oneida Community, the Taiping Rebellion, and the Mormons during the Nineteenth Century'. *Communal Societies* 31 (1):1–28.

Foucault, Michel. 1979. *Discipline and Punish: The Birth of the Clinic*. Translated by Alan Sheridan. New York: Vintage.

Frame, Tom. 2002. 'Local Differences, Social and National Identity, 1930–1966'. In *Anglicanism in Australia: A History*, edited by Bruce Kaye, 100–23. Melbourne: Melbourne University Press.

Franz-Willing, Georg. 1972. 'Die Ideologie der Taiping'. *Zeitschrift für Religions und Geistesgeschichte* 24:316–36.

French, Paul. 2014. *North Korea: State of Paranoia*. London: Zed Books.

Friedmann, Robert. 1973. *The Theology of Anabaptism: An Interpretation*. Harrisonburg: Herald.

Friesen, Abraham. 1965. 'Thomas Müntzer in Marxist Thought'. *Church History* 34 (3):306–27.

Friesen, Abraham. 1990. *Thomas Muentzer, a Destroyer of the Godless: The Making of a Sixteenth-Century Religious Revolutionary*. Berkeley: University of California Press.

Furr, Grover. 2011. *Khrushchev Lied*. Kettering: Erythros.

Gabel, Paul. 2005. *And God Created Lenin: Marxism vs. Religion in Russia, 1917–1929*. Amherst: Prometheus.

Gao Wangzhi. 1996. 'Y.T. Wu: A Christian Leader Under Communism'. In *Christianity in China: From the Eighteenth Century to the Present*, edited by Daniel Bays, 338–52. Stanford: Stanford University Press.

Gapon, Georgi. 1905. *The Story of My Life*. London: Chapman Hall.

Garaudy, Roger. 1970. *Marxism in the Twentieth Century*. London: Collins.

Garaudy, Roger, Denis Kenny, Leo Clareborough, Max Charlesworth, Brian Stanfield, and Ron Marstin. 1967. 'Marxist-Christian Dialogue'. *Australian Left Review* 10 (7–27).

Garaudy, Roger, and Quentin Lauer. 1968. *A Christian-Communist Dialogie*. Garden City: Doubleday.

Garaudy, Roger, Karl Rahner, and Johann Metz. 1967. *From Anathema to Dialogue: The Challenge of Marxist-Christian Cooperation*. Translated by Luke O'Neill and Edward Quinn. London: Collins.

Garber, Jeremy. 2006. 'Reading the Anabaptists: Anabaptist Historiography and Luther Blissett's *Q*'. *Conrad Grebel Review* 24 (1):82–94.

Gardavský, Vítězslav. 1973. *God is Not Yet Dead*. Harmondsworth: Penguin.

Garff, Joachim. 2007. *Søren Kierkegaard: A Biography*. Translated by Bruce Kirmmse. Princeton: Princeton University Press.

Garnsey, David. 1947. 'Preface'. In *Religion and Revolution*, edited by Farnham Maynard and Kurt Merz, 2. Melbourne: Fraser & Morphet.

Geras, Norman. 1983. *Marx and Human Nature: Refutation of a Legend*. London: Verso.

Getty, John Arch. 1985. *Origins of the Great Purges: The Soviet Communist Party Reconsidered, 1933–1938*. Cambridge: Cambridge University Press.

Girardi, Giulio. 1968. *Marxism and Christianity*. London: Gill and Son.

Girardi, Giulio. 1988. 'Marxism Confronts the Revolutionary Religious Experience'. *Social Text* 19–20:119–51.

Goertz, Hans-Jürgen. 2000. *Thomas Müntzer: Apocalyptic, Mystic and Revolutionary*. Edinburgh: T & T Clark.

Goldmann, Lucien. 1964. *The Hidden God: A Study of the Tragic Vision in the Pensées of Pascal and the Tragedies of Racine*. Translated by Philip Thody. New York: The Humanities Press.

Goldstein, Warren. 2014. 'Reconstructing the Classics: Weber, Troeltsch, and the Historical Materialists'. *Method and Study in the Theory of Religion* 26: 470–507.

Gore, Charles, ed. 1889 [2009]. *Lux Mundi: A Series of Studies in the Religion of the Incarnation*. Cambridge: Cambridge University Press.

Gottwald, Norman. 1992. 'Sociology of Ancient Israel'. In *Anchor Bible Dictionary*, Vol. 6, edited by David Noel Freedman, 79–89. New York: Doubleday.

Graeber, David. 2011. *Debt: The First 5,000 Years*. New York: Melville House.

Graham, Billy. 2007. *Just As I Am: The Autobiography of Billy Graham*. New York: HarperOne.

Graham, W. Fred. 1978. *The Constructive Revolutionary: John Calvin and His Socio-Economic Impact*. Atlanta: John Knox.

Gramsci, Antonio. 1994. *Letters from Prison*. Translated by Raymond Rosenthal. Vol. 1. New York: Columbia University Press.

Gramsci, Antonio. 1996. *Prison Notebooks*. Translated by Joseph A. Buttigieg. Vol. 2. New York: Columbia University Press. Original edition, Quaderni del carcere, 1975.

Grayson, James. 2002. *Korea: A Religious History*. London: Routledge.

Gregory, J.S. 1963. 'British Missionary Reaction to the Taiping Movement in China'. *Journal of Religious History* 2 (3):204–18.

Grimshaw, Patricia, and Peter Sherlock. 1997. 'One Woman's Concerns for Social Justice: The Letters of Helen Baillie to Farnham Maynard 1933–36'. In *Anglo-Catholicism in Melbourne: Papers to Mark the 150th Anniversary of St Peter's Eastern Hill 1846–1996*, edited by Colin Holden, 85–97. Parkville: Department of History, University of Melbourne.

Gritsch, Eric. 1989. *Thomas Müntzer: A Tragedy of Errors*. Minneapolis: Fortress.

Guevara, Che. 1998. *Guerilla Warfare*. Lincoln: University of Nebraska Press.

Gutiérrez, Gustavo. 1969 [2001]. *A Theology of Liberation*. Translated by Caridad Inda and John Eagleson. London: SCM.

Habeck, Robert. 2003. 'Ein ermordetes Gespenst. Was der Roman "Q" von Luther Blissett mit Identitätslosigkeit zu tun hat'. *Literaturkritik.de* 5:194–96.

Haenchen, Ernst. 1985. *The Acts of the Apostles: A Commentary*. Oxford: Blackwell.

Hald, Mette Marie. 2008. *A Thousand Years of Farming: Late Chalcolithic Agriultural Practices at Tell Brak in Northern Mesopotamia*. Oxford: Archaeopress.

Hamza, Agon, ed. 2016. *Althusser and Theology: Religion, Politics and Philosophy*. Leiden: Brill.

Harding, Neil, ed. 1983. *Marxism in Russia: Key Documents 1879–1906*. Cambridge: Cambridge University Press.

Harding, Neil. 1984. 'Socialism, Society and the Organic Labour State'. In *The State in Socialist Society*, edited by Neil Harding, 1–50. Oxford: Macmillan.

Harnack, Adolf von. 1902. *What is Christianity?* Translated by Thomas Saunders. New York: G.P. Putnam's Sons.

Havet, Étienne, and Lucas Gaudreau. 2010. *Without Freedom of Religion or Belief in North Korea*. Hauppauge: Nova Science Publishers.

Hebblethwaite, Peter. 1977. *The Christian-Marxist Dialogue: Beginnings, Present Status, and Beyond*. London: Darton, Longman and Todd.

Hess, Moses. 1837. *Die Heilige Geschichte der Menschheit*. Stuttgart.

Hess, Moses. 1841. *Die europäische Triarchie*. Leipzig.

Hess, Moses. 2004. *The Holy History of Mankind and Other Writings*. Edited by Shlomo Avineri. Cambridge: Cambridge University Press.

Hilliard, David. 1997. 'Anglo-Catholicism in the Religious Ecology of Melbourne'. In *Anglo-Catholicism in Melbourne: Papers to Mark the 150th Anniversary of St Peter's Eastern Hill 1846–1996*, edited by Colin Holden, 169–87. Parkville: Department of History, University of Melbourne.

Hinkelammert, Franz. 1986. *The Ideological Weapons of Death: A Theological Critique of Capitalism*. Translated by Phillip Berryman. Maryknoll: Orbis.

Holden, Colin. 1986. 'Catholic Socialism'. In *The Anglican Church Today: Catholics in Crisis*, edited by Francis Penhale, 121–39. London: Mowbray.

Holden, Colin. 1996. *From Tories at Prayer to Socialists at Mass: A History of St Peter's, Eastern Hill, Melbourne, 1846–1990*. Melbourne: Melbourne University Press.

Holden, Colin. 1997a. 'Introduction: Sharing a Place in the Sun: the Position of Anglo-Catholics in Australia's Metropolitan Dioceses at the Beginning of the 20th Century'. In *Anglo-Catholicism in Melbourne: Papers to Mark the 150th Anniversary of St Peter's Eastern Hill 1846–1996*, edited by Colin Holden, 1–20. Parkville: Department of History, University of Melbourne.

Holden, Colin. 1997b. 'Political Pilgrimages and Pilgrims: Farnham E. Maynard as Anglo-Catholic Socialist'. In *Anglo-Catholicism in Melbourne: Papers to Mark the 150th Anniversary of St Peter's Eastern Hill 1846–1996*, edited by Colin Holden, 69–84. Parkville: Department of History, University of Melbourne.

Home, Stewart. 2013. 'Wu Ming'. *Art Review* 67:72–74.

Höpfl, Harro. 1982. *The Christian Polity of John Calvin*. Cambridge: Cambridge University Press.

Hopkins, David. 1985. *The Highlands of Canaan: Agricultural Life in the Early Highlands*. Sheffield: Almond.

Horkheimer, Max. 1963 [1985]. 'Theismus – Atheismus'. In *Gesammelte Schriften*, Vol. 7, 173–86. Frankfurt am Main: Fischer Taschenbuch.

Horkheimer, Max. 1996. *Critique of Instrumental Reason*. Translated by Matthew O'Connell et al. New York: Continuum.

Hornik, Heidi, and Mikael Parson. 2017. *The Acts of the Apostles Through the Centuries*. Oxford: Wiley-Blackwell.

Horsley, Richard. 2014. 'Social Movements in Galilee'. In *Galilee in the Late Second Temple and Mishnaic Period, Volume 1: Life, Culture, and Society*, edited by David Fiensy and James Strange, 167–74. Minneapolis: Fortress.

Horsley, Richard, and John Hanson. 1985. *Bandits, Prophets, and Messiahs: Popular Movements in the Time of Jesus*. Philadelphia: Trinity Press International.

Hou Jundan. 2014. 'Xiaqi yu minqing: shiji zhongye difang junshihua yanbian zhong de shehui zhuanxing'. *Chinese Journal of Sociology / Shehui* 34 (3):61–91.

Howe, Renate. 1997. 'Town and Gown: Father Maynard and the Student Christian Movement'. In *Anglo-Catholicism in Melbourne: Papers to Mark the 150th Anniversary of St Peter's Eastern Hill 1846–1996*, edited by Colin Holden, 109–22. Parkville: Department of History, University of Melbourne.

Israel, Joachim. 1971. *Alienation from Marx to Modern Sociology: A Macrosociological Analysis*. Boston: Allyn and Bacon.

Jameson, Fredric. 1981. *The Political Unconscious: Narrative as a Socially Symbolic Act*. Ithaca: Cornell University Press.

Jankowska, Ninel. 1969. 'Extended Family Commune and Civil Self-Government in the Fifteenth-Fourteenth Century B.C'. In *Ancient Mesopotamia: Socio-Economic History. A Collection of Studies by Soviet Scholars*, edited by Igor Diakonoff, 235–52. Moscow: 'Nauka' Publishing House.

Jankowska, Ninel. 1991. 'Asshur, Mitanni, and Arrapkhe'. In *Early Antiquity*, edited by Igor Diakonoff and Philip Kohl, 228–60. Chicago: University of Chicago Press.

Jen Youwen. 1973. *The Taiping Revolutionary Movement*. New Haven: Yale University Press.

Jewett, Robert. 2007. *Romans*. Minneapolis: Fortress.

Jo Song Baek. 1999. *The Leadership Philosophy of Kim Jong Il*. Pyongyang: Foreign Languages Publishing House.

Johnston, Ian. 2010. *The Mozi: A Complete Translation*. New York: Columbia University Press.

Judge, Edwin. 1960. *The Social Pattern of the Christian Groups in the First Century*. London: Tyndale.

Judge, Edwin. 2008. *Social Distinctives of the Christians in the First Century: Pivotal Essays*. Peabody: Hendrickson.

Kallander, George. 2013. *Salvation Through Dissent: Tonghak Heterodoxy and Early Modern Korea*. Honolulu: University of Hawaii Press.

Kallas, James. 1965. 'Romans XIII:1-7: An Interpollation'. *New Testament Studies* 11: 365–74.

Kan Baoping. 1997. 'Theology in the Contemporary Chinese Context'. *Word and World* 17 (2):161–67.

Käsemann, Ernst. 1980. *An die Römer*. Tübingen: J.C.B. Mohr (Paul Siebeck).

Kautsky, Karl. 1888a [1979]. *Thomas More and His Utopia*. Translated by Henry James Stenning. London: Lawrence and Wishart.

Kautsky, Karl. 1888b [1947]. *Thomas More und seine Utopie, mit einer historischen Einleitung*. 3rd ed. Berlin: Dietz.

Kautsky, Karl. 1892a [1910]. *The Class Struggle (Erfurt Program)*. Translated by William Bohn. Chicago: Charles Kerr.

Kautsky, Karl. 1892b [1899]. *Das Erfurter Programm in seinem grundsätzlichen Theil erläutert von Karl Kautsky*. 6 ed. Stuttgart: Dietz.

Kautsky, Karl. 1895. *Die Vorläufer des neueren Sozialismus I: von Plato bis zu den Wieder-täufern*. Stuttgart: Dietz.

Kautsky, Karl. 1897. *Communism in Central Europe in the Time of the Reformation*. Translated by J.L. Mulliken and E.G. Mulliken. London: Fisher and Unwin.

Kautsky, Karl. 1903. 'Social Democracy and the Catholic Church'. *The Social Democrat* 7:162–69, 234–43, 359–62, 430–36.

Kautsky, Karl. 1908a [2007]. *Foundations of Christianity*. Translated by H.F. Mins. London: Socialist Resistance.

Kautsky, Karl. 1908b [1977]. *Der Ursprung des Christentums: Eine historische Untersuchung*. Stuttgart: Dietz.

Kautsky, Karl. 1910. *Ethik und materialistische Geschichtsauffassung*. Stuttgart: Dietz.

Kautsky, Karl. 1932. *Jidujiao zhi jichu*. Translated by Tang Zhi and Ye Qifang. Shanghai: Shenzhou guoguang she.

Kautsky, Karl, and Paul Lafargue. 1922. *Die Vorläufer des neueren Sozialismus III: Die beiden ersten grossen Utopisten*. Stuttgart: Dietz.

Kautsky, Karl, Paul Lafargue, Eduard Bernstein, and Hugo Lindemann. 1895. *Die Vorläufer des neueren Sozialismus II: von Thomas More bis zum Vorabend der Französischen Revolution*. Stuttgart: Dietz.

Keener, Craig. 2005. *1–2 Corinthians*. Cambridge: Cambridge University Press.

Kerševan, Marko. 1985. 'Atheism: Is It Essential to Marxism?' *Journal of Ecumenical Studies* 22 (3):501–4.

Khalidi, Tarif, ed. 1984. *Land Tenure and Social Transformation in the Middle East*. Beirut: American University of Beirut Press.

Kilcourse, Carl. 2014. 'Son of God, Brother of Jesus: Interpreting the Theological Claims of the Chinese Revolutionary Hong Xiuquan'. *Studies in World Christianity* 20 (2): 124–44.

Kilcourse, Carl. 2016. *Taiping Theology: The Localization of Christianity in China, 1843–64*. Basingstoke: Palgrave Macmillan.

Kim Heung Soo. 2009. 'Recent Changes in North Korean Christianity'. *Asian Christian Review* 3 (1):10–19.

Kim Heung Soo, and Ryu Dae Young. 2002. *Bughanjong-gyoui sae loun ihae*. Seoul: Dasan Press.

Kim Il Bong. 2017. *Understanding Korea, 10: Unification Question*. Translated by Kim Myong Chan and Pak Hyo Song. Pyongyang: Foreign Languages Publishing House.

Kim Il Sung. 1930 [2011]. 'The Path of the Korean Revolution: Report to the Meeting of Leading Personnel of the Young Communist League and the Anti-Imperialist Youth League Held in Kalun, June 30, 1930'. In *Complete Works*, Vol. 1, 32–41. Pyongyang: Foreign Languages Publishing House.

Kim Il Sung. 1936a [2011]. 'The Ten-Point Programme of the Association for the Restoration of the Fatherland'. In *Complete Works*, Vol. 1, 279–80. Pyongyang: Foreign Languages Publishing House.

Kim Il Sung. 1936b [2011]. 'The Inaugural Declaration of the Association for the Restoration of the Fatherland'. In *Complete Works*, Vol. 1, 282–85. Pyongyang: Foreign Languages Publishing House.

Kim Il Sung. 1937 [2011]. 'Appeal to All Korean Compatriots'. In *Complete Works*, Vol. 1, 346–50. Pyongyang: Foreign Languages Publishing House.

Kim Il Sung. 1945 [2011]. 'On the Question of the National United Front'. In *Complete Works*, Vol. 2, 416–31. Pyongyang: Foreign Languages Publishing House.

Kim Il Sung. 1955 [1982]. 'On Eliminating Dogmatism and Formalism and Establishing Juche in Ideological Work'. In *Works*, Vol. 9: 395–417. Pyongyang: Foreign Languages Publishing House.

Kim Il Sung. 1972. *On the Three Principles of National Reunification: Conversations with the South Korean Delegates to the High-Level Political Talks between North and South Korea, May 3 and November 3, 1972*. Pyongyang: Foreign Languages Publishing House.

Kim Il Sung. 1975. *On the Occasion of the 30th Anniversary of the Foundation of the Workers' Party of Korea*. Pyongyang: Foreign languages Publishing House.

Kim Il Sung. 1992. *Let the North and South Open the Way to Peace and the Reunification of the Country in a United Effort: Talk to the Delegates to the North-South High-Level Negotiations from Both Sides, February 20, 1992*. Pyongyang: Foreign Languages Publishing House.

Kim Il Sung. 1993. *10-Point Programme of the Great Unity of the Whole Nation for the Reunification of the Country*. Pyongyang: Foreign Languages Publishing House.

Kim Il Sung. 1994. *With the Century*. 8 vols. Pyongyang: Foreign Languages Publishing House.

Kim Il pyong, J. 2003. *Historical Dictionary of North Korea*. Lanham: Scarecrow.

Kim Ji Ho. 2017. *Understanding Korea, 9: Human Rights*. Translated by Kim Yong Nam and Ri Chung Hyon. Pyongyang: Foreign Languages Publishing House.

Kim Jong Il. 1982 [1995]. 'On the Juche Idea: Treatise Sent to the National Seminar on the Juche Idea Held to Mark the 70th Birthday of the Great Leader Comrade Kim Il Sung, March 31, 1982'. In *On Carrying Forward the Juche Idea*, 7–78. Pyongyang: Foreign Languages Publishing House.

Kim Jong Il. 1983 [1995]. 'Let Us Advance Under the Banner of Marxism-Leninism and the Juche Idea: On the Occasion of the 165th Birthday of Karl Marx and the Centenary of His Death, May 3, 1983'. In *On Carrying Forward the Juche Idea*, 111–41. Pyongyang: Foreign Languages Publishing House.

Kim Jong Il. 1987 [1995]. 'On Establishing the Juche Outlook on the Revolution: Talk to the Senior Officials of the Central Committee of the Workers' Party of Korea, October 10, 1987'. In *On Carrying Forward the Juche Idea*, 190–212. Pyongyang: Foreign Languages Publishing House.

Kim Jong Il. 1991 [1995]. 'Our Socialism Centred on the Masses Shall Not Perish: Talk to the Senior Officials of the Central Committee of the Workers' Party of Korea, May 5, 1991'. In *On Carrying Forward the Juche Idea*, 252–90. Pyongyang: Foreign Languages Publishing House.

Kim Kwang Il, Pak Hak Il, and Han Jong Yon. 2013. *Anecdotes of Kim Il Sung's Life, 2.* Pyongyang: Foreign Languages Publishing House.

Kim Myong Chol. 2003. 'Significance of Chinese Economic Success to North Korea'. In *North Korea in the World Economy*, edited by E. Kwan Choi, E. Han Kim and Yesook Merrill, 18–23. London: Routledge Curzon.

Kim Sukjoo. 2011. *Liang Fa's Quanshi liangyan and Its Impact on the Taiping Movement,* Baylor University, Waco.

Kim Yunk Suk, and Kim Jin Ho, eds. 2013. *Reading Minjung Theology in the Twenty-First Century: Selected Writings by Ahn Byung-Mu and Modern Critical Responses*. Eugene: Wipf and Stock.

Kirk, Andrew. 1976a. 'The Meaning of Man in the Debate Between Christianity and Marxism'. *Themelios* 1 (2):41–49.

Kirk, Andrew. 1976b. 'The Meaning of Man in the Debate Between Christianity and Marxism (Part 2)'. *Themelios* 1 (3):85–93.

Klaassen, Walter. 1973. *Anabaptism: Neither Catholic nor Protestant*. Waterloo: Conrad.

Knight, Douglas. 2011. *Law, Power, and Justice in Ancient Israel, Library of Ancient Israel*. Louisville: Westminster John Knox.

Koester, Helmut. 2000. *Introduction to the New Testament, Volume II: History and Literature of Early Christianity*. 2nd ed. New York: Walter de Gruyter.

Kohn, Richard, and Joseph Harahan, eds. 1988. *Strategic Air Warfare: An Interview with Generals Curtis E. LeMay, Leon W. Johnson, David A. Burchinal, and Jack J. Catton* Washington: Office of Air Force History United States Air Force.

Kolakowski, Leszek. 1981. *Main Currents of Marxism*. Translated by P.S. Falla. Vol. 1. Oxford: Oxford University Press.

Kolonitskii, Boris Ivanovich. 2004. "Democracy in the Political Consciousness of the February Revolution". In *Revolutionary Russia: New Approaches*, edited by Rex Wade, 75–90. New York: Routledge.

Kong Jong-won. 1974. *Earth Without Heaven: How Religion Was Extinguished in North Korea*. Seoul: Kwangmyong Publishing Company.

Kouvelakis, Stathis. 2003. *Philosophy and Revolution: From Kant to Marx*. Translated by G.M. Goshgarian. London: Verso.

Krišto, Jure. 1985. 'Marxist Critique of Religion and Croatian Catholic Culture'. *Journal of Ecumenical Studies* 22 (3):474–86.

Kroeber, Clifton. 1996. 'Theory and History of Revolution'. *Journal of World History* 7 (1):21–40.

Krupskaya, Nadezhda. 1930 [1960]. *Reminiscences of Lenin*. New York: International Publishers.

Kuczyński, Janusz 1979. *Christian-Marxist Dialogue in Poland*. Warsaw: Interpress.

Kuhn, Philip. 1967. 'The T'uan-lien Local Defense System at The Time of The Taiping Rebellion'. *Harvard Journal of Asiatic Studies* 27:218–55.

Kwan, Simon Shui-Man. 2014. *Postcolonial Resistance and Asian Theology*. London: Routledge.

Kwok Pui-lan. 2016. 'Postcolonial Intervention in Political Theology'. *Political Theology* 17 (3):223–25.

Lankov, Andrei. 2007. *North of the DMZ: Essays on Daily Life in North Korea*. Jefferson: McFarland.

Lash, Nicholas. 1981. *A Matter of Hope: A Theologian's Reflections on the Thought of Karl Marx*. London: Darton, Longman and Todd.

Lauer, Quentin. 1968. 'The Atheism of Karl Marx'. In *Marxism and Christianity: A Symposium*, edited by Herbert Aptheker, 40–55. New York: Humanities Press.

Le Blanc, Paul. 1990. *Lenin and the Revolutionary Party*. Amherst: Humanity Books.

Lee Sang Taek. 1996. *Religion and Social Formation in Korea: Minjung and Millenarianism*. Berlin: Mouton de Gruyter.

Lenin, V.I. 1894a [1960]. 'What the "Friends of the People" Are and How They Fight the Social-Democrats (A Reply to Articles in *Russkoye Bogatstvo* Opposing the Marxists)'. In *Collected Works*, Vol. 1, 129–332. Moscow: Progress Publishers.

Lenin, V.I. 1894b [1967]. 'Čto takoe «druz′â naroda» i kak oni voûût protiv social-demokratov? (Otvet na stat′i «Russkogo Bogatstva» protiv marksistov). Vesna–leto 1894 g'. In *Polnoe sobranie sochinenii*, Vol. 1, 125–346. Moscow: Izdatel'stvo politicheskoi literatury.

Lenin, V.I. 1895a [1960]. 'Draft and Explanation of a Programme for the Social-Democratic Party'. In *Collected Works*, Vol. 2, 93–121. Moscow: Progress Publishers.

Lenin, V.I. 1895b [1967]. 'Proekt i ob"iasnenie programmy sotsial-demokraticheskoĭ partii'. In *Polnoe sobranie sochinenii*, Vol. 2, 81–110. Moscow: Izdatel'stvo politicheskoi literatury.

Lenin, V.I. 1899a [1960]. *The Development of Capitalism in Russia: The Process of the Formation of a Home Market for Large-Scale Industry*. In *Collected Works*, Vol. 3, 21–607. Moscow: Progress Publishers.

Lenin, V.I. 1899b [1967]. *Razvitie kapitalizma v Rossii. Protsess obrazovaniia vnutrennego rynka dlia krupnoĭ promyshlennosti*. In *Polnoe sobranie sochinenii*, Vol. 3, 1–609. Moscow: Izdatel'stvo politicheskoi literatury.

Lenin, V.I. 1903a [1961]. 'The Autocracy is Wavering...'. In *Collected Works*, Vol. 6, 346–51. Moscow: Progress Publishers.

Lenin, V.I. 1903b [1967]. 'Samoderzhavie kolebletsia...'. In *Polnoe sobranie sochinenii*, Vol. 7, 123–28. Moscow: Izdatel'stvo politicheskoi literatury.

Lenin, V.I. 1905a [1962]. 'A Militant Agreement for the Uprising'. In *Collected Works*, Vol. 8, 158–66. Moscow: Progress Publishers.

Lenin, V.I. 1905b [1967]. 'O boevom soglashenii dlia vosstaniia'. In *Polnoe sobranie sochinenii*, Vol. 9, 274–82. Moscow: Izdatel'stvo politicheskoi literatury.

Lenin, V.I. 1905c [1962]. 'Revolutionary Days'. In *Collected Works*, Vol. 8, 101–23. Moscow: Progress Publishers.

Lenin, V.I. 1905d [1967]. 'Revoliutsionnye dni'. In *Polnoe sobranie sochinenii*, Vol. 9, 205–29. Moscow: Izdatel'stvo politicheskoi literatury.

Lenin, V.I. 1905e [1966]. 'Socialism and Religion'. In *Collected Works*, Vol. 10, 83–87. Moscow: Progress Publishers.

Lenin, V.I. 1905f [1968]. 'Sotsializm i religiia'. In *Polnoe sobranie sochinenii*, Vol. 12, 142–47. Moscow: Izdatel'stvo politicheskoi literatury.

Lenin, V.I. 1907a [1962]. 'Draft for a Speech on the Agrarian Question in the Second State Duma'. In *Collected Works*, Vol. 12, 267–99. Moscow: Progress Publishers.

Lenin, V.I. 1907b [1972]. 'Proekt rechi po agrarnomu voprosu vo vtoroĭ Gosudarstvennoĭ dume'. In *Polnoe sobranie sochinenii*, Vol. 15, 127–60. Moscow: Izdatel'stvo politicheskoi literatury.

Lenin, V.I. 1907c [1963]. 'The Agrarian Programme of Social-Democracy and the First Russian Revolution, 1905–1907'. In *Collected Works*, Vol. 13, 217–431. Moscow: Progress Publishers.

Lenin, V.I. 1907d [1973]. 'Agrarnaia programma sotsial-demokratii v pervoĭ russkoĭ revoliutsii 1905–1907 godov'. In *Polnoe sobranie sochinenii*, Vol. 16, 193–413. Moscow: Izdatel'stvo politicheskoi literatury.

Lenin, V.I. 1908a [1962]. *Materialism and Empirio-Criticism: Critical Comments on a Reactionary Philosophy*. In *Collected Works*, Vol. 14, 17–361. Moscow: Progress Publishers.

Lenin, V.I. 1908b [1968]. *Materializm i émpiriokrititsizm. Kriticheskie zametki ob odnoĭ reaktsionnoĭ filosofii*. In *Polnoe sobranie sochinenii*, Vol. 18, 7–384. Moscow: Izdatel'stvo politicheskoi literatury.

Lenin, V.I. 1908c [1963]. 'Leo Tolstoy as the Mirror of the Russian Revolution'. In *Collected Works*, Vol. 15, 202–9. Moscow: Progress Publishers.

Lenin, V.I. 1908d [1968]. 'Lev Tolstoĭ, kak zerkalo russkoĭ revoliutsii'. In *Polnoe sobranie sochinenii*, Vol. 17, 206–13. Moscow: Izdatel'stvo politicheskoi literatury.

Lenin, V.I. 1909a [1963]. 'The Attitude of the Workers' Party to Religion'. In *Collected Works*, Vol. 15, 402–13. Moscow: Progress Publishers.

Lenin, V.I. 1909b [1968]. 'Ob otnoshenii rabocheĭ partii k religii'. In *Polnoe sobranie sochinenii*, Vol. 17, 415–26. Moscow: Izdatel'stvo politicheskoi literatury.

Lenin, V.I. 1909c [1963]. 'Classes and Parties in their Attitude to Religion and the Church'. In *Collected Works*, Vol. 15, 414–23. Moscow: Progress Publishers.

Lenin, V.I. 1909d [1968]. 'Klassy i partii v ikh otnoshenii k religii i tserkvi'. In *Polnoe sobranie sochinenii*, Vol. 17, 429–38. Moscow: Izdatel'stvo politicheskoi literatury.

Lenin, V.I. 1910a [1963]. 'The Capitalist System of Modern Agriculture'. In *Collected Works*, Vol. 16, 423–46. Moscow: Progress Publishers.

Lenin, V.I. 1910b [1968]. 'Kapitalisticheskiĭ stroĭ sovremennogo zemledeliia'. In *Polnoe sobranie sochinenii*, Vol. 19, 319–44. Moscow: Izdatel'stvo politicheskoi literatury.

Lenin, V.I. 1910c [1963]. 'Heroes of "Reservation"'. In *Collected Works*, Vol. 16, 368–73. Moscow: Progress Publishers.

Lenin, V.I. 1910d [1973]. 'Geroi «ogovorochki»'. In *Polnoe sobranie sochinenii*, Vol. 20, 90–95. Moscow: Izdatel'stvo politicheskoi literatury.

Lenin, V.I. 1910e [1963]. 'L.N. Tolstoy'. In *Collected Works*, Vol. 16, 323–27. Moscow: Progress Publishers.

Lenin, V.I. 1910f [1973]. 'L.N. Tolstoĭ'. In *Polnoe sobranie sochinenii*, Vol. 20, 19–24. Moscow: Izdatel'stvo politicheskoi literatury.

Lenin, V.I. 1910g [1963]. 'L.N. Tolstoy and the Modern Labour Movement'. In *Collected Works*, Vol. 16, 330–32. Moscow: Progress Publishers.

Lenin, V.I. 1910h [1973]. 'L.N. Tolstoĭ i sovremennoe rabochee dvizhenie'. In *Polnoe sobranie sochinenii*, Vol. 20, 38–41. Moscow: Izdatel'stvo politicheskoi literatury.

Lenin, V.I. 1910i [1963]. 'Tolstoy and the Proletarian Struggle'. In *Collected Works*, Vol. 16, 353–54. Moscow: Progress Publishers.

Lenin, V.I. 1910j [1973]. 'Tolstoĭ i proletarskaia bor'ba'. In *Polnoe sobranie sochinenii*, Vol. 20, 70–71. Moscow: Izdatel'stvo politicheskoi literatury.

Lenin, V.I. 1911a [1963]. 'Lev Tolstoi and His Epoch'. In *Collected Works*, Vol. 17, 49–53. Moscow: Progress Publishers.

Lenin, V.I. 1911b [1973]. 'L.N. Tolstoĭ i ego ėpokha'. In *Polnoe sobranie sochinenii*, Vol. 20, 100–4. Moscow: Izdatel'stvo politicheskoi literatury.

Lenin, V.I. 1913a [1966]. 'To Maxim Gorky, Second Half of November, 1913'. In *Collected Works*, Vol. 35, 127–29. Moscow: Progress Publishers.

Lenin, V.I. 1913b [1970]. 'A.M. Gor'komu. Vtoraia polovina noiabria'. In *Polnoe sobranie sochinenii*, Vol. 48, 230–33. Moscow: Izdatel'stvo politicheskoi literatury.

Lenin, V.I. 1913c [1963]. 'What Goes on Among the Narodniks and What Goes on in the Countryside'. In *Collected Works*, Vol. 18, 555–61. Moscow: Progress Publishers.

Lenin, V.I. 1913d [1973a]. 'Chto delaetsia v narodnichestve i chto delaetsia v derevne?' In *Polnoe sobranie sochinenii*, Vol. 22, 363–69. Moscow: Izdatel'stvo politicheskoi literatury.

Lenin, V.I. 1914–16a [1968]. 'Conspectus of Hegel's Book *The Science of Logic*'. In *Collected Works*, Vol. 38, 85–237. Moscow: Progress Publishers.

Lenin, V.I. 1914–16b [1973]. 'Konspekt knigi Gegelia «Nauka Logiki»'. In *Polnoe sobranie sochinenii*, Vol. 29, 77–218. Moscow: Izdatel'stvo politicheskoi literatury.

Lenin, V.I. 1916a [1964]. 'Imperialism, the Highest Stage of Capitalism: A Popular Outline'. In *Collected Works*, Vol. 22, 185–304. Moscow: Progress Publishers.

Lenin, V.I. 1916b [1969]. 'Imperializm, kak vysshaia stadiia kapitalizma (Populiarnyĭ ocherk)'. In *Polnoe sobranie sochinenii*, Vol. 27, 299–426. Moscow: Izdatel'stvo politicheskoi literatury.

Lenin, V.I. 1917a [1964]. 'The State and Revolution'. In *Collected Works*, Vol. 25, 385–497. Moscow: Progress Publishers.

Lenin, V.I. 1917b [1969]. 'Gosudarstvo i revoliutsiia. Uchenie marksizma o gosudarstve i zadachi proletariata v revoliutsii. Avgust–sentiabr′ 1917 g.; ranee 17 dekabria 1918 g'. In *Polnoe sobranie sochinenii*, Vol. 33, 1–120. Moscow: Izdatel'stvo politicheskoi literatury.

Lenin, V.I. 1917c [1964]. 'Statistics and Sociology'. In *Collected Works*, Vol. 23, 271–7. Moscow: Progress Publishers.

Lenin, V.I. 1917d [1973]. 'Statistika i Sotsiologiia'. In *Polnoe sobranie sochinenii*, Vol. 30, 349–56. Moscow: Izdatel'stvo politicheskoi literatury.

Lenin, V.I. 1917e [1967]. 'To Inessa Armand, January 30, 1917'. In *Collected Works*, Vol. 35, 279–81. Moscow: Progress Publishers.

Lenin, V.I. 1917f [1970]. 'I.F. Armand. 17 (30) ianvaria 1917 g'. In *Polnoe sobranie sochinenii*, Vol. 49, 377–79. Moscow: Izdatel'stvo politicheskoi literatury.

Lenin, V.I. 1921a [1970]. 'To N. Osinsky, March 1, 1921'. In *Collected Works*, Vol. 45, 90–92. Moscow: Progress Publishers.

Lenin, V.I. 1921b [1970]. 'N. Osinskomu. 1 marta 1921 g'. In *Polnoe sobranie sochinenii*, Vol. 52, 85–86. Moscow: Izdatel'stvo politicheskoi literatury.

Leopold, David. 2007. *The Young Karl Marx: German Philosophy, Modern Politics, and Human Flourishing*. Cambridge: Cambridge University Press.

Lévi-Strauss, Claude. 1989. *Tristes Tropiques*. Translated by John Weightman and Doreen Weightman. London: Pan.

Li Jieli. 1998. 'Geopolitical Dynamics of State Change: A Comparative Analysis of the U.S. Civil War and the Chinese Taiping Rebellion'. *Michigan Sociological Review* 12:24–49.

Liang Fa. 1965. *Quanshi liangyan*. Taibei: Taiwan xuesheng shuju.

Liang, Grace Hui. 2008. 'Interpreting the Lord's Prayer from a Christian-Confucian Perspective: Wu Leichuan's Practice and Contribution to Chinese Biblical Hermeneutics'. In *Reading Christian Scriptures in China*, edited by Chloë Starr, 118–33. London: T & T Clark.

Liao Sheng. 2005. 'Minzhong xinli xuqiu yu taiping tianguo de xingwang'. *Shixue yuekan* 10:108–17.

Liao Sheng, and Wang Xiaonan. 2004. 'Taiping tianguo guafu zai jia wenti bianxi: Jian lun guafu zai jia bu neng zuo wei taiping tianguo jiefang funü zhi lunju'. *Shixue yuekan* 7:93–99.

Lichtman, R. 1968. 'The Marxian Critique of Christianity'. In *Marxism and Christianity: A Symposium*, edited by Herbert Aptheker, 65–121. New York: Humanities Press.

Liew, Tat-siong Benny. 1999. 'Tyranny, Power and Might: Colonial Mimicry in Mark's Gospel'. *Journal for the Study of the New Testament* 73:7–31.

Lih, Lars. 2007. 'Lenin and the Great Awakening'. In *Lenin Reloaded: Towards a Politics of Truth*, edited by Sebastian Budgen, Stathis Kouvelakis and Slavoj Žižek, 183–96. Durham: Duke University Press.

Lincoln, Bruce. 2000. *Theorizing Myth: Narrative, Ideology, and Scholarship*. Chicago: University of Chicago Press.

Lindemann, Hugo, and Morris Hillquit. 1922. *Die Vorläufer des neueren Sozialismus* IV. Stuttgart: Dietz.

Lischer, Richard. 1973. 'The Lutheran Shape of Marxian Evil'. *Religion in Life* 42 (4):549–58.

Liu Kwang-Ching. 1981. 'World View and Peasant Rebellion: Reflections on Post-Mao Historiography'. *The Journal of Asian Studies* 40 (2):295–326.

Liu Xun. 2009. 'In Defense of the City and the Polity: The Xuanmiao Monastery and the Qing Anti-Taiping Campaigns in Mid-Nineteenth Century Nanyang'. *T'oung Pao* 95 (4/5):287–333.

Liu Yan. 2016. 'The Rewriting of Jesus Christ: From the Saviour to the Proletarian: A Comparative Study of Zhu Weizhi's *Jesus Christ* and *Jesus the Proletarian*'. *Asian and African Studies* 25 (2):173–190.

Lobkowicz, Nicholas, ed. 1967a. *Marx and the Western World*. Notre Dame: Indiana University Press.

Lobkowicz, Nicholas. 1967b. 'Marx's Attitude Toward Religion'. In *Marx and the Western World*, edited by Nicholas Lobkowicz, 303–35. Notre Dame: Indiana University Press.

Lochman, Jan. 1970a. *Church in a Marxist Society: A Czechoslovak View*. London: SCM.

Lochman, Jan. 1970b. 'Marxism, Liberalism, and Religion: An East European Perspective'. In *Marxism and Radical Religion: Essays Towards a Revolutionary Humanism*, edited by John Raines and Thomas Dean, 11–26. Philadelphia: Temple University Press.

Lochman, Jan. 1972. 'Platz für Prometheus: Das gemeinsame Erbe von Christentum und Marxismus'. *Evangelische Kommentare* 5:136–41.

Lochman, Jan. 1978. 'The Place for Prometheus: Theological Lessons from the Christian-Marxist Dialogue'. *Interpretation* 32 (3):242–54.

Lochman, Jan. 1985. 'Christ and/or Prometheus: Theological Issues in the Encounter Between Christians and Marxists'. *Journal of Ecumenical Studies* 22 (3):440–53.

Longenecker, Richard. 1990. *Galatians. Word Biblical Commentary*, Vol. 41. Waco: Word Books.

Lossky, Vladimir. 1978. *Orthodox Theology: An Introduction*. Translated by Ian Kesarcodi-Watson and Ihita Kesarcodi-Watson. Crestwood: St Vladimir's Seminary Press.

Losurdo, Domenico. 2008. *Stalin: Storia e critica di una leggenda nera*. Rome: Carocci editore.

Löwith, Karl. 1949. *Meaning in History: The Theological Implications of the Philosophy of History*. Chicago: University of Chicago Press.

Löwy, Michael. 1996. *The War of Gods: Religion and Politics in Latin America*. London: Verso.

Lukács, Georg. 1971. *Theory of the Novel: A Historico-Philosophical Essay in the Forms of Great Epic Literature*. Translated by Anna Bostock. Cambridge: MIT.

Lukács, Georg. 1972. *Studies in European Realism: A Sociological Survey of the Writings of Balzac, Stendhal, Zola, Tolstoy, Gorki and Others*. Translated by Edith Bone. London: Merlin.

Lunacharsky, Anatoly Vasil'evich. 1905. 'K iubileiu 9 ianvaria'. *Proletarii* 13 (9 August):3–4. http://lunacharsky.newgod.su/lib/pesy/stihi-lunacharskogo-TOC-9-.

Lunacharsky, Anatoly Vasil'evich. 1908a. 'Ateizm'. In *Ocherki po filosofii marxisma*, edited by V.A. Bazarov, M. Berman, A.V. Lunacharsky, P.S. Yushkevich, A. Bogdanov, I. Gelfond and S. Suvorov, 107–61. St. Petersburg.

Lunacharsky, Anatoly Vasil'evich. 1908b. *Religiia i sotsializm: Tom 1*. Moscow: Shipovnik.

Lunacharsky, Anatoly Vasil'evich. 1911. *Religiia i sotsializm: Tom 2*. Moscow: Shipovnik.

Lunacharsky, Anatoly Vasil'evich. 1919. *Velikii perevorot*. St. Petersburg.

Lunacharsky, Anatoly Vasil'evich. 1963–1967. *Sobranie sochinenii*. Moscow: Khudozhestvennaia literatura.

Lunacharsky, Anatoly Vasil'evich. 1973. *On Literature and Art*. Moscow: Progress Publishers.

Lunacharsky, Anatoly Vasil'evich. 1981. *On Education: Selected Articles and Speeches*. Moscow: Progress Publishers.

Lunacharsky, Anatoly Vasil'evich. 1985. *Religiia i prosveshchenie*. Edited by V.N. Kuznetsova. Moscow: Sovetskaia Rossiia.

Luo Ergang. 1951. *Taiping tianguo shigao*. Beijing: Kaiming Shuju.

Luo Ergang. 1991. 'Taiping tianguo de bingfa'. *Fuyin baokan ziliao: Zhongguo jindai shi* 4:30–41.

Luther, Martin. 1540. *An die Pfarrherrn wider den Wucher zu predigen*. Wittenberg.

Luther, Martin, and Desiderius Erasmus. 1969. *Luther and Erasmus: On the Bondage of the Will and On the Freedom of the Will*. Edited by E.G. Rupp and P.S. Watson. Vol. 17, *Library of Christian Classics*. London: SCM.

Luxemburg, Rosa. 1905a [1970]. 'Socialism and the Churches'. In *Rosa Luxemburg Speaks*, edited by Mary-Alice Waters, 131–52. New York: Pathfinder Press.

Luxemburg, Rosa. 1905b [1982]. *Kirche und Sozialismus*. Frankfurt am Main: Stimme-Verlag.

Lyons, William John. 2016. 'Realizing Calvin's Radical Potential: Interpreting Jeremiah 48:10 during the English Revolution'. *Relegere: Studies in Religion and Reception* 6 (1):1–18.

Ma Tong Hui. 2010. *Reunification of Korea is a Major Security Issue on the Korean Peninsula: The North Korean Perspective*. Stockholm: Institute for Security and Development Policy.

Macherey, Pierre. 1992. *A Theory of Literary Production*. London: Routledge.

Machovec, Milan. 1965. *Marxismus und dialektische Theologie: Barth, Bonhoeffer und Hromádka in atheistisch-kommunistischer Sicht*. Zürich: EVZ-Verlag.

Machovec, Milan. 1980. *Jesus für atheisten*. Gütersloh: Gütersloher Verlagshaus.

MacIntyre, Alasdair. 1971. *Marxism and Christianity*. Harmondsworth: Penguin.

Macintyre, Stuart. 1998. *The Reds: The Communist Party in Australia from Origins to Illegality*. St Leonards: Allen and Unwin.

Mackay, Christopher. 2016. *False Prophets and Preachers: Henry Gresbeck's Account of the Anabaptist Kingdom of Münster*. Kirksville: Truman State University Press.

Macmurray, John. 1936. *Creative Society: A Study of the Relation of Christianity to Communism*. New York: Association Press.

Malek, Roman. 2004. *Verschmelzung der Horizonte: Mozi und Jesus zür Hermeneutik der chinesisch-christlichen Begegnung nach Wu Leichuan (1869–1944)*. Leiden: Brill.

Malina, Bruce, and John Pilch. 2008. *Social Science Commentary on the Book of Acts*. Minneapolis: Fortress.

Malinowski, Bronislaw. 1932. *Argonauts of the Western Pacific: An Account of Native Enterprise and Adventure in the Archipelagoes of Melanesian New Guinea*. London: Routledge.

Mann, William. 2001. 'Augustine on Evil and Original Sin'. In *The Cambridge Companion to Augustine*, edited by Eleonore Stump and Norman Kretzmann, 40–48. Cambridge: Cambridge University Press.

Mao Zedong. 1917a [1992]. 'Letter to Li Jinxi (August 23, 1917)'. In *Mao's Road to Power: Revolutionary Writings 1912–1949*, Vol. 1, edited by Stuart Schram, 130–36. Armonk: M.E. Sharpe.

Mao Zedong. 1917b [1990]. 'Zhi Li Jinxi xin (1917.08.23)'. In *Mao Zedong zaoqi wengao, 1912.6-1920.11*, 84–91. Changsha: Hunan chubanshe.

Mao Zedong. 1926a [1994]. 'Some Points for Attention in Commemorating the Paris Commune'. In *Mao's Road to Power: Revolutionary Writings 1912–1949*, Vol. 2, 365–68. Armonk: M.E. Sharpe.

Mao Zedong. 1926b [1993a]. 'Jinian bali gongshe de zhongyao yiyi'. In *Maozedong wenji*, Vol. 1, 33–36. Beijing: Renmin chubanshe.

Mao Zedong. 1928a [1995]. 'Resolutions of the Sixth Congress of Party Representatives from the Fourth Red Army'. In *Mao's Road to Power: Revolutionary Writings 1912–1949*, Vol. 3, 122–27. Armonk: M.E. Sharpe.

Mao Zedong. 1928b [1987]. 'Hongjun disijun diliuci dangdaibiao dahui jueyi'an'. In *Jinggangshan geming genjudi*, Vol. 1, 199–204. Beijing: Zhonggong dangshi ziliao chubanshe.

Mao Zedong. 1935a [1999]. 'On Tactics Against Japanese Imperialism'. In *Mao's Road to Power: Revolutionary Writings 1912–1949*, Vol. 5, 86–102. Armonk: M.E. Sharpe.

Mao Zedong. 1935b [1991a]. 'Lun fandui riben diguozhuyi de celüe'. In *Maozedong xuanji*, Vol. 1, 142–69. Beijing: Renmin chubanshe.

Mao Zedong. 1937a [1965]. 'On Contradiction'. In *Selected Works of Mao Tse-Tung*, Vol. 1, 311–47. Beijing: Foreign Languages Press.

Mao Zedong. 1937b [1952]. 'Maodunlun'. In *Maozedong xuanji*, Vol. 1, 299–340. Beijing: Renmin Chubanshe.

Mao Zedong. 1937c [2004]. 'On Dialectical Materialism'. In *Mao's Road to Power: Revolutionary Writings 1912–1949*, Vol. 6, 573–667. Armonk: M.E. Sharpe.

Mao Zedong. 1938a [2004]. 'On Protracted War'. In *Mao's Road to Power: Revolutionary Writings 1912–1949*, Vol. 6, 319–89. Armonk: M.E. Sharpe.

Mao Zedong. 1938b [1991b]. 'Lun chijiuzhan'. In *Maozedong xuanji*, Vol. 2, 439–518. Beijing: Renmin chubanshe.

Mao Zedong. 1938c [2004c]. 'On the New Stage'. In *Mao's Road to Power: Revolutionary Writings 1912–1949*, Vol. 6, 458–541. Armonk: M.E. Sharpe.

Mao Zedong. 1938d [1991c]. 'Lun xin jieduan'. In *Zhonggong zhongyang wenjian xuanji*, Vol. 11, 557–662. Beijing: Zhonggong zhongyang dangxiao chubanshe.

Mao Zedong. 1939a [2005]. 'The Chinese Revolution and the Chinese Communist Party'. In *Mao's Road to Power: Revolutionary Writings 1912–1949*, Vol. 7, 279–306. Armonk: M.E. Sharpe.

Mao Zedong. 1939b [1991]. 'Zhongguo geming he zhongguo gongchandang'. In *Maozedong xuanji*, Vol. 2, 621–56. Beijing: Renmin chubanshe.

Mao Zedong. 1939c [2005]. 'The May Fourth Movement'. In *Mao's Road to Power: Revolutionary Writings 1912–1949*, Vol. 7, 66–68. Armonk: M.E. Sharpe.

Mao Zedong. 1939d [1991]. 'Wusi yundong'. In *Maozedong xuanji*, Vol. 2, 558–60. Beijing: Renmin chubanshe.

Mao Zedong. 1939e [2005]. 'Speech at the Meeting in Yan'an in Commemoration of the Twentieth Anniversary of the May Fourth Movement'. In *Mao's Road to Power: Revolutionary Writings 1912–1949*, Vol. 7, 69–79. Armonk: M.E. Sharpe.

Mao Zedong. 1939f [1991]. 'Qingnian yundong de fangxiang'. In *Maozedong xuanji*, Vol. 2, 561–69. Beijing: Renmin chubanshe.

Mao Zedong. 1939g [2005]. 'Women, Unite'. In *Mao's Road to Power: Revolutionary Writings 1912–1949*, Vol. 7, 44–49. Armonk: M.E. Sharpe.

Mao Zedong. 1939h [1993]. 'Funümen tuanjie qilai'. In *Maozedong wenji*, Vol. 2, 166–72. Beijing: Renmin chubanshe.

Mao Zedong. 1940a [2005]. 'On New Democracy'. In *Mao's Road to Power: Revolutionary Writings 1912–1949*, Vol. 7, edited by Stuart R. Schram, 330–69. Armonk: M.E. Sharpe.

Mao Zedong. 1940b [1991]. 'Xin minzhuzhuyi lun'. In *Maozedong xuanji*, Vol. 2, 662–711. Beijing: Renmin chubanshe.

Mao Zedong. 1944a [2015]. 'Letter to Guo Moruo (21 November 1944)'. In *Mao's Road to Power: Revolutionary Writings 1912–1949*, Vol. 8, 657–58. New York: Routledge.

Mao Zedong. 1944b [1983]. 'Zhi Guo Moruo'. In *Maozedong shuxin xuanji*, 241–43. Beijing: Renmin chubanshe.

Marcuse, Herbert. 1970. 'Marxism and the New Humanity: An Unfinished Revolution'. In *Marxism and Radical Religion: Essays Towards a Revolutionary Humanism*, edited by John Raines and Thomas Dean, 3–10. Philadelphia: Temple University Press.

Marie, Jean-Jacques. 2008. *Lénine 1870–1924*. Paris: Editions Balland.

Marković, Mihailo. 1985. 'Atheism is Not Essential to Marxism; Critique of Religion Is'. *Journal of Ecumenical Studies* 22 (3):528–34.

Marquardt, Friedrich-Wilhelm. 1972. *Theologie und Sozialismus: Das Beispiel Karl Barths*. Munich: Kaiser.

Martin, Bradley. 2006. *Under the Loving Care of the Fatherly Leader: North Korea and the Kim Dynasty*. New York: St. Martin's.

Martin, Dale. 1999. *The Corinthian Body*. New Haven: Yale University Press.

Martin, Terry. 2001. 'An Affirmative Action Empire: The Soviet Union as the Highest Form of Imperialism'. In *A State of Nations: Empire and Nation-Making in the Age of Lenin and Stalin*, edited by Ronald Grigor Suny and Terry Martin, 67–90. Oxford: Oxford University Press.

Martyn, J. Louis. 2004. *Galatians, Anchor Yale Bible Commentaries*. New Haven: Yale University Press.

Marx, Karl. 1841a [1975]. 'Difference Between the Democritean and Epicurean Philosophy of Nature with an Appendix'. In *Marx and Engels Collected Works*, Vol. 1, 25–106. Moscow: Progress Publishers.

Marx, Karl. 1841b [1975]. 'Differenz der demokritischen und epikureischen Naturphilosophie nebst einem Anhange'. In *Marx Engels Gesamtausgabe*, Vol. I.1, 5–92. Berlin: Dietz.

Marx, Karl. 1843a [1975]. 'Contribution to the Critique of Hegel's Philosophy of Law'. In *Marx and Engels Collected Works*, Vol. 3, 3–129. Moscow: Progress Publishers.

Marx, Karl. 1843b [1982]. 'Zur Kritik der Hegelschen Rechtsphilosophie'. In *Marx Engels Gesamtausgabe*, Vol. I:2, 3–137. Berlin: Dietz.

Marx, Karl. 1844a [1975]. 'Contribution to the Critique of Hegel's Philosophy of Law: Introduction'. In *Marx and Engels Collected Works*, Vol. 3, 175–87. Moscow: Progress Publishers.

Marx, Karl. 1844b [1982]. 'Zur Kritik der Hegelschen Rechtsphilosophie. Einleiting'. In *Marx Engels Gesamtausgabe*, Vol. I:2, 170–83. Berlin: Dietz.

Marx, Karl. 1844c [1975]. 'Economic and Philosophic Manuscripts of 1844'. In *Marx and Engels Collected Works*, Vol. 3, 229–346. Moscow: Progress Publishers.

Marx, Karl. 1844d [1982]. 'Ökonomisch-philosophische Manuskripte (Erste Wiedergabe)'. In *Marx Engels Gesamtausgabe*, Vol. I:2, 187–322. Berlin: Dietz.

Marx, Karl. 1844e [1982]. 'Ökonomisch-philosophische Manuskripte (Zweite Wiedergabe)'. In *Marx Engels Gesamtausgabe*, Vol. I:2, 323–444. Berlin: Dietz.

Marx, Karl. 1844f [1975]. 'On the Jewish Question'. In *Marx and Engels Collected Works*,
Vol. 3, 146–74. Moscow: Progress Publishers.

Marx, Karl. 1844g [1982]. 'Zur Judenfrage'. In *Marx Engels Gesamtausgabe*, Vol. I:2,
138–69. Berlin: Dietz.

Marx, Karl. 1845a [1976]. 'Theses on Feuerbach (original version)'. In *Marx and Engels
Collected Works*, Vol. 5, 3–5. Moscow: Progress Publishers.

Marx, Karl. 1845b [1973]. 'Thesen über Feuerbach (original version)'. In *Marx Engels
Werke*, Vol. 3, 5–7. Berlin: Dietz.

Marx, Karl. 1847a [1976]. 'Moralising Criticism and Critical Morality: A Contribution to
German Cultural History Contra Karl Heinzen'. In *Marx and Engels Collected Works*,
Vol. 6, 312–40. Moscow: Progress Publishers.

Marx, Karl. 1847b [1972a]. 'Die moralisierende Kritik und die kritisierende Moral. Beitrag zur Deutschen Kulturgeschichte. Gegen Karl Heinzen von Karl Marx'. In *Marx
Engels Werke*, Vol. 4, 331–60. Berlin: Dietz.

Marx, Karl. 1847c [1976]. 'The Poverty of Philosophy: Answer to the *Philosophy of Poverty* by M. Proudhon'. In *Marx and Engels Collected Works*, Vol. 6, 104–212. Moscow:
Progress Publishers.

Marx, Karl. 1847d [1972b]. 'Das Elend der Philosophie. Antwort auf Proudhons „Philosophie des Elends"'. In *Marx Engels Werke*, Vol. 4, 63–182. Berlin: Dietz.

Marx, Karl. 1852a [1979]. 'The Eighteenth Brumaire of Louis Bonaparte'. In *Marx and
Engels Collected Works*, Vol. 11, 99–197. Moscow: Progress Publishers.

Marx, Karl. 1852b [1985]. 'Der achtzehnte Brumaire des Louis Bonaparte'. In *Marx Engels Gesamtausgabe*, Vol. I:11, 96–189. Berlin: Dietz.

Marx, Karl. 1853 [1975]. 'Revolution in China and Europe'. In *Marx Engels Collected
Works*, Vol. 12, 93–100. Moscow: Progress Publishers.

Marx, Karl. 1859a [1987]. 'A Contribution to the Critique of Political Economy'. In *Marx
and Engels Collected Works*, Vol. 29, 257–417. Moscow: Progress Publishers.

Marx, Karl. 1859b [1961]. 'Zur Kritik der Politischen Ökonomie'. In *Marx Engels Werke*,
Vol. 13, 3–160. Berlin: Dietz.

Marx, Karl. 1861–63a [1989]. *Economic Manuscript of 1861–63 (Continuation): A Contribution to the Critique of Political Economy*. In *Marx and Engels Collected Works*, Vol.
32. Moscow: Progress Publishers.

Marx, Karl. 1861–63b [1991]. *Economic Manuscript of 1861–63 (Continuation): A Contribution to the Critique of Political Economy*. In *Marx and Engels Collected Works*, Vol. 33.
Moscow: Progress Publishers.

Marx, Karl. 1861–63c [1976–82]. *Zur Kritik der Politischen Ökonomie (Manuskript 1861–1863)*.
In *Marx Engels Gesamtausgabe*, Vol. II:3. Berlin: Dietz.

Marx, Karl. 1867a [1996]. *Capital: A Critique of Political Economy, Vol. 1*. In *Marx and
Engels Collected Works*, Vol. 35. Moscow: Progress Publishers.

Marx, Karl. 1867b [1983]. *Das Kapital. Kritik der politischen Ökonomie. Erster Band. Hamburg 1867*. In *Marx Engels Gesamtausgabe* II.5. Berlin: Dietz.

Marx, Karl. 1868 [1985]. 'Remarks on the Programme and Rules of the International Alliance of Socialist Democracy'. In *Marx and Engels Collected Works*, Vol. 21, 207–11. Moscow: Progress Publishers.

Marx, Karl. 1871a [1986]. 'The Civil War in France'. In *Marx and Engels Collected Works*, Vol. 22, 307–59. Moscow: Progress Publishers.

Marx, Karl. 1871b [1986]. 'Record of Marx's Speech on the Seventh Anniversary of the International'. In *Marx and Engels Collected Works*, Vol. 22, 633–34. Moscow: Progress Publishers.

Marx, Karl. 1872a [1988]. 'On the Hague Congress: A Correspondent's Report of a Speech Made at a Meeting in Amsterdam on September 8, 1872'. In *Marx and Engels Collected Works*, Vol. 23, 254–56. Moscow: Progress Publishers.

Marx, Karl. 1872b [1973a]. 'Rede über den Haager Kongreß'. In *Marx Engels Werke*, Vol. 18, 159–61. Berlin: Dietz.

Marx, Karl. 1875a [1989]. 'Critique of the Gotha Programme'. In *Marx and Engels Collected Works*, Vol. 24, 75–99. Moscow: Progress Publishers.

Marx, Karl. 1875b [1985]. 'Kritik des Gothaer Programms'. In *Marx Engels Gesamtausgabe*, Vol. I:25, 3–25. Berlin: Dietz.

Marx, Karl. 1881a [1992]. 'Marx to Ferdinand Domela Nieuwenhuis in the Hague, London, 22 February 1881'. *Marx and Engels Collected Works*, Vol. 46, 65–67. Moscow: Progress Publishers.

Marx, Karl. 1881b [1973]. 'Marx an Ferdinand Domela Nieuwenhuis 22.Februar 1881'. In *Marx Engels Werke*, Vol. 35, 159–61. Berlin: Dietz.

Marx, Karl. 1881c [1992]. 'Marx to Vera Zasulich, Geneva, 8 March 1881'. In *Marx and Engels Collected Works*, Vol. 46, 71–72. Moscow: Progress Publishers.

Marx, Karl. 1881d [1973]. 'Marx an Vera Iwanowna Sassulitsch in Genf, 8.März 1881'. In *Marx Engels Werke*, Vol. 35, 166–67. Berlin: Dietz.

Marx, Karl. 1890 [1991]. *Das Kapital. Kritik der politischen Ökonomie. Erster Band. Hamburg 1890*. In *Marx Engels Gesamtausgabe*, Vol. II:10. Berlin: Dietz.

Marx, Karl. 1894a [1998]. *Capital: A Critique of Political Economy, Vol. III*. In *Marx and Engels Collected Works*, Vol. 37. Moscow: Progress Publishers.

Marx, Karl. 1894b [2004]. *Das Kapital. Kritik der politischen Ökonomie. Dritter Band. Hamburg 1894*. In *Marx Engels Gesamtausgabe*, Vol. II:15. Berlin: Akademie Verlag.

Marx, Karl, and Friedrich Engels. 1845a [1975]. *The Holy Family, or Critique of Critical Criticism*. In *Marx and Engels Collected Works*, Vol. 4, 5–211. Moscow: Progress Publishers.

Marx, Karl, and Friedrich Engels. 1845b [1974]. *Die heilige Familie oder Kritik der kritischen Kritik*. In *Marx Engels Werke*, Vol. 2, 3–223. Berlin: Dietz.

Marx, Karl, and Friedrich Engels. 1845–46a [1976]. *The German Ideology: Critique of Modern German Philosophy According to Its Representatives Feuerbach, B. Bauer and*

Stirner, and of German Socialism According to Its Various Prophets. In *Marx and Engels Collected Works*, Vol. 5, 19–539. Moscow: Progress Publishers.

Marx, Karl, and Friedrich Engels. 1845–46b [1973]. *Die deutsche Ideologie. Kritik der neuesten deutschen Philosophie in ihren Repräsentanten Feuerbach, B. Bauer und Stirner und des deutschen Sozialismus in seinen verschiedenen Propheten*. In *Marx Engels Werke*, Vol. 3, 9–530. Berlin: Dietz.

Marx, Karl, and Friedrich Engels. 1846a [1976]. 'Circular Against Kriege'. In *Marx and Engels Collected Works*, Vol. 6, 35–51. Moscow: Progress Publishers.

Marx, Karl, and Friedrich Engels. 1846b [1972]. 'Zirkular gegen Kriege'. In *Marx Engels Werke*, Vol. 4, 3–17. Berlin: Dietz.

Marx, Karl, and Friedrich Engels. 1852a [1979]. 'The Great Men of the Exile'. In *Marx and Engels Collected Works*, Vol. 11, 227–326. Moscow: Progress Publishers.

Marx, Karl, and Friedrich Engels. 1852b [1985]. 'Die großen Männer des Exils'. In *Marx Engels Gesamtausgabe*, Vol. I:11, 219–311. Berlin: Dietz.

Masani, Pesi. 1979. 'The Common Ground of Marxism and Religion'. *Journal of Ecumenical Studies* 16 (3):472–95.

Matera, Frank. 2007. *Galatians*. Collegeville: Liturgical Press.

Maynard, Farnham. 1929. *Economics and the Kingdom of God*. Melbourne: SCM.

Maynard, Farnham. 1935. 'Editorial'. *The Defender: The Quarterly Magazine of the Australian Church Union* 15 (4):1–8.

Maynard, Farnham, and Kurt Merz. 1947. *Religion and Revolution*. Melbourne: Fraser & Morphet.

McCain, Paul, ed. 2005. *Concordia: The Lutheran Confessions*. St Louis: Concordia Publishing House.

McGovern, Arthur. 1985. 'Atheism: Is It Essential to Marxism?' *Journal of Ecumenical Studies* 22 (3):487–500.

McKinnon, Andrew. 2006. 'Opium as Dialectics of Religion: Metaphor, Expression and Protest'. In *Marx, Critical Theory and Religion: A Critique of Rational Choice*, edited by Warren Goldstein, 11–29. Leiden: Brill.

McPherson, Albert. 2000. 'Maynard, Farnham Edward'. In *Australian Dictionary of Biography*. Canberra: National Centre of Biography, Australian National University.

Mecchia, Giuseppina. 2009. 'Wu Ming: Anonymous Hatchet Throwers at the Dawn of the 21st Century'. In *Creative Interventions: The Role of Intellectuals in Contemporary Italy*, edited by Eugenio Bolongaro, Mark Epstein and Rita Gagliano, 195–214. Newcastle Upon Tyne: Cambridge Scholars.

Meeks, Wayne. 2003. *The First Urban Christians: The Social World of the Apostle Paul*. New Haven: Yale University Press.

Mehring, Franz. 1931. *Zur deutschen Geschichte*. Berlin: Soziologische Verlagsanstalt.

Merz, Kurt, Ralph Gibson, and Farnham Maynard. 1944. *A Fair Hearing for Socialism*. Melbourne: Fraser & Morphet.

Metz, Johann Baptist. 1977. *Faith in History and Society: Toward a Practical Fundamental Theology*. New York: Crossroad.

Meyer-Fong, Tobie. 2003. *What Remains: Coming to Terms with Civil War in Nineteenth-Century Century China*. Stanford: Stanford University Press.

Michael, Franz, and Chung-li Chang. 1966. *The Taiping Rebellion: History and Documents*. 3 vols. Seattle: University of Washington Press.

Milbank, John. 1990. *Theology and Social Theory: Beyond Secular Reason*. Oxford: Blackwell.

Miner, Steven Merritt. 2003. *Stalin's Holy War: Religion, Nationalism, and Alliance Politics, 1941–1945*. Chapel Hill: University of North Carolina Press.

Moffett, Samuel. 2005. *A History of Christianity in Asia, Vol. 2, 1500–1900*. Maryknoll: Orbis.

Mojzes, Paul. 1968. *Christian-Marxist Dialogue in Eastern Europe*. Minneapolis: Augsburg.

Moltmann, Jürgen. 1965. *Theology of Hope*. Translated by James W. Leitch. London: SCM.

Moltmann, Jürgen. 1976. *Im Gespräch mit Ernst Bloch. Eine theologische Wegbegleitung*. Munich: Kaiser.

Moltmann, Jürgen. 1999. 'Liberating and Anticipating the Future'. In *Liberating Eschatology: Essays in Honor of Letty M. Russell*, edited by Margaret Farley and Serene James, 189–208. Louisville: Westminster John Knox.

Montero, Roman. 2017. *All Things in Common: The Economic Practices of the Early Christians*. Eugene: Wipf and Stock.

Moore, Stephen. 2006. *Empire and Apocalypse: Postcolonialism and the New Testament*. Sheffield: Sheffield Phoenix.

Morawski, Stefan. 1965. 'Lenin as Literary Theorist'. *Science and Society* 29 (1):2–25.

Müntzer, Thomas. 1988. *The Collected Works of Thomas Müntzer*. Translated by Peter Matheson. Edinburgh: T & T Clark.

Murphy, Francis. 1974. '"La Main Tendue": Prelude to Christian-Marxist Dialogue in France, 1936–1939'. *The Catholic Historical Review* 60 (2):255–70.

Nadan, Amos. 2003. 'Colonial Misunderstanding of an Efficient Peasant Institution'. *Journal of the Economic and Social History of the Orient* 46:320–54.

Nadan, Amos. 2006. *The Palestinian Peasant Economy under the Mandate: A Story of Colonial Bungling*. Cambridge: Harvard University Press.

Nettl, John Peter. 1966. *Rosa Luxemburg*. 2 vols. London: Oxford University Press.

Nicholls, Paul. 1997. '"Supporting the Book Without Reservation": Melbourne, Mother and the 1927–8 Revision of the B.C.P'. In *Anglo-Catholicism in Melbourne: Papers to Mark the 150th Anniversary of St Peter's Eastern Hill 1846–1996*, edited by Colin Holden, 49–68. Parkville: Department of History, University of Melbourne.

Norris, Russell. 1974. *God, Marx and the Future: Dialogue with Roger Garaudy*. Philadelphia: Fortress.

Oestreicher, Paul, ed. 1969. *The Christian Marxist Dialogue: An International Sympo-sium*. Basingstoke: Macmillan.

Offord, Derek. 1986. *The Russian Revolutionary Movement in the 1880s*. Cambridge: Cambridge University Press.

Olgin, Moissaye Joseph. 1917. *The Soul of the Russian Revolution*. New York: Henry Holt.

Ovan, Sabrina. 2005. 'Q's General Intellect'. *Cultural Studies Review* 11 (2):69–76.

Packull, Werner. 1977a. *Mysticism and the Early South German-Austrian Anabaptist Movement, 1525–1531*. Scottsdale: Herald.

Packull, Werner. 1977b. 'Thomas Müntzer Between Marxist-Christian Diatribe and Dia-logue'. *Historical Reflections / Réflexions Historiques* 4 (1):67–90.

Palmer, Carol. 1999. 'Whose Land Is it Anyway? An Historical Examination of Land Tenure and Agriculture in Northern Jordan'. In *The Prehistory of Food: Appetites for Change*, edited by Chris Gosden and Jon Hather, 282–99. London: Routledge.

Pannenberg, Wolfhart. 1991–93. *Systematic Theology*. Translated by Geoffrey William Bromiley. 3 vols. Grand Rapids: Eerdmans.

Pelagius. 1993. *Pelagius's Commentary on St Paul's Epistle to the Romans*. Translated by Theodore De Bruyn. Oxford: Clarendon.

Pervo, Richard. 2009. *Acts: A Commentary*. Minneapolis: Fortress.

Petterson, Christina. 2012. *Acts of Empire: The Acts of the Apostles and Imperial Ideology*. Taipei: Sino-Christian Studies.

Petterson, Christina. 2015. 'Imagining the Body of Christ'. In *Sexuality, Ideology and the Bible: Antipodean Engagements*, edited by Caroline Blythe and Robert Myles, 35–55. Sheffield: Sheffield Phoenix.

Petterson, Christina. 2016. '"A Plague of the State and the Church": A Local Response to the Moravian Enterprise'. *Journal of Moravian History* 16 (1):45–60.

Petterson, Christina. In press. *Herrnhut: A Community of Selves in Eighteenth Century Saxony*. Leiden: Brill.

Piediscalzi, Nicholas, and Robert Thobaben, eds. 1985. *Three Worlds of Christian-Marxist Encounters*. Philadelphia: Fortress.

Piga, Emanuela. 2010. 'Metahistory, Microhistories and Mythopoeia in Wu Ming'. *Journal of Romance Studies* 10 (1):51–67.

Platt, Stephen. 2012. *Autumn in the Heavenly Kingdom: China, the West and the Taiping Civil War*. New York: Alfred A. Knopf.

Plekhanov, Georgi. 1974. *Selected Philosophical Works*. Vol. 5. Moscow: Progress Publishers.

Qin Baoqi. 2010. 'Taiping tianguo de "xiao tiantang", "renjian tiantang" zongjiao lixiang de zhongguo shijian'. *Qing History Journal* 80 (4):70–77.

Raines, John, and Thomas Dean. 1970. 'Introduction'. In *Marxism and Radical Religion: Essays Toward a Revolutionary Humanism*, edited by John Raines and Thomas Dean, ix–xvi. Philadelphia: Temple University Press.

Rapp, John. 2008. 'Clashing Dilemmas: Hong Rengan, Issachar Roberts, and a Taiping "Murder" Mystery'. *Journal of Historical Biography* 4:27–58.

Rauschenbusch, Walter. 1907. *Christianity and the Social Crisis*. New York: Macmillan.

Rees, Brinley Roderick. 1998. *Pelagius: Life and Letters*. Martlesham: Boydell & Brewer.

Reilly, Thomas. 2004. *The Taiping Heavenly Kingdom: Rebellion and the Blasphemy of Empire*. Seattle: University of Washington Press.

Reznik, Vladislava. 2003. 'Soviet Language Reform: Practical Polemics Against Idealist Linguistics'. *Slovo* 15 (1):33–47.

Riekkinen, Vilho. 1980. *Römer 13: Aufzeichnung und Weiterführung der exegetischen Diskussion*. Helsinki: Aufzeichnung und Weiterführung der exegetischen Diskussion.

Roberts, Brian. 1996. *Landscapes of Settlement: Prehistory to the Present*. London: Routledge.

Roslov, Edward. 2002. *Red Priests: Renovationism, Russian Orthodoxy, and Revolution*. Bloomington: Indiana University Press.

Rubenstein, Annette. 1995. 'Lenin on Literature, Language, and Censorship'. *Science and Society* 59 (3):368–83.

Rumscheidt, Martin. 2001. 'Socialists May be Christians; Christians Must be Socialists. Karl Barth Was!' *Toronto Journal of Theology* 17 (1):107–18.

Russell, Peter. 1977. 'Christian Millenarianism and the Early Taiping Movement: Reopening a Debate'. *Social History / Histoire Sociale* 9:114–33.

Ryu Dae Young. 1997. 'An Odd Relationship: The State Department, Its Representatives, and American Protestant Missionaries in Korea, 1882–1905'. *The Journal of American-East Asian Relations* 6:261–87.

Ryu Dae Young. 2003. 'Treaties, Extraterritorial Rights, and American Protestant Missions in Late Joseon Korea'. *Korea Journal* 43 (1):174–203.

Ryu Dae Young. 2004. 'Korean Protestant Churches' Attitude towards War: With a Special Focus on the Vietnam War'. *Korea Journal* 44 (4):191–222.

Ryu Dae Young. 2006. 'Fresh Wineskins for New Wine: A New Perspective on North Korean Christianity'. *Journal of Church and State* 48:659–75.

Ryu Dae Young. 2017. 'Political Activities and Anti-Communism of Korean Protestant Conservatives in the 2000s'. *Asian Journal of German and European Studies* 2 (6):1–18.

Sasson, Aharon. 2010. *Animal Husbandry in Ancient Israel: A Zooarchaeological Perspective on Livestock Exploitation, Herd Management and Economic Strategies*. London: Equinox.

Saucier, Gerard, Laura Geuy Akers, Seraphine Shen-Miller, Goran Knežević, and Lazar Stankov. 2009. 'Patterns of Thinking in Militant Extremism'. *Perspectives on Psychological Science* 4 (3):256–71.

Sayer, Derek. 1991. *Capitalim and Modernity: An Excursus on Marx and Weber*. London: Routledge, Chapman and Hall.

Schäbler, Birgit. 2000. 'Practicing Musha': Common Lands and the Common Good in Southern Syria under the Ottomans and the French (1812–1942)'. In *Rights to Access, Rights to Surplus: New Approaches to Land in the Middle East*, edited by Roger Owen, 241–309. Cambridge: Harvard University Press.

Schmitt, Carl. 2005. *Political Theology: Four Chapters on the Concept of Sovereignty*. Translated by George Schwab. Chicago: University of Chicago Press.

Schuler, Peter. 1975. 'Karl Marx's Atheism'. *Science and Society* 39 (3):331–45.

Schwartz, Peter. 1989. 'Imagining Socialism: Karl Kautsky and Thomas More'. In *Karl Kautsky and the Social Science of Classical Marxism*, edited by John H. Kautsky, 44–55. Leiden: Brill.

Scott, Tom. 1989. *Thomas Müntzer: Theology and Revolution in the German Reformation*. London: St. Martins Press.

Seebaß, Gottfried. 2002. *Müntzers Erbe: Werk, Leben und Theologie des Hans Hut*. Gütersloh: Gütersloher Verlagshaus.

Shih, Vincent. 1967. *The Taiping Ideology: Its Sources, Interpretations, and Influences*. Seattle: University of Washington Press.

Shorrock, Tim. 2015. 'Can the United States Own Up to Its War Crimes During the Korean War?' *The Nation*, 30 March, https://www.thenation.com/article/can-united-states-own-its-war-crimes-during-korean-war/.

Siebert, Rudolf. 1977a. 'The New Religious Dimension in Western Marxism, I'. *Horizons* 3 (2):217–31.

Siebert, Rudolf. 1977b. 'The New Religious Dimension in Western Marxism, II'. *Horizons* 4 (1):43–59.

Siegelbaum, Lewis. 1988. *Stakhanovism and the Politics of Productivity in the USSR, 1935–1941*. Cambridge: Cambridge University Press.

Slezkine, Yuri. 2000. 'The Soviet Union as a Communal Apartment, or How a Socialist State Promoted Ethnic Particularism'. In *Stalinism: New Directions*, edited by Sheila Fitzpatrick, 313–47. London: Routledge.

Smith, James. 2005. *Marks of an Apostle: Deconstruction, Philippians, and Problematizing Pauline Theology*. Atlanta: Society of Biblical Literature.

Snow, Edgar. 1937 [1994]. *Red Star Over China*. New York: Grove.

Sohn Won Tai. 2003. *Kim Il Sung and Korea's Struggle: An Unconventional Firsthand History*. Jefferson: McFarland.

Song Du-yul. 1995. *Korea-Kaleidoskop: Aktuelle Kontexte zur Wiedervereinigung*. Osnabrück: Secolo.

Sorokin, Boris. 1979. *Tolstoy in Prerevolutionary Russian Criticism*. Columbus: Ohio State University Press.

SPD. 1891a. 'Erfurt Program'. In *German History in Documents and Images: Wilhelmine Germany and the First World War, 1890–1918* Vol. 5, edited by Chickering, Roger, Steven Chase Gummer and Seth Rotramel.

SPD. 1891b. "Protokoll des Parteitages der Sozialdemokratischen Partei Deutschlands: Abgehalten zu Erfurt vom 14. bis 20. Oktober 1891". http://www.marxists.org/ deutsch/geschichte/deutsch/spd/1891/erfurt.htm.

Spence, Jonathan. 1996. *God's Chinese Son: The Taiping Heavenly Kingdom of Hong Xiuquan.* Hammersmith: HarperCollins.

Stalin, I.V. 1906a–1907a [1954]. 'Anarchism or Socialism?' In *Works*, Vol. 1, 297–373. Moscow: Foreign Languages Publishing House.

Stalin, I.V. 1906b–1907b [1946a]. 'Anarkhizm ili sotsializm?' In *Sochineniia*, Vol. 1, 294–372. Moscow: Gosudarstvennoe izdatel'stvo politicheskoi literatury.

Stalin, I.V. 1938a. *History of the Communist Party of the Soviet Union (Bolsheviks): Short Course.* New York: International Publishers.

Stalin, I.V. 1938b [1946b]. *Istoriia Vsesoiuznoĭ Kommunisticheskoĭ Partii (Bol'shevikov): Kratkiĭ kurs.* Moscow: OGIZ Gospolitizdat.

Stark, Rodney. 1996. *The Rise of Christianity: How the Obscure, Marginal Jesus Movement Became the Dominant Religious Force in the Western World.* Princeton: Princeton University Press.

Stark, Rodney. 2006. *The Victory of Reason: How Christianity Led to Freedom, Capitalism, and Western Success.* New York: Random House.

Stark, Rodney. 2011. *The Triumph of Christianity: How the Jesus Movement Became the World's Largest Religion.* San Francisco: HarperCollins.

Ste Croix, G.E.M. de. 1981. *The Class Struggle in the Ancient Greek World: From the Archaic Age to the Arab Conquests.* London: Duckworth.

Steinmetz, David Curtis. 1995. *Calvin in Context.* New York: Oxford University Press.

Stevenson, William. 1999. *Sovereign Grace: The Place and Significance of Christian Freedom in John Calvin's Political Thought.* New York: Oxford University Press.

Stevenson, William. 2004. 'Calvin and Political Issues'. In *The Cambridge Companion to John Calvin*, edited by Donald McKim, 173–87. Cambridge: Cambridge University Press.

Stirner, Max. 1845a [2005]. *The Ego and His Own: The Case of the Individual Against Authority.* Translated by Steven Byington. Mineola: Dover.

Stirner, Max. 1845b. *Der Einzige und Sein Eigentum.* Leipzig: Philipp Reclam.

Strauss, David Friedrich. 1835. *Das Leben Jesu, kritisch bearbeitet.* Tübingen: C.F. Osiander.

Strauss, David Friedrich. 1902. *The Life of Jesus: Critically Examined.* Translated by George Eliot. London: Swan Sonnenschein.

Stromberg, Roland. 1979. 'Marxism and Religion'. *Studies in Soviet Thought* 19 (3):209–17.

Suda, Max Josef. 1978. 'The Critique of Religion in Karl Marx's Capital'. *Journal of Ecumenical Studies* 15 (1):15–28.

Swancutt, Diana. 2004. 'Sexy Stoics and the Reading of Romans 1.18-2.16'. In *A Feminist Companion to Paul*, edited by Amy-Jill Levine and Marianne Blickenstaff, 95–97. London: T & T Clark International.

Talbert, Charles. 2005. *Reading Acts: A Literary and Theological Commentary on the Acts of the Apostles*. Revised ed: Smyth & Helwys.

Tang Baolin. 2012. *The Complete Biography of Chen Duxiu*. 3 vols. Hong Kong: Chinese University of Hong Kong.

Tee An Chu. 2012. *A Study of Bishop Ting Kuanghsün's Theological Reconstruction in China*, PhD Thesis. School of Arts, Histories and Cultures, Manchester University, Manchester.

Tellbe, Mikael. 2001. *Paul Between Synagogue and State: Christians, Jews and Civic Authorities in 1 Thessalonians, Romans and Philippians*. Stockholm: Almqvist & Wiksell.

Thiemann, Ronald. 1985. 'Praxis: The Practical Atheism of Karl Marx'. *Journal of Ecumenical Studies* 22 (3):544–49.

Thistleton, Anthony. 2000. *The First Epistle to the Corinthians*. Grand Rapids: Eerdmans.

Thoburn, Nicholas. 2011. 'To Conquer the Anonymous: Authorship and Myth in the Wu Ming Foundation'. *Cultural Critique* 78:119–50.

Thurston, Robert. 1986. 'On Desk-Bound Parochialism, Commonsense Perspectives, and Lousy Evidence: A Reply to Robert Conquest'. *Slavic Review* 45 (2):238–44.

Ting, K.H. 1990. 'What We Can Learn from Y.T. Wu Today'. *International Bulletin of Missionary Research* 14 (4):158–61.

Tolstoy, Leo. 1857 [1889]. 'Lucerne'. In *A Russian Proprietor and Other Stories*. Translated by Nathan Dole, 87–122. New York: Thomas Y. Crowell.

Tolstoy, Leo. 1877 [1918]. *Anna Karenina*. Translated by Louise Maude and Almer Maude. New York: Oxford University Press.

Tolstoy, Leo. 1885 [1902]. *What I Believe (My Religion)*. Christchurch: Free Age.

Tolstoy, Leo. 1887 [1934]. 'On Life'. In *On Life and Essays on Religion*. Translated by Almer Maude, 1–167, Oxford: Oxford University Press.

Tolstoy, Leo. 1889 [1890]. *The Kreutzer Sonata*. Boston: Benjamin Tucker.

Tolstoy, Leo. 1900 [1972]. *The Slavery of Our Times*. London: John Lawrence.

Toscano, Alberto. 2010a. *Fanaticism: On the Uses of An Idea*. London: Verso.

Toscano, Alberto. 2010b. 'Preface: The Resurrections of Thomas Müntzer'. In *Wu Ming Presents Thomas Müntzer: Sermon to the Princes*, edited by Wu Ming, vii–xviii. London: Verso.

Troeltsch, Ernst. 1992. *The Social Teaching of the Christian Churches*. Translated by Olive Wyon. 2 vols. Louisville: Westminster John Knox.

Troeltsch, Ernst. 1911. *Die Soziallehren der christlichen Kirchen und Gruppen*. 2 vols. Tubingen: J.C.B. Mohr.

Van Kley, Dale. 1999. *The Religious Origins of the French Revolution: From Calvin to the Civil Constitution 1560–1791*. 2nd ed. New Haven: Yale University Press.

Van Leeuwen, Arendt Theodoor. 2002. *Critique of Heaven*. Cambridge: James Clarke.

Vereš, Tomo. 1985. 'The Ambivalence of Marx's Atheism'. *Journal of Ecumenical Studies* 22 (3):549–60.

Voegelin, Eric. 1989–2009. *The Collected Works of Eric Voegelin.* 34 vols. Columbia: University of Missouri Press.

Voelz, James. 1999. 'A Self-Conscious Reader-Response Interpretation of Romans 13:1-7'. In *The Personal Voice in Biblical Interpretation*, edited by Ingrid Rosa Kitzberger, 156–69. London: Routledge.

Vogler, Günter. 1989. *Thomas Müntzer.* Berlin: Dietz.

Volkoff, Alex, and Edgar Wickberg. 1979. 'New Directions in Chinese Historiography: Reappraising the Taiping: Notes and Comment'. *Pacific Affairs* 52 (3):479–90.

Vvedensky, Aleksandr Ivanovich. 1925 [1985]. 'Sodoklad A.I. Vvedensky'. In *Religia i prosveshchenie*, edited by V.N. Kuznetsova, 186–93. Moscow: Sovetskaia Rossiia.

Waddell, Peter. 2014. *Charles Gore: Radical Anglican.* London: Canterbury Press.

Wagner, Rudolf. 1982. *Reenacting the Heavenly Vision: The Role of Religion in the Taiping Rebellion.* Berkeley: University of California, Institute of East Asian Studies.

Walton, Steve. 2008. 'Primitive Communism in Acts? Does Acts Present the Community of Goods (2:44–45; 4:32–35) as Mistaken?' *The Evangelical Quarterly* 80: 99–111.

Wang Shaomin, and Xiao Daming. 1989. 'Cong "Tianfu tianxiong shengzhi" kan taiping tianguo funu de shiji diwei'. *Fuyin baokan ziliao: Zhongguo jindai shi* 10:53–54.

Ward, Graham. 2002. *True Religion.* Oxford: Wiley-Blackwell.

Weber, Max. 1992. *The Protestant Ethic and the Spirit of Capitalism.* Translated by Talcott Parsons. London: Routledge.

Weems, Benjamin. 1964. *Reform, Rebellion and the Heavenly Way.* Tucson: University of Arizona Press.

Wei Wanlei. 1987. 'Taiping tianguo baiwang de jiti xinli fenxi'. *Shiexue yuekan* 10: 30–36.

Weitling, Wilhelm. 1838–1839. *Die Menschheit. Wie Sie ist und wie sie sein sollte.* Bern.

Weitling, Wilhelm. 1845a [1969]. *The Poor Sinner's Gospel.* Translated by Dinah Livingstone. London: Sheed & Ward.

Weitling, Wilhelm. 1845b [1967]. *Das Evangelium des armen Sünders.* Leipzig: Reclam.

Weller, Robert. 1987. 'Historians and Consciousness: The Modern Politics of the Taiping Heavenly Kingdom'. *Social Research* 54 (4):731–55.

West, Charles. 1958. *Communism and the Theologians.* London: Westminster.

Wetzel, James. 2001. 'Predestination, Pelagianism and Foreknowledge'. In *The Cambridge Companion to Augustine*, edited by Eleonore Stump and Norman Kretzmann, 49–58. Cambridge: Cambridge University Press.

Wickeri, Philip. 1988. *Seeking the Common Ground: Protestant Christianity, the Three-Self Movement, and China's United Front.* Maryknoll: Orbis.

Wickeri, Philip. 2007. *Reconstructing Christianity in China: K.H. Ting and the Chinese Church.* Maryknoll: Orbis.

Wilkinson, Tony. 2003. *Archaeological Landscapes of the Near East.* Tucson: University of Arizona Press.

Wilkinson, Tony. 2010. 'The Tell: Social Archaeology and Territorial Space'. In *Development of Pre-State Communities in the Ancient Near East*, edited by Dianne Bolger and Louise Maguire, 55–62. Oxford: Oxbow.

Willis-Watkins, David. 1989. 'Calvin's Prophetic Reinterpretation of Kingship'. In *Probing the Reformed Tradition*, edited by E. McKee and B. Armstrong, 116–34. Louisville: Westminster John Knox.

Winstanley, Gerrard. 1983. *The Law of Freedom and Other Writings*. Edited by Christopher Hill. Cambridge: Cambridge University Press.

Wood, Ellen Meiksins. 2008. *Citizens to Lords: A Social History of Western Political Thought from Antiquity to the Middle Ages*. London: Verso.

Worden, Robert, ed. 2008. *North Korea: A Country Study*. Washington: Federal Research Division Library of Congress.

Wu Leichuan. 1925. 'Zhudao wenyan cizhiqi'. *Zhenlizhoukan* 52 (23 March).

Wu Leichuan. 1936. *Jidujiao yu zhongguo wenhua*. Shanghai: Qingnian xiehui shuju.

Wu Leichuan. 1940. *Modi yu Yesu*. Shanghai: Qingnian xiehui shuju.

Wu Ming. 2001. 'From the Multitude of Europe Rising Up against the Empire and Marching on Genoa (19–20 July 2001)'. Available at http://www.wumingfoundation.com/english/giap/Giap_multitudes.html.

Wu Ming. 2010. 'Spectres of Müntzer at Sunrise: Greeting the 21st Century'. In *Thomas Müntzer: Sermon to the Princes*, edited by Wu Ming, xix–xliv. London: Verso.

Wu Yaozong. 1934. *Shehui fuyin*. Shanghai: Qingnian xiehui shuju.

Wu Yaozong. 1947. 'Jidujiao yu zhengzhi'. *Tian Feng* 59 (15 February).

Wu Yaozong. 1948a. *Meiyouren kanjianguo shangdi*. Shanghai: Qingnian xiehui shuju.

Wu Yaozong. 1948b [1963]. 'The Present Day Tragedy of Christianity'. In *Documents of the Three-Self Movement: Source Materials for the Study of the Protestant Church in Communist China*, edited by Frances Jones, 1–5. New York: National Council of the Churches of Christ in the U.S.A.

Wu Yaozong. 1949. *Hei'an yu guangming*. Shanghai: Qingnian xiehui shuju.

Xia Chuntao. 1992. 'Taiping tianguo dui "sheng jing" taidu de yanbian'. *Lishi yanjiu* 1:139–54.

Xia Chuntao. 2003. 'Taiping jun zhong de hunyin zhuangkuang yu liang xing guanxi tanxi'. *Jindaishi yanjiu* 1:5–37.

Xia Chuntao. 2004. 'Taiping tianguo funü diwei jianti zai yanjiu'. *Fuyin baokan ziliao: Zhongguo jindai shi* 8:45–48.

Xie Qizhang 1989. 'Lun hong xiuquan zongjiao zhengzhi sixiang de xingcheng'. *Fuyin baokan ziliao: Zhongguo jindai shi* 8:45–48.

Yeung King-To. 2005. 'Repressing Rebels, Managing Bureaucrats: The Qing State's Counter-Mobilization Against the Taiping Rebellion, 1851–68'. In *American Sociological Association Conference Proceedings*, 2005. Philadelphia.

Yieh, John. 2009. 'Jesus the "Teacher-Saviour" or "Saviour-Teacher": Reading the Gospel of Matthew in Chinese Contexts'. *Tiologiese Studies / Theological Studies* 65 (1):525–33.

Yin Changfu. 1989. 'Nongmin geming zhanzheng yu "xiliya shi kuangxiang" – taiping tianguo yundong yu deguo nongmin zhanzheng de bijiao yanjiu. *Fuyin baokan ziliao: Zhongguo jindai shi* 7:34–40.

Yuan Chung Teng. 1963. 'Reverend Issachar Jacox Roberts and the Taiping Rebellion'. *Journal of Asian Studies* 23 (1):55–67.

Zabłocki, Janusz. 1979. 'In the Interest of Dialogue and Cooperation'. *International Journal of Politics* 9 (1):89–97.

Zeng Guofan. 1854 [1999] 'A Proclamation against the Bandits of Guangdong and Guangxi' (1854). In *The Search for Modern China: A Documentary Collection*, edited by Pei-kai Cheng, Michael Lestz, and Jonathan Spence, 146–49. London: W.W. Norton.

Zhang Baohui. 2000. 'Communal Cooperative Institutions and Peasant Revolutions in South China, 1926–1934'. *Theory and Society* 29 (5):687–736.

Zhang Daye. 2013. *The World of a Tiny Insect: A Memoir of the Taiping Rebellion and Its Aftermath*. Translated by Tian Xiaofei. Seattle: University of Washington Press.

Zhang Zhenzhi. 1929. *Geming yu zongjiao*. Shanghai: Minzhi shuju.

Zhao Xiaoyang. 2010. 'Taiping tianguo kan yin shengjing diben yuanliu kaoxi'. *Qing History Journal* 79 (3):75–82.

Zheng Jianshun 2000. 'Guanyu taiping tianguo shi yanjiu de jige wenti'. *Shixue yuekan* 6:61–67.

Zheng Xiaowei. 2009. 'Loyalty, Anxiety, and Opportunism: Local Elite Activisim During the Taiping Rebellion in Eastern Zhejiang, 1851–1864'. *Late Imperial China* 30 (2):39–83.

Zhu Congbing. 1991. 'Taiping tianguo zhaoshuya kaobian'. *Lishi Yanjiu* 5:90–103.

Zhu Dong'an. 1990. 'Taiping tianguo "tuixing shenquan zhengzhi" shuo zhi yi'. *Lishi yanjiu* 5:3–11.

Zhu Weizhi. 1950. *Wuchanzhe Yesu zhuan*. Shanghai: Guang xuehui.

Zucchi, Stefan Matthias. 2007. 'Luther und Münzer – Forte und Blissett: Darstellung und Interpretation historischer Ereignisse in der mitteleuropäischen Gegenwartsliteratur'. *Arcadia* 42 (2):415–30.

Index

CPSIA information can be obtained
at www.ICGtesting.com
Printed in the USA
LVHW022240070523
746371LV00013B/448